Hizb'allah in Lebanon
The Politics of the Western Hostage Crisis

Magnus Ranstorp
Department of International Relations
University of St Andrews
Fife

Foreword by Terry Waite, CBE

St. Martin's Press
New York

St. Martin's Press, Scholarly and Reference Division,
175 Fifth Avenue, New York, N.Y. 10010

First published in the United States of America in 1997

This book is printed on paper suitable for recycling and
made from fully managed and sustained forest sources.

Printed in Great Britain

ISBN 0–312–16288–X (cloth)
ISBN 0–312–16491–2 (paperback)

Library of Congress Cataloging-in-Publication Data
Ranstorp, Magnus.
Hizb'allah in Lebanon : the politics of the western hostage crisis
/ Magnus Ranstorp ; foreword by Terry Waite.
p.   cm.
Includes bibliographical references (p.   ) and index.
ISBN 0–312–16288–X (cloth). — ISBN 0–312–16491–2 (pbk.)
1. Hizballah (Lebanon)   2. Hostages—Lebanon.   3. Lebanon–
–History—Civil War, 1975–   I. Title.
DS87.5.R367   1996
956.92—dc20   96–20970
                                                          CIP

This book is dedicated to my grandparents, Carl and Ester Ranstorp and to my father Per, for never doubting and for the opportunities...

Contents

Preface

The picturesque Scottish seaside town of St. Andrews would seem unlikely to naturally lend itself to the study of religious fundamentalism in any form. Yet, the historical remnants of this medieval town today, which predate the origins of the University of St. Andrews in 1411, bear witness to a period of fervent religious fundamentalism at the heart of the town's existence, whose first victim of the Scottish reformation became the martyred university student Patrick Hamilton. Any sense of detachment from the study of religious fundamentalism was also lost with the discovery of my belonging to the University's college of St. Leonard, the patron saint of hostages adopted by noblemen and soldiers away on the Crusades, most notably Bohemund, the first prince of Antioch, who were held captive in Muslim hands in the battles between Christendom and Islam in the Middle Ages. Notwithstanding the power of saints to those unjustly imprisoned and forgotten as hostages in solitary confinement for several years, the release of hostages either during the Crusades or in contemporary Lebanon depended not only on the importance of the hostages as a bargaining instrument but also on an ability and a willingness by the political masters at home to pay a ransom for their release. While the abduction of Bohemund during the Crusades embodied an effort by Islam to contain militant Christendom from recovering the holy place of Jerusalem from Muslim rule, the abduction of Westerners in Lebanon encapsulated the resurgence of a wider pan-Islamic effort to expel foreigners from the region in an attempt to liberate Jerusalem under non-Islamic control. The practice of hostage-taking has an old tradition in the Middle East, dating back to the early days of the Crusades. However, contemporary Western efforts to understand or deal with the hostage-incidents in Lebanon have been a surprising failure given that the "rules of the game" for the resolution of the hostage-crisis have changed little since Bohemund's days. Both the West's fear and inability to comprehend the enemy's willingness to sacrifice their own lives was also surprising given our own practice of martyrdom during the Crusades.

Despite the many historical parallels, this book focuses on the inner dynamics of the Hizb'allah (the Party of God), one of the most important, yet least understood, terrorist organisations in the Middle East, whose activity has wrecked havoc for Western governments for over a decade. The main aim of this study is not only to contribute to a fuller understanding of the labyrinthine complexity of the dynamics of the hostage-crisis in

Lebanon but also to bridge the gap between a detailed case-study of a terrorist group as well as its relationship with Iran and Syria, and the evaluation of Western government responses to this form of foreign policy crisis. This approach is necessary in order to more closely resolve the fundamental dilemma of the duty by Western democratic states to protect their citizens taken hostage abroad without any major sacrifice in the conduct of foreign policy. In this task, an understanding of the mechanisms governing the behaviour of one of the most complex and secretive terrorist organisations in the Middle East as well as the constraints and opportunities in the crisis environment within which the American, French, and British government have been forced to operate, is a step in the right direction. While beyond the scope of this study, it is essential to recognize that the Western hostages have unfairly received public and media exposure especially since over 10,000 Lebanese nationals became innocent victims and pawns in the warfare between the various indigenous militins in a particularly cruel and tragic hostage affair since many of these are still missing and unaccountable for despite the end of the Lebanese civil war.

A project of this magnitude could not have been completed without the assistance of patient and supportive colleagues, friends and family, to whom I would like to publicly express my gratitude to for services beyond any call of duty or responsibility. I am deeply grateful and indebted to staff and colleagues at the Department of International Relations, University of St. Andrews, who have offered invaluable ideas, criticism and suggestions. A few in particular deserve special mention. First, and foremost, I owe special gratitude to Professor Paul Wilkinson for providing me with invaluable and endless encouragement as well as advice throughout the research. I am also deeply grateful to Gina Wilson, who deserves a sainthood for her assistance in administrative matters, always with great humour and diligence. I would also like to extend special gratitude to Dr Bruce Hoffman and his wife Donna as well as Drs Ali Watson and Peter Macmillan for their unwavering support and encouragement as well as friendship. A number of other colleagues and friends deserve mention for advice and assistance at some stage of my research, most notably Gazman Xhudo, Peter Hirst, Amit Merothra, Katherine Edward, Vivian Jabri, Shaun McCarthy, Guy Sanan, Jan Axlund, Eva Sandberg, Ann Cameron, Anita Hedin and many others who know who they are. I am also indebted to Ambassador Per Haugestad and his wife Karin for their always generous hospitality, encouraging advice and for the opportunity to gain an insider's view on the mechanics of third party diplomacy and mediation which assisted me in my work.

Finally, I owe special gratitude to my friend Ellen Thelin-Haugestad, who provided me with necessary inspiration and advice throughout my research and writing. Her advice and support proved to be invaluable in keeping my work in perspective, especially when the magnitude of the project periodically became overwhelming.

Apart from research in the United Kingdom, I also had an opportunity to make several research trips to Israel, France, Egypt, and United States to interview government, intelligence and security officials with special knowledge of the Hizb'allah and the hostage-crisis in Lebanon. Many of these interviews provided invaluable and unique insights into the organisation as events unfolded and I am deeply grateful to those I have met, some who, due to the nature of their profession, would prefer to remain anonymous. To those I can mention, I owe special thanks to Ariel Merari Martin Kramer and Xavier Raufer.

I would also like to thank my editor Annabelle Buckley for her patience and advice as well as Linda Auld for her great editorial skills.

Finally, I want to acknowledge the inexhaustible support and encouragement of my parents, especially Per, Britt-Marie and my sister Cecilia, whose unending belief in my ability and endless support is finally starting to pay off. I also want to express a long overdue gratitude and acknowledgment to Bernard and Lynn Tome for their friendship, advice and support during the early and crucial years of my academic career.

Foreword by Terry Waite, CBE

Dr Magnus Ranstorp has made a valuable contribution towards understanding one of the most confused and clandestine periods of public and private diplomacy – the Lebanese hostage-crisis of the 1980s.

In 1979 I took up a new job on the private staff of the newly appointed Archbishop of Canterbury. My responsibilities were varied. The designation – Advisor on Anglican Communion Affairs – indicated that I was expected to keep the Archbishop briefed on matters concerning the worldwide Anglican Communion. I was also required to travel with him and from time to time deal with issues on his behalf. Almost immediately a major problem occurred in the small Anglican Community in Iran. Several lay and clerical members of the Church disappeared and anxious relatives and friends turned to the Archbishop of Canterbury for assistance. The problem landed on my desk. This is not the place to describe the dynamics of that particular event. Suffice to say that after a great deal of effort involving several visits to Iran the individuals were located and finally released. Little did I realise then that the 1980s would prove to be a decade in which hostage-taking and allied acts of terrorism would predominate. No sooner was the Iran problem resolved when British subjects disappeared in Libya. Once again, acting as a humanitarian envoy I visited that country and eventually the matter was resolved.

The Lebanon was a very different matter indeed. Before the problem in Libya was concluded individuals were being abducted in Beirut. One of the first to disappear was an American Presbyterian clergyman – The Revd Ben Weir. Officials from his Church in the United States visited Lambeth Palace in London. They knew of our involvement in hostage-situations and requested our assistance. Initially we were most reluctant to be involved and in this book Dr Ranstorp gives a clear indication of the reasons for that reluctance. First, we recognised the political complexities of the region and questioned whether the situation was open to humanitarian involvement. Second, at the time no one had any clear idea as to who was directly responsible for the abduction of the hostages or of the exact demands being made. Acting in concert with Anglican colleagues throughout the world I attempted to make a preliminary analysis of the situation. The British authorities were cautious, even, one might say, reluctant, to see any involvement by the Archbishop. They were either unwilling or unable to provide any information as to the identity of the hostage-takers beyond confirming what was generally known; that they probably came from radical groups within the Lebanese Shi'a community. Initially we had no contact with the American administration but were in touch with Syrian, Iranian and Lebanese informants. Such information that we received from these sources lacked clarity and more often than not seemed contradictory. Dr Ranstorp gives an account of the various political agendas being pursued by the principal actors in this drama and this analysis explains some of the reasons for our difficulty in gaining an accurate picture of the problem.

We finally took up the matter on humanitarian grounds when relatives and colleagues of hostages expressed their frustration at the apparent unwillingness of their governments to be involved in seeking the release of the abducted individuals.

The first main question to be dealt with was simple to express but difficult to answer. Who was holding the hostages and why? As Magnus Ranstorp makes clear, the hostage-takers used a variety of cover names in order to disguise their true identity and cause confusion. This posed a very real problem for a potential mediator. Whom should one contact and how? The major powers within the region were unable or unwilling to provide any direct link and so an alternative approach had to be developed. This involved the potential negotiator taking a high public profile, building on a previous reputation for fair dealing and hoping that this would engender a response from the abductors. The story has been told elsewhere.* Suffice to say that I was able to establish face to face contact with the Lebanese captors of the Western Hostages, obtain positive proof that they had direct contact with the hostages and receive from the captors their demands.

It is at this point where we get into the problem of the both complementary and contradictory nature of the conflicting agendas discussed by Dr Ranstorp. As he explains, Syria, Iran and Hizb'allah shared some goals in common. They also had their own agendas which were both supported and neglected by their respective allies according to the dominant political agenda of the moment. The initial approach to me (which came in the form of a letter, signed by four American hostages, and delivered to Lambeth Palace) was made by the Lebanese captors. Eventually when I met with them in Beirut they communicated to me their demands which concerned the welfare and eventual release of their blood relatives being held in Kuwait (*al-Da'wa al-Islamiyyah*).

As is made clear in this book, Kuwait constantly denied me entry to the country to visit the *al-Da'wa* prisoners. I did not believe then, nor do I

*Terry Waite, *Taken on Trust*, Hodder and Stoughton, London, 1993.

believe now that had I been able to make a humanitarian visitation that would have been sufficient to put an end to the Western hostage-crisis. It would have eased the situation somewhat and certainly given me extra credibility with Hizb'allah. At my request the Archbishop of Canterbury did write a letter to the Emir of Kuwait requesting him not to execute the prisoner under sentence of death. Such an action by the Emir would have further endangered the Western hostages. The Emir did not carry out the death sentence on any of the prisoners, although it is impossible to know what effect the letter had on his decision.

At the time I was puzzled as to why I did not seem to get any political support from either Britain or the United States to make a compassionate visit to Kuwait. I was told by American officials that requests for my visit had been made and refused. I believed that if requests had been made they had been half-hearted to say the least. When the Iran-Contra affair broke to me and to the world for the first time it became clear that other political games were being played out. The Iran-Iraq war came higher up the agenda for Iran than did the prisoners in Kuwait.

Iran-Contra faced me with an acute dilemma and there is no need to detail it here. Enough to say that my decisions regarding my next move had to be taken from the base from which I was operating. That base was *primarily* humanitarian and *not* political. As a humanitarian negotiator I felt obliged to maintain faith both with the captives *and* their captors. During captivity my experience of interrogation by Hizh'ballah would support Dr Ranstorp's multiple agenda theory. Questions concentrated on the activities of Oliver North and of the arms deal with Iran. I was in the fortunate position of knowing nothing at all about arms dealing and thus was able to give totally truthful answers. On reflection I believe that it is possible that Hizb'allah were also taken by surprise and may have broken faith with me out of a desire to: (a) discover what I could tell them about arms dealing (long before I was captured they knew I was in touch with the American Administration); and/or (b) recognising that as I was making no significant progress with Kuwait, detain me as a potential bargaining counter. As is explained in this book that particular ploy was forestalled.

The political machinations outlined by Magnus Ranstorp serve not only to indicate the problems raised in seeking the release of innocent hostages caught in the midst of such a complex trap, but also raises the question of the appropriate relationship between humanitarian intermediaries and political agents. This is a subject for further exploration.

There is only space for me to make two final comments. During my initial negotiations with and subsequent incarceration by the hostage-takers, it became clear to me that they were operating within a very tight command structure. Such a structure requires an advanced degree of organisation. Their concern for security was so great that during the final period of captivity, when I was confined with three other hostages, we were all subject to a twenty-four hour video and audio surveillance. Naturally this made me cautious then about expressing opinions on any subject which might have been of interest to my captors. As is suggested in this book, efficient organisation and rigorous security were two factors which enabled the hostage saga to develop as it did.

I have no doubt that the author has got the broad picture right in this book. Given the complexity, high degree of secrecy, and desire to "save face" following the event it is not surprising that certain areas remain in the shadows. Some individuals and some Governments have escaped exposure of their involvement by a narrow margin. Dr Ranstorp has produced a valuable analysis of a complex issue and I would commend this book to anyone who would wish to gain further insight into events that so dominated the 80s.

Terry Waite, CBE

1 Introduction

"Muster against them [the believers] all the men and cavalry at your disposal, so that you may terrorize the enemies of Allah and the faithful"[1]
"Therefore, when ye meet the Unbelievers (in fight), smite at their necks, at length, when ye have thoroughly subdued them, bind a bond firmly (on them): thereafter (is the time for) either generosity or ransom: until the war lays down its burden"[2]

The seizure of American diplomats as hostages at the U.S. embassy in Teheran in 1979, and their subsequent incarceration for 444 days, was widely considered, at the time, an anomaly in the conduct of contemporary international relations and unique to the dynamics of revolutionary efforts by Iranian clerics to use the hostage-crisis in the foreign policy arena for internal gains in the establishment of a theocratic regime. As made clear by U.S. President Jimmy Carter, the event was "[u]nprecedented in human history."[3] From this it was clear that the handling of the U.S. embassy siege exposed the vulnerability of a Western democracy to this special form of terrorism used by a non-Western adversary as a foreign policy instrument and particularly the difficulty in applying conventional tools of statecraft to deal with this new form of foreign policy crisis. It also represented a landmark event in which hostage-taking situations would become a permanent feature in Middle East politics for Western governments, especially within the context of the civil war in Lebanon. In a ten-year period, between 1982 and 1992, almost one hundred foreign citizens were abducted in Lebanon by a number of enigmatic pro-Iranian Shi'ite organisations, seemingly loosely or closely affiliated with the Hizb'allah movement.[4] Unlike the 1979 U.S. embassy siege in Teheran, the hostage-taking of foreign citizens in Lebanon differed in many ways in the prolongation and complexity of the incidents. While the preceding hostage-crisis involved 52 American diplomats used collectively by revolutionary clerics in Iran in an extremely aggressive confrontation with the United States, the abduction of foreigners in Lebanon was perpetrated by non-identifiable groups with pro-Iranian affiliation, operating within the confines of a protracted civil war, in the pursuit of an array of demands ranging from each respective group's own requirements to the advancement of specific foreign policy objectives either directly or indirectly benefiting Iran and Syria. Apart from the fact that the 1979 Iranian incident involved the incarceration of U.S. hostages for 444 days in a clearly defined barricade/siege

1

situation in a hostile but identifiable country, the average time of confinement of American, French and British hostages in Lebanon was 782 days occurring within the confines of the anarchial environment of Lebanon's civil war. In many cases, these Lebanese hostage-taking situations caused major crises for Western governments in the conduct of foreign policy in the regional and international arena. Most Western governments, whose citizens are held hostage, pursue an official declared policy of no-concessions to terrorists. Official U.S. policy repeatedly underlined that: "[t]he U.S. government will make no concessions to terrorists. It will not pay ransoms, release prisoners, change its policies or agree to other acts that might encourage terrorism."[5] Similarly, the Council of Europe adheres to the principle of: "no concessions to the coercion of terrorists and those who support them."[6] Despite these public postures, their actual conduct towards the foreign hostage-crisis in Lebanon has often had a chequered history with secret concessions to secure the release of some of their hostages.[7] Over the last decade the balance-sheet for responses to the hostage-crisis in Lebanon also underlines the inherent difficulties for Western democratic states to resolve the dichotomy between the duty to protect its citizens abroad and the governmental obligation in hostage-taking situations to maintain the national interest in the conduct of foreign policy. This has been aptly demonstrated by David Clinton in that:

> "[a] state whose leaders and people forget or dismantle the ties that bind them into a community with a recognized national interest does more than run the risk of an internal 'war of every man against every man'. As the recent example of Lebanon and the American hostages makes clear, it also becomes a danger to any international ties, since its inability to maintain civil order allows internal violence to spill over into the outside world and threaten innocent third parties. What international society there is relies on states to undergird it by safeguarding their own national interests as functioning communities."[8]

This problem has been present regardless of the adoption of either a resolute hardline approach, as in the case of measures adopted by Great Britain characterized by firmness and refusal to make any concessions despite executions of hostages, or a softer approach, as in the case of the American and French dual-track measures characterized by the pursuit of a public hardline position while engaged in secret negotiations and concessions to secure the release of its hostages. In both cases, the targeted Western governments have been viewed as weak, incompetent and discredited through diminished public trust and confidence in the government in conjunction with maintaining a publicly enunciated policy by the abandonment of their citizens abroad or by the disclosure of the existence of negotiations or even deals. As a unique crisis or problem in the foreign policy arena, the nature of the foreign hostage-incidents in Lebanon as well as responses by Western governments have not only appeared to be enigmatic and secretive to the public and policymakers, even with the benefit of hindsight after the complete dénouement of the hostage-file in 1991–2, but have also been inadequately dealt with by academic research and within decision-making circles in studies of the management of these situations and in the application of prescribed lessons for any future incidents under similar conditions. This must be considered quite surprising given the duration and significant ramifications of these hostage-taking incidents on the conduct of foreign policy by Western democratic states operating in a veritable atmosphere of crisis over the last decade. As a consequence, the hostage-crisis in Lebanon underlines both the complexity and the difficulty in the successful resolution of hostage-situations for many Western governments and the importance of devoting considerable academic and policy attention to this issue in view of its ability and continued potential for affecting international relations.

This study examines, through a case-study approach, the complex nature and dynamics of the foreign hostage-crisis in Lebanon perpetrated by the Hizb'allah organisation with special reference to the multiple abductions of American, British, and French citizens between the period of 1982-1992. It also addresses in detail the multitiered relationships between the Hizb'allah and its patrons, Iran and Syria, as a prerequisite for the accompanying evaluation of the corresponding policies and responses adopted by the United States and the two European states within the framework of the application of crisis-management requirements and techniques.

This present chapter examines the nature of hostage-taking as a unique form of foreign policy crisis for Western governments and the theoretical applicability of crisis-management as an instrument to confront it. It also provides the methodological *raison d'être* for the study as well as a literature review of past and present material.

In the second chapter, an indepth historical background of the formation of the Hizb'allah movement in 1982 is provided to explain the close deference by the movement to Iran and the metamorphosis of a traditionally non-activist Lebanese Shi'a community into an extremely militant Islamic movement with a pan-Islamic ideology and strategy.

A third chapter provides analysis of Hizb'allah's organisational structure and its connections with Iran's clerical establishment and with Syria in order to establish the influences on the movement's decision-making process. These influences are superimposed onto Hizb'allah's practice of hostage-taking of American, French, and British citizens, within the framework of the movement's interaction with the constantly changing internal Lebanese environment.

The fourth chapter analyses the basis for the dynamics of the Iranian-Syrian relationship and its impact on the Hizb'allah within Lebanon with reference to opportunities and constraints in the abduction and release of foreign hostages.

A fifth chapter provides analysis of the performance of crisis management responses by the American and two West European states to the hostage-crisis. It draws on the analysis of the previous chapters to which Western governmental performance in these crises are evaluated in accordance with conformity to the established requirements for successful crisis-management and to the dynamics of the hostage-crisis as presented through the case-study.

The sixth and final chapter draws conclusions from the preceding evaluation of the hostage-crisis and the application of crisis-management techniques in order to assess the effectiveness of Western responses and its applicability for future hostage-incidents in the Middle East.

THE DEFINITION OF HOSTAGE-TAKING

The act of "hostage-taking" is among the most common manifestations of political terrorism. Its practitioners have been uniformly codified in international law as:

> "Any person who seizes or detains and threatens to kill, to injure or to continue to detain another person in order to compel a third party, namely, a State, an international intergovernmental organization, a natural or juridical person, or a group of persons, to do or abstain from doing any acts as an explicit or implicit condition for the release of the hostage."[9]

By employing the definition provided by the Hostage Convention, it is possible to discern certain key characteristics of hostage-taking in order to separate it from other forms of political terrorism.[10] In this context, the term hostage-taking will only relate to acts which are international in nature. An act of hostage-taking can be considered international when it is; "(1) directed at foreigners or foreign targets; (2) concerted by the governments or factions of more than one state; or (3) aimed at influencing the policies of a foreign government."[11] Within the framework of this definition, it is possible to obtain and identify four constitutive elements indispensable to the act of hostage-taking on the assumption that the dynamics of hostage-taking acts, and the behaviour of all parties involved, will be governed by the same fundemental principles and processes which apply to all social interactions.[12] As a consequence, the hostage-takers are treated as rational actors, in which rationality only implies that the actor has a reason for the execution of his actions and that the actor believes the action itself is not only useful in obtaining his goals but also that it maximises effect and possible outcomes.[13]

The first of the four necessary elements of hostage-taking is the seizure or detention of another person. Although acts of hostage-taking may assume a wide variety of ways in which the actual seizure or detention may be carried out, it is useful to classify hostage-incidents into two major categories: barricade/siege and hostage concealment situations. The distinction between these two types of hostage-situations is necessary as both differ in logistical and physical terms and require almost inevitably different policy and tactical responses. In a hostage barricade/siege situation, the hostage-takers and their victims are besieged in a location known to and controlled by the authorities. This severely restricts the mobility of the hostage-takers and often the duration of the incident. In a hostage concealment situation, the perpetrators detain hostages at an unknown location. These incidents are usually longer in duration as they provide the hostage-takers with anonymity, security and mobility.[14] In relation to the situation in Lebanon, the concealment of the hostages is not only a function of efficient operational secrecy by the terrorist organisation but also can be attributed to the chaotic environment caused by the protracted civil war which complicates the process of any response by governments. As such, the hostage-crisis in Lebanon is unique and precedent-setting since it does not conform to previous models of hostage-taking as the concealment is merely a technique or mechanism rather than an end itself.

A second element of the act of hostage-taking involves the threat to kill, to injure or to continue the detention of a hostage in order to compel a third party. A major underlying assumption of hostage-taking is that the act itself is carried out in order to affect the choices of a third party. As succinctly observed by Thomas Schelling: "[h]ostages represent the power to hurt in its purest form."[15] The selection of choices by a third party is dependent on the expected response of the hostage-taker to a particular decision and its preference for humanitarian values. The death of a hostage is threatened by the hostage-taker, as a last resort, in order to compel a third party to comply with any demand[s]. This rests on the presumption that a third party must consider the death of a hostage to be worse than complying with the demand[s]. Consequently, the threat in itself requires credibility which means that a third party will resist compliance to demands if the threat to kill hostages is not believable. Herein, the hostage-taker faces the dilemma that the credibility to carry out the threat is actually undermined by the fact that a third party's compliance with any demand is dependent on the survival of the hostage. However, this dilemma may be resolved by multiple abduction of hostages while the credibility of a threat can be enhanced through sequential killings of hostages, whereby the hostage-taker increases the costs for a third party for non-compliance. In the case of the abductions in Lebanon, the hostage-takers repeatedly threatened to execute their hostages to force compliance to its demands, yet only a relatively limited number of hostages were executed. In hindsight, between 1982 and 1992, only five Western hostages either died or were executed by the Hizb'allah. These were: Michel Seurat (1986); Peter Kilburn (1986); William Buckley (1985); William Higgins (1988); and Alberto Molinaro (1992). While only a few bodies of hostages were found, the hostage-takers used the presumed deaths of hostages and through silence regarding the hostage, as a means of reinforcing the credibility of their threats.

The third element of hostage-taking is that the aforementioned threat against hostages compels a third party to do or abstain from doing specified act[s]. All acts of hostage-taking must be considered goal-oriented activity, either motivated by economic, financial and/or political reasons. It is also assumed that all hostage-takers genuinely seek compliance rather than resistance from a third party in response to any demand[s].[16] In the bargaining process between a hostage-taker and a third party, the hostage-taker faces two options in any attempts to achieve concessions from a third party: either to raise the level of the threat for a third party to force submission or, subsequently, reward any compliance. In turn, the main goal of the hostage-taker is to compel a third party to either take any action or refrain from certain activity.

A final element of hostage-taking is compliance by a third party to the demands of the hostage-taker as an explicit or implicit condition for the release of the hostage[s]. It is important to recognize that the outcome of a hostage-incident, regardless of the nature of demands, is implicitly or explicitly the *quid pro quo* for the submission of the third party to the compulsion.[17] At its most basic level, the process of bargaining in hostage-taking incidents assumes that a hostage-taker attempts to achieve maximum objectives, while the third party seeks to resolve the situation by conceding the minimum amount possible.[18] As a consequence, the relationship between the hostage-taker and a third party is conducted through a zero-sum framework, whereby if one party wins then the other must necessarily lose.

HOSTAGE-TAKING IN LEBANON AS A FORM OF FOREIGN POLICY CRISIS

Over the last decade, incidents of hostage-taking of foreigners in Lebanon have had a disproportionate effect on foreign and domestic policy for many Western governments compared to other forms of crisis in foreign affairs, given the nature of the problem and the actual number of victims involved in these incidents. Even in comparison to other forms of international terrorism and in relation to incidents carried out in previous years, the phenomenon of hostage-taking in the 1980s neither increased significantly in number of incidents or fatalities.[19] Despite the actual reality of the low-level threat posed by hostage-taking to vital national interests and security of Western governments, there has been a close association of the hostage-taking incidents in Lebanon with the notion of "crises". This has been reinforced by the rhetoric of major Western political leaders in response to the hostage-incidents in Lebanon. While President Reagan stated that: "[i]f we permit terrorism to succeed anywhere, it will spread like cancer, eating away at civilized societies and sowing fear and chaos everywhere", the issue of the hostages in Lebanon became an obsession for the French political candidates in the national elections in 1986 and 1988.[20] Although the prolonged hostage-incidents in Lebanon have presented foreign governments with unique and unprecedented foreign policy problems as well as challenges, it is essential to determine the degree of conformity of these hostage-taking acts to necessary criteria of what constitutes a crisis in the foreign policy arena and to determine the way in which hostage-taking differs from other more conventional foreign policy crises.

The term "crisis" itself is frequently used indiscriminately by journalists, academics and policymakers alike to describe conditions of conflict and disagreement in international politics. While agreement exists that crisis, stemming from the etymology of the word, involves a turning-point from a condition of peace to the possibility of war,[21] there is no generally agreed definition of the term. In fact, as conceded by many analysts, the concept of crisis has been rendered hollow and useless as it is applied to all situations which are essentially difficult to diagnose, distressful to confront, and whose course is unpredictable with any great degree of certainty.[22] The main reason for the wide variety of definitions of the term stems not only from the methodological approach adopted but also from the actual context within which the crisis occurs, in terms of the diverse actors and means as well as the length of the struggle in many grey areas of conflict.[23] From the etymological roots of the term crisis and its subsequent development, it is possible to discern a number of recurring components. Apart from the notion of decision and turningpoint, crises also signify a threat to vital goals and objectives, a moment of truth for those confronted with it, short time for decisions, as well as a sense of opportunity, the last most evidently revealed by the Chinese definition of crisis depicted by a double ideogram representing both danger and opportunity.[24]

While scholars have offered a wide range of definitions of crisis, usually dependent on the context, the term has been defined descriptively in accordance to certain key traits or sets of characteristics. As most attempts to define crisis focus on high-threat situations restricted to the military and security areas alone between two or more *state* actors, especially within the context of the conventional application of crisis-management, it is necessary to find suitable and broad definitions of crisis for situations created by non-territorial political groups against territorial entities, especially within the context of the so-called "grey areas" of conflict. Instead, as advanced by Alexander George, crisis-situations are usually heavily context-dependent.[25]

Among the most frequently used and classical definitions of crisis has been offered by Charles Hermann, who defines it as a "situation that (1) threatens high-priority goals of the decision-making unit; (2) restricts the amount of time available for response before the decision is transformed; and (3) surprises the members of the decision-making unit by its occurrence."[26] While this definition has been valuable for the decision-making approach to crisis behaviour, some argue it is limited as it cannot be applied to many situations which fail to conform to "stringent requirements of coherent decision-making by a group perceiving itself to be in a situation of high threat, short time and surprise."[27] The application of this definition to the hostage-situation in Lebanon reveals its limitations due to the longevity of the situation, in many cases hostages had been held for several years, as well as by the recurring repetition of these abductions which minimised any element of surprise. As a consequence, it is more useful to adopt a broader definition which includes two characteristics of any crisis, commonly accepted by the scholarly community as: [1] a severe threat to important values and [2] a finite time for coping with the threat.[28]

The assessment of the level of the threat of the Lebanon hostage-taking acts is based on various components: firstly, the importance of values for decision-makers of Western governments, whose citizens have been held hostage in Lebanon; secondly, they must be placed within the context of the perceived degree of the threat to national interests; thirdly, this will be influenced by the previous experience in countering terrorism; and fourthly, the constraints imposed by the dynamics of the incident itself for governments in responding effectively and rapidly for its resolution.

At its core, acts of hostage-taking constitute a direct assault on commonly held principles and values of all citizens within liberal democracies, most notably the maintenance of order by a state to ensure that the lives of its citizens are secure against violence. All societies, according to Hedley Bull, attempt to sustain order through the pursuit of three primary goals: "[t]o ensure that life will be in some measure secure against violence resulting in death or bodily harm…that promises, once made, will be kept, or that agreements once undertaken, will be carried out…pursue the goal of ensuring that the possession of things remain stable to some degree, and will not be subject to challenges that are constant and without limit."[29] As such, a government has a required responsibility, especially in hostage-taking situations, to be viewed as doing all in "its power to defend the life and limb of its citizens" not only within its own borders but also abroad.[30] The claim that the state has a duty to protect its citizens and their welfare rests on the reciprocal duty by the citizen, as a priviledge of receiving this protection, to risk his or her life for the state at certain times. In this task, the concerned government faces a fundamental dilemma to balance its individual responsibility towards its citizens taken hostage abroad with its requirement to safeguard the maintenance of other collective national interests. It should be the case, according to George F. Kennan, that: "[g]overnment is an agent, not a principal. Its primary obligation is to the interests of the national society it represents, not to the moral impulses that individual elements of that society may experience."[31] An underlying reason for this dilemma has been that many governments have moved to integrate their strategy to confront and combat international terrorism as, inturn an integral component of their foreign policy. As a consequence, the handling of the hostage-issue in Lebanon by governments has not only been influenced by efforts to confront state-sponsored terrorism by proxy but has also been closely affected by internal Lebanese, regional and international affairs. While the integration of efforts to confront terrorism as components of foreign policy has made the issue of handling the hostage-situation in Lebanon susceptible to the opportunities and constraints arising from the conduct of wider foreign policies in the Middle East, it has also been subject to a wide variety of pressures, most notably associated with the perceptions of the threat and lack of available options for its resolution based on the previous assessment.

The salience of the hostage-situation in Lebanon to Western governments' foreign policy agendas was inextricably linked to the perceived serious challenge of the rise and spread of militant Islamic fundamentalism in the Middle East, embodied in the establishment of an Islamic theocracy in Iran and in its drive to export its revolution beyond its borders, to the detriment of regional stability and against Western interests in the broader Muslim world. While Iran's most direct and sustained influence pertained to their co-religionists in Lebanon, direct violent acts under the banner of militant Islam against Western citizens and property, coupled with anti-Western demonology and promises of a holy war against the enemies of Islam, exacerbated the perception among Western policymakers and publics that Islam could be equated with fanaticism and terrorism. This image was reinforced by the October 1983 twin-suicide attacks against American and French Multinational Forces (MNF) contingencies in Lebanon, resulting in the deaths of 300 servicemen, which elevated the problem of Islamic terrorism to the level of a major national security issue. While the incidents were symptomatic of the problems faced by the West in their involvement in Lebanon and in attempts to find a resolution to the intractable civil war, their impact was also compounded by the subsequent systematic abduction of foreign citizens by shadowy pro-Iranian groups, operating under the cover of an anarchial environment. Although these incidents were closely reminicent of the 1979 Iranian hostage-crisis for policymakers and public, the hostage-situation in Lebanon differed from the previous situation in the complexity of the issues, the longevity of the incidents as well as the multiplicity of involved parties.

As a manifestation of the threat of Iran's attempts to spread Islamic fundamentalism in the Middle East, the hostage-taking incidents in Lebanon were viewed by Western policymakers through the application of a narrow Western ideological prism depicting Islam against the West. This approach ignored the causes of the rise of the Shi'a community in Lebanon, from political quietism to militant activism against the background of confessional warfare, and consequently suffered from the misperception of the Hizb'allah as merely a creation of revolutionary Iran, and a tool orchestrated and directed from Teheran in a holy war against the West. This image of the adversary, as fanatical and dangerous, and the nature of its links with Iran was also reinforced in the West by Hizb'allah's public deference to Iran in all spheres of its activities.[32] As a consequence, the hostage-issue in Lebanon became not only viewed as a logical extension of the West's wider foreign policy efforts to contain Iranian influence in the region but also contributed to its treatment by Western governments as an issue both of assault on individual lives of its citizens and on national integrity.

While the treatment by the West of the hostage-incidents in Lebanon within the confines of wider foreign policy efforts to contain Iran naturally elevated the issue of the hostages on the foreign policy agenda, the nature and dynamics of these incidents contributed to the athmosphere of crisis in efforts by their governments to extract Western hostages. For example, after the revelation of the Iran-Contra affair, President Reagan's approval rating dropped from 67 percent to 46 percent, the largest single drop for a U.S. president ever.[33] The elevation of the hostage-incidents to the status of foreign policy crisis stemmed from pressures on Western decision-makers in failing to effectively confront and rapidly secure the release of their own citizens from captivity. Apart from the sensational and spectacu-lar nature of these acts, the pressures faced by Western governments from within their own borders were related to the public discrepancy between the expression of concern for the welfare of citizens taken hostage abroad as well as promises made for their safe return and a publicly enunicated firm policy of "no concessions" to any terrorist demands. While the pub-licly enunciated policy of no concessions reduced government flexibility in the handling of the hostage-crisis, as credibility would be seriously damaged by the subsequent disclosure of any dealings with terrorists, it also increased the pressure on government decisionmakers from the public and media, who regarded their respective governments as weak and soft, in concurrence with the continued prolongation of these incidents despite assurances of a rapid resolution. The creation of heightened and unrealistic expectations by governments in dealing with the hostage-taking incidents when, in reality, there were no simple solutions, underlined the unique contradictory pressures created by hostage-taking situations on govern-ments compared to other forms of more conventional foreign policy crisis. The actual cost inflicted by abandoning previous public rhetoric and promises resulted in "[l]osses in credibility and prestige which may impair the defaulting parties' political effectiveness."[34] In particular, a distin-guishing pressure for decision-makers in dealing with these hostage-incidents relates to the human dimensions of the crisis, most notably the identification of an individual predicament.[35] The knowledge by a govern-ment leader of the actual identity of a particular Western hostage incarcer-ated in Lebanon removed any bureaucratic sense of impersonality towards the issue and in the application of any delineated policies and principles. In his memoirs, President Reagan admitted that he: "[f]elt a heavy weight on (his) shoulders to get the hostages home."[36] In turn, these pressures were continuously reinforced by the terrorists, through the release of peri-odic personal appeals by the hostages, through intense scrutiny of any action or inaction by targeted governments by the media and by the victims' families, through various pressure groups. As described by Thomas Twetten in his testimony to the Tower Commission:

"[t]he real thing that was driving this was…a lot of pressure from the hostage families…and there were articles in the magazines about the forgotten hostages, and there were alot of things being said about the U.S. Government isn't doing anything… And there [was] alot of fear about the yellow ribbons going back up and that this President would have the same problems that the last President had had with the Iranian hostages."[37]

This fear was further compounded by the perceived innocence of the suffering hostages themselves, only guilty of being at the wrong place at the wrong time.[38]

Unlike most other forms of foreign policy crisis, the hostage incidents were also extremely long in duration. As a crisis, the degree of intensity was closely dependent on the nature of threats by the terrorist for the execution of a hostage unless the government meet certain political demands. While the sense of urgency was dependent on the credibility of the hostage-taker to carry out the threat, it also led to constant readjustment of escalation and de-escalation along the crisis ladder by governments in response to new abductions, threats, and demands by the terrorists over an extensive period of time.

As a unique form of foreign policy crisis, the hostage-incidents in Lebanon have constituted a serious problem for many Western governments, which at the core underlines the fundamental dilemma for liberal democracies in finding a remedy for the inbalance between safeguarding its moral obligation towards protecting its individual citizens while maintaining longterm foreign policy interests.[39] In response to the search for an equilibrium between interests and obligations in these hostage-crises, Western governments have usually vacilliated between the extremes of either underreacting or overreacting in a seemingly *ad hoc* manner in response to pressures from the public and from foreign states or for the advancement of foreign policy agendas and the fortunes of individual political leaders. Although hostage-incidents exhibit unique pressures for decisionmakers compared to other more conventional crises, all types of crisis restrict the maneuverability of government responses. As the primary goal of all governments in response to any type of crisis must be to contain and minimize the effects of a crisis while maximizing their available initiatives, the employment of traditional principles and techniques of crisis-management to the handling of a hostage-crisis by governments can provide a useful instrument for the evaluation of the crisis itself as well as a guideline in order to cope and manage these complex forms of crisis more effectively and successfully.

CRISIS-MANAGEMENT AND ITS APPLICATION TO
HOSTAGE-CRISES

The term "crisis-management" has been indiscriminately employed in the field of social sciences by academics and policymakers in attempts to exercise control over an array of "crisis" situations, ranging from nuclear confrontation between the two superpowers to terrorism incidents and natural disasters. Although the literal meaning of the term "management" itself denotes efforts "to control" and "to take charge of" crisis situations, it has been regarded as somewhat misleading for the activity at hand. As pointed out by Coral Bell:

> "[t]he overtones of the word 'management' imply a rational, dispassionate, calculating, well considered activity, conducted with judgement and perhaps even at a leisurely pace with a view to long term as against short term interests. Actual crisis decisonmaking is not usually at all like that: it is improvised at great pressure of time and events by men working in a fog of ambiguity."[40]

At its core, the inherent paradox and dilemma of crisis-management has been the necessity of taking certain actions in order to protect one's vital interests while avoiding actions that may result in undesired costs and risks.[41] While the conventional application of the craft of crisis-management has centered on efforts to minimize chances of crisis-situations between two or more state-actors from escalating into war,[42] which led to the establishment of certain conventions and instruments in the management of crises, it is possible to discern and apply a number of these underlying principles of crisis-management to violent crisis-situations, most notably in response to the hostage-crisis in Lebanon.

The most central task of crisis-management is to ensure the resolution of a crisis on a satisfactory basis, in which the vital interests of the state are secured and protected, through a process of coercion and accommodation in order to achieve effectively a maximum amount of concession from the adversary and, at the same time, maintain one's own position relatively intact.[43] The process of coercion and accommodation must be carefully balanced in order to prevent either the escalation of a crisis or capitulation to the wishes of the adversary at any price.[44] In this task, the ability to manage the crisis for a policymaker is dependent on the understanding of the nature and degree of threats to his country's interests in order to gain control over the crisis-situation and on the evaluation of employment of instruments and policy preferences, an assessment of the way in which the adversary views the crisis situation, and a determination of the probable consequences of different courses of action designed to influence the adversary's behaviour in order to secure specific objectives in a crisis. While crisis-management involves the ability to communicate resolve and intent to an adversary, the instruments for this purpose can be distinguished into two basic categories in confronting a specific crisis involving hostage-taking, namely physical acts and verbal statements of intent.[45] The verbal dimensions of crisis-management may precede the actual application of the instruments but are always present as reinforcement used in combination with the physical acts.[46]

The physical instruments of crisis-management in a hostage-crisis involve either military actions or nonmilitary instruments of statecraft.[47] The military dimensions of crisis-management in hostage-crisis situations involves the movement of military forces to designated positions as a signal of commitment and resolution. This may involve the threat or actual use of limited violence against the adversary either to force a change in its position to achieve concessions or to punish for non-conciliatory behaviour. In order to achieve control over the application of military force to avoid an unwanted escalation of the crisis, it is important to recognize the limited applicability of the use of military instruments, either in isolation of other nonviolent instruments of statecraft or for the resolution of the crisis itself.[48] According to Casper Weinberger, U.S. Secretary of Defense, five basic conditions, reminiscent of just war theory, must be met before applying military force to a situation: "[t]he force must be timely, appropriate, have public support, have a high probability of success and should be used only as a last resort."[49] Although the use of military force must be closely integrated with a diplomatic strategy, avoidance of the application of military force is also appealing as an inexpensive approach in that it reduces the political and psychological costs involved in the crisis.[50]

The other physical instrument of crisis-management assumes greater importance than violent means and must be considered more complex as it involves the combined use of an array of political tools of statecraft. While these can be broadly categorized within the field of diplomacy, economics, and international law, their use is far more flexible and applicable to a hostage-crisis situation, than just applying military force, as they consist of a variety of combined resources, utilized within the framework of a crafted strategy to alter the behaviour of an adversary in accordance with one's own interests. This strategy relies on a mixture of these political instruments of crisis-management, either in isolation or in combination, through a process of "persuasion, coercive threats or actions, accommodative offers and concessions".[51] While the components of the political instruments of statecraft may assume a coercive nature, ranging from the rupture of diplomatic relations with states closely associated with the hostage-takers to the active apprehension and prosecution of hostage-takers in accordance with domestic or international law, or may become conciliatory, ranging from lifting economic sanctions to the release of imprisoned terrorists, the actual application of these instruments to a crisis-situation involves the *techniques* of crisis-management.[52] The exact nature of these techniques vary from crisis to crisis as crisis-management is highly context-dependent, subject to the interplay of all involved actors and to an array of important factors affecting the crisis-situation.[53] As a consequence, the application of a crisis-management approach to hostage-situations in Lebanon will have to be adapted to the individual character of the crisis, in terms of actors as well as to the dynamics of the situation, which will determine the political constraints and opportunities under which to apply different techniques of crisis-management. While crisis-management involves the choice between coercion and accommodation, or a mixture of the two, any application of crisis-management techniques is dependent on the employment of a strategy. In this sense the concept of strategy conforms to the ideas of Thomas Schelling that it needs to be broadly based in terms of how one state-actor attempts to get another actor to do something it might not otherwise do.[54] As the hostage-crisis in Lebanon involved not only the Hizb'allah organisation itself but also two identifiable state-actors, Iran and Syria, the application of crisis-management instruments through various techniques as well as the devising of any strategy for their employment had to be conducted at two levels, accounting for both the advancement of Hizb'allah's own interests and the interests of its two patron states. This differentiation becomes necessary as both Iran and Syria have been not only closely involved in the activities of the Hizb'allah but also have exploited their roles as intermediaries in the hostage-crisis, in which these two states have actively used their influence over the Hizb'allah to release Western hostages through coercion and accommodation, in order to gain substantial advancements in their own foreign and domestic policy agendas. While the interests of Hizb'allah may converge with the interests of its patrons, as a range of demands by the organisation is presented in conjunction with those of the sponsoring states, it is necessary to clarify the salience of these demands to either adversary in order to discern the necessary strategy and direction of the application of crisis-management techniques. In fact, the selection of a strategy must be appropriate to the character of the crisis which offers a reasonable chance of achieving required political objectives in a crisis-situation. This issue underlines the existence of certain requirements of crisis-management in order to select appropriate instruments of statecraft, to deploy these through effective techniques, and to devise a useful strategy for their deployment with a view to achieving the successful resolution of the crisis itself in accordance with clear and obtainable political objectives.[55] Although the requirements of crisis-management vary in different types of crisis, these should be regarded as general principles for more effective management of hostage-crisis situations for policymakers rather than necessary conditions in the stricter sense, as stressed in all major works of crisis-management. These political and operational requirements of crisis-management in terrorist crisis situations, within the framework of the hostage-crisis in Lebanon, can be limited to: the limitation of political objectives pursued in a crisis; the limitation of means employed in pursuit of these objectives; accurate and timely intelligence on the adversary and on the crisis-situation; the maintenance of communication with the adversary; access to and experience with crisis-management machinery; search for a broad platform of support; and consideration of the precedent effect of crisis-behaviour.[56]

Requirements of Crisis-Management

The first requirement of the limitation of political objectives in a crisis for effective crisis-management means that a policymaker must realize that in most cases he/she will be unable to achieve its maximum political objectives. It can be expected that the increased intensity of the pursuit of political objectives at the expense of the adversary will be proportional to the increased will to resist by the adversary. It is also necessary to define the political objectives in a crisis within the framework of opportunities and constraints in the given crisis-environment for the establishment of the boundaries for the application of crisis-management.[57]

A second requirement for effective crisis-management, the limitation of means employed in pursuit of these political objectives, is essential in order to avoid an unnecessary escalation of a crisis situation.[58] This must entail a cost-benefit analysis that posits the risks to be run in pursuit of these political objectives as well as the costs of compromising these same objectives. It is also crucial to provide various ways in which the adversary can retreat without losing face in order to provide an avenue for the resolution of the crisis itself without too much cost.[59] This may be achieved by the involvement of an international organisation or through mediation by a third party.

The third requirement of crisis-management, accurate and timely intelligence on the adversary and on the crisis-situation, involves the identification of the adversary and the dynamics of the crisis as a fundamental pre-requisite to base any application of crisis-management. As the failure to provide reliable and timely intelligence at the onset of the crisis and through its development leads to major errors in estimating an adversary's intentions in the crisis and reactions to employed responses, it is critical to rely on accurate and timely intelligence in order to determine whether the selection of crisis-management instruments are likely to be effective in eliciting a favoured response, where to apply these instruments, and when the application of these techniques is likely to be effective.

A fourth requirement of crisis-management, the maintenance of communication with the adversary, is imperative as a means to avoid misunderstanding and miscommunication with the adversary, either through the means of direct channels or through an intermediary.[60] As crisis-management involves the signaling of coercion and accommodation, means of communication with the adversary become more valuable during a crisis as the likelihood of being misunderstood is greater.[61] In order to utilize the crisis-management instruments, even in the absence of diplomatic relations with an adversary, it is necessary to find alternative means of communication in order to maintain the balance between coercion and accommodation. Often the employment of a third party as an intermediary is advantageous in situations which prevent direct negotiations with an adversary and as a shield to delay the urgency of the crisis. In order to maintain communication channels and to reduce the possibility of escalatory effects of a crisis, there must be restraint in the use of language through avoidance of ideological and moralising posturing towards the adversary and the crisis itself.[62]

The fifth requirement of crisis-management, access to and experience with crisis-management machinery, is essential for preparedness and effectiveness in any given crisis-situation. The existence of crisis-management machinery will directly affect the outcome of success or failure in any efforts to employ various instruments and techniques to a crisis and to limit the effects of the situation for policymakers. In order to be effective, the crisis-management machinery must serve as the operational and support requirement for crisis-management and negotiations as well as be able rapidly and accurately to adapt itself to the changing dynamics of the crisis-situation.[63]

A sixth requirement of crisis-management, the search for a broad platform of support, is crucial in the domestic and international context in order to obtain endorsement of measures already implemented or planned in the future. In the domestic context, it is necessary to educate the public over the inherent difficulties of responding to the crisis in order to limit the effects of the crisis on the political leadership as well as to search for political support for any course of action prior to and throughout the crisis. In the international context, it is necessary to seek political support from allies for the co-ordination and implementation of any course of action in order to avoid tension and cross-purpose activity.

The final requirement of crisis-management, consideration of the precedent effect of crisis-behaviour, must be present in order to avoid setting unfavourable precedents for similar situations in the future. Apart from ensuring the legality of adopted measures in accordance with domestic and international law, the course of action adopted and implemented must be in accordance with previous agreements entered into with other states in order to avoid undermining either the credibility of promises made with allies or the actions of other states confronted by a similar crisis. An assessment must be made whether the behaviour in the handling of the crisis either encourages or discourages more crisis-situations of a similar nature.[64]

These requirements of crisis-management should serve as a guideline in the task of formulation of an effective strategy which takes into account the necessary diplomatic desiderata in order to reconcile, as closely as possible, the policy dilemmas of crisis-management, namely the dichotomy between the protection of national interests in a crisis and avoidance of measures that would escalate any crisis to undesirable and uncontrollable levels.[65] They can also serve as a useful guideline to the evaluation of any government performance in confronting the hostage-crisis in Lebanon. Using crisis-management instruments and techniques as adherence to these requirements should make for a more effective and consistent policy as well as path in efforts to resolve the dilemma of fulfillment of the duty by a state to protect its citizens abroad taken hostage without sacrifice of its national interests in the conduct of foreign policy.

METHODOLOGICAL APPROACH

In any field of academic study there exist an array of levels of analysis, each distinguished by different concepts, research questions and methodologies. While insight into any one level will bring out a particular segment of analysis, although valuable in itself, it is the actual *linkage* of the findings at all levels into an aggregate whole which is the most difficult but also the most valuable exercise for academic researchers.[66] A main point of departure for this study is that the focus on a single and one-dimensional level of analysis is deficient as a framework for full comprehension of the hostage-crisis in Lebanon. An examination of the dynamics of the crisis itself, and the application of crisis-management to it, through the employment of a multilayered case-study approach, would enable us to move beyond the position of blind men attempting to grasp the elephant (as aptly described in North's famous analogy).[67]

Any methodological approach to studying the hostage-crisis in Lebanon would seem to lend itself naturally to the use of a systems analysis in order to discern definable and regular patterns of interaction between the constituent actors.[68] Using systems theory as a framework for understanding the hostage-crisis in Lebanon could provide academics with an analytical tool to identify, measure, and examine the interaction between Hizb'allah, Syria, and Iran within the environment of a regional subsystem. Although systems theory has valuable merits as an approach with wide application, it also has some severe limitations from a foreign policy approach in dealing with the complex interactions between the triangular relationship between Hizb'allah-Iran-Syria. As systems theory is geared towards determination of predictability in the interaction between the constituent actors within the regional sub-system as well as with the international system,[69] it has been criticized for failing to achieve this objective.[70] A major problem with systems analysis, as delineated by Stanley Hoffman, is the construction of a model of the behaviour of interacting groups within a system on certain hypotheses, which are often questionable, abstract, and arbitrarily derived and thus far removed from reality.[71] In theory, this flaw can be effectively demonstrated by treating systems analysis as a broad-based funnel, which originates at its widest base with all actors involved in a particular hostage-crisis situation and begins with some general assumptions by policymakers, based upon preconceived notions and information about a particular actor or several actors. In crisis-situations, Richard Ned Lebow argues that policymakers are often strongly committed to particular policies from the outset of the crisis and either ignore or interpret any new information to make it consistent with their own expectations.[72] Moving along the narrower base of the funnel towards the crisis-situation itself, these general assumptions become increasingly modified in order to adapt to a particular situation or actor. However, as the move away from the broad-based original assumptions occurs through modification, it often leads to the application of a new set of assumptions, at times in total contradiction to the original broad-based theory. For example, the question of the relationship between Hizb'allah and Iran has vacilliated between total control and total independence. In the event that this occurs across a general area, it leads to a series of several assumptions with no linkage between each other as the original base has been perverted. The perversion of the base of original assumptions may explain some of the reasons for the failure to pursue a coherent policy throughout the hostage-crisis. In practice, this can be demonstrated by the systems analysis approach adopted by the Western policymakers to the hostage-crisis in Lebanon, both in terms of assumptions about the relationship between Hizb'allah and Iran as well as the applicability of traditional hostage-negotiation strategy and tactics to the situation. A major original and broad-based belief among Western policymakers has been that Hizb'allah's relationship with Iran has been monolithic and static, as the movement was considered merely an Iranian autonom.[73] Another assumption has been that traditional counterterrorism policy and techniques, crafted and applied to the broader areas of confronting state-sponsored terrorism in the Middle East and other forms of political violence elsewhere, were not only applicable but also adequate for effective responses to the hostage-crisis in Lebanon. As these original and broad-based assumptions moved towards the narrower base of the funnel in interaction with the multitiered dynamics of the hostage-crisis in Lebanon, it resulted in a series of new uncoordinated assumptions for policymakers, fundamentally different from the assumption from which policy and approach were based upon originally. This problem has been eloquently echoed by Paul Wilkinson that the tendency to oversimplify and generalize tends to produce simplistic and dangerous proposals for panaceas. Wilkinson went on to accurately observe that "[c]ontext is all in the analysis of political violence. In view of the enormous diversity of groups and aims involved, generalizations and evaluations covering the whole field of modern terrorism should be treated with considerable reserve."[74] As a consequence, this fundamental problem necessitates a different type of approach, namely that: "[i]ndividual cases rather than a series of abstract assumptions can credibly constitute the 'building blocks' of theory formation".[75] In terms of this study, using a case-study approach to the hostage-crisis in Lebanon, through the employment of the same funnel from systems analysis, translates into a "bottom-up" approach without any general assumptions from the start.[76] A case-study analysis of the hostage-crisis in Lebanon involves a thorough study of the particular situation at hand and the multitiered dynamics of all involved actors (Hizb'allah, Iran and Syria), all interconnected at various levels, in order to evaluate and formulate a specific policy for a particular situation. In the event that this can be done with several individual hostage-crises with similar dynamics, the various crises can be examined for linkage and commonality which, in turn, forms the framework for a new broad theory.[77]

The employment of systems analysis with a high degree of generalization will automatically also not achieve the expected positive results or predictability of using crisis-management to the hostage-crisis. As stated by J.L. Gaddis: "[f]or in coping with unsimulatable situations, theory – which is only past experience projected forward – is, and should be, of little help: variables overwhelm the capacity for generalization; generalizations, if attempted, are almost certain to mislead."[78] This can be explained by the fact that the generalizations of systems analysis fail to account for the dynamics of a continuous fluctuation in the environment *vis-à-vis* the interaction between Hizb'allah-Iran-Syria. While identifying the *breadth* of linkages between Hizb'allah-Iran-Syria becomes essential for any analysis of the hostage-crisis, it is equally important to understand its *depth*. In many ways, the configuration of the hostage-crisis in Lebanon is reminiscent of a cobweb in which the interaction of the Hizb'allah with its environment; the interaction between Hizb'allah and Iran and Syria, respectively; and the interaction between Iran and Syria superimpose themselves on the ground in Lebanon, resulting in a multitiered system of constant interaction, a process vital to the understanding of the mechanics of the hostage-crisis itself and, in particular, to the application of any crisis-management techniques. In order for policymakers to avoid a one-dimensional general approach, it is necessary to opt for an integrated multilayered framework of analysis as a base for a case-study from which it is possible to superimpose the instruments and techniques of crisis-management used by Western governments to evaluate its effectiveness in the past and its applicability for the future. As aptly observed by Charles Kegley, Jr.:

"[m]erely asking the question, 'Is a particular act of terrorism accounted for by domestic or external influences?' requires us to consider the possibility that it was not determined exclusively by only one set of factors, but by a number in combination. This allows complexity to be captured and serves as an antidote to inaccurate stereotypes and invalid inferences."[79]

A main underlying criteria for evaluating the effectiveness of crisis-management is not only adherence to certain requirements of effective crisis-management strategy but also its employment in accordance with the dynamics of the crisis-situation itself. As a consequence, in agreement with Robert Jervis, when not only many factors are at work, but also the relationships among them are varied, case-studies will make the greatest contribution to understanding.[80]

LITERATURE REVIEW

The literature on the hostage-crisis in Lebanon can be characterized by the discrepancy between the enormous quantity of sources available in the public domain and the relatively limited quantity and quality of analysis pursued by academics and policymakers on the subject. While the quantitative aspects of the hostage-crisis literature can be related to the sensational nature of this form of foreign policy crisis, the hostage-issue has been amplified as a subject, as it occurred within a protracted civil war environment, but has also suffered from constraint by the same environment, in terms of the availability and scope of information on the hostage-taking organisations acting under the umbrella of the Hizb'allah. The complexity of operating within the chaotic environment of Lebanon's civil war has contributed to the difficulty in accurately identifying the nature of the hostage-takers themselves. It has been compounded by the obsession of the Hizb'allah movement for operational secrecy. The lack of accurate intelligence on the Hizb'allah movement, exacerbated by an abundance of rumours, has presented academic analysts and journalists with special barriers to overcome in order to provide a composite picture over the dynamics of the hostage-crisis. While these inherent problems have led most academics to dismiss the possibility of unravelling the inner dimensions of Hizb'allah activity in any meaningful way for a fuller and better understanding of the hostage-crisis, it has also contributed to a countless array of unreliable Western journalistic accounts based on unconfirmed rumours and faulty assumptions. The lack of indepth analysis by academics into the Hizb'allah movement has forced them into no other avenue than reliance on systems theory to provide a general approach to a complex subject. Herein lies the inherent inconsistency of analysis for those who study these movements, such as academics, and, more importantly, policymakers, who are handcuffed into making specific crisis-management decisions with only a general composite picture. As accurately pointed out by the eminent Middle East scholar John Esposito:

> "[m]ore often than not, Islamic movements are lumped together; conclusions are drawn based on stereotyping or expectation than empirical research. The problem owes less to the secrecy of individuals and organizations than to more mundane factors: the less we know, the more we tend to generalize or deductively conclude from that which we do know."[81]

Like a giant jigsaw puzzle, the real dilemma for any serious scholar has been not only to decipher the valuable information from either dis- or mis-information as well as seperating facts from fiction, but also to describe and interpret the bigger picture, especially the contexts of international and domestic politics present during the crisis. The need to conduct post-mortems of Western responses to the hostage-crisis are obvious given the failure of most states to adequately minimise its impact on domestic and foreign policy affairs and its destabilizing effect during the last decade on intra-state relations in the international system which has served to perpetuate past and present Middle East conflicts.

A number of valuable scholarly contributions exist on the transformation of the Lebanese Shi'a community from political quietism to militant activism, shedding light on the conditions that facilitiated its active political and military entry within a civil war environment. Yet, this only contributed to a limited amount of direct academic analysis on the Hizb'allah movement itself. While few academic studies have dealt with certain aspects of Hizb'allah's practice of terrorism and hostage-taking, more recent efforts have focused on Hizb'allah's political readjustment within Lebanon's post-civil war environment.

The exisiting academic literature on Hizb'allah and its use of political violence against foreigners make valuable individual contributions to the overall picture of the true nature of the movement and its activity. While a few studies have concentrated on exploration of certain aspects of the movement's relationship with Iran, most small fragments of information on the dynamic interaction between Hizb'allah and its environment as well as with Iran and Syria must be extracted from other more general academic studies on Middle East politics and from domestic as well as foreign press reports. The denouement of the hostage-crisis in Lebanon in 1991, coupled with a more openness of the Hizb'allah as a parliamentary political party from 1992, has made the study of the movement not only more feasible and accessible in terms of new information about the movement than previous academic attempts to overcome the secrecy barriers of the subject, but also more salient in terms of providing a broad and indepth understanding of a phenomenon that plagued the conduct of foreign policy for most Western governments for over a decade. This becomes more pressing given the parallel resurgence of Islamic movements in other Arab states, who increasingly employ political violence against Western targets for whom the Hizb'allah serves as an example to emulate.

In contrast to information surrounding the hostage-crisis in Lebanon, the academic literature on the subject, as opposed to theory, of crisis-management and its application to specific hostage-situations in unknown environments is still in its infancy. This is due to the fact that many of these hostage-crisis situations are not fixed, rather part of an ongoing process. As such, they remain static which means that indepth comprehensive and accurate accounts of their study are subject to scrutiny. While previous analysis has focused on the mechanics of using crisis-management machinery to specific barricade/siege situations, the void in the academic field of using crisis-management as an applied instrument and guideline for the evaluation of Western government response to the hostage-crisis in Lebanon needs to be filled in order to bridge efforts to reconcile the inherent policy dilemmas displayed by the chequered history of Western government response to this form of foreign policy crisis. Apart from the inherent tendency by these Western governments to veil their past performance to the hostage-crisis in complete secrecy, the emerging literature on uncovered secret initiatives by policymakers is useful not only as a justification that performance in managing hostage-taking situations needs to be significantly enhanced in order to limit its effect in the conduct of foreign policy, but also as a rich source of information to the whole range of problems facing policymakers trying to extract themselves from these forms of crisis. While the majority of these exposés, most notably the Iran-Contra debacle, have provided fuller insights into the inner sanctum of foreign policy-making in hostage-crisis situations, few have drawn valuable lessons for the improvement of Western government responses in the past or for the future. This study intends not only to contribute to a fuller understanding of the labyrinthine complexity of the dynamics of the hostage-crisis in Lebanon but also to bridge the gap between a detailed case-study of a terrorist group, sponsored by outside states, and the evaluation of Western government responses to this foreign policy crisis using crisis-management as an instrument to evaluate their effectiveness and success.

2 Background to the Formation of the Hizb'allah in Lebanon

INTRODUCTION

Prior to the organisational formation of Hizb'allah in June 1982, the Lebanese Shi'a community was largely regarded, by other militias as well as outside observers, as politically irrelevant in Lebanon.[1] This came as no surprise given the Shi'a community's historical background as socially excluded, economically deprived and politically marginalised within Lebanon, itself reinforced by the institutionalized political system of confessionalism which disadvantaged the representation of the Muslims. Apart from the *Harakat al-Mahrumin* (Movement of the Dispossessed) and later its militia Amal movement, founded in 1974 by Imam Musa al-Sadr,[2] the Shi'a of Lebanon remained a predominantly poor and disorganized religious community. When the political mobilization of the Shi'a into militant Islamic movements occurred, it was largely overshadowed by the dimensions of civil war in Lebanon. Subsequently, the emergence of Hizb'allah in 1982·was perceived by the West largely within the context of Iran's revolutionary efforts to export its revolution following Israel's 1982 invasion of Lebanon. However, it would be erroneous, as pointed out by Augustus Richard Norton, to assume that the Shi'a emerged to prominence on the Lebanese scene in 1982 as a mere creation by Iran.[3] Although recognizing that Iran played a decisive role in the emergence of Hizb'allah, from being initially a small group spearheaded by senior Shi'i clergy without a distinct organisational apparatus to a full-fledged participant in the mainstream of Lebanese politics, the political mobilization of Lebanon's Shi'i community has occurred in stages which preceded the Islamic revolution in Iran and Hizb'allah's entry as a radical and militant organisation in June 1982 by several decades.

THE NAJAF-BACKGROUND OF HIZB'ALLAH

Although the actual *creation* of the Hizb'allah movement occurred in June 1982 when a breakaway faction from Amal, the *Islamic Amal* party,

merged with a network of radical Shi'ites from other Lebanese movements, such as the *Lebanese al-Da'wa*, the *Association of Muslim Uluma
in Lebanon*, and the *Association of Muslim Students*, the various strands
of these Shi'ite movements and organisations which formed into one
political entity under the umbrella of Hizb'allah could trace their origins
to the activities during the 1960–70s of the Shi'i religious academies in
the south of Iraq most notably in the Shi'i shrine city of Najaf. Both
Najaf and Karbala were foremost centers of Shi'i theology as both cities
holds pre-eminence in the history of Islam as the place of martyrdom of
two of the first three Shi'i Imams. Individual Lebanese Shi'ite clergy,
who were students at the Najaf seminary, were also closely associated
and connected with the emergence of the clandestine Iraqi revolutionary
movement *al-Da'wa al-Islamiyya* (the Islamic Call or *Da'wa*), formed in
1968.[4] At these theological schools, a cadré of young Shi'ite scholars
from Iran, Iraq, Lebanon and other Arab states were educated and
influenced by radical Islamic theories from prominent senior Iraqi and
Iranian Shi'a clergy, who customarily took up residence and taught
there.[5] As Islam does not recognize the concept of nationality, leading to
the foundation of a pan-Islamic ideology, it was natural that most senior
clergy and their disciples at Najaf and Karbala forged close and personal
friendships regardless of nationality. In fact, the activity of the Shi'i
clergy in Najaf has been at the heart of most revivalist or revolutionary
movements in the Muslim world and has contributed to most of Islam's
current political vitality. In particular, it was in Najaf that Rúhallah al-
Khomeini spent fourteen years in exile and where he formulated his own
revolutionary brand of Shi'i Islam, as delivered in his famous 1969–70
lectures on the nature of Islamic government and clerical rule. His
Islamic vision was, of course, transformed into reality with the Islamic
revolution in Iran in 1979 and has subsequently served as a great source
of inspiration and guidance not only to Lebanon's Shi'a community but
also to most contemporary Islamic movements across the Middle East
and far beyond. Within this context, it should be noted that Iran had
already particularly close sentiments with Lebanon given its longstanding
cultural, religious and historical ties to the Shi'as of Jabal Amil (south
Lebanon), which dates back to the sixthteenth century when the Safavids
established Shi'ism as the official religion of the Persian Empire. This
historical tie was also the source of extensive family and personal bonds
between the two areas, as evidently displayed by the involvement of
Sheikh Raghib Harb, a south Lebanese cleric, in assisting Muhammad
Baqer al-Sadr with an early draft of Iran's constitution after the revolution in 1979.

While the religious indoctrination of radical Islamic theory that the future Hizb'allah clerics received at Najaf provided the ideological foundation for the organisation and led to the forging of close-knit relationships and personal networks between eminent leaders of the Shi'a community across the Middle East, the involvement of Lebanese Najaf-educated clerics, who later became prominent Hizb'allah leaders, with other radical clergy in the activities of the Iraqi *al-Da'wa al-Islamiyya* directly influenced the Shi'a resurgence in Lebanon. In particular, the confrontation with the Ba'athi regime had a strong influence on the political mobilization of the Shi'a community. Apart from an extensive campaign of antireligious repression against Shi'i clergy and institutions in Iraq, the Ba'th regime launched a policy resulting in the massive deportation of foreign clerics.[6] As a consequence, a number of Najaf-schooled Lebanese clerics returned to Lebanon where they established Shi'ite educational institutions, based on the Najaf model, to a young generation of students, indoctrinated in radical Islamic theory.[7] Other Najaf-educated clerics were either forcibly removed or fled for their safety and returned to Lebanon where they formed a Lebanese twin organisation of the Iraqi *al-Da'wa al-Islamiyya*, the *Lebanese al-Da'wa* party.[8] This party, under the spiritual guidance of Sheikh Muhammad Hussein Fadlallah,[9] would later become a core component in the establishment of the Hizb'allah movement in 1982. It is, therefore, essential to understand that the Najaf-background of most members of Hizb'allah's command leadership as well as the activity of Iraq's *al-Da'wa al-Islamiyya*, as a forerunner to the creation of the Hizb'allah, was the antecedent to the revolutionary ideological basis of, and the organisational evolution of, the current movement in Lebanon as well as the influence of the close friendships forged between Hizb'allah clergy and members of Iran's clerical establishment.

It is important to recognize the manner in which the historical background of Shi'i militancy in Iraq served as a precursor to the ideological foundation and organisational framework for the creation of the Hizb'allah movement. Firstly, the genesis of both Iraq's *al-Da'wa al-Islamiyya* and Lebanon's Hizb'allah followed similar concerns over the spread and influence of secular ideologies over their respective Islamic communities. In response to these threats, young and prominent Shi'a uluma in Najaf served as the ideological moving force behind the Shi'a resurgence in Iraq, and later in Lebanon, by providing an Islamic alternative to the rival doctrines of nationalism and communism. In this task, the chief ideologues were Muhammad Baqir al-Sadr in Iraq (who founded the *al-Da'wa al-Islamiyya*) and Sheikh Muhammad Hussein Fadlallah in Lebanon, alongside Ayatollah Khomeini's own clerical activity, who together aroused the

Islamic conciousness of the younger generation and fostered a more radical ideology and vision of an Islamic order through their literary works and religious sermons on Islamic theory and especially its capacity to answer the challenges of the modern world. Specifically, the Shi'i intellectual contribution of both al-Sadr and Fadlallah, as the ideological moving force behind the resurgence of political and social activism of their respective communities, originated in a similar crisis milieu. While the actual founding of the *al-Da'wa al-Islamiyya* in 1968/69 by al-Sadr came in response to the repression of the Shi'i religious academies in Najaf by the Iraqi Ba'ath regime, the more activist position of Sheikh Fadlallah developed only after the outbreak of the Lebanese civil war, especially in reaction to his growing fears that Muslims were threatened by the popularity of secular and non-Islamic movements. This was reinforced in July 1976 when the Shi'a community, among them Sheikh Fadlallah, was forcibly evicted from the al-Na'ba slum district of Beirut by the Christian militias of the Lebanese Front. He resettled in the Bir al-'Abed quarter in the southern suburbs of Beirut and served as a rallying point for Shi'ite activists through his political sermons and writings on radical Islamic theory while providing guidance on how the Lebanese Shi'a community could best confront and handle contemporary issues.

Secondly, it was only natural that the Lebanese *al-Da'wa*, under the spiritual guidance of Sheikh Fadlallah, had closely fashioned itself after, and was influenced by, the activities of *al-Da'wa al-Islamiyya* in Iraq. Apart from the fact that both organisations emphasized extreme secrecy and underground activity, in alignment with traditional Shi'i doctrine of protecting the community against persecution by regimes (adopted ever since the martyrdom of al-Husayn at Karbala in AD 680), the Lebanese *al-Da'wa* was religiously subordinated to the ideological guidance and directives by Muhammad Baqer al-Sadr. A forceful manifestation of the closeness of this relationship was the unsuccessful assassination attempts on Sheikh Fadlallah by the Iraqi Ba'ath regime for his connections with the party. Yet, the most visible sign followed the execution of Baqer al-Sadr by the Ba'ath regime, on 9 April 1980, when the Lebanese *al-Da'wa* began to dissolve as an organisation. While former al-Da'wa members reiterated the dissolution of the movement in Lebanon, the actual disbandonment occurred when its senior leaders worked to reorganise its members within the framework of Hizb'allah. Yet, the legacy of the Lebanese *al-Da'wa* party had, and continues to have, a strong impact on the ideology, direction and organisational structure of the Party of God.

The background to the establishment of Hizb'allah can also be attributed to an array of other factors and events both within and external to Lebanon.

Parallel to the activities of the religious academies in Iraq and *al-Da'wa al-Islamiyya*, the Lebanese Shi'a community emerged as a major political and military force against the background of social exclusion and economic deprivation within Lebanon. While the history of the Lebanese Shi'ites had been traditionally marked by political submission and lament, the advent of Imam Musa al-Sadr's charismatic leadership over the Shi'a community transformed it into one of rebellion and social protest.[10] Yet, Shi'a activism was not only the product of political and socioeconomic grievances combined with an effective charismatic religious leadership, that used key religious symbolism to mobilize Shi'i Muslims into protest and revolutionary movements.[11] It was also profoundly influenced between 1975 and 1982 by a number of major events. Apart from the breakdown of the Lebanese state signified by the onset of civil war in 1975, a number of events, both within and external to Lebanon, changed the Shi'i community from a marginal entity to a major political and military force within Lebanon. Three major events, preceding Israel's 1982 invasion of Lebanon, transformed the Shi'a into political action: firstly, the disappearence of Imam Musa al-Sadr in Libya in August 1978 became a focal point for the mobilisation and radicalization of the Shi'a community.[12] Secondly, Israel's invasion of southern Lebanon in 1978, with the consequent loss of Shi'i lives and destruction of their homes, revitalized Amal and reinforced the image of Israel as the enemy of Islam, and thirdly, the establishment of a Shi'a Islamic state in Iran, which followed Khomeini's successful overthrow of the Pahlavi dynasty in 1979, reverberated among the Shi'a community in Lebanon and provided them with an effective model for political action. The manner in which these internal Lebanese events affected and contributed to the Shi'i resurgence in Lebanon, in combination with the activity by the radical clergy in Najaf and the revolutionary underground movement, the *al-Da'wa al-Islamiyya*, as an antecedent to the ideological foundation and organisational framework of the Hizb'allah, were important components to the transformation of a politically assertive Shi'a community into a militant Islamic movement in Lebanon, as embodied in the Hizb'allah. It also provides a vital assessment of the movement's close personal ties to their co-religionists in Iran as well as its ready assimilation of Iranian post-revolutionary Shi'ite ideological principles in the struggle against an array of enemies and in their ideological commitment to the establishment of an Islamic Republic of Lebanon.

Although the political mobilization of the Shi'i community was accelerated by these factors and events, the 1982 Israeli invasion became a seminal event as it facilitated not only Iran's direct involvement with the Shi'a community, through the deployment of a small Iranian contingent to the Biq'a area of Lebanon, but also led to the proliferation of a number of radical and militant Shi'a movements. These groups merged into the establishment of a main revolutionary Shi'a movement, the Hizb'allah, an organisational umbrella composed of a coalition of radical movements under the leadership of a small select group of Najaf-educated clergy.

THE INFLUENCE OF ISRAEL'S 1982 INVASION FOR THE CREATION OF HIZB'ALLAH

Israel's invasion of June–September 1982 and its subsequent occupation of southern Lebanon profoundly influenced the political mobilization and radicalization of the Shi'a community. Although the Lebanese Shi'a community initially welcomed Israel's decision to eradicate the PLO presence, any Shi'a euphoria soon developed into resentment and militancy following the realization that Israel would continue to occupy southern Lebanon.[13] For Iran, Lebanon represented the most ideal test-case for the export of the revolution more than any other place, given the anarchy of the ensuing civil war, exacerbated by Israel's continued occupation, the resultant economic crisis hitting the Shi'a community the hardest, and the close historical as well as personal ties between the Iranian clerical establishment and Lebanon's Shi'ite clergy. Actively encouraged by Iran, the more radical Najaf-educated clergy abandoned the Lebanese *al-Da'wa* party as a vechicle for increased political activism as its mass appeal and effectiveness was hindered by the secretive and underground nature of the party. Many former al-Da'wa members (now prominent Hizb'allah leaders) were critical of the party's ideas and methods, especially its central doctrine of underground activity. Instead Iran encouraged these former *al-Da'wa* members to join and infiltrate Amal in order to disseminate a more radical revolutionary message to a wider audience and to challenge the secular and moderate orientation of Amal. A notable individual within the *al-Da'wa,* adopting this route, was Sheikh Hassan Nasserallah, who became an Amal official after serving as a group official in the *al-Da'wa party.* Some of these former members, who would later occupy important positions within Hizb'allah, managed not only to rise through the ranks of Amal but also to pose a serious threat to Nabih Berri's leadership of the movement. In particular, Nabih Berri's reaction to the Israeli invasion, seeking political accommodation rather than military confrontation to the crisis, precipitated the moment for a major split within the Amal movement by more radical officials, who were actively encouraged by official Iran to establish an Islamic alternative to Amal.[14]

The major event, which led to division within Amal's hierarchy between moderates and those adopting a hardline Islamic approach, occurred when Nabih Berri decided to join the National Salvation Committee, which was formed by president Ilyas Sarkis in mid-June 1982 to deal with Israel's occupation and siege of Beirut. For the more radical Amal members, who were inspired by Ayatollah Khomeini and viewed Amal as the vanguard of revolutionary struggle in Lebanon based on the model and ideals of the Iranian revolution, Nabih Berri's participation was not only contrary to the line adopted by Amal at its fourth congress but also judged un-Islamic.[15] In practical terms, Amal's secular leadership had rejected the establishment of an Islamic Republic of Lebanon, modelled on Iran, and underlined its commitment to the national sovereignty and territorial integrity of Lebanon. The most vocal opposition came from Husayn al-Musawi, deputy head and official spokesman of the movement, who was closely sympathetic to the Iranian revolution, after being influenced by the ideas and writings of Ali Shari'ati (an Iranian Islamic intellectual) and had advanced a programme for Lebanon based on the Iranian Islamic model. As such, al-Musawi not only openly opposed Berri's decision but also directly challenged the Amal leadership by calling for Iranian arbitration of the matter.[16] While the Iranian ambassador to Lebanon, Moussa Fakhr Rouhani, requested Berri's withdrawal from the Committee, Iran's newly-appointed ambassador to Syria, Ali Akbar Mohtashemi, became involved as arbitrator and issued a ruling on the matter in favor of al-Musawi.[17] Subsequently, when Berri did not abide by the Iranian ruling, al-Musawi resigned from the Amal movement.[18]

Disillusioned with Amal's political moderation and actively encouraged by Iran, al-Musawi and some other members, mostly residents of the Biqa, left Amal's Beirut headquarters and moved to Baalbek.[19] When Berri participated at the first session of the six-man National Salvation Committee, on 21 June 1982, al-Musawi announced from Baalbek the creation of his own movement, the *Islamic Amal*.[20] While al-Musawi denounced Amal's Berri for having deserted the Islamic line of Imam Musa al-Sadr, which necessitated the creation of *Islamic Amal*, he clearly emphasised that *Islamic Amal* was not a rival movement but rather assumed the role of the authentic Amal.[21] According to al-Musawi, this was also necessary as Amal as an organisation strongly opposed the idea of pledging allegiance to Ayatollah Khomeini.[22] Apart from the fact that Amal believed Iranian revolutionary solutions would not solve Lebanon's sectarian problems, the tension between Amal and Iran was also rooted in Iranian inaction over the 1979 disappearence of Imam Musa al-Sadr as well as the fact that Amal's extensive support for Iranian opposition activity against the Shah's regime, through military training of senior Iranian revolutionaries in Lebanon in camps under Amal's auspices, failed to translate into extensive support for the movement in the aftermath of the 1979 Islamic revolution. The latter reason was reinforced by the fact that several of Amal's most loyal friends within Iran's clerical establishment either disappeared or were killed or ousted by Ayatollah Khomeini in the period between 1980–81. Friction between Amal and Iran was exacerbated by the fact that Iran supported and encouraged the Palestinian Liberation Organisation (PLO), as a natural spearhead in the holy war against Israel, especially since PLO activity brought considerable trouble and hardship to the south Lebanese Shi'ites.

Another main challenge to Nabih Berri's participation in the National Salvation Committee came from Sheikh Ibrahim al-Amin, Amal's representative in Iran. After unsuccessful appeals to Nabih Berri from the Iranian ambassador to Lebanon at the time, Moussa Fakhr Rouhani, Iran encouraged Sheikh Ibrahim al-Amin to publicly challenge Berri's decision.[23] Simultaneous with the announcement by al-Musawi's of the creation of *Islamic Amal*, Sheikh al-Amin criticized Nabih Berri at a press conference in Teheran and publicly announced his split from Amal.[24]

As demonstrated by the defections of al-Musawi and Sheikh al-Amin from Amal, the split within Amal was symptomatic of the fact that the movement was structurally a broad-based and loose organisation. Amal's secular orientation and lack of political independence, as Amal served as Syria's political and military vechicle in Lebanon, made the movement not only less receptive to Iran as a suitable instrument to transmit its revolutionary message to the Shi'as of Lebanon but also more vulnerable to defections and challenges from within, especially by those who preferred the Iranian regime as a patron. This opposition was spearheaded by the more fundamentalist elements within Amal, who with active Iranian support managed to not only defect but also remove a sizeable number of followers from the mainstream movement, especially in the Biq'a area. In this task, al-Musawi received close advice and support from Iran's ambassador to Syria, Mohtashemi, who had requested from him a list of all those Amal members who were sympathetic to the Iranian revolution and its cause. However, the fact that Husayn al-Musawi and other *al-Da'wa* members represented a minority view within Amal, coupled with the fact that other Najaf-educated clerics failed to organise themselves effectively under a united banner, meant that Iran had previously limited success in the establishment of a revolutionary movement within *one* organisational framework.

While Iran actively seized the opportunity to use its influence with pro-Iranian and leading Amal members to provoke a serious internal challenge within the movement over Berri's secular orientation, especially concerning his decision to participate with the National Salvation Committee, Israel's invasion provided Iran with another opportunity to exert direct involvement and influence over their Shi'a co-religionists in Lebanon through the deployment of an Iranian contingent of Revolutionary Guard Corps units (IRGC or Pasdaran) to the Biq'a valley. Their entry into the Biq'a town of Ba'albek in mid-1982 was the culmination of earlier Iranian efforts, though blocked by Syria, to aquire a limited warfighting-capability against Israel in Lebanon. This was intially announced as early as 1980 by Ayatollah Montazeri's son in Beirut, signalling the imminent arrival of Pasdaran expeditionary units enroute to Lebanon as displayed by the presence of approximately 170 Iranian Pasdaran members, who remained stationed in the Hamorriyah training camp near Damascus until they departed for the frontlines in the Iran-Iraq war. This was later formalized through Iranian Majlis legislation in June 1981 which allowed for the IRGC to be dispatched to fight Israel in southern Lebanon.[25] However, the possibility of direct Pasdaran engagement, alongside Syria's military forces, had been blocked by Syria as well as Khomeini himself for strategic reasons and thus the actual size of the Iranian contingent dispatched to Lebanon remained too small for a direct combat role.[26] The Iranian Pasdaran contingent's arrival in Lebanon and presence after July 1982 directly contributed to ensure the survival and growth of Husayn al-Musawi's newly-created small militia, *Islamic Amal*, and the Pasdaran actively supervised in the formation and development of Hizb'allah in late 1982.[27] In the formation of the Hizb'allah, Ayatollah Ali Akbar Mohtashemi, who served as Iran's ambassador to Syria and would later become Iran's Minister of the Interior, played a pivotal role (having spent considerable time in Najaf with his mentor Ayatollah Khomeini until the latter's expulsion from Iraq and had forged close relationships with future Hizb'allah clerics during this time) as he actively supervised the creation of the movement by merging the *Lebanese al-Da'wa*; the *Association of Muslim Students*; *al-Amal al-Islamiyya*; and other radical Shi'ite movements initially within the framework of the Department for Islamic Liberation Movements run by the Iranian Pasdaran, and after 1986 by the Iranian Ministry of Foreign Affairs.[28]

THE ESTABLISHMENT AND EXPANSION OF THE HIZB'ALLAH

The establishment of Hizb'allah, with active Iranian supervision, in Lebanon occurred in three phases and the movement divided its operations into three main geographical areas: the Biq'a; Beirut; and the South. Each of these regional divisions were lead by high-ranking Hizb'allah clergy with local background and affiliation to a network of loyal supporters.

Phase I: The Establishment of Hizb'allah in the Biq'a

Immediately following Israel's invasion, Iran urged Syria to allow the deployment of a small Iranian contingent into Lebanon and also to turn the war in Lebanon into a religious war against Israel.[29] As a result of the imminent threat posed by the Israeli invasion, Syria signed a military agreement with Iran which allowed the entry of Iranian Pasdaran into Lebanon in return for Iranian oil supply.[30] Initially, Syria allowed the establishment of an Iranian headquarters in the Syrian border village of Zebdani,[1] while a second contingent of 800 Iranian Pasdaran, supervised by Mohsen Rafiqdust, were deployed into Ba'albek.[32] This contingent was later reinforced by another 700 Pasdaran, who were distributed in a number of smaller villages in the Biq'a valley. Although the Iranian contingent was largely composed of military instructors and fighters, it also included senior clergy who intensively engaged in religious indoctrination into the religio-political teachings of Ayatollah Khomeini to Hizb'allah and Islamic Amal cadres.[33] In particular, the Pasdaran's non-military support role as spiritual mentors has not only been vital in Hizb'allah's rapid growth, combativeness and degree of religious fervour but also as an institution the movement could depend on in times of crisis, whether it was militarily and politically challenged from within Lebanon by other militias and by Syria or subjected to pressure from different elements within Iran's clerical establishment. Despite the Iranian contingent's proximity to IDF frontlines in the southern part of the Biq'a, coupled with Iran's call for a jihad against Israel, the Pasdaran did not engage in any military combat with Israel which underlined that the main nature of Iran's mission was geared towards aiding the formation of an organisational basis and infrastructure for a new revolutionary Shi'a group through extensive military training and religious guidance.[34] As admitted by Hadi Reza Askari, the Pasdaran commander in Lebanon, in an interview in 1991: "[t]he guard is not a militia; our mission is to train the people to fight Israel."[35] This was echoed by Hizb'allah's Sheikh Naim al-Qassim: "[t]he Iranian Islamic Revolutionary Guard does not fight in southern Lebanon. However, it is known that some of its members are present in the al-Biq'a area; they play an educational and training role and do not participate in other matters."[36]

While the Iranian Pasdaran provided regular military training to the militiamen of *Islamic Amal*, it concentrated mainly on the systematic recruitment and ideological indoctrination of radical Shi'ites in the Biq'a area.[37] Under guidance from the Pasdaran, leading Najaf-educated Lebanese clerics with local background spearheaded the formation of a nucleus leadership of the new revolutionary Shi'a organisation and began the process of recruitment and indoctrination of Shi'i residents in Ba'albek, through translating Iran's revolutionary message from Persian into Arabic.[38] The two individuals most closely identified as the initial founders of the Hizb'allah were Sayyid Abbas al-Musawi and Sheikh Subhi al-Tufayli, who both founded religious institutions and were regarded as the spiritual leaders in Ba'albek.[39] These religious figures were closely supported by units of Iranian Revolutionary Guards, under direct command of Ahmad Kan'ani, not only in the creation of a first Hizb'allah military unit in the Biq'a, and later its security agency, but also in the imposition of Islamic fundamentalism on all citizens of the Ba'albek. For example, this latter point was evident by Hizb'allah and Islamic Amal units, supported by the Pasdaran, who enforced strict Islamic dress-codes and banned anti-Islamic Western-style behaviour of Bi'qa residents through a campaign of kidnapping and harassment.[40] In the autumn of 1982, under the aegis of the then Pasdaran-controlled *Office of Liberation Movements,* the core Hizb'allah clergy drafted the movement's preliminary charter and constitution for the establishment of an Iranian-style Islamic regime in Lebanon. On December 26, 1982, Sheikh al-Tufayli was appointed as the "president of the Islamic Republic" in Ba'albek.[41]

Although the activities of the Iranian Pasdaran rapidly transformed the Biq'a area into a citadel for the Hizb'allah and *Islamic Amal*, they encountered resistance from segments within the Shi'i community and, more importantly, from the Lebanese armed forces.[42] This was evident from the Pasdaran unit's attack on the Lebanese army barracks in Ba'albek on November 22, 1982 (Lebanon's Independence Day). A key factor in the successful transformation of the Biq'a area was Syria's acquiesence to anarchy in a territory under its control and responsibility. Apart from the Iranian-Syrian military agreement for the deployment of Iranian Pasdaran to Lebanon, Syria's lack of effort to control the activities of the various Shi'a groups, buttressed by the Iranian Pasdaran, was based on the desire not to offend its Iranian ally, especially in the confrontation with the Americans and the Lebanese government over the 17 May 1983 Israeli-Lebanese Agreement, which constituted the second Arab-Israeli peace treaty after the 1979 Camp David Accord. Although the Lebanese government severed diplomatic relations with Iran, on 23 November 1983, after many attacks by the Iranian Pasdaran on the remaining Lebanese army units in the Biq'a and the seizure of the Sheikh Abdallah barracks,

Syria began only to reassert its authority and restrain the activity of the pro-Iranian groups and the Pasdaran after the abrogation of the May 17 1983 Agreement in March 1984.[43] Prior to mid-1984, Hizb'allah and *Islamic Amal*, in concert with Iran's Pasdaran, were able to rapidly recruit and indoctrinate a large number of Shi'a followers as the Iranian contingent was also supported by large Iranian funds. These substantial funds were used by the Iranian Pasdaran to support the Hizb'allah in running an array of social welfare and financial services for the Shi'a community, including religious schools, clinics and hospitals, as well as cash subsidies to Shi'ite families below the poverty line, which naturally boosted the popularity and growth of the pro-Iranian movement in the Biq'a.[44] The funds were also used to provide sophisticated armaments and military training for young Hizb'allah and *Islamic Amal* militiamen.[45] In July 1984, the Iranian Pasdaran established six military centers in the Bi'qa for training of Hizb'allah and Islamic Amal fighters. The Pasdaran units, supported by generous funds, had no problem attracting new recruits among the local impoverished Shi'a community as the pay for joining as a fighter far exceeded what other militias were able to offer. For example, newly-trained Hizb'allah and *Islamic Amal* fighters in the Biq'a received approximately $150–$200 per month.[46] In addition, these fighters are also offered special privileges in terms of cost-free education and medical treatment for themselves and their families. It is, therefore, not surprising that a sizeable number of Amal fighters defected regularly to the ranks of Hizb'allah and that the pay of South Lebanon Army (SLA) fighters, Israel's proxy in southern Lebanon, is indexed against those received by their Islamic enemies.

Parallel to the creation of Hizb'allah and its subsequent rapid growth in the Biq'a, under the leadership of Sheikhs Abbas al-Musawi and Subhi al-Tufayli, the movement spread to other areas heavily populated by Shi'a, to the southern suburbs of Beirut and to the villages and towns in southern Lebanon.

Phase II: Hizb'allah's Expansion Into Beirut

In Beirut, Hizb'allah's natural source for organising Shi'ites was to work within the framework of existing radical Shi'ite organisations and religious institutions. Apart from recruiting more fundamentalist elements within Amal, who followed the example set by the departure of Husayn al-Musawi and Sheikh Ibrahim al-Amin, the involvement of Sheikh Muhammad Hussein Fadlallah proved to be important for Hizb'allah as he commanded a considerable number of Shi'a followers in the Bir al-'Abed quarters of southern Beirut, through his activity in the mosque of al-Sallum. Arriving from Najaf to Beirut in 1966, Sheikh Fadlallah's high-ranking religious stature was due both to his longstanding charitable work among the poor urban Shi'ite community, who arrived from southern Lebanon and the Biq'a, as well as to his preaching and writings, in which he advocated political activism and force as a means to preserve and defend Islam in favour of traditional Shi'ite policy of quietism and dissimulation. A central personality in the Lebanese Shi'a community in his capacity as head of the Council of Shi'ite Religious Scholars, Sheikh Fadlallah was crucial for the movement's legitimacy and growth as he also wielded unrivalled influence over the activity of religious movements, most notably within the *Association of Muslim Students,* the student cover-organisation of *al-Da'wa* party, and among former Lebanese *al-Da'wa* members.[47] As one of the three most prominent Shi'i clergymen in Lebanon, Sheikh Fadlallah's active involvement in the Lebanese political arena, through his criticism of foreign intervention in Lebanon and appeals for the establishment of an Islamic Republic, led to the emergence of Sheikh Fadlallah as the spiritual guide and the most senior cleric associated with the Hizb'allah.[48] In fact, Sheikh Fadlallah had publicly dissolved the Lebanese *al-Da'wa,* as advocated by Iran, and in return, he agreed to join the Hizb'allah, which needed a senior spiritual guide in close alignment with Islamic Iran. Although Sheikh Fadlallah had rejected the claim of "spiritual guide" of the movement, his role as the leader of the defunct Lebanese *al-Da'wa* meant that his standing within the Hizb'allah was bolstered by the fact that a considerable number of its newly recruited members in Beirut had previous affiliation with the *al-Da'wa.*[49] A number of other prominent clergymen in Beirut joined the Hizb'allah, who brought with them their own memberships and followers which gradually merged within one organisational framework. Among the initial founders of the first Hizb'allah units in Beirut were Sheikh Muhammad Ismail al-Khaliq and Sheikh Hassan Nasserallah, both prominent *al-Da'wa* members, who used their prominent *hawzat* in Beirut *(Hawzat al-Rasul al-Akram)* as a base for recruitment, and Sheikh al-Amin, who returned from Iran to Beirut to act as Hizb'allah's official spokesman.[50] These clergymen managed to expand their influence not only through the Najaf-styled religious Shi'ite academies in Beirut but also with Iranian technical and financial assistance through Iran's embassies in Beirut and Damascus.[51] Furthermore, the Hizb'allah was practically assisted by the expansion of the Iranian Pasdaran from Ba'albek into Beirut beginning in April 1983.[52]

While the influx of Iranian Pasdaran and substantial financial support, coupled with Iranian assistance in the indoctrination and recruitment process, contributed to the rapid growth of Hizb'allah in Beirut, it was also assisted by the suicide attacks against the US and French contingents of the Multinational Force (MNF) on October 23, 1983. As later explained by Hizb'allah: "[o]n the morning of 23 October 1983, two martyr mujahidin set out to inflict upon the U.S. Administration an utter defeat not experienced since Vietnam, and a similar one upon the French Administration."[53] Although the exact identity of the bombers remains uncertain, the alleged complicity of Hizb'allah promoted the movement as the spearhead of the sacred Muslim struggle against foreign occupation. The subsequent withdrawal of the United States and France from Lebanon was hailed as a major victory for the Hizb'allah, both in terms of establishing itself as a revered militia and in driving away foreign enemies of the Lebanese Shi'ites. The Hizb'allah attacks, which went under the nom de guerre *al-Amal al-Islami*, also underlined the major role of Iranian support and guidance to the movement's activities, especially in Beirut. Apart from logistical support provided by Iran's diplomatic representatives in Lebanon and Iranian Pasdaran, Hizb'allah enjoyed close cooperation with Iran's embassy in Syria, most notably with its ambassador, Ali Akbar Mohtashemi.[54]

Phase III: Hizb'allah's Expansion Into Southern Lebanon

In southern Lebanon, Hizb'allah's expansion was hindered initially by the dominance of Amal's authority. However, the failure of Amal to confront the challenge posed by Israel's military presence in southern Lebanon, exacerbated by the power vacuum left by PLO's defeat and departure from the area, led to the emergence of more militant organisations in the spring of 1983, led by local radical clergy with ideological ties to Iran, which united under the banner of the *Association of the Uluma of Jabal Amil*.[55] Beneath this coalition was a number of small organized Shi'i cells, headed by Sheikh Rageb Harb (another Najaf student), who both planned and carried out persistant resistance attacks against Israel.[56] These young and fire-brand clerics provided the core foundation for the extension of Hizb'allah in the South and their resistance activity not only undermined the influence of Amal in the area but also seriously challenged Israel's presence, especially through self-martyring operations. It is clear the growth of the Hizb'allah units in the South can be attributed to the infusion of Iranian aid and the arrival of Iranian Pasdaran. This link with Iran was highlighted by Sheikh Ragib Harb, who stated: "[m]y house in Lebanon is the embassy of the Islamic Republic of Iran".[57] Yet, Hizb'allah's rapid expansion was also due to the increased militancy by

these units both in response to Israel's military activity and, more importantly, to raised prospects for an Israeli withdrawal. This was fuelled by
Israel's withdrawal from the Shouf Mountains in September 1983 and the
decision by Sheikh Muhammad Shams al-Din (vice president of the
Higher Shi'ite Assembly of Lebanon) to issue a *fatwa* (an official religious
decree), calling on all Muslims to conduct "comprehensive civil opposition" to the Israeli occupation, following Israel's desecration of the Shi'a
Ashura commemoration in Nabatiya.[58] The 1984 assassination of Sheikh
Harb, allegedly by Israeli agents, served to increase the fanaticism of his
followers and the militancy of Hizb'allah. The deadly effectiveness of
Hizb'allah suicide attacks, as manifested by the destruction of IDF headquarters in Tyre on 4 November 1983, not only earned the movement
prestige among the southern Shi'a residents but also directly contributed to
Israel's decision to announce a withdrawal in January 1985. The newly-
formed military wing of Hizb'allah, which adopted the name of *Islamic
Resistance (al-Muqawama al-Islamiyya)*, claimed that Israel's withdrawal
was achieved by its persistent attacks and was a major victory for Islam as
well as a direct prelude for the liberation of Jerusalem.[59]

The rapid growth and popularity of the Hizb'allah in these three regions
was achieved not only by a successful combination of ideological indoctrination and material inducement by Hizb'allah through the infusion of
Iranian aid and military assistance. It was also achieved by the ability of
the Hizb'allah leaders to mobilize a destitute Shi'i community, disaffected
with the continuing Israeli occupation, and unite it within the framework
of an organisation with clearly defined and articulated political objectives.
This was achieved through the provision of concrete and workable solutions to the fundamental political, social, and economic needs of the Shi'a
community in the absence of any central Lebanese authority and in the
presence of civil war. The establishment of an efficient Hizb'allah propa-
ganda-machinery (through its *al-Ahd* newspaper, its television-station *al-
Manar,* as well as its radio-station *Voice of the Oppressed*) served to
reinforce Iran's visible and direct influence over the movement as well as
Hizb'allah's own achievements and popularity. Hizb'allah's rationale for
the massive infusion of assistance to residents in the South was also a calculated move to become the sole representative of the Lebanese Muslim
community and to gain the support of local inhabitants for its military
activities in southern Lebanon. Apart from providing a social and financial
infrastructure for the Shi'i community, which was deeply affected by the
economic crisis exacerbated by Israel's 1982 invasion, the Hizb'allah
effectively gained supporters as the movement projected itself as the
spearhead of the struggle against the main enemies of Islam, namely the

United States and Israel. In this task, the Hizb'allah exploited central Shi'a symbols, especially through the *Ashura* processions which annually commemorates the seventh-century martyrdom of Imam Husayn, to enlist support and promulgate revolutionary activism based on the struggle against tyranny, disinheritance, and social injustice. The exploitation of Shi'ite symbolism was used by the Hizb'allah as a political weapon to embody the condition of the oppressed and disinherited Shi'ite community under the Lebanese confessional system. This was coupled with a display of ideological deference to Ayatollah Khomeini's pan-Islamic vision, in which the movement would expel foreign influence from Lebanon, establish an Islamic regime based on social justice and finally set the stage for the liberation of Jerusalem.[60] When Hizb'allah successfully forced the departure of the multi-national force from Lebanon and the retreat of Israel into a narrow zone in southern Lebanon, through a combination of relentless guerilla warfare and self-martyring operations, it was viewed a major achievement by Hizb'allah and Iran as no other force had been able to accomplish the expulsion of both the United States and Israel from its soil.[61] This point was not lost on Iranian clerics who underscored that Hizb'allah's achievement was unprecedented as the Arabs had lost the previous four wars with Israel. To this end, it not only raised the self-esteem of the entire Shi'a community but also naturally boosted the popularity of the Hizb'allah and enhanced the movement's credibility as the promoter of the sacred struggle against heretic oppression and foreign occupation.

THE IDEOLOGICAL FOUNDATION OF THE HIZB'ALLAH

Hizb'allah's radicalization of the Shi'a community, through the exploitation of Shi'i symbols, and its declared allegiance to the Islamic Republic of Iran and Ayatollah Khomeini, underlined the movement's close ideological and spiritual deference to Islamic Iran's pan-Islamic vision and authority. At its simplest level, the very adoption of the name of Hizb'allah derived from the Quran (V, 56), which denotes the body of Muslims, symbolizes the revolutionary character of the movement, namely that the followers of Allah *(hizb'allah)* would triumph over the followers of Satan *(hizb-ush-Shaytan)*.[62] Sheikh Fadlallah, in his book *Islam and the Logic of Force*, referred to this Islamic struggle between *Hizb'allah* and *Hizb-ush-Shaytan* when he called on Muslims to organize along party lines in order to safeguard the survival of Islamic values and movements against the threat of powerful secular parties.[63] In this task, the ideologists of Hizb'allah justified not only the leadership structure of the movement but also most of its activities on the Quranic tenents, most notably based on traditional authority and leadership in Twelver Shi'ism.

Ideology and Structure

A fundamental feature of the Hizb'allah leadership structure was the central role of the *uluma* (pre-eminent Islamic scholars) within the movement. Although many Hizb'allah leaders maintained that the movement was "not an organisation, for its members carry no cards and bear no specific responsibilities",[64] the leadership of the movement was strictly composed of *uluma* and the actual structure based on the centrality of this religious hierarchy.[65] Accordingly, the central role of the *uluma* in Hizb'allah concentrated all authority and powers to a small élite clerical group which ensure strict discipline and obedience by the followers to the rulings and orders of their religious leaders, whose decisions flow from the *uluma* down the entire community. In this structure, decisions made by the collective clerical Hizb'allah leadership were reached through consensus and delegated to a regional *alim* (Islamic scholar) of a certain district, who presents his followers with the required actions and their general outlines. In turn, the manner in which a certain act is executed is left to the initiative of these followers under the guidance of the *alim,* as they carry out the actual reconnaissance and execution of the operation under local conditions and as it ensures operational secrecy and compartmentalisation.[66] The highest authority in the Hizb'allah clerical hierarchy is not only allotted to the most learned practitioners of Islamic jurisprudence, obtained only after many years of religious training and scholarly activity, but is·also based on the number of students and followers belonging to each cleric.

As in Iran, the prominent role of the *uluma* within Hizb'allah's leadership confers them with religio-political legitimacy in the eyes of their followers. Apart from ensuring strict obedience by followers to decisions taken by the Hizb'allah leadership, the authority of the Hizb'allah *uluma* extends all the way to the religious and political authority of Iran's Ayatollah Khomeini, to whom they appeal for guidance and directives in cases when Hizb'allah's collective leadership are too divided over issues and fail to reach a consensus.[67] The ultimate authority and allegiance to the Islamic Republic of Iran and Khomeini by the Hizb'allah was most evidently displayed by the publication of an official manifesto in February 1985 in which they pledged absolute loyalty to Khomeini, whom they described as their leader *(al-qa'id).*[68] In the words of Sheikh al-Amin: "we don't have an authoritative leadership in Lebanon. Our leadership is Khomeini's".[69] In fact, the absence of an opinion and ruling by Ayatollah Khomeini on certain matters created divisions within, and problems for, Hizb'allah's clerical leadership in the execution and justification of actions within the framework of Islamic law.[70] A clear example of this dilemma was Hizb'allah's practice of suicide attacks and the abduction of foreign citizens which seemed to violate some principles of Islamic law. In the former case, the problem centered around the strong Islamic prohibition against suicide, and in the latter case that the seizure of innocent hostages was irreconcilable with Islamic law. As Ayatollah Khomeini has offered no formal opinion on the legality of these issues, primarily because Iran has disavowed any direct involvement, the most senior Hizb'allah leaders have offered their own interpetation in accordance with what they perceive to be the tacit approval of the Imam.[71] For example, prior to any suicide mission, senior Hizb'allah commanders always request a fatwa from the most senior Shi'ite clergy to justify that the act is permissible according to Islamic law. In the task of interpretation, Sheikh Fadlallah emerged an important figure for Iran and the rank and file of Hizb'allah as he offered Iran a medium for translating and conveying the Islamic Republic's message to the Hizb'allah followers as well as providing them with spiritual guidance on specific matters as the chief *Mujtahid*, arbiter of Islamic law, of the Shi'ite community in Lebanon. Sheikh Fadlallah's importance as the locus of spiritual and political authority of the Hizb'allah, as its most senior and learned cleric, and his deference to Ayatollah Khomeini was evidently revealed by the fact that he was referred to as the "Khomeini of Lebanon".[72] Sheikh Fadlallah's stature is evident from the substantial financial contributions made to social services by his own office, collected through mosques and other Muslim contributions independent from Iran's assistance. Yet Hizb'allah's denial that Sheikh Fadlallah serves within the organisation is deliberate deception in order to protect him against outside charges of involvement in any operational activity, as evident by early accusations of having "blessed" the suicide operations against Western targets in October 1983. It also provides Hizb'allah, as admitted by Sheikh Nasserallah, with an intermediary, who shields the organisation in any dealings or negotiations with hostile adversaries.[73] While Sheikh Fadlallah occupied a crucial position as a bridge between Hizb'allah's Iranian patrons and its Lebanese clients, he also gradually pursued his own independent agenda which created considerable tension with Iranian leaders as well as with other leading clerical leaders of Hizb'allah. Apart from his supreme religious standing to the rank-and-file of Hizb'allah, Sheikh Fadlallah's more independent line from Iran and other organisational leaders over certain issues can be viewed as a deliberate strategy to bolster his own religious standing within the Shi'ite community even beyond Lebanon, especially in the post-Khomeini period with the religiously disputed nomination of a worthy successor to the guardianship of *jurisconsult*. With the death of Ayatollah Khomeini and later the demise of Sayyids Abolqasem Kho'i and Reza Golpayegani, the two most supreme Shi'a religious authorities in Iraq and Iran, Sheikh Fadlallah felt that he had no *absolute* obligation to follow the appointed successor Khameini, the supreme Jurisconsult, in guidance matters as Fadlallah considered himself more learned and knowledgeable in Islamic treatise.[74] With the exception of Ayatollah Montazeri, who was designated successor to Khomeini until he was suddenly removed and closest to the Supreme Leader in religious stature, Ayatollah Khameini's lack of adequate religious credentials in the Shi'i world has led to splits within the religious hierarchy and ranks. This issue is exacerbated by the fact that Ayatollah Kho'i and, subsequently, his representative Sheikh Fadlallah have long criticized the concept of the *Velayat-e-Faqih*. Notwithstanding Fadlallah's wider religious leadership aspirations, a main area of contention with Iran and other Hizb'allah leaders has centered around the feasibility of establishment of an Islamic state in Lebanon in the near future, especially as the 1989 Ta'if accords reformed the Lebanese political system along sectarian lines rather than abolished it altogether. Hizb'allah uniformly rejects the Ta'if accords as it serves as a fundamental stumbling block to seizing political power through majority vote but differ within the rank-and-file whether it is practically possible to overcome this obstacle in the near term. Yet, this only served to highlight that Hizb'allah was not a monolithic body with total subservience to Iran but rather a coalition of clerics, who each had their own views and networks of followers as well as ties to Iran's clerical establishment. This was highlighted by Sheikh Nasserallah who admitted that "not everyone in Hizb'allah thinks the same. Views are usually raised. But differences are always settled through a higher religious authority".[75] In this respect, the existence of divergent views within Hizb'allah clerical ranks and the settlement of disputes through reference to higher religious guidance from Iran's clerical establishment have become increasingly pronounced as Hizb'allah evolved as an organisation. This can be explained by the fact that each individually practising Shi'a Muslim belonging to the Hizb'allah movement at grassroots level has always the freedom to choose which high-ranking cleric to follow as a guide, based on particular preference for their religious stature within the local community, their clerical code of conduct and their local community-based programme. As such, allegiances to high-ranking clergy naturally vary and are dependent or dictated, to a large extent, on the geographical locality or the local background of the learned Shi'ite authorities vis-a-vis rank-and-file members. This was clearly illustrated by the fact that the two first Secretary-Generals of Hizb'allah, who ruled over the movement in its first decade of existence, originated from the Biq'a area. It is also, of course, dependent on, and complicated by, parallel allegiances of local members determined by specific past or present professions within Hizb'allah, especially in its military or security branches. For example, the existence of professional allegiances, compounded by the issue of local background, was evidently displayed by Sheikh Nasserallah's decision to replace certain military commanders in southern Lebanon, as they pledged allegiance to his rival Sheikh al-Tufayli and came from his home area in the Biq'a, with for him more trusted and loyal operational members. Another example of this is displayed by the continued existence of the so-called *al-Da'wa* trend within Hizb'allah ranks which is determined by their previous party affiliation and typified by uncompromising militancy, as seen by the fact that this trend initiated Hizb'allah's warfare with Amal in 1987 under the command of Sheikh Nasserallah. As such, any sharp difference between Hizb'allah clergy tends to correspond to regional conditions and differences affecting the direction of the movement's strategy. Apart from this complex web of allegiances within Hizb'allah ranks, political differences within Hizb'allah's command leadership is also the by-product of the fact that each high-ranking religious cleric has his own pledged allegiance within the Iranian clerical establishment (in some cases also the Iraqi clerical hierarchy) to more learned Shi'a religious authorities, in most instances governed by the legacy of a teacher-student relationship based on personal friendship and religious rank forged during scholarship in any of the Shi'a shrine seminary centers. For example, while Sheikh Fadlallah was the personal representative of Ayatollah Abu al-Qasim al-Musawi al-Khoi, whom he studied under in Najaf between 1950 until 1966, Sheikh Muhammad Ismail al-Khaliq was appointed Ayatollah Montazeri's representative in Lebanon. In particular, the importance of this network was most evident by al-Khaliq's role, in his capacity as Montazeri's emissary, in leaking the so-called U.S.-Iranian arms-for-hostages deal to the pro-Syrian newspaper al-Shira in 1986. Similarly, sharp political differences over the supreme leadership of the Shi'a community have been clearly displayed between Sheikh Fadlallah, on the one hand, and Sheikh Muhammad Yazbek, the personal representative of Iran's spiritual leader, Ayatollah Ali Khameini.

The concentration of the supreme powers of the Hizb'allah movement in the hands of a select few, coupled with the mechanism of implementation of decisions through delegation at a lower level, reflected not only the ability of Hizb'allah to protect its leaders from persecution and elimination in an extremely hostile environment as well as the effectiveness of its operations but also the *depth* of Hizb'allah's clerical relationship with Iran. Although leading Hizb'allah clergy and Iranian officials deny that the movement had a clearly defined organisational structure, the Hizb'allah was secretly governed on the national and local level by the supreme political-religious leadership, composed of a small and select group of Lebanese *uluma*. The supreme decision-making bodies of the Hizb'allah were divided between the *Majlis al-Shura* (the Consultative Assembly), which was headed by twelve senior clerical members with responsibility for tactical decisions and supervision of overall Hizb'allah activity throughout Lebanon,[76] and the *Majlis al-Shura al-Karar* (the Deciding Assembly), headed by Sheikh Muhammad Hussein Fadlallah and composed of eleven other clerics with responsibility for all strategic matters.[77] Within the *Majlis al-Shura*, there existed seven specialized committees dealing with ideological, financial, military, political, judicial, informational and social affairs.[78] In turn, the *Majlis al-Shura* and these seven committees were replicated in each of Hizb'allah's three main operational areas (the Biq'a, Beirut, and the South). They functioned as the principal governing body on daily activity while advising the main *Majlis al-Shura* on the result of their efforts.[79] Furthermore, the Islamic Republic of Iran was also represented in the *Majlis al-Shura* by one or two Iranian military and diplomatic representatives from either the Pasdaran contingent or Iran's embassies in Beirut and Damascus.[80] The presence of Iranian officials within the *Majlis al-Shura* underlined the close co-operation and supervision of activities between Iran and Hizb'allah. In fact, Hizb'allah's *Majlis al-Shura*, which was instituted by Iran's Fazlollah Mahallati in 1983, met infrequently until 1986,[81] which would suggest that Iran was able to exert more direct control over Hizb'allah activity, especially during Ayatollah Ali Akhbar Mohtashemi's tenure as Iran's Ambassador to Syria. However, the supreme governing body of the Hizb'allah assumed a more central and independent role with the intensity of factionalism within Iran's clerical establishment and following the death of Ayatollah Khomeini in 1989.

The composition of the *Majlis al-Shura* underlined the close personal affiliation between Hizb'allah's clerical elite and Iran's clerical establishment, as most of the members of Hizb'allah's leadership received their education at the Najaf religious academies and were influenced by Ayatollah Khomeini, both before and after his departure in 1978. Apart from Sheikh Fadlallah, who returned to Beirut in 1966 after his studies under Abu al-Qasem al-Musawi al-Khoi, the most senior clergy of the

Hizb'allah leadership are all graduates of the Najaf religious academies who returned to Lebanon in the mid-1970s.[82] Both Sheikh Abbas al-Musawi and Sheikh Subhi al-Tufayli, who spearheaded the formation of Hizb'allah and the movement in the Biq'a area, spent respectively eight and nine years studying theology in Najaf.[83] Similarly, Hizb'allah's current Secretary-General, Sheikh Hassan Nasserallah received his theological education in Najaf under the tutelage of Ayatollah Khomeini. The Najaf experience of the Hizb'allah leadership explains both the depth of personal ties between leading Hizb'allah and Iranian leaders as well as the movement's ready assimilation of, and adherence to, Islamic Iran's ideological doctrines.

While Hizb'allah's structure were based on a close-knit and secret leadership and a broad based political movement, which made it more capable of engaging in successful covert operations while shielding the movement's leaders from elimination, the method of organisation was not only fashioned after but also closely reflected the ideological principles of the Islamic revolution in Iran. In particular, Hizb'allah's close ideological identification and its adherence to the line and authority of Ayatollah Khomeini, was most evidently displayed by the movement's subscription to the principle of government by the *just jurisconsult (al-wali al-faqih).*[84] Hizb'allah's adoption of this political theory, made famous by Ayatollah Khomeini during his exile in Najaf and enshrined in the 1979 constitution of the Islamic Republic of Iran, makes it a duty for the movement to obey the decisions and authority of the *just jurisconsult* in the absence of the twelfth Imam. As Hizb'allah clerics professed absolute allegiance to the authority of Ayatollah Khomeini, the movement also embraced many other principles of Iran's Islamic ideology. Following Iran, Hizb'allah viewed itself as a movement under the guidance of Imam Khomeini and struggling against the injustices of imperialism and colonialism, followed by the stand of "no-East and no-West, only Islam".[85] Taking the cue from Iran, it was not surprising that Hizb'allah's ideology attributes all disasters and the condition of the historically oppressed Muslims to the foreign imperialists and infidel Westerners, especially spearheaded by the United States and its regional manifestation, Israel. In a dialectic fashion, Hizb'allah divides the world into the oppressors *(mustakbirun)* and the oppressed *(mustad'afun)* in which the struggle for justice and equality can only be achieved through a revolutionary process and activism. To this end, an important instrument employed by both Iran and Hizb'allah has been the martyrdom of Imam Husayn as a symbol for the struggle against all contemporary tyrants. This symbolism used during the *Ashura* processions heightens the historical feelings of deprivation and injustice of the

Shi'a community and revives annually Shi'i commitments to struggle against the enemies of Islam. In order to relieve the oppressed from the socio-economic reality of the Shi'a community, as well as take revenge on the oppressors, Hizb'allah's revolutionary ideology calls for a comprehensive *jihad* under the guidance of leading religious officials, the Shi'i *uluma*. This symbolism, however, was not confined to the annual *Ashura* processions but translated into self-martyrdom through a series of suicide-operations against the enemies of Islam, following the lead and example set by Iranian shock troops at the Iraqi front in the battle of truth against falsehood. As succinctly described by Fouad Ajami, "this is a seventh-century battle, a primitive, atavistic struggle being refought with the arguments and the weapons of the 20th century".[86] Yet, the defensive nature of this holy war was echoed by Sheikh Fadlallah's justification: "[w]hen Islam fights a war, it fights like any other power in the world, defending itself in order to preserve its existence and its liberty, forced to undertake preventive operations when it is in danger."[87]

The central position of the Shi'a *uluma*, as the vanguard of revolutionary struggle and social change, stems from its perceived independence from political rulers and tyrants and a closeness to the oppressed Shi'a masses. As such, the Lebanese Shi'a *uluma*, under the divine guidance of Ayatollah Khomeini, has rejected the Western model of secularism as well as sectarianism, especially within the context of Lebanon's political system as it caused and fuelled the civil war as well as exacerbated sectarian injustices and inequities.[88] As a result, Hizb'allah's declaratory aim, evidently outlined in its 1985 manifesto, has been the complete overthrow of the confessional system and the establishment of an Islamic state in Lebanon governed by *Sharia* law.

Although disagreements exist within Hizb'allah ranks over the feasibility of establishing an Islamic state in Lebanon in the near future, the movement's central doctrine of rule by the *just juristconsult*, whereby Hizb'allah subjects itself to authority from outside its own nation-state, means that it rejects the very idea of nationalism. Instead, Hizb'allah's revolutionary vision of the creation of an Islamic state in Lebanon must be viewed within a larger pan-Islamic context.[89] This was clearly evident, for example, in Hizb'allah's call to an emergency meeting in the wake of the 1989 Ta'if accord in which new measures were needed "with a view to liberating Lebanon, Jerusalem, and the entire holy land".[90] This was necessary as Hizb'allah viewed the al-Ta'if accord to be an American document based on the 1943 accord, designed to make Lebanon come under American hegemony. As the principle of rule by *just juristconsult* occupies a central position within the Hizb'allah's ideology, the movement

does not recognize what they perceive to be articifical territorial boundaries, which divide Islam, in its wider quest for the creation of an Islamic
state. On the contrary, Hizb'allah's embrace of a pan-Islamic identity
means that the movement viewed itself as an extension of a worldwide
Islamic movement under the guidance of Ayatollah Khomeini. This is
evident by Sheikh Fadlallah's own analogy, describing Hizb'allah's relationship with Iran, that "Lebanon is a lung through which Iran breathes."[91]
As such, Hizb'allah's strategy of creating an Islamic state in Lebanon was
part and parcel of a grander design which aimed to restore Lebanon's
Muslims to the *Dar al-Islam* (the bode of Islam), in other words to establish one great Islamic state or nation, uniting the entire region.[92]
Hizb'allah's grand strategy is closely linked to not only the internal conditions within Lebanon's borders but, more importantly, to regional Islamic
victory in adjacent territories. As a result, Iran's war with Iraq was viewed
by the Hizb'allah as an Islamic struggle between "Truth and Falsehood",
in which Iranian victory would not only result in Islam's triumph in Iraq
but also set the stage for Hizb'allah's own victory in Lebanon.[93] After
Iran's acceptance of UN resolution 598 in 1988, the Hizb'allah substituted
the setback in the Gulf war, in terms of achieving its pan-Islamic vision,
with the revival of Islamic fundamentalism within the Palestinian uprising
(intifada) in the Israeli occupied territories.[94] As such, Hizb'allah viewed
the internal conflict in Lebanon not within the confines of confessional
strife but rather as a battle for the liberation of *al-Quds* (Jerusalem).

Hizb'allah's grand strategy of implementing "the one Islamic world
plan" was set to proceed in four stages: armed confrontation with Israel;
overthrow of the Lebanese regime; the liberation of any form of intervention by the Great Powers in Lebanon; and finally the establishment of
Islamic rule in Lebanon which will be joined by other Muslims in the creation of a greater Islamic community *(umma)*.[95] While the order of priorities were continuously redefined by leading Hizb'allah ideologists,
reflecting the changing internal and external context for Hizb'allah, the
pan-Islamic premise of the movement furnished the ideological *raison
d'etré* for most of Hizb'allah's political and military activity. At its most
basic level, Sheikh Nasserallah described Hizb'allah as a movement composed along two main axis: firstly, a belief in the rule by the *just jurisconsult* and adherence to Khomeini's leadership; and secondly, the continued
need to struggle against the Israeli enemy.[96] As a result, Iran occupied a
central role as the vanguard for Hizb'allah since it embodied both the revolutionary struggle and model that the movement itself was attempting to
achieve in Lebanon. "We learned a truth from Imam Khomeini",
explained Sheikh Nasserallah, "that any country – if an army comes and

occupies it, no matter how strong – if the people of this country rise up and are ready for sacrifice, they will achieve victory in the end."[97] In turn, Hizb'allah received major support and guidance from Iran not only because it translated, disseminated, and defended Iran's pan-Islamic message among the Shi'a community but also as it performed important functions for Iran's foreign policy in the Lebanese, regional and international arena.

HIZB'ALLAH'S PAN-ISLAMIC IDEOLOGY AND STRATEGY

The pan-Islamic premise of Hizb'allah was a defining characteristic of the movement's relationship with Iran. While Hizb'allah's pan-Islamic strategy reflected the specific conditions of the Lebanese Shi'a community, which led to the establishment of radical Shi'a movements, it was also predicated in a larger context on the ideological and political unity between the Hizb'allah and the Islamic revolution in Iran. Apart from professing absolute allegiance to the authority of Ayatollah Khomeini, Hizb'allah's implementation of its pan-Islamic strategy was closely linked to Iran's ability to project successfully its foreign policy of exporting the Islamic revolution abroad while consolidating and protecting it at home. This order of priority has been evident by Sheikh Fadlallah's own views that "we should first defend the Islamic Revolution and Iran before considering the formation of a second Islamic state".[98] In a pan-Islamic context, this symbiotic relationship between Hizb'allah and Iran manifested itself in many different ways in Lebanon.

Liberation of Jerusalem

The pan-Islamic goal of liberating Jerusalem through armed confrontation against Israel had been not only a reflection of suffering by the Shi'a community, following Israel's invasion and subsequent occupation of southern Lebanon, but also used by Hizb'allah as a pretext to mobilize support for the overthrow of the secular Lebanese regime and the establishment of an Islamic state. Hizb'allah's successful and relentless guerilla activity, which led to Israel's withdrawal in 1985, served to enhance the movement's role as protector of the Shi'a community in southern Lebanon while it bolstered the movement's support and image, among both followers and adversaries alike, as an implacable foe of Israel and other enemies of Islam. While Hizb'allah succeeded initially to fill the power-vacuum created by Israel's withdrawal at the expense of Amal, the race for the

leadership of the Shi'a community in southern Lebanon was not only a
battle between the Hizb'allah and Amal but also between Iran and Syria.
Apart from expanding Iran's position within the Shi'a community through
Hizb'allah, by a successful combination of ideological indoctrination and
material inducement, Iran's support for Hizb'allah was also based on
Lebanon's geostrategic position allowing Iran to participate actively in the
wider context of Middle East politics, especially in the Arab-Israeli
conflict. As such, Iran's support for the Hizb'allah in the South was particularly important, if not critical, towards this end as it could operate relatively unhindered compared to its limited ability to function and operate in
Syrian-controlled Beirut and Biq'a area. The Arab-Israeli arena is
absolutely crucial to Iran, for without having the ability to be a key player,
Iran's leadership role over, and credibility within, the Islamic community
would be severely undermined since "the liberation of Palestine" is at the
central core of Iran's revolutionary discourse and struggle, especially as
the Palestine question embodies a series of key issues: justice for Muslims,
defense of the oppressed and dispossessed Shi'a community, Islamic
Iran's revolutionary vanguard position as the leader of the Muslim world,
and US hegemony in the region. Iran's staunch dedication to the
Palestinian cause, calling for the defeat and obliteration of Israel from its
existence, can be seen as a vital instrument in the mobilisation of the revolutionary Muslim masses, especially as it transcends the Arab/Persian as
well as the Sunni/Shi'ite divides. As such, Iranian officials have continu-
ally declared the question of Palestine as the most important issue in the
Muslim world. For Hizb'allah, the question of Palestine assumed a symbolic level of solidarity as the oppressed Lebanese Shi'ites found a natural
ally in the dispossessed Palestinian community in the common struggle
against the *mustakbirun* (oppressors), specifically in the struggle to resist
Israeli occupation and restore the Arab-Muslim historical rights in
Palestine. This solidarity with the Palestinians was clearly evident by the
fact that Hizb'allah publicly emerged in September 1984, for the first time,
and announced its existence on the second anniversary of the massacre of
Palestinians at the Sabra and Shatila refugee camps. It was also consistently shown by Hizb'allah's close support to the Palestinians during the
Amal-Hizb'allah "war of the camps". As a stumbling block to Syria's
plans for the future of Lebanon, Iran actively promoted the destabilisation
of security in southern Lebanon, through proxy, in order to obstruct any
prospects for accommodation in the Arab-Israeli conflict. For example,
prior to the 1991 Madrid meeting, the increased militancy of the
Hizb'allah was a joint effort with Iran to sabotage the scheduled Middle
East peace process. In autumn 1991 meetings with Sheikh Mohammad

Jawad Khonsari, director of the Middle East and African department at the Iranian Foreign Ministry, the Hizb'allah discussed the coordination of the resistance work to liberate the South of Lebanon and holy Jerusalem.[99] The anarchic situation in the South also provided Iran with a forum to expand its influence in other areas of regional politics while paving the way for the Hizb'allah in the establishment of an Islamic state in Lebanon. As a result, both Iran and Hizb'allah were vehemently opposed to UN resolution 425, partly as a practical measure as the continous deployment of UNIFIL obstructed the obligatory *jihad* against Israel, but also as the resort to force was the only option available to the movement against Israel, whom they believed had neither any intention nor interest in a withdrawal from southern Lebanon. Also, Hizb'allah rejected the acceptance of UN Resolution 425 as it implied admitting the existence of Israel as a legitimate state or entity. Any recognition of, or settlement with, Israel amounts to treachery and a surrender to the principles of Islam as outlined by the Islamic Amal leader, Husayn al-Musawi: "[o]n our part we do not accept any peace as long as Israel is in existence and Israel must be obliterated".[100] In fact, any dealing with Israel was prohibited by the movement's spiritual leader, whether or not other Arab states reconciled with Israel. Both Iran and Hizb'allah were also opposed to the implementation of the 1989 Ta'if Accord, the blueprint for national reconciliation with reform towards a more equitable political system for all confessional groups, and which attempted to end the civil war through the disarmament and dissolution of Lebanon's militias under Syrian auspices and control.[101] In the latter case, Hizb'allah's permission to maintain their armed presence in the South and in the eastern Biq'a, as the Hizb'allah claimed to be a resistance movement rather than a militia, came as a result of a *modus vivendi* between Iran and Syria.[102] This underlines that the fate of Hizb'allah has not only been dependent on the regional relationship between Iran and Syria with regard to Lebanon but also that the movement's position vis-á-vis Israel reflected both its own internal agenda as well as Iran's foreign policy interests.

Establishment of an Islamic Republic in Lebanon

Hizb'allah's pan-Islamic goal of overthrowing the secular Lebanese regime was inspired by the revolutionary achievement set by the establishment of the Islamic Republic of Iran in 1979. While Iran proved that it was possible to achieve the impossible in the face of oppression and injustice, Hizb'allah's rejection of the confessional system was based on the adherence by the movement to governance by the *just juristconsult*

(al-walih al-faqi) as its ideological foundation. As such, Hizb'allah
viewed its revolutionary struggle in Lebanon not within the confines of
geographical borders but rather as a chapter in the liberation of Jerusalem
and the establishment of one great Islamic *umma*. Although Iran and
Hizb'allah shared the conviction that Islamic rule will ultimately triumph
in Lebanon, there existed divergence over methods and their feasibility,
even within Hizb'allah ranks.[103] The Hizb'allah sceptics, with Sheikh
Fadlallah at its fore, acknowledged that the conditions in Lebanon were
both more complex and difficult than those which existed in pre-
revolutionary Iran. Unlike Iran, the situation in Lebanon was complicated
by the multiplicity of, and opposition by, other religious militias supported
by powerful foreign involvement.[104] In particular, Syria was alarmed over
Hizb'allah's emergence not only as its agenda was directly juxtaposed
with Syria's hegemony in Lebanon but also as the movement posed the
only real challenge to Asad's attempts to resurrect the defunct Lebanese
political system. As Syria showed uncompromising determination to
reassert its suzerainty over Lebanon, especially within the framework of
the Ta'if Accord, Hizb'allah readjusted its grand strategy of overthrowing
the secular regime through armed struggle towards a willingness to participate in mainstream Lebanese politics, a move already visible within the
context of Hizb'allah's warfare against Amal in 1988 but more directly
inspired by the decisive victory in the Algerian elections of the Muslim
fundamentalist grouping, the *Front Islamique du Salut (FIS)*.[105] While
Hizb'allah is staunchly against the confessional system of Lebanese government and politics, its readjustment demonstrated not only flexibility
within the movement in the post-Khomeini era, with diminished Iranian
support and limited maneuverability in the post-civil war period in
Lebanon, but also its susceptibility to changes in the regional and international arena. As such, the creation of an Iranian-styled revolutionary
Shi'ite Islamic state in Lebanon has been dependent on Hizb'allah's willingness to abandon violence and patiently work within the Lebanese confessional system, and perhaps more importantly, by tempering their
pan-Islamic zeal both in terms of expansion into Syria and willingness to
accept the present *Pax Syriana* in Lebanon, a position adopted at least for
the moment until the eventual demise of the confessional system. In addition, the prospects for an Islamic state in Lebanon, and to a larger extent,
the future of Hizb'allah is predicated on not only Iran's ability to sustain
its support for the movement but also the direction of Islamic Iran's
foreign policy and the intensity of factionalism within Iran's clerical
establishment.

Liberation of Lebanon from Foreign Presence and Influence

Hizb'allah's third pan-Islamic goal of "the liberation of Lebanon from any form of political and military intervention by the Great Powers"[106] mirrors Islamic Iran's foreign policy of exporting the revolution as well as the continued Shi'a predicament in Lebanon and the country's vulnerability to foreign interests and foreign intervention. While the Lebanese Shi'a community's anti-Western hostility was deeply rooted in the historical legacy of Western colonialism and intervention, it was exaggerated by the dynamics of a protracted civil war; the Israeli invasion and subsequent occupation; and the imposition of Western political and military order. In many ways, Hizb'allah's hostility towards the United States could be seen as an wider symbolic extension of the Iranian revolutionary struggle against outside intervention and colonialism, as epitomised by the U.S. embassy siege in Teheran. This hostility by the Hizb'allah was early crystallized and most evidently demonstrated towards the American and French participation in the Multinational Forces, deployed after the massacres in the West Beirut refugee camps of Sabra and Shatila. The movement regarded the MNF not as a peace-keeping force but rather as pro-Israeli and anti-Muslim due to its image as supporter and protector of the Gemayel regime.[107] In an effort designed to end any foreign military presence and political influence, the Hizb'allah executed a series of suicide attacks, with active support from Syria and Iran, most notably against the headquarters of the U.S. and French contingents which led to the multinational evacuation from Lebanon in 1984. Hizb'allah also spearheaded the armed campaign which led to the 1985 Israeli withdrawal from the Shouf Mountains and Beirut to a narrow security zone in South Lebanon, while it contributed to the political climate that pressured Amin Gemayel to abrogate the 1983 May 17th Agreement with Israel. Although the Hizb'allah was successful in precipitating the American and Israeli withdrawals from Lebanon, which earned the movement prestige and revolutionary credence among the Shi'a community, the achievement also underlined the close co-operation and convergence of interests between Hizb'allah, Syria, and Iran. For Syria, Hizb'allah's activity contributed to the re-emergence of Syria's political and military dominance in Lebanon after its influence had been diminuated by military defeat, following Israel's 1982 invasion and occupation of areas formerly controlled by Syria, and by foreign intervention, which secured U.S. hegemony in Lebanon. For Iran, Hizb'allah's activity provided it with both a crucial means to participate actively militarily in the Arab-Israeli conflict by proxy and a forum to confront Israeli and American designs in Lebanon and elsewhere in the Middle East.

In the aftermath of the American and Israeli withdrawals from Lebanon, Iran's and Syria's operational co-operation against common enemies, through Hizb'allah as their proxy, was pursued through the abduction of foreign citizens, both as a means to influence Western policy in Lebanon and as a way to exploit the issue for their own foreign policy agendas in the regional context. While the abductions by Hizb'allah forced the departure of Westerners from Lebanon, particularly after the January 1987 incidents, the decision to initiate the hostage-takings was primarily based on Iranian foreign policy calculations and interests, which in most cases coincided with Hizb'allah's own agenda. As such, both Iran and Hizb'allah were able not only to remove military and political obstacles for the creation of an Islamic state in Lebanon but also use the hostage issue against their common enemies for a wide array of political purposes. Although the hostage-takings by Hizb'allah and its militancy against Western targets was motivated by the movement's own agenda in Lebanon, Iran was able to use the foreign hostages as a useful instrument to extract political, military and financial concessions from the Western world.

Syria's acquiesence to Hizb'allah's practice of hostage-taking, as it controlled the Biq'a area from which Iranian Pasdaran and Hizb'allah operated, has been based primarily on its relationship with Iran. Although Hizb'allah activity was indirectly serving Syria's ambition for local hegemony, by the expulsion of foreign military and political presence from Lebanon, the hostage issue has also proved to be a liability for Syria. In its vigorous efforts to establish a *Pax Syriana* in Lebanon, Syria's close identification with the Hizb'allah undermined its ability to attract economic support from the Western world and shed its regional and international isolation. In addition, the abduction of foreign hostages by Hizb'allah, coupled with the movement's attacks against Israel, not only damaged Syria's ability to control activity within Lebanese territory but also threatened to bring Syria into an armed confrontation with Israel in and over Lebanon. As a result, Syrian protection and support for Amal was used to counter any uncontrolled Hizb'allah militancy against Israel and in the struggle for control of the Shi'a community in southern Lebanon. This intra-Shi'i warfare over the control of Shi'i regions in Lebanon culminated in February 1988, following the kidnapping of U.S. Marine Lieutenant Colonel William Higgins, and continued until January 1989 when Iran and Syria co-sponsored an agreement between Amal and Hizb'allah.[108] However, Syrian restraint towards, and at times complicity with, Hizb'allah hostage-taking activity underlined that Syria's tolerance was based on its larger converging interests with Iran, as long as an enlarged Iranian role in Lebanon through Hizb'allah did not threaten either to spill over the borders and encourage Islamic movements to challenge the Asad regime nor limit Syrian designs in Lebanon, rather than based on bowing to regional and international pressures.

Creation of Wider Islamic Community Beyond Lebanon's Borders

Hizb'allah's final pan-Islamic goal of linking the establishment of Islamic rule in Lebanon as part in the creation of a single Islamic community underscored not only that Hizb'allah's revolutionary struggle rejected the principles of Arab and Persian nationalism, which divides the Muslims along artificial lines, but also that the movement is incorporated in a larger Islamic strategy led by the *just jurisconsult* Ayatollah Khomeini. As the Hizb'allah viewed itself as a component of a larger movement composed of all downtrodden Muslims who struggle under the guidance of Ayatollah Khomeini against the injustices of imperialism and colonialism, the movement's wider ideological outlook was a reflection of a total identification with Ayatollah Khomeini's revolutionary vision and the vanguard position of the Islamic Republic of Iran. Within this ideological framework, Hizb'allah viewed Arab nationalism as a complete failure since it has led not only to Arab disunity, especially in terms of a resolution to the Palestinian issue, and Arab accommodation with Israel, as exemplified by the 1979 Camp David Accords, but also to worsened socio-economic difficulties for the Arab masses due to weak and illegitimate Arab political systems.[109] A manifestation of Hizb'allah's rejection of Arab nationalism was the way in which the movement viewed the war between Iran and Iraq. In accordance with Iran, Hizb'allah adopted a pan-Islamic justification for Iran's continuation of its war with Iraq, in which the problem was viewed as a wider battle against the usurper of the *dar al-Islam* (the territory of Islam) rather than within the confines of a conflict between the Iraqi President Saddam Hussein and the Iranian government.[110] As explained by Sheikh Fadlallah: "[t]he war imposed by Iraq on the Islamic Republic of Iran, is a war waged by the entire world of blasphemy against Islam."[111] When Ayatollah Khomeini's accepted UN Resolution 598, Hizb'allah abandoned the overthrow of Saddam Hussein's regime as a necessary first step to restore control of al-Quds (Jerusalem) to the *dar al-Islam* and turned towards supporting the Islamic elements within the Palestinian uprising, especially as Hamas outright contested the legitimacy of the PLO since its secular and nationalist ideology was considered un-Islamic. Hizb'allah's concentration on Palestine reinforced the

movement's pan-Islamic premise as the struggle for the liberation of
Palestine not only drew attention to the dominance of the United States
and Israel in the region but also because it was directly predicated on the
liberation of Jerusalem.

Hizb'allah functioned as an important conduit for Iran in efforts to
spread Ayatollah Khomeini's universalist message across ethnic, linguistic, and sectarian barriers, both in terms of disseminating Iran's political
views and in educating the Arab masses about its Islamic ideology.[112]
Hizb'allah's refutation of secular nationalism as an alien ideology derived
from the West and harmful to the unity of the Islamic *umma*, means that
the movement repudiates the idea of Iran as a distinct state with its own
interests.[113] While Iranian pan-Islamists have been compelled by the constraints of realpolitik to subordinate the radical philosophy of the revolution for the pragmatic interests of the state (as exemplified by the
Iran-Contra affair and the acceptance of a cease-fire with Iraq in 1988), the
Hizb'allah showed greater loyalty to the pan-Islamic vision not only by
the fact that it can afford to be as a revolutionary movement but also as it
has been dependent on pan-Islam for its sense of purpose and mission.
However, Hizb'allah's pan-Islamic revolutionary struggle has been predicated on Islam's triumphs in adjacent territories, spearheaded by the
Islamic Republic of Iran and under the guidance of the Ayatollah
Khomeini. As a result, while Iran has been forced to demonstrate greater
flexibility in its revolutionary dogma, in terms of the transnational notion
of a *Pax Islamica*, in order to safeguard the very survival of the Islamic
regime, Hizb'allah not only veiled its own revolutionary struggle in pan-
Islamic motifs but also linked it to the success of Iran's ability to export its
revolution.

While Hizb'allah's ruling élite viewed its revolutionary struggle in
Lebanon through the ideological prism of pan-Islam, which was reflected
by the linkage of its activity with Islamic Iran's foreign policy within
Lebanon and on the regional and international level, the rank and file of
the movement was also deeply affected by the realities imposed by
Lebanon's confessional problems, as manifested through, and exacerbated
by, a decade of protracted warfare. As such, Hizb'allah viewed the possibility of the final implementation of a *Pax Islamica* as occurring only
through the completion of all constituent elements or parts of Hizb'allah's
pan-Islamic strategy.[114] Unlike Iran, the confessional nature of Lebanon,
given the opposition from an array of other religious communities with
powerful foreign support, had forced Hizb'allah to readjust the movement's pan-Islamic priorities in accordance with the varying conditions
of feasibility. Although all pan-Islamic goals of the Hizb'allah are

intertwined with each other, the Islamic resistance in southern Lebanon, and its eventual extension into the liberation of Jerusalem, served as a basic premise for the movement's political actions. Apart from providing Hizb'allah with legitimacy, the movement's resistance activity and pursuit of the liberation of Jerusalem, was not only secondary to but also the pretext for a more pressing concern: the struggle for Lebanese power and the establishment of Islamic rule.[115] As such, Hizb'allah's resistance activity can be seen as an instrument to enhance the movement's popularity and credibility among the Lebanese Shi'a community in a wider effort to achieve the implementation of an Islamic regime. Hizb'allah's order of priorities must also be seen within the context of conducive elements that determines the level of achievement of these pan-Islamic goals in the near future. In terms of the liberation of Jerusalem, Hizb'allah recognized that the elimination of Israel was a protracted pan-Islamic strategy extending over many years. As pledged by Sheikh al-Tufayli, during his speech at the funeral of Hizb'allah Secretary-General al-Musawi in 1992, "we know that we will not triumph in one or even several years but have prepared for a battle of centuries".[116] The centrality of Hizb'allah's holy war against Israel is continously reiterated by its leaders in all their speeches, confirming that they would readily martyr themselves for this cause rather than being forced to submit to either Israel or the U.S. As outlined by Sheikh al-Tufayli: "[i]f the whole world makes peace with Israel, Hizb'allah will continue to fight the Jews – even if Israel withdraws from south Lebanon. The peace documents will be torn up, there will be no normalization with the enemy, and the resistance will continue."[117] Hizb'allah's re-orientation towards, and solidarity with, the Palestinian Intifada, through its support and cooperation with the emergence of *Hamas* and *Islamic Jihad*, was a manifestation of raised expectations within the movement for the near accomplishment of the liberation of Jerusalem. This was further elevated by the resurgence of Islamist movements across the Maghreb and Mashriq and the seriousness of this challenge to the legitimacy, and stability, of the Arab ruling élites, a challenge most notably spearheaded by Algeria's FIS and Egypt's *al-Gamma al-Islamiyya*. However, Hizb'allah itself has gradually been forced to adopt a two-phased approach to the liberation of Jerusalem which focuses primarily on the liberation of Lebanese territory from Israeli occupation and then towards the struggle for the liberation of Palestine. This dual-phased approach is necessary as Hizb'allah recognizes that the condition and regional situation for the liberation of either Lebanon or Palestine differ. Yet, the unequivocal nature of this struggle was underlined by Sheikh Nasserallah, who maintained that the Hizb'allah "do not officially recognize the existence or continuation of the Israeli government."[118] As such, according to the Hizb'allah leader, it was the movement's responsibility to eliminate the Israeli usurpation of the land of Palestine. Similarly, the Hizb'allah has been divided over the feasibility for the transformation of Lebanon into an Islamic republic in the immediate future. The division within Hizb'allah ranks reflected not only scepticism over the applicability of the Iranian model within Lebanon's multiconfessional system but also the necessity of a readjustment in the movement's pan-Islamic strategy to ensure its own survival, especially in the post-Khomeini period and under the Ta'if Accords with the extension of a *Pax Syriana* in Lebanon. As a result, Hizb'allah's military activity was confined to southern Lebanon, where it escalated its attacks against Israel in order to justify its armed existence as a resistance movement rather than a militia, while the movement's political wing participated in the autumn 1992 Lebanese elections, in which they scored a surprising electoral success. The eight elected Hizb'allah parliamentary reresentatives were obliged to pursue a strategy based on three principles: "putting pressure on the government to support the anti-Zionist resistance, opposing the idea of negotiation with Israel, and urging the government to assist people living in war-stricken areas".[119] Hizb'allah's shift in strategy should not be viewed as an ideological departure from its pan-Islamic goal of creating an Islamic Republic in Lebanon but rather a carefully crafted move, which has been officially blessed by Iran's Ayatollah Khameini, to facilitate a revolution from within the Lebanese political system. As admitted by Sheikh Nasserallah, Hizb'allah's electoral participation was a move "trying to topple the government through peaceful means."[120]

CONCLUSIONS

An understanding of the historical antecedent to the formation of the Hizb'allah is a fundamental prerequisite for the application of crisis management to the hostage-crisis for a number of reasons. Firstly, the Najaf origins of the movement and its subsequent development within Lebanon provides a frame of reference for the extent to which the close personal friendships forged between future Iranian and Hizb'allah leaders have been instrumental not only in governing the Lebanese movement's ideological deference to Iran but also that its past and present activities are guided more by the evolution of a series of complex clerical networks than bound by a duty to profess absolute obedience to any Iranian orders. Apart from the close allegiance between Hizb'allah's clerical élite and members of Iran's clerical establishment, rooted in their shared theological experience at Najaf and previous assistance to the anti-Shah revolutionary activity, the rank and file of the movement is also far from monolithic but rather bound and guided by a complex web of relationships, extending from the élite clerical leadership down to ties with family, neighbourhoods and individual religious clergy.[121] This has meant that the movement's members have been not only divided over loyalty to Hizb'allah's pan-Islamic vision over their collective Lebanese identity but also over the nature of authority, as manifested through different allegiances by its members and frequent disagreements within the movement as well as towards its relations with Iran. The existence of varying allegiances within the Hizb'allah and towards Iran are essential to gauge to the advantage of crisis-management at a general level, to understand the depth and breadth of clerical networks, and at a more specific level, to monitor fundamental divisions within the movement and areas of disagreements with Iran. This determines the willingness of Hizb'allah to act on behalf of Iranian orders or more independently.

Secondly, the evolution of the movement and its ideology within the Lebanese environment is also a necessary prerequisite for comprehending its animosity towards the West, as displayed by its violent behaviour, and its wider relationships with other internal actors, most notably within the Shi'a community. However, the anarchial Lebanese environment has led to a latent tension between Hizb'allah's ideological vision for Lebanon, and its recent exercise of caution and restraint in safeguarding its existence and achievements as a militant Islamic movement. Hizb'allah's hostage-taking activity provides the most revealing area in which these constraints and opportunities have been displayed.

3 Hizb'allah and the Hostage-crisis Within Lebanon

INTRODUCTION

In a ten-year period, between 1982 and 1992, a number of enigmatic and obscure organisations, seemingly loosely or indirectly affiliated with the Hizb'allah organisation in Lebanon, not only launched spectacular and deadly suicide operations against the Western presence but also engaged in political acts of hostage-taking of Western citizens. While the shadowy Hizb'allah movement has denied any active involvement in these acts of terrorism, though applauding these operations in concert with Iran, its self-proclaimed main enemies of the United States, Great Britain, and France, collectively sustained casualties of over 300 individuals killed by the organisation while it has held over 45 citizens in captivity for various lengths of time over a ten-year period.[1] While the chaos and insanity of the fifteen-year protracted civil war in Lebanon contributed to the difficulty in extricating the Western hostages from among a multitude of confessional militias, it also led to the association and image of Hizb'allah in the West as a crazy and fanatic religious group, bent on martyrdom through suicide-operations, and engaged in the random abduction of foreigners, under the assumed strict control and direction of Iran's clerical establishment.

Although the West crossed paths in Lebanon with the radical and militant aspects of the Shi'a community and the Islamic Republic of Iran through Hizb'allah's abductions of foreign citizens, the highly complex nature of the internecine conflict involving an array of confessional warring factions with foreign patrons, prevented a clearly defined understanding of the Hizb'allah's motives and organisation from emerging. In the murky underworld of Lebanon's civil war, where conduct was regulated by regional, national, sectarian and family interest, the nature of the shadowy groups, acting under the umbrella of Hizb'allah, further compounded the complexity of the hostage-crisis and the involvement of Iran. The ambiguous nature of the organisation itself and its affiliation with Iran lead to an array of misperceptions and miscalculations by Western governments and outside observers in their attempts to both understand and

60

confront the prolonged hostage-crisis in Lebanon, at times with disastrous consequences.

The problems of looking at hostage-taking by the Hizb'allah are: firstly, any complete analysis of the hostage-crisis requires a comprehensive understanding of Hizb'allah as an organisation and its *relationship* with elements within Iran's clerical establishment as well as *interaction* with Iranian institutions. While information provided by hostages on their release yield limited insight into the way in which the Hizb'allah operates as well as interacts with Iran, most previous analyses dismiss the possibility of unravelling the dimensions of the network of personal contacts and relationships between Hizb'allah and Iranian clergymen. As accurately advanced by John Calabrese:

> "[f]rom the days of Musa Sadr, the Iranian-Lebanese Shia connection has been built on a network of personal contacts and relationships. Hezbollah as an 'organisation', Iran as a 'state', and the 'association' between them have been, and still are, impenetrable and unfathomable: knowing what they are depends on knowing who the key personalities are within them, and how these key players relate to one another."[2]

Secondly, the approach of viewing both Hizb'allah and Iran as unitary rational actors is not only based on a misconception but ignores the political reality of the internal dimensions of Lebanon's civil war as well as the permanent projection of clerical factionalism in Iran onto the Lebanese arena through the Hizb'allah's activity, especially in terms of hostage-taking of foreigners. In particular, the importance of understanding clerical factionalism in Iran and its superimposition on the Hizb'allah is essential since "[t]he Iranian political and social systems decree that one deal with personalities and not with institutions, the personal relationship to this day transcends any formal or institutionalized relationship."[3] As a militant Islamic organisation, the Hizb'allah is far from a uniform body as displayed by continuous *clerical factionalism* between its leading members over the direction of the movement and the constant readjustments of the movement's position within Lebanon's warring factions. This is influenced by the dynamics of the relationship with Iranian clerical factions and institutions at work within the movement.

Thirdly, the hostage-crisis is also influenced by multi-layered Lebanese, regional, and international politics. This influence affects the process of the hostage-crisis as Westerners are abducted and released for *individual* Hizb'allah motives or *in convergence* with Iranian and, to a lesser extent, Syrian interests.

Fourthly, in terms of Hizb'allah as an organisation, it requires deciphering the affiliation and position of the shadowy sub-groups under its
umbrella, who claim responsibility for these abductions. It is also necessary to examine the nature and dynamics of Hizb'allah's *command leadership* and its *decision-making* with reference to the process of
hostage-taking of Westerners.

Finally, this must be balanced against the dynamics of Hizb'allah's
institutionalized relationships with Iran and Syria in Lebanon in accordance with internal Lebanese factors and external developments, creating
opportunities and constraints in the practise of hostage-taking.

USE OF COVERNAMES AND CONCEALMENT IN HIZB'ALLAH
ABDUCTION OF FOREIGNERS

A myriad of different names have appeared attributed to organisations
claiming responsibility for the abduction of Western hostages in Lebanon.
This has led to a great deal of confusion among policymakers and academics alike in attempts to determine whether the perpetrating group has
acted within the framework of Hizb'allah's umbrella, semi-independently,
or completely independently. As a senior Israeli Defense Ministry official
succintly phrased the problem in a 1987 interview: "[w]e don't know anything about them – where they are, who they are and how to deal with
them". As these groups have managed to maintain almost complete
secrecy surrounding their identity and operations, any determination of
their status and affiliation to Hizb'allah is a difficult task. Nevertheless, it
is necessary and, more importantly, possible to discern the *raison d'être*
by the perpetrating organisation for the concealment of their identity as
well as their connection with the Hizb'allah.

Although Hizb'allah's spiritual leader, Sheikh Muhammad Hussein
Fadlallah, debunked the idea of *taqiyya*, or dissimulation, when he urged
his followers to organize along party lines with the publication of *Islam
and the Logic of Force* in 1976, the Shi'a tradition of concealment, as
practised by the Shi'a minority when religiously persecuted in ancient
times, has been frequently used by the Hizb'allah when operating covertly,
especially in the abduction of foreigners.[4] The use of different cover
names during covert operations has shielded the Hizb'allah movement and
its leaders from persecution and reprisals, while the cover names themselves have been employed not only to confuse the enemy but also to
signify the currents inside the movement at a particular time.[5] While the
nom de guerre of *Islamic Jihad*, or "Holy War", emerged in connection

with Hizb'allah's multiple suicide operations in 1983, many Hizb'allah leaders openly admitted both involvement in *Islamic Jihad* operations and that the organisation did not exist as such, but rather was merely a "telephone organisation",[6] whose name was "used by those involved to disguise their true identity".[7] The use of the term *Jihad* by the Hizb'allah denoted the combat activity against the enemies of Islam and lent revolutionary credence to the movement in the eyes of the Shi'ite community. It was also used by the Hizb'allah in the abduction of foreigners from 1984 until mid-1985, which symbolically reflected the movement's accelerated efforts to expel any Western political and military presence in Lebanon. Therefore, it was not surprising that *Islamic Jihad* as a cover name ceased to be used in new abductions of foreigners after Hizb'allah's successful victory in forcing not only the earlier departure of the Multinational Forces but also Israel's partial withdrawal from Lebanon in June 1985.

The emergence of another organisation, using the *nom de guerre* of the *Revolutionary Justice Organisation*, in claiming responsibility for the abduction of foreigners during 1986, signified Hizb'allah's concern over the imprisonment of a number of its members in France as most abductions involved French citizens. When the cover name was used in abductions of three Americans in September-October 1986, (shortly preceding the revelation of the US-Iran arms-for-hostages deal) it was believed the name signified a split within the Hizb'allah which mirrored Iranian clerical factionalism.[8] As later revealed by the confinement of these French and American hostages with other hostages held by *Islamic Jihad*, coupled with the unified position within Hizb'allah rejecting any US-Iranian *rapprochement*, this was not the case.

Apart from a single abduction of a French citizen in January 1987 by the *Revolutionary Justice Organisation*, Hizb'allah's shift towards using the *nom de guerre, Islamic Jihad for the Liberation of Palestine,* reflected not only solidarity with imprisoned Hizb'allah and Shi'ite Palestinians held by Israel but also the movement's political and military orientation in the struggle for the "liberation of Jerusalem" through armed confrontation in southern Lebanon. This also signified Hizb'allah's co-operation with *Fatah* elements instituted in 1987 for the escalation of the armed confrontation with Israel.[9] While a number of other cover names were subsequently used by Hizb'allah, the common feature of these names signified the release of imprisoned Hizb'allah members, as evident by the use of the names *The Organisation for the Defense of Free People* or *Holy Strugglers for Freedom*, and, more importantly, symbolized the fate of the Shi'a as a deprived and humiliated community, as evident by the use of the title *Organization of the Oppressed on Earth*.[10] This is evidently apparent by the choice of name of Hizb'allah's own radio station, *Voice of the Oppressed.*[11]

While the employment of these cover names by Hizb'allah reflected the concerns and direction of the movement in Lebanon, the fact that many hostages were held with other hostages taken by different groups is evidence that the names have not necessarily represented separate and different groups, either within or outside the organisational structure of the Hizb'allah.[12] In fact, as demonstrated by the testimony of many former hostages, the core group of kidnappers of Western hostages only involved a dozen men from various Hizb'allah clans, most notably the Mugniyya and Hamadi clans.[13] The fact that these two clans have been continuously pinpointed by authorities for alleged involvement in the kidnappings of foreigners underlines not only the importance of the Lebanese clan system as a basis for Hizb'allah's organizational structure and activity but also the personal and ideological loyalty within the Hizb'allah to higher religious authority. This has led to an extremely close-knit structure capable of engaging in successful covert operations. Even IDF Military Intelligence (AMAN) found it extremely difficult to infiltrate the organisation as its membership was based solely on religious or family bonds, which compounded the difficulty in unraveling "its compartmentalized ultrasecretive cells and cryptic communications".[14] While clan loyalty and individual clerical relationships have provided the basis for the movement and the framework for its hostage-taking activity, it functions under the jurisdiction of a centralized and well organized leadership structure. Although leading Hizb'allah clergy deny the movement has a clearly defined organisational structure, the Hizb'allah is secretly governed on the national and local level by a supreme political-religious board of authority, composed of a small and select group of Lebanese *uluma*. Due to the absolute nature of the supreme religious authority of the Hizb'allah's command leadership, all decisions or activities relating to hostage-taking by regional or clan leaders had to be approved at the highest level.[15] As a result, the idea that Hizb'allah's hostage-taking activity were pursued independently by individual Hizb'allah clans, either without the knowledge of leading clergy or not through a chain of command, ignores not only the nature of religious authority exercised over every aspect of the movement's activity but also the institutionalized cooperation and coordination with both Iran and Syria in some of these operations. According to PLO's Salah Khalaf (Abu Iyad), all the different names adopted by Hizb'allah are merely covers for its operational wing.[16] Although a number of abductions of foreigners were initiated in alignment with individual interests of certain Hizb'allah clans, all acts of hostage-taking also coincided with the collective interest of the organisation as a whole. As a consequence, it is necessary to analyse the nature of Hizb'allah's command leadership, its decision-making structure as well as policy with specific reference to the movement's hostage-taking activity. It is also necessary to examine the nature of the involvement of Iranian clergy and institutions at work in Lebanon as well as Syrian military and intelligence services in terms of their influence within and over Hizb'allah activity.

HIZB'ALLAH'S COMMAND LEADERSHIP[17]

On the first anniversary of the martyrdom of Sheikh Ragheb Harb, on February 16, 1985, Hizb'allah publicly announced for the first time not only its ideological progamme and strategy in a manifesto but also appeared as a unified organisation with the assembly of the entire Hizb'allah command leadership.[18] Although the Hizb'allah revealed only the position of Sheikh Ibrahim al-Amin as its official spokesman, the movement was secretly governed by a supreme religious body, which had been instituted by Iran's Fazlollah Mahallati in 1983, fashioned after the upper echelons of Iran's clerical leadership. The composition of the highest authority within this supreme religious body in Lebanon reflected the core group of individual Shi'ite clergy who assisted in the foundation of the Hizb'allah in July 1982. Apart from the position of Husayn al-Musawi, as the only non-clerical member of the religious leadership, the composition of Hizb'allah's leadership council was also reflective of the religious authority of these clergymen in terms of their command of a substantial number of followers in each of the three main Shi'ite regions in Lebanon: the Biq'a; Beirut; and southern Lebanon.

Bekaa Valley

In the Biq'a area, the Hizb'allah is headed by Sheikh Subhi al-Tufayli, who was considered the highest religious authority in Ba'albek as evident by his nomination of "president of the Islamic Republic" in Ba'albek in 1984,[19] and Sheikh Abbas al-Musawi. Along with Husayn al-Musawi and his *Islamic Amal*, these two religious figures occupied not only the most senior positions as spiritual leaders of the Hizb'allah in the Biq'a but also played an instrumental role as liaison with the Iranian Pasdaran and Iran while maintaining overall control over Hizb'allah's irregular and semi-regular military units.[20] Sheikh al-Tufayli acted as the head of the Hizb'allah headquarters in Ba'albek and was the movement's main liaison with Teheran.[21] Sheikh al-Musawi was operational head of the Hizb'allah's Special Security Apparatus between 1983–85 and later of the movement's military wing, the *Islamic Resistance* (a position held between late-1985 until April 1988).[22] Another main leader of Hizb'allah military activity in the Biq'a was Sheikh Husayn al-Khalil, who maintained a senior position within Hizb'allah's command leadership. Prior to his promotion as head of the Politbureau in 1989–90, al-Khalil was credited with having established the movement's security apparatus and acted as operational coordinator of Hizb'allah's military units in co-operation with *Islamic Amal*, which was subordinated organisationally within Hizb'allah from 1984 onwards under the personal authority of Husayn al-Musawi.[23] A lesser Hizb'allah figure in the Biq'a with an important function was Mustafa Mahmud Madhi, who is responsible for the arms shipments received from Iran at the Sheikh Abdallah barracks (or Sakaneh Imam Ali base).[24]

Beirut

In Beirut and the surrounding suburbs, the Hizb'allah was headed by Sheikh Muhammad Hussein Fadlallah, the overall spiritual guide of the movement, who mustered a substantial following within exisiting Shi'ite religious institutions and other Shi'ite radical movements. While Sheikh Fadlallah denies any official position within Hizb'allah, the main leaders were seen to be Sheikh al-Amin, the official spokesman, and Sheikh Hassan Nasserallah, who mustered support from the activists and former *al-Da'wa* members within the movement and were operationally responsible for certain aspects involving military and terrorist operations.[25] Both Sheikh al-Amin and Sheikh Nasserallah acted as liaison officers with Iran through its embassy in Beirut, most notably with Mohammad Nourani, the chargé d'affaires between 1981–1985.[26] Another senior Hizb'allah cleric was Sheikh Muhammad Ismail Khaliq, who is the personal representative of Iran's Ayatollah Montazeri in Lebanon.[27]

Southern Lebanon

In southern Lebanon, the Hizb'allah was headed by Sheikh Raghib Harb until his death in 1984.[28] While he was succeeded by Sheikh Abd al-Karim Obeid as Imam of Jibshit and in his position within Hizb'allah's command leadership, the regional leadership of the movement is divided between local commanders and religious clergymen in the Hizb'allah districts of Nabatiya and Sidon-Zahrani in southern Lebanon, most notably under the

direction of Sheikh 'Afif al-Nabulsi and Sheikh Muhammad Fannish.[29]
Hizb'allah's military units in southern Lebanon are headed by local commanders, who recruit young Shi'ites from the villages with in-depth
knowledge of the local terrain.[30] The military units of *Islamic Resistance*
(al-Muqawama al-Islamiyya) are organized by Iranian Pasdaran officers
into the structure of a regular army and are composed of a total of
300–400 core fighters and at least 1,500 armed sympathisers. Their
strength is limited compared to Hizb'allah's military strength of 2,500
fighters in the Biq'a and 1,000 in Beirut but overall the movement can
muster a standing reserve of over 25,000 men. The number of Islamic
Resistance fighters increased drastically in 1991 to a potential of 5,000
men when its Beirut and Biq'a contingents were forced to relocate to the
South in order to comply with the Ta'if accord, though the number of
active fighters is estimated around 600 according to IDF's Northern
Command. While Hizb'allah's military actions against Israel were initiated by the local commanders, all military activity was subject to approval
by Hizb'allah's military command, headed by twelve Hizb'allah clergymen. Until his death in August 1988, assassinated by Amal, Sheikh Ali
Karim was the head of Hizb'allah operations center in south Lebanon.[31]
This decision-making authority is divided between section commanders
and the military forces headquarters in Ba'albek, headed by Abdullah
Kassir,[32] who is in command of a considerable weapons arsenal which
most notably includes M-113 APCs, ex-Soviet "Sagger-3" anti-tank
weapons, LAWs (Light Anti-Tank Weapons) and SAM-7 anti-aircraft
missiles. The main weapon used against Israeli targets by the Hizb'allah is
the Katyusha rocket (or BM-21), a Soviet-designed solid propellant rocket
with a range of approximately 13 miles.

Hizb'allah's Decision-Making: the Majlis al-Shura and the Majlis al-Shura al-Karar

These prominent regional Hizb'allah clergymen and commanders were
represented on the *Majlis al-Shura*, the supreme decision-making authority of the Hizb'allah on the national level, that first adjourned on May 28,
1986, on a regular basis.[33] Within the *Majlis al-Shura*, there are seven specialized committees dealing with ideological, financial, military, political,
judicial, informational and social affairs.[34] In turn, the *Majlis al-Shura* and
these seven committees are replicated in each of Hizb'allah's three main
regional and operational areas. They function as the principal governing
body on local daily activity while advising the main *Majlis al-Shura* on
the result of their efforts.[35] All Hizb'allah activity is regulated by decisions

taken by the main *Majlis al-Shura*, which issued general directives to the regions, which in turn were left to implement the decisions on the operational level. While Sheikh Fadlallah presided over the national *Majlis al-Shura* as its overall leader in his capacity as spiritual leader of Hizb'allah, the main clergymen who excerise control over the movement are the ones responsible for a specific committee or portfolio.[36]

The restructuring of the movement in 1989 with the addition of an new organ, the *Executive Shura (Majlis al-Shura al-Karar)* which ranks after the main *Majlis al-Shura* as the second highest leadership authority, and a *Politbureau (Maktab al-Siyassi)*, a supervisory organ which coordinates the work of the various committees under the *Jihad al-Bina'* (Holy Reconstruction Organ). These changes have meant a "Lebanonization" of the Hizb'allah where the control of the overall organisation has been made more open and expanded. The control of specific portfolios has become more important and increasingly subject to factionalism.[37] Although Hizb'allah's newly established central decision-making body has led to a greater openness within the organisation (as evidenced by the formation of an "information department" which supervises its radio and television broadcasts as well as papers), in conjunction with an effort by Hizb'allah to raise its profile and move into mainstream Lebanese politics, it has continued to maintain strict operational secrecy in the field of military and security affairs.

Special Security Apparatus

Within the military committee on Hizb'allah's main *Majlis al-Shura* and in the three regional areas, there exists a separate body, the so-called Special Security Apparatus (SSA), responsible for intelligence and security matters.[38] In turn, the Hizb'allah's security apparatus is divided into three subgroups: the central security apparatus, the preventative security apparatus and an overseas security apparatus.[39] The central security apparatus is further divided into two groups responsible for either East or West Beirut.[40] While Sheikh al-Musawi was the overall head of Hizb'allah's SSA until late 1985 and thereafter headed by Sheikh Wafic Safa, the central security apparatus is headed by Imad Mughniya and Abd al-Hadi Hamadi and was chiefly responsible for Hizb'allah's hostage-taking activity of foreigners.[41] On the operational level, it was mainly family members from both the Mughniya and Hamadi clans that were involved in the hostage-takings which ensured loyalty to the senior commanders and secrecy surrounding the operations. Apart from Mughniya and Hamadi, other senior members of the national central security apparatus were Sheikh Hussein Ghabris, who acted as Mughniya's deputy, Sheikh Hussein Khalil, who was the main liaison between Hizb'allah's security and intelligence, Nabil Kaouk, head of the SSA in southern Lebanon, Hamze Zakaria, Muhammad Ali Mikdad, and Hassan Izzeldine, who was responsible for Hizb'allah's international relations and was most notably closely involved in the 1985 TWA-847 and 1988 KU422 hijacking as well as the negotiations concerning the Western hostages.[42] This division of Hizb'allah's SSA has also been effective in the infiltration of its own members within rival movements and in the elimination of military and political opponents in Lebanon, most notably revealed by the Amal movement's dismissal of a number of leading members after discovering their dual allegiance to Hizb'allah in 1988.[43] Hizb'allah's national preventative security apparatus was headed by Salah Nun and Muhammad Hammud and was in charge of the personal security of prominent Hizb'allah clergymen.[44] The functions of Hizb'allah's central security apparatus and the overseas security apparatus, in charge of special operations abroad, overlapped as Hussein Khalil, Ibrahim Aqil, Imad Mughniya, Muhammad Haydar, Kharib Nasser and Abd al-Hamadi, were the senior commanders of the Hizb'allah operations in Europe.[45] Waid Ramadan acted as the chief coordinator of Hizb'allah with Iran concerning these European operations.[46] During the frequent absence of Mughniya from Lebanon, the influence of his *de facto* deputy, Ali Karekeh, increased within the SSA.[47]

While Hizb'allah's SSA managed to maintain operational secrecy due to its employment of mainly family and clan members, this can also be attributed to the previous experience by some of its commanders in Fatah Force 17, the PLO's intelligence and security organisation.[48] In particular, Imad Mughniya had been not only the personal bodyguard of Sheikh Fadlallah before he was elevated in position within the Hizb'allah after the successful hijacking of TWA 847, but also served with Force 17 as a lieutenant prior to Israel's invasion in 1982.[49] The decision by Hizb'allah's SSA to abduct foreign citizens is usually initiated at the highest level in the main *Majlis al-Shura* within the Hizb'allah through consultation with its senior clergy and two permanent representatives from Iran.[50] After reaching consensus on the future nationality of the hostage, Hizb'allah's *Majlis al-Shura* delegated either specific details of a certain individual intended for abduction, or broadly issued directives relating to the nationality and profession of the victim, to the commanders of Hizb'allah's national SSA.[51] A similar method was used with regard to military operations by the *Islamic Resistance*, formed in 1983, whereby the attacks were initiated by local commanders with confirmation from the supreme *Majlis al-Shura*, in alignment with general directives connected to the political situation.

In the execution of the abductions authorized by Hizb'allah's national SSA, the operational officers maintained close liaison with official representatives from Iran's embassies in Beirut and Damascus as well as with Pasdaran officials. While Muhammad Haydar was Hizb'allah's main liaison with the Pasdaran, three senior Hizb'allah operatives maintained liaison with Iranian intelligence, VEVAK *(Vezarat-e Ettela'at Va Amniyat-e Keshvar)*, most notably Hussein al-Khalil.[52] Apart from the well-known and close role of Ali Akbar Mohtashemi, the former Iranian Ambassador to Syria and Interior Minister, in both the formation of the Hizb'allah and continued guidance over the movement, Iranian diplomatic staff provided intelligence on targets while the Iranian Pasdaran supplied weaponry and training.[53] In particular, the Lebanese Pasdaran contingent, under the command of Hussein Moslehi, had an early involvement in planning and supervising Hizb'allah attacks in 1983 as evident by the US Marine barracks bombing in Beirut. While Iran's embassy in Beirut was previously active with Hizb'allah under the helm of Muhammad Nourani, the Iranian chargé d'affaires, most of the liaison for security reasons between Hizb'allah and Iran occurred through the Iranian embassy in Syria, headed by ambassador Hasan Akhtari, who issued the main instructions to Hizb'allah's networks in Lebanon. However, Ali Akbar Rahimi and Muhammad Javad of the Iranian embassy in Beirut maintained close liaison with Hizb'allah's national SSA.[54] The role of the Iranian embassy in Beirut assumed increased importance over the mission in Damascus due to the constraints imposed by the Amal-Hizb'allah clashes.[55] While Iran's military attaché in Damascus coordinated activities between Iran's Pasdaran contingent in Ba'albek and its headquarters in the Syrian border village of Zebdani, the Pasdaran contingent and Iran's military attaché in Beirut were involved not only in supplying the cadres of Hizb'allah SSA with training and military equipment but also in its hostage-taking activity, as evident by their role in the intitiation as well as interrogation and housing of some of the foreign hostages.

The role of the Pasdaran with Hizb'allah was formally institutionalized through, and controlled by, the presence of a high-ranking IRGC representative on the *Majlis al-Shura*.[56] Despite attempts by Iran's clerical establishment to impose a degree of clerical control over the Pasdaran, the Lebanese contingent has shown a capacity for institutional autonomy and radicalism by its previous and present commanders, most notably under the command of Hosein Deqan, in terms of conforming to the wishes of the political leadership in Iran, especially *vis-à-vis* the release of Western hostages.[57] In particular, this was evident by the efforts of Iran's Rafsanjani to assign a more loyal and pliable IRGC unit to the Pasdaran contingent in 1989.[58]

The Hizb'allah command leadership and its security and intelligence service were also in close liaison with Syrian military intelligence[59] which actively participated in the planning of Hizb'allah actions until the withdrawal of the Multinational Forces from Beirut in early 1984. Syria pursued a calibrated policy of tacit cooperation with Hizb'allah and support for its abductions of foreigners, as long as they were in accordance with Syrian strategic interest in Lebanon. Simultaneously it was forced to clamp down on Hizb'allah in order to reassert Syrian hegemony and to limit Iran's influence and avoid a military confrontation with Israel.[60] For example, Syria warned Hizb'allah in 1985 about its overt activity, urging the establishment of an Islamic Republic, by threatening to kill Sheikh Fadlallah unless this activity was ceased.[61] While Syria has pursued a public policy of disassociation from Hizb'allah's hostage-taking activity, its relationship with the movement's SSA was pursued by Syrian military intelligence, under the command of Brigadier Ghazi Kan'an.[62] As Syria has been in firm control over the Biq'a area from which Pasdaran and Hizb'allah operate, Syrian military intelligence not only facilitated the transfer of hostages to Ba'albek from Beirut, but also acted as a conduit for the release of the foreign hostages through the hands of Syrian military intelligence officers. A main liaison between Hizb'allah and Syrian military intelligence was Mustafa al-Dirani, the former head of Amal's security service who defected from Amal in late-1988 and joined the Hizb'allah in 1989.[63] Al-Dirani served also as the main coordinator of Hizb'allah's security moves against Syria.

The relationship between Hizb'allah's SSA and Syrian military intelligence has been characterized by periods of conflict and cooperation, largely dictated by the shifting internal situation in Lebanon. Syrian sanction for the presence of Pasdaran and tolerance towards Hizb'allah activity had often been dependent on its relationship with Iran as well as coupled with Syrian complicity in drug-trafficking in Lebanon.[64] In terms of the latter, Hizb'allah clergymen encourage the drug trade as it serves to weaken the three great enemies of Islam and openly cultivate hashish and opium in the Syrian-controlled Biq'a valley.[65] Despite cooperation in certain areas, friction between Syria and Hizb'allah has been manifest by retaliatory abductions and the threat, or actual use, of military force. A prominent example is the 1988 Syrian arrest warrant against Imad Mughniya. Apart from direct Syrian military intervention or through the use of its proxy, Amal, in the search for foreign hostages, Syria increased the pressure on both the Hizb'allah and the Pasdaran by confining them to the Biq'a area or searching for the hostages in Hizb'allah safe-houses in Beirut and its southern suburbs. However, frictions between Syria and Hizb'allah over the hostage-taking of foreigners were the exception rather than norm, as displayed by their increased coordination of military operations against Israel, closely supervised and controlled by Syria's deputy chief of the general staff, Ali Aslane, and cooperation in the release of hostages. For example, Sheikh Subhi al-Tufayli meet the Syrian leader Hafez al-Assad in 1987, who promised support and supply of weapons for the organisation, and they also agreed that all Hizb'allah military operations would be coordinated with the Syrian headquarters in Lebanon.[66] At any rate, Syria controlled the surrounding territory of the Biq'a and authorized not only the presence of the Pasdaran and the Hizb'allah, but also their movement beyond this area. Despite Syrian rhetoric to contain Hizb'allah activity, the first real intervention against the movement occurred in March 1994 with the arrest of eleven Hizb'allah fighters during the course of a violent demonstration to mark Jerusalem Day held in Ba'albek, who were handed over to the Lebanese Army. Yet, the significance of this event should be viewed in the larger context of Syrian tacit approval of most Hizb'allah activity. In particular, Syria continues to supply weapon consignments to Hizb'allah for its anti-Israeli operations through a fixed route: from Teheran to Damascus and onwards under Syrian protection to Beirut's southern suburbs and then to Hizb'allah strongholds near the security zone.

The Nature of Clerical Factionalism Within Hizb'allah

Apart from the Hizb'allah decision-making apparatus and the institutionalized relationship with Iran and Syria through military and civilian channels at work in Lebanon, Hizb'allah's mechanism for hostage-taking of foreigners was also subject to influence from clerical factionalism within the organisation itself and to a web of clerical relationships extending from members of the national *Majlis al-Shura* to various clergy within Iran's civilian and military establishment. While the clerical factionalism within Hizb'allah can be monitored by the ascendancy or demotion of clergyman over the leadership of the movement, as shown by the election of a new Hizb'allah Secretary-General every two years, it is also a guide to not only the direction of the movement in Lebanon but also to the affiliation and loyalty of Hizb'allah's leadership with clerical factions and institutions in Iran. Although the Hizb'allah command leadership is a cohesive organisation, the main differences between leading Hizb'allah clergymen are over methods rather than aims, as evidently displayed by the 1988 dispute between Sheikh al-Tufayli and Sheikh Fadlallah over the question of the feasibility of the establishment of an Islamic republic in Lebanon.[67] While Sheikh Subhi al-Tufayli, supported by Sheikh Ibrahim al-Amin, argued that an Islamic Republic should be established as soon as possible and all means should be pursued for this purpose, Sheikh Fadlallah disagreed. Similarly, Sheikh al-Tufayli has been at the heart of a dissident faction within the command leadership over the issue of a new leader of the movement, in the wake of the February 1992 assassination of Sheikh al-Musawi. This faction vehemently objected to Hizb'allah member's participation in the Lebanese parliamentary elections held between 23 August and 6 Septemeber 1992, in which the movement won 12 out of a total of 128 seats.[68] However, the position of the Secretary-General and his deputy are fundamental to monitor for an understanding of Hizb'allah as they directly control all the affairs of the movement and are *ex-officio* in charge, and have direct access to, clerical commanders of the regional *Majlis al-Shuras*.[69] For example, the Deputy Secretary-General is in charge of the financal and military affairs of the movement.[70]

While Hizb'allah's national *Majlis al-Shura* was established in 1986, no particular leading cleric emerged as undisputed leader until the ascendancy of Sheikh al-Tufayli in late 1987, a noted radical with particularly close personal ties with Ali Akbar-Mohtashemi in Iran. Sheikh al-Tufayli's position as leader of the Hizb'allah remained uncontested until the death of Ayatollah Khomeini in 1989, when the organisation faced unprecedented challenges within Lebanon and, consequently, displayed intensified rivalry between Hizb'allah clergymen over the position and direction of the movement. As a result of meetings held in Teheran in Octobèr and December 1989, Hizb'allah submitted to major structural changes, as evident by the establishment of an *Executive Shura*, also known as the Supreme Shura (consisting of nine leading Hizb'allah clergy).[71] While the composition of the new *Executive Shura* corresponds with the the so-called *Consultative Shura*, or the *Majlis al-Shura*, the former decision-making body assumed the second highest authority of the Hizb'allah and set mainly strategic matters in the overall administration of the movement.[72] It also led to the establishment of a *"Politbureau"*, a supervisory committee composed of fifteen clergy in charge of Hizb'allah's co-ordination of recruitment, propaganda and support services on the regional and local level.[73]

Although Sheikh al-Tufayli retained his position as Secretary-General of the Hizb'allah in December 1989, the meetings underlined strong clerical factionalism within the Hizb'allah's hierarchy.[74] In particular, the

meetings revealed intense rivalry between the nominated leadership and
elements from *Lebanese al-Da'wa*, the *Islamic Resistance*, and members
of the Special Security Apparatus, as evident by their rejection of the main
Hizb'allah decisions at the meeting and the delay in the reappointment for
another two months of Sheikh al-Tufayli until the December 1989
meeting.[75] The militant position of Sheikh Hassan Nasserallah was also
revealed by his vocal opposition to compromises made to Amal in 1989 by
his clerical colleagues. The structural changes within Hizb'allah's leadership also led to the dismissal of four leading Hizb'allah officials while it
bolstered the positions of Sheikh al-Tufayli, Sheikh Naim Qassem, and
Sheikh Nasserallah within the leadership of Hizb'allah's national *Majlis
al-Shura*. Under the renewed command of Sheikh al-Tufayli, the
Hizb'allah leadership was considered closer to Iran's radical faction, led
by Ali Akbar-Mohtashemi, than to Hashemi Rafsanjani.

   While the tenure of Sheikh al-Tufayli as leader of Hizb'allah was
marked by friction with Iran's newly-elected president, the election of
Sheikh al-Musawi as the Secretary-General of Hizb'allah, and Sheikh al-
Amin as his deputy, in May 1991[76] came after settlement of uncertainty
within Hizb'allah ranks concerning disarmament of all militias in accordance with implementation of the Ta'if agreement.[77] The appointment of
Sheikh al-Musawi, the former head of the *Islamic Resistance*, came as a
response to a *quid pro quo* arrangement between the organisation and Iran
and Syria which permitted the movement to maintain their armed presence in the South and in the eastern Biq'a, as it claimed to be a resistance
movement rather than a militia.[78] Unlike his predecessor, Sheikh al-
Musawi appeared to be more pragmatic as evident by the fact that he
presided over Hizb'allah through the denouement of the Western hostage
crisis while he readjusted the organisation's grand strategy from creating
an Islamic Republic of Lebanon through armed struggle to a willingness to
participate in mainstream Lebanese politics. In order to engineer this readjustment through increased control of the movement's cadres, Sheikh al-
Musawi reduced the number of members on the *Majlis al-Shura* to eight
clergy, compared to over twenty members under al-Tufayli's reign.
Although his pragmatism was a reflection of Hizb'allah's effort to confront the challenges posed by a post-militia phase of Lebanese politics and
that the position of Sheikh al-Musawi was closer to the line of Iran's
Hashemi Rafsanjani than that of his clerical colleagues within the
Hizb'allah, it was also the result of increased Iranian influence and pressure.[79] Unlike his predecessor, Sheikh al-Musawi had previously voiced
his explicit opposition against Ayatollah Montazeri while pledging close
allegiance to Ayatollah Khameini and Rafsanjani.

The assassination of Sheikh al-Musawi by Israeli missile-firing heli-copters on February 16, 1992, after he and a number of other high-ranking Hizb'allah officials attended an annual memorial service in the village of Jihshit in order to mark the eight anniversary of the death of Sheikh Harb, strengthened Hizb'allah's militancy and allegiance to Iran's more radical clergy.[80] In an attempt to assure its own cadres that al-Musawi's death had not seriously affected the organisation, Hizb'allah immediately announced the election of Sheikh Nasserallah as its new leader. However, internal rivalry within Hizb'allah between Nasserallah factions and those support-ing al-Tufayli became apparent by the influence and intervention of Iran into the appointment of the new Hizb'allah leader.[81] Despite the fact that Nasserallah received a majority vote in *Majlis al-Shura* elections in May 1991 to the post of Secretary-General of the movement, which he yielded to Sheikh al-Musawi out of "humility", Sheikh Nasserallah bolstered his own position within the *Majlis al-Shura* under Sheikh al-Musawi's leader-ship[82] as he held control over finances and military matters, thereby restricting the maneuverability of Sheikh al-Musawi and turning himself into the real *de facto* leader. This was initially troublesome for the less radical wing within the Hizb'allah as Sheikh Nasserallah also maintained a far more closer relationship with Iran's revolutionist faction, most notably with Ali-Akbar Mohtashemi, than his predecessor.[83] His more radical stance had been evidently displayed during Hizb'allah's warfare with Amal, which he initiated and spearheaded over the control of the Iqlim al-Tuffah area. After the Amal-Hizb'allah cease-fire, Sheikh Nasserallah had begun a carefully calibrated policy of tempering his uncompromising mili-tancy as a move to project a more "obedient" image in his dealings with Iran both in alignment with the political realities confronting the organisa-tion within Lebanon and, perhaps more importantly, to bolster his own political standing within the party and with official Iran. However, Iranian pressure to appoint Sheikh Nasserallah to the post of the incumbent Secretary-General of Hizb'allah over the hardline contender and previous leader, Sheikh al-Tufayli, led to an intense dispute by dissident factions loyal to al-Tufayli.[84] In particular, the internal rivalry within the Hizb'allah leadership came over the decision by certain leaders to partici-pate in Lebanon's parliamentary elections, held between 23 August and 6 September 1992, which the followers of the al-Tufayli faction vehe-mently objected to as solid evidence of abandonment of the movement's pan-Islamic goal of resistance against Israel by redirecting the move-ment's focus towards Lebanese internal politics.[85] While threats of sabo-tage by Sheikh al-Tufayli to Hizb'allah's participation in the parliamentary elections (most notably the burning of the voting-centres in

his home village of Brital) failed to matcrialize,[86] challenges to the leadership of Sheikh Nasserallah by al-Tufayli supporters in the Biq'a area
assumed the form of independent resistance attacks against Israel immediately following the procurement by the Hizb'allah of 12 electoral seats out
of 128 in the Lebanese parliamentary elections.[87] As a consequence, the
divisions within the Hizb'allah, in the wake of the death of Sheikh al-
Musawi, have been between Nasserallah's efforts to reorientate Hizb'allah
more towards political rather than military activity through acceptance of
the realities of Lebanon's systems and the dissident faction led by Sheikh
al-Tufayli, supported by the Iranian revolutionist faction, towards undermining the more moderate position of the new Secretary-General and to
press on with a perpetual *jihad* against Israel at all costs.[88] Nasserallah has
increasingly stressed his commitment to the armed strategy of the Islamic
Resistance against Israel, most notably through the creation of a new
organ, the *al-Jihad Council,* bringing in all various factions under a central
umbrella to coordinate all anti-Israeli activity (headed by Sheikh Hachem
Safieddine). This meant that he could skilfully control the dissident Biq'a
valley wing led by Sheikh al-Tufayli, both as a means to prevent any
attempts of independent action against Israel through bringing this hardline faction's fighters and commanders strictly into the fold and, at the
same time, demonstrate resolve to the organisation's cadres of a renewed
resolve in combating Israel in southern Lebanon.

   Sheikh Nasserallah also underlined that Hizb'allah's parliamentary participation was a calibrated move as well as an incremental strategy to challenge and overthrow the Lebanese government from within. Hizb'allah's
participation as a party represented in the Lebanese parliament was also a
joint Hizb'allah-Iranian strategy, as outlined by Rafsanjani in several
meetings with the movement and blessed by Ayatollah Khameini, to legit-
imize the movement in order to guarantee its survival and insulate itself
from internal/external persecution in post-civil war Lebanon. As admitted
by Sheikh Nasserallah: "[o]ur entry to the ranks of parliamentary
representatives gives us the opportunity to defend our resistance on the
political plane."

   The internal rivalry between Nasserallah and al-Tufayli clearly demonstrated the existence of clerical factionalism within the hierarchy of the
movement. It also underlined the importance of understanding divisions
among its leaders and their ability to muster a substantial number of followers as a guide to the activity of the movement as well as allegiances of
dissident factions. In this particular rivalry, the fact that Sheikh
Nasserallah comes from southern Lebanon (from the village of
Bazuriyah), rather than as his predecessors from the Biq'a area, meant that

he was more susceptible to losing control over the loyalty of commanders and fighters of the *Islamic Resistance*. In fact most of these senior fighters traditionally come from the Biq'a and pledge closer allegiance to Sheikh al-Tufayli.[89] This became apparent by Sheikh Nasserallah's replacement of military commanders in southern Lebanon and to the separation of the *Islamic Resistance* from the political framework of the Hizb'allah for operational expediency and security after the assassination of Sheikh al-Musawi.[90] An example of the Secretary-General's effort to achieve firm control over the movement's military activity was the appointment of Nabil Kaouk as the general coordinator of military operations in southern Lebanon as well as his moves to disband and bring groups close to the movement within the organisational fold, most notably the *Believers Resistance* Movement *(al-Mukawama al-Moumna)*. However, the failure of Sheikh al-Tufayli to regain the leadership post of the Hizb'allah in its leadership elections in May 1991, February 1992, April/May 1993, and July 1995 have led to an erosion in the influence of the extremist and radical camp of the movement which is parallel to the decline of its closest allies in Iran, the revolutionist faction under the leadership of Hojjatolislam Mohtashemi. This has been most apparent by the relegation of Sheikh al-Tufayli to a position as a mère member of the main *Majlis al-Shura* without any specific portfolio. As admitted by Sheikh al-Tufayli in a July 1994 interview with *L'Orient-Le Jour:* "I am an ordinary militant, and I do not participate in decision-making. This has been true since the time of the legislative elections."[91] As such, the control over the Hizb'allah depends on the ability of individual clergy in ousting political opponents from key positions as well as on their navigation skill in steering a balanced and unprovocative political course between Iranian and Syrian influence as well as requirements while ensuring and maximising the movement's own position. To this end, Sheikh Nasserallah has been very successful in increasing the powers of those who pledge loyalty to the Secretary-General and to appoint these to head the most crucial positions within the movement while reducing these institutional positions in number. This success has stemmed from the fact that Sheikh Nasserallah was able to muster a substantial number of followers, given his previous position as Hizb'allah mobilisation officer in the Biq'a area and his current prominent role within the so-called *al-Da'wa* trend within the movement. The latter was displayed by his appointment of other notable *al-Da'wa* activists to key decision-making posts in the *Majlis al-Shur*a in the July 1995 Hizb'allah elections, most notably Sheikh Naim Qassem (deputy Secretary-General), Sheikh Hussein al-Khalil (special counsel to Nasserallah) and Sheikh Muhammad Raad, at the expense of the more radical Biq'a wing with the exception of Sheikh Muhammad Yazbek, retained for his role as Ayatollah Khameini's representative in Lebanon. In many ways Sheikh Nasserallah's reign also represents a gradual generational shift within the Hizb'allah leadership away from the radical 'old guard', who founded the movement, to a younger circle of cadres, who are more adept and tuned into the changes necessary for the movement in order for it to successfully survive the challenges imposed by Lebanon's post-civil war environment. As a result, Hizb'allah appointments of a new Secretary-General demonstrated that the election of a particular senior Hizb'allah cleric was not only dependent on the applicability of his previous experience to a current situation confronting the movement within Lebanon and on the level of support and followers the candidate manage to muster within the movement but also to his links with factions and institutions within Iran's clerical establishments.

HIZB'ALLAH'S RELATIONSHIP WITH IRANIAN CLERGY AND INSTITUTIONS

Apart from the influence of close personal relationships, the conduct of both formal and informal consultations between Hizb'allah clergymen and Iranian officials occurs through a variety of channels and institutions. While official Iran has attempted to exert influence over Hizb'allah activity through various Iranian agencies at work in Hizb'allah, ranging from the Pasdaran contingent and Iran's personal representatives in Damascus and Beirut to Iran's Foreign Ministry and the *Martyrs' Foundation*, Hizb'allah clergymen are also influenced by individual Iranian clergy with personal and political aspirations, at times, contrary to the official position and policy of Iran's ruling clerical élite.[92] The degree of divergence between Hizb'allah's subordination, in principle, to the supreme religious and political authority of Ayatollah Khomeini, and the disobedience and disagreements displayed within Hizb'allah ranks towards Iran's official leadership and its willingness to sacrifice ideology to achieve pragmatic foreign and domestic policy objectives, depends on Hizb'allah's and individual clergymen's interaction with official Iranian institutions as well as on clerical factionalism in Iran. In turn, any discord or harmony in Hizb'allah's relationship with Iran is influenced by the impact of Iranian clerical factionalism on the institutions at work in Hizb'allah.

As a revolutionary movement, the pan-Islamic ideological position of the Hizb'allah and its command leadership is naturally attuned to the revolutionist faction within Iran's clerical establishment. The more doctrinnaire and radical faction within Iran's clerical establishment is led by: Hojjat al-Islam Muhammad Musavi Kho'iniha; Ayatollah Ali Meshkini; Ayatollah Montazeri; Mir Hussein Musavi; Hojjat al-Islam Ali-Akbar Mohtashemi; Musavi Khoeiniha; and Mehdi Hashemi.[93] This closeness in radical ideology stemmed from the position of Ayatollah Khomeini. It also mirrors the involvement by several Iranian members of the revolutionist factions with prominent Lebanese Shi'ite clerics both prior to and, more importantly, in the formation and development of Hizb'allah in Lebanon. The personal relationships between some Iranian clergymen and Hizb'allah's command leadership, forged at the religious centers in Najaf (and some in Qum) as well as in Lebanon during the early 1970s, translated not only in their close involvement in the actual formation of Hizb'allah in 1982, but also in the appointments of these Iranian clergy to the official Iranian institutions at work in Hizb'allah.[94] This facilitated the rapid growth and expansion of Hizb'allah as well as forged ties to the inner sanctum of Iran's clerical establishment. The movement also became gradually susceptible to clerical factionalism in Iran, as evident by the dismissal and appointment of Iran's radical clergy within these Iranian institutions.[95]

The Role of Ali-Akbar Mohtashemi

Among the most influential and strongest relationships between an individual Iranian clergyman and the Hizb'allah command leadership was the role of Ali-Akbar Mohtashemi, the former Iranian ambassador to Syria and former Interior Minister. Arriving in Damascus in 1982 as newly-appointed Iranian ambassador, Mohtashemi had forged close relationships with many future Hizb'allah leaders during his stay and studies under Ayatollah Khomeini. This personal network proved vital to Hizb'allah's growth and access to Iranian clerics and institutions, especially given that Mohtashemi had been Ayatollah Khomeini's personal secretary during the latter's exile in Paris. Apart from his pivotal role in the creation of the Hizb'allah in 1982 and his role as liaison between Iran and the movement in Lebanon during his tenure in Syria until 1986, Mohtashemi's radical position in ideological terms has resonated within the movement in Lebanon, especially when Hizb'allah has been at odds with the official Iranian leadership.[96] While Mohtashemi has cultivated a broad base of support within the movement, his closest relationship within Hizb'allah's command leadership has been with the radical activists, most notably Sheikh al-Tufayli and Sheikh Nasserallah.[97] Hizb'allah's spiritual leader, Sheikh Fadlallah, reportedly was not a supporter of Mohtashemi.[98]

Although the promotion of Mohtashemi as Interior Minister within Iran's clerical establishment in 1986 meant the loss of his position as Iranian representative within Hizb'allah's national *Majlis al-Shura*, he maintained an independent relationship with the movement's leadership, as evident from his frequent visits to Lebanon and Syria as well as his outspoken views on Hizb'allah's position with particular reference to the abduction and release of foreign hostages.[99] Although the dismissal of Mohtashemi in the post-Khomeini cabinet, under the leadership of Hashemi-Rafsanjani, in 1989 weakened his influence within Iran's clerical establishment, it also translated into an attempt by Mohtashemi to upstage Rafsanjani's pragmatic foreign policy, through Hizb'allah, by blocking the release of Western hostages. Notwithstanding the prominent role of Mohtashemi in the initiation of abductions of foreigners, his influence over radical clergy within Hizb'allah provided him with an instrument to both sabotage moderate and pragmatic overtures by the Iranian leadership in the foreign policy arena as well as to bolster his position within the clerical factionalism in Iran. However, Mohtashemi's ability to manipulate Hizb'allah activity was limited by changes in the movement's position within the Lebanese environment, as evident by the denouement of the hostage crisis in 1991 despite strong opposition from Mohtashemi, and by the presence of a more pragmatic Hizb'allah leader, Sheikh al-Musawi, in charge of the organisation. These limitations have been reinforced by the fact that Sheikh Nasserallah removed himself from Mohtashemi's inner circle of loyal followers after his ascendancy to the post of Secretary-General in 1992 and continues to skilfully steer himself between the official leaderships in Teheran and Damascus and their respective attempts to impose their influences on the organisation's position and direction in Lebanon.

Ayatollah Montazeri and the Office of Islamic Liberation Movements

Another prominent Iranian cleric for the Hizb'allah is Khomeini's designated heir, Ayatollah Husayn Ali Montazeri.[100] Apart from his early active role in the promotion of Iranian involvement in Lebanon through Hizb'allah, Montazeri's position as supervisor of the *Office of Islamic Liberation Movements*, operated by his relative Mehdi Hashemi and in charge of coordination of Iran's revolutionary support and activity abroad, provided him with an official channel to Hizb'allah's command leadership. This was also reinforced by the fact that both Mohammad Montazeri and Mehdi Hashemi had obtained guerrilla training in Lebanon before 1979 and were deeply involved in promoting the Iranian Pasdaran's presence.[101] As the *Office of Islamic Liberation Movements* had been originally a formal arm of the Revolutionary Guard until 1983, it transformed into a semi-independent institution of the IRGC headed by Montazeri's protege, Medhi Hashemi, which coordinated the operational cooperation between Iran and the Hizb'allah.[102] Hashemi's efforts to foment revolutionary activity and terrorism abroad damaged Iran's war effort with Iraq and led to his arrest in 1986. The retaliatory abductions of American hostages and revelation of the U.S.-Iranian arms-for-hostages deal by Ayatollah Montazeri's personal representative in Lebanon, Sheikh Ismail al-Khaliq, coupled with the kidnapping of Iyad Mahmoud, the Syrian chargé d'affaires to Iran, was a clear manifestation of the connection between Iranian clerical factionalism and Hizb'allah activity.[103] It also led to the final separation of the *Office of Islamic Liberation Movements* from the IRGC and its transfer to the Ministry of Foreign Affairs in late 1986, in an effort by Rafsanjani to achieve a greater degree of Iranian control over Hizb'allah activity.[104] This was also evident by Rafsanjani's appointment of a noted protégé, Hojjat al-Islam Hadi Khosrowshahi, in 1987 to head the *Office of Islamic Liberation Movements*, and the nomination of Rafsanjani's brother, Mahmud Hashemi, to head the Lebanon desk within Iran's Ministry of Foreign Affairs.[105] Mohtashemi established his own parallel institution with its own budget to aid the movement, thus making Hizb'allah's official links to the revolutionary Iranian clergy more difficult. Yet Mohtashemi had difficulty in competing with the financial resources of the Office of Islamic Liberation Movements, who had an operational budget of $150 million after 1986.[106] Even worse, the dismissal of Khomeini's designated heir Montazeri in March 1989 and the death of Ayatollah Khomeini three months later left the movement in disarray over its future position in Lebanon.

In the post-Khomeini period, Ahmad Salek has headed the Office of Islamic Liberation Movements which is significant in that he is closely associated with Ayatollah Khameini and serves as his representative to the Pasdaran. This has meant that Hizb'allah has enjoyed a closer relationship with this institution under Sheikh Nasserallah's reign as Secretary-General, given his closer relationship to Ayatollah Khameini than his more radical opponent within the movement Sheikh al-Tufayli, especially at a time when the movement has been dependent on large Iranian financial contributions for its expansion.

Iranian Ministry of Foreign Affairs

While Montazeri maintained relations with Hizb'allah through another Iranian institution, the Ministry of Islamic Guidance,[107] several radical

Iranian clergy held senior positions within Iran's Ministry of Foreign
Affairs and strongly supported the movement in Lebanon. Among the
most helpful foreign ministry officials has been Director for Arab Affairs,
Hosein Sheikh-ol-Islam, who coordinated with the Pasdaran to position its
members in Iranian embassies abroad and participate in Hizb'allah operations.[108] Another radical Iranian ally of Hizb'allah was Javad Mansuri,
Undersecretary for Cultural and Consular Affairs in the Ministry of
Foreign Affairs, who controlled the Iranian embassies abroad. After the
appointment of Rafoanjani in 1989, both Sheikh-ol-Islam's and Mansuri's
positions were formally demoted in the Ministry of Foreign Affairs.[109] As
a consequence, Hizb'allah downgraded the role and influence of the
Iranian Ambassadors to Syria and Lebanon on both its *Executive* and
Consultative Shuras.[110] However, Hizb'allah maintain a non-adversarial
relationship with Muhammad Kazem Khansari, the head of the Africa and
Middle East department at the Iranian Ministry of Foreign Affairs.

Martyrs' Foundation and Foundation of the Oppressed

Other influential Iranian institutions at work within the Hizb'allah are the
Martyrs' Foundation, under the command of Ayatollah Mehdi Karrubi,
and the *Foundation of the Oppressed*, headed by Hojjat al-Islam
Mohammad Ali-Rahmani.[111] These two Iranian institutions have been
responsible for helping the families of those killed in the revolution and the
redistribution of material and financial assistance to lower class families in
need. They are funded by the government, religious trusts and by income
from confiscation of exiled Iranians' properties. They also serve as a
channel for Iran's substantial injection of resources to the Hizb'allah in
Lebanon. Iran's financial contributions, which averaged $60 million a year,
were vital for the Hizb'allah in running an array of social and financial services for the Shi'a community, including religious schools, hospital clinics,
agricultural co-operatives and building projects.[112] The Hizb'allah religious
hawzats and mosques have served a vital role in the indoctrination process
of countless young Shi'ites, reinforced by Iranian support for Hizb'allah's
three radio stations, one television station and two publications.[113]

   The Hizb'allah organ *Jihad al-Bina'* (Holy Reconstruction Organ)
serves as the main coordinating body, divided into eight committees, for
the social and financial needs of the movement's members.[114] Through
Iran's generous financial support, the *Islamic Health Committee* established two major hospitals in Ba'albek and in the southern suburbs of
Beirut in 1986 and an array of medical centres and pharmacies throughout
the various regions in Lebanon.[115] *The Financial Aid Committee*, in close

cooperation with the *Martyrs' Foundation*, distributed over $90 million between 1982–86 to families whose dependants had died or were wounded, and the *Martyrs' Foundation* provides approximately $225,000 monthly to martyrs' families.[116] Apart from aid to those who had fallen or were wounded in the fight against the enemies of Islam, the *Financial Aid Committee* has extended generous loans intended for marriages, school expenses, and small business ventures.[117] The importance of the *Reconstruction Committees* has been made obvious by the repair during 1988–91 of over 1,000 homes in southern Lebanon damaged by Israeli attacks.[118] Apart from Hizb'allah's dependence on Iranian financial support to sustain these services and projects, Hizb'allah's ability to capture the hearts and minds of the Shi'a community, through a skillful combination of financial inducements and ideological indoctrination, partially depended on Iran's willingness to extend available resources. Likewise, in the armed struggle the Pasdaran provided the Hizb'allah with other military-related equipment and sources. According to *al-Dustur,* approximately one-third of Iran's financial support for "liberation movements" is allocated to the Hizb'allah in Lebanon.[119] Iranian aid to Hizb'allah steadily increased from $30 million in 1985 to over $64 million in 1988,[120] most of which were channelled to the movement through the Iranian embassies in Damascus and Beirut.

However, these aid institutions were subject to Iranian clerical factionalism.[121] In particular, the involvement of Ayatollah Mehdi Karrubi in the 5 April 1988 hijacking of KU422 by Hizb'allah pointed to an effort by the Iranian cleric to influence the forthcoming Iranian *Majlis* elections.[122] Control over Iranian funds to Hizb'allah, through the leader of the *Martyrs' Foundation*, was also used by Hashemi-Rafsanjani in 1989 in an effort to control Hizb'allah. This was evident by his move to downgrade support for the movement in Lebanon and by the dismissal of Ayatollah Karrubi, who was replaced by the only non-radical former IRGC Minister and Rafsanjani's nephew, Mohsen Rafiqdust.[123] In the wake of the release of the remaining Western hostages in 1991, reports spoke of much reduced Iranian aid to the Hizb'allah, in some cases as high a reduction as 90 percent.[124] Although Iran has faced financial constraints after the 1988 end of the First Gulf war, Hizb'allah's expansion of its social services and financial assistance to the Lebanese Shi'ites would indicate otherwise. For example, the delay in Iranian financial assistance to Hizb'allah in October 1993 was caused by a financial crisis in the Bank of Iran rather than any Iranian attempts to reduce aid to the movement.[125] Infact, evidence would suggest that Iran's current annual financial contribution to the Hizb'allah amounts to over $100 million in order to sustain its vast non-military activities and to renew as well as expand its weapons arsenal.

The Iranian Revolutionary Guards Corps (Pasdaran)

Although Hizb'allah's command leadership has been affected by the availability of Iranian financial and material resources, the military institution of the *Revolutionary Guards,* especially the *al-Qods* (Jerusalem) forces under the command of Ahmad Valildi, was least affected by Iranian clerical factionalism and remained the most reliable and loyal ally of the Hizb'allah.[126] As demonstrated by the Pasdaran contingent in Lebanon, it has remained the most radical and least pliable Iranian institution with close ties to Iran's clerical revolutionist faction. The Pasdaran's semi-institutional autonomy from the civilian leadership in Iran, coupled with its own financial infrastructure, has meant that Hizb'allah has been able to resist attempts of co-option by Iran through support from the IRGC. Attempts by Iranian political leaders to exert pressure on the IRGC contingent in Lebanon, as evident by proposals for its withdrawal and the release of the remaining hostages in Lebanon in 1991, were unsuccessful. Rafsanjani offered more weaponry and authority to the Pasdaran, which would enable it to pursue more hardline political and military objectives in the strengthening of the Islamic revolution and its spread to other countries.[127] This became apparent through the assurance of Hadi Reza Askari, commander of the Iranian Pasdaran contingent, that it would remain in Lebanon until Israel withdrew its troops from southern Lebanon. The lack of control by Iran's political leadership over IRGC support for Hizb'allah was clearly revealed by the Pasdaran's close training and military support of the Hizb'allah in its repeated armed clashes during 1987–1990 with Amal, despite official efforts by Iran to broker an end to the conflict in order to preserve its relationship with Syria. As the IRGC's Lebanon contingent was led and manned by the most ideologically radical military-officials and demonstrated a degree of institutional autonomy from civilian political control, it enabled Hizb'allah to exercise a certain amount of independence, at times in violation of specific orders, in terms of its activity in Lebanon, especially in the abduction and release of foreign hostages.[128] However, the political necessity of close affiliation with Iran's official leadership for its continued survival in Lebanon under the Ta'if agreement contributed to Hizb'allah's decision, under the helm of Sheikh Nasserallah, to hand over the Sheikh Abdallah barracks in Baalbek to the Lebanese Army in the summer of 1992. Meanwhile the organisation retained a base for training and weaponry storage in the eastern Biq'a in close cooperation with Pasdaran officials.

Iran and the Hostage-Taking

Notwithstanding the various influences of factionalism within Hizb'allah and the Iranian clerical establishment, coupled with the movement's relationship with Iranian and Syrian military institutions, Hizb'allah and offical Iran coordinated some of the movement's abductions of foreigners, from a basis of convergence of mutual interest, through a formally defined chain of command from Iran to Hizb'allah. At the highest level in Iran, the Islamic Republic's *Supreme National Security Council*, which is the central decision-making body of the military-security establishment (instituted by the 1989 Iranian constitutional reform to ensure coordination between national security and foreign policy matters),[129] is the main vehicle for policy formulation, decisions and guidance to Hizb'allah relating to hostage-taking in Lebanon and operations abroad. While this Council, composed of the Iranian President, the intelligence minister, Ali Fallahian, and the IRGC commander of the *al-Qods* force, Ahmad Vahidi, is formally in charge of the policy formulation *vis-á-vis* Hizb'allah, the implementation of specific operational directives was delegated to the *Office of Islamic Liberation Movements*. In turn, this body delegated the specific tasks through Iran's diplomatic representatives in Damascus and, to a lesser extent, Beirut as well as to the Pasdaran contingent in Lebanon.[130] Although Iran's operational policy with Hizb'allah remained particularly close until the removal of Mehdi Hashemi in the autumn of 1986 and the reassignment of Mohtashemi from his post as Ambassador to Syria to Minister of Interior, it became increasingly subject to clerical factionalism in Iran. The reassignment of the *Office for Islamic Liberation Movements* to Iran's Ministry of Foreign Affairs, and the appointment of Hojjat al-Islam Khosrowshahi to head the control-mechanism of Iran's official contacts with Hizb'allah,[131] underlined not only the clerical factionalism in Iran but also that control over Hizb'allah activity was excerised both through official Iranian institutions and independent channels loyal to the revolutionist faction within Iran's clerical establishment.

In particular, it has been suggested that Iran, in an attempt to control Hizb'allah abductions, recalled senior Hizb'allah SSA commanders to Iran in April 1987 either because of increased disagreements between Hizb'allah and Iran over the movement's claims for independence or as an internal safety precaution to prevent their capture by Syrian intelligence in Lebanon due to their involvement in attacks against Syrian armed forces in West Beirut.[132] It would seem likely that Imad Mughniya and Abd al-Hadi Hamadi remained in Iran for training and security reasons rather than for detention, as both were subsequently elevated within Hizb'allah's operational command leadership.[133] This hypothesis can be further supported by the parallel Iranian efforts to upgrade the Hizb'allah's military capability through increased funding and sophisticated weaponry.[134] While Mughniya has periodically been absent from Lebanon (October-Dececember 1987 in northern Iran; in January 1988 at Qum; and his return to Lebanon in July 1990), both Hamadi and Mughniya took refuge in Iran for security reasons following the Israeli kidnapping of Mustafa al-Dirani in May 1994 as well as the assassination of Imad's brother Fuad Mughniya in Beirut in December 1994, possibly carried out by the Lebanese army's *Deuxieme Bureau*.[135]

THE ABDUCTION OF FOREIGNERS BY THE HIZB'ALLAH

As previously demonstrated, the nature of understanding Hizb'allah activity, such as its abductions of foreigners, involves analysis of a complex network of interactions both within and external to the movement in Lebanon. Apart from the Hizb'allah's centralized decision-making apparatus, clerical factionalism within the command leadership of the organisation was compounded by the influence of an array of Iranian and Syrian individuals and institutions at work within the movement. Aside from individual Iranian clergy, these include: Iranian Pasdaran; Iran's Ministry of Foreign Affairs; Iran's *Office of Islamic Liberations Movements*; the *Supreme National Security Council*; Iran's Ministry of Guidance; Iran's Martyr Foundation; Iran's diplomatic representatives in Beirut and Damascus; and Syrian military and civilian *Mukhabarat*. In turn, these external influences on the movement affected its activity to varying degrees, as Hizb'allah showed disobedience and disagreement towards both Iran and Syria at different times. Although Hizb'allah activity often converged with the interests of Iranian and Syrian official policy, it is necessary to examine the movement's hostage-taking activity in Lebanon in terms of its *own* organisational requirements and individual motivations by Hizb'allah members as well as interests by Iran and Syria.

The majority of abductions of Western citizens by the Hizb'allah, with very few exceptions, occurred within the framework of a specific and limited time period.[136] As these abductions occurred within concentrated time periods, the decision by Hizb'allah's command leadership to abduct individual foreign citizens was intitiated in direct response to an array of factors affecting the organisation within Lebanon. These factors can be identified as a direct response by the organisation to a number of major events affecting its own position within Lebanon's civil war over a ten-year period, either for the purposes of survival or for the advancement of its pan-Islamic goals. It is equally important to recognize that Hizb'allah activity, as manifested by the abduction of foreigners, was directly related to the collective as well as individual interests of high-ranking Hizb'allah clergy. As a result, it is necessary to examine Hizb'allah hostage-taking activity not only in relation to the evolution of the organisation itself within Lebanon but also to the individual interests of high-ranking Hizb'allah clergy.

Apart from the often converging interests between Hizb'allah as an organisation and the individual interests of its leading clergy, it is necessary to examine the influence and involvement of Iranian clergy and institutions at work in Lebanon on Hizb'allah's hostage-taking activity. The convergence or divergence of Iranian interests in the abduction of foreigners by Hizb'allah must be understood within the context of the array of official and unofficial interaction between Iran and the Hizb'allah as manifest through hostage-taking. The participation of Iranian clergy and institutions in Hizb'allah activity needs to be examined in order to understand the nature of these abductions in terms of being in alignment with the motivations of official Iran or as a manifestation of Iranian clerical factionalism. In turn, this assessment must be balanced against Hizb'allah's own requirements for its position within the internal Lebanese environment.

The abductions of American, French, and British citizens by the Hizb'allah have occurred within specific phases:

- *July 1982–February 1984*: the expansion of the movement and attacks against foreign presence;
- *February 1984–January 1985*: the arrest of *Lebanese al-Da'wa* members in Kuwait;
- *March 1985–June 1985*: the successful actions of the movement in seeking to bring about the expulsion of Western presence and Israel's withdrawal from Lebanon;
- *February 1986–May 1986*: accelerated confrontation with Israel and UNIFIL in southern Lebanon;
- *September 1986–October 1986*: undermining U.S.-Iranian *rapprochement* through the revelation of the Iran-Contra scandal and anti-American abductions;
- *January 1987–January 1988*: arrest of leading Hizb'allah members in Germany and increased armed confrontation with Amal in Lebanon;

- *February 1988–February 1989*: challenges to Amal's authority in southern Lebanon;
- *April 1989–April 1991*: confronting major internal challenges and clerical factionalism in Iran;
- *May 1991–December 1992*: preparation for a post-militia phase of Lebanese politics, participation within the democratic process, and confrontation with Israel.

These phases have reflected not only the movement's own position within the Lebanese environment as a confessional group, but also the individual as well as the collegiate interests by leading Hizb'allah clergy in the abduction of Western foreigners. Apart from Hizb'allah's own requirements, these phases also reflect the interaction between Hizb'allah and Iranian clergy and institutions as well as Syrian influence over its activity. As a result, the examination of Hizb'allah's hostage-taking activity provides a composite picture of the various influences imposed on Hizb'allah's decision-making process in decisions to abduct individual foreigners as well as the underlying *raison d'être* for these abductions. This picture becomes increasingly complex as Hizb'allah developed within Lebanon and was subjected to an array of internal and external constraints as well as opportunities in its hostage-taking activity.

First Phase: July 1982–February 1984

The first abduction by the Hizb'allah of a foreign Western citizen occurred on July 19, 1982, with the kidnapping of David Dodge, the acting president of the American University of Beirut (AUB). Apart from being the most prominent American citizen in Lebanon next to the U.S. Ambassador, the abduction of David Dodge came directly in response to the previous kidnapping of four employees of the Iranian Embassy in Beirut by the Israeli-backed Phalangist militia on July 5, 1982. The importance of these Iranian hostages for Iran became apparent with the revelation of their identity, most notably Ahmad Motevaselian, the Ba'albek commander of the Pasdaran contingent, and Mohsen Musavi, the Iranian chargé d'affaires to Lebanon.[137] While it seems clear that the abduction of David Dodge was initiated by the Pasdaran contingent in Lebanon in an effort to exert American pressure on the Phalangist militia to release their commander, Ahmad Mohtaveselian, the operation was executed by Husayn al-Musawi's *Islamic Amal*.[138] The involvement of the *Islamic Amal* in the abduction of David Dodge was seen not only by the fact that the militia spearheaded Hizb'allah's first military units but also by the confinement of the Pasdaran to the Biq'a area.[139] In particular, the close cooperation between *Islamic Amal* and Pasdaran was revealed by the immediate transfer of David Dodge from Beirut to the Biq'a area, where he was handed over to the Pasdaran contingent in the Syrian border village of Zebdani. Furthermore, the transfer of David Dodge to Iran in April 1983, where he was interrogated by senior Pasdaran officials while held at Evin prison, is evidence that the abduction of Dodge was not only closely coordinated by *Islamic Amal* and the Pasdaran but also initiated solely in accordance with Iran's interest in securing the release of its own captives.[140]

Although the abduction of David Dodge, who subsequently was released after Syrian intervention, on July 21, 1983, failed to achieve the release of the Iranian captives, it had no immediate repercussions and remained an isolated incident of hostage-taking by an Hizb'allah-affiliated organisation. A main reason for the absence of any abductions of other foreign citizens, until the beginning of 1984, can be attributed to the concentration of efforts by the Hizb'allah in the expansion of the movement from Ba'albek into Beirut and southern Lebanon. While Hizb'allah was able to recruit rapidly and indoctrinate a large number of Shi'ite followers in these areas, assisted by the expansion of the Pasdaran from Ba'albek into Beirut in April 1983,[141] the movement's activity was closely aligned with Iran. Notwithstanding the close coordination between Hizb'allah and the Pasdaran in the consolidation of the Hizb'allah movement's activities in Ba'albek and in Beirut, the major role of Iranian support and guidance over the movement was revealed by the close cooperation between Hizb'allah's leading clergy and Iran's official representatives in Beirut and Damascus. In particular, the pattern of Hizb'allah activity during this period, with special concentration on suicide-attacks against foreign targets, underscored not only close alignment and convergence with Iran's foreign policy in Lebanon but also the heavy influence of certain Iranian revolutionary clergy within and over Hizb'allah's decision-making process. This influence was also clearly demonstrated by the subsequent infrequent meetings of Hizb'allah's national *Majlis-al-Shura* from 1983 until 1986 during the tenure of Iran's Ambassador to Syria, Ali Akhbar Mohtashemi. Apart from his prominent and active role in the establishment of the Hizb'allah, Mohtashemi appears to have played an active role, with the Pasdaran and Syrian military intelligence, in the supervision of Hizb'allah's suicide bomb attacks against the American embassy in Beirut in April 1983, the American and French contingents of the Multinational Force (MNF) in October 1983 and the American embassy annex in September 1984.[142] While this close influence over Hizb'allah activity by Iran continued until the reassignment of the *Office of Islamic Liberation* to Iran's Ministry of Foreign Affairs in 1986,

Hizb'allah's activity was also aligned with its pan-Islamic strategy of expelling foreign influence and presence in Lebanon.

Hizb'allah's open warfare against Western political and cultural imperialism in Lebanon began with the bombing of the American embassy on April 18, 1983, which coincided with the arrival of Pasdaran to Beirut. The decision by Hizb'allah to confront the United States, France, the United Kingdom and Israel in Lebanon was based not only on their status as the four principal enemies of the Islamic Republic of Iran but also on their political and military intervention within Lebanon's civil war. Apart from the traditional American and French support for the Christian-dominated Lebanese government, US and French military participation in the MNF, deployed after the massacres in the West Beirut refugee camps of Sabra and Shatila, not only exacerbated Shi'i hostility but also served to obstruct any efforts to overthrow the confessional system and towards the establishment of an Islamic state in Lebanon. For Hizb'allah, American and, to a lesser degree, French military participation, inserted to maintain peace between the warring factions in the absence of an effective Lebanese army, became increasingly associated with support for the discredited Gemayel regime as they became gradually drawn into the civil war as active participants.[143] The rejection by Hizb'allah of the American-sponsored 17 May agreement, coupled with direct military engagement between Hizb'allah and the American MNF contingent, backed by the presence offshore of massive U.S. naval support, led to a comprehensive effort by the Lebanese Shi'ite organisation to destroy any foreign military presence and political influence in Lebanon. Hizb'allah's execution of a series of suicide attacks, with the active support of Iran and Syria, against the American and French MNF contingents in Beirut on October 23, 1983, resulted not only in the disintegration of the MNF through the withdrawal of both the American and French contingents in the early months of 1984, but also earned the movement prestige and revolutionary credence in its battle with Amal for the hearts and minds of the Shi'a community.[144] While the withdrawal of the MNF from Lebanon represented a major victory for the Hizb'allah, in terms of achieving its pan-Islamic goal of liberating Lebanon from all forms of political and military intervention by the Western powers, the organisation accelerated its efforts to confront Israel's military presence through an armed campaign while it concentrated on the removal of any remaining Western presence through attacks on, and kidnappings of, foreigners. This determination by Hizb'allah was clearly manifested in conjunction with the departure of the American MNF contingent through the assassination of Malcolm Kerr, who had replaced the kidnapped David Dodge as president of the AUB. While the assassination of Malcolm Kerr occurred as a retaliatory response to Hizb'allah's armed conflict with the U.S. Marines and the U.S. Navy's 6th Fleet, it also served both as a direct affront on AUB, as the most clear remnant bastion of the United States' cultural and political presence in Lebanon, and as a message that all Western foreign citizens were no longer safe.

Although the Hizb'allah would subsequently abduct an array of Westerners as a means of removing any remaining Western presence from Beirut, the organisation's next campaign of abductions was inextricably tied to the participation of individual Hizb'allah members with Iraqi *al-Da'wa al-Islamiyya* elements in the multiple terrorist attacks in Kuwait, on December 12, 1983, most notably against the U.S. and French embassies. In particular, Hizb'allah's abduction campaign, between February and March 1984, of three American citizens and a Frenchman was initated in direct response to the arrest and conviction of two *Islamic Amal* members in Kuwait, who were relatives of high-ranking Hizb'allah and *Islamic Amal* officials in Lebanon. Despite Iran's close involvement in the Kuwaiti incidents with Iraqi *al-Da'wa al-Islamiyya* and in the abduction of the five Westerners in Lebanon by the Hizb'allah, the individual interests of some leading Hizb'allah clergy in the case of their imprisoned relatives in Kuwait dominated the decision by the organisation regarding the nationality of future hostages as well as the ideal time for their abduction. In particular, all of these abductions in the next phase occurred as a direct response to decisions made concerning the fate of imprisoned Hizb'allah members.

Second Phase: February 1984–January 1985

The second phase of Hizb'allah abductions in Lebanon came as a response to the arrest by Kuwaiti authorities, in the wake of the December 1983 multiple terrorist attacks, of 25 suspects, three of whom were Lebanese Shi'ites (Elias Fuad Saab; Hussein al-Sayed Yousef al-Musawi; and Azam Khalil Ibrahim).[145] While it soon became apparent that the Iraqi *al-Da'wa al-Islamiyya*, headquartered in Iran, was responsible for the attacks, two of the three Lebanese Shi'ites arrested were related to Husayn al-Musawi, leader of *Islamic Amal*, and Imad Mughniyah, formerly a bodyguard of Sheikh Fadlallah as well as the operational leader of Hizb'allah's SSA (Hussein al-Sayed Yousef al-Musawi is a first-cousin to *Islamic Amal* leader Husayn al-Musawi. Elias Fouad Saab is the brother-in-law and cousin to Imad Mughniya).[146] While the involvement of these Lebanese *al-Da'wa* members, operating within the framework of *Islamic Amal* and Hizb'allah, in the Kuwaiti bomb attacks pointed not only to close cooperation with the Iraqi *al-Da'wa al-Islamiyya* but also to coordination with Iranian officials, Hizb'allah's decision to abduct foreign citizens in Lebanon closely followed the conclusion of trial of the 21 *al-Da'wa* defendants in Kuwait. In connection with the initiation of the trial of the 21 *al-Da'wa* defendants, on February 11, 1984, Hizb'allah retaliated with the abductions of American Frank Regier and Frenchman Christian Joubert in Lebanon. The decision by Hizb'allah to abduct an American and a French citizen mirrored not only alignment with Iran's foreign policy, most notably in an attempt to deter both the American and French administrations as well as Persian Gulf governments from extending financial and military assistance to Iraq. It was also a means by the organisation to place dual pressure on Kuwait for either the release of the *al-Da'wa* defendants or, at least, to receive leniency in treatment and sentencing. As the *al-Da'wa* trial progressively moved towards conclusion, at the end of March 1984, Hizb'allah abducted two other American citizens, Jeremy Levin and William Buckley. In comparison to the previous kidnappings of Regier and Joubert, the Hizb'allah abduction of Levin and Buckley revealed not only careful selection of targets in order to maximize the pressure on Kuwait from the American administration but subsequently also close Iranian involvement, especially in the case of the abduction of William Buckley, the chief of CIA's Lebanese operations. While the Hizb'allah abductions were motivated by the family connections between leading *Islamic Amal* officials and their imprisoned relatives held in Kuwait, the nature of the close cooperation between Hizb'allah and Iran was reinforced by the transfer of William Buckley to Iran, through the hands of the Pasdaran contingent in the Biq'a area.[147]

In conjunction with the conviction of the *al-Da'wa* defendants, on March 27, 1984, most notably with the imposition of a death sentence on Elias Fuad Saab, the Hizb'allah threatened to kill its hostages in an effort to prevent the Kuwaiti government from carrying through the planned execution of the *al-Da'wa* prisoners. In March 1984, Kuwait's State Security Court had sentenced Elias Fuad Saab to death, together with four Iraqi *al-Da'wa* members, while Hussein al-Sayed Yousef al-Musawi received life-imprisonment and Azam Khalil Ibrahim received 15 years imprisonment.[148] While the Hizb'allah kidnapped American Benjamin Weir in May 1984, in another effort to pressure Kuwait to accede to its demands of freedom or leniency for the prisoners, there then followed a brief period in which no other Westerners were abducted until December 1984. Hizb'allah's respite can be attributed to the lack of suitable Western citizens, as manifested by the drastic reduction of U.S. official presence in Lebanon (from 190 personel in 1983 to 6 in 1984),[149] and to the focus by the movement on guerilla attacks against Israel. The resumption of kidnappings by the Hizb'allah occurred in connection with the hijacking of a Kuwaiti airliner, KU 221, by four members of the *al-Da'wa al-Islamiyya* on December 4, 1984, in another concerted effort to obtain the release of the imprisoned *al-Da'wa* 17 members in Kuwait. The Kuwaiti hijacking and the abduction of Briton Peter Kilburn, which occurred the previous day in Lebanon, appears to have been perpetrated by *Islamic Amal* with close Iranian involvement. Evidence of close co-operation between *Islamic Amal* and Iran in the case of the Kuwaiti hijacking was supported by the hijackers' use of falsified Lebanese passports and, more importantly, by the previous presence of *Islamic Amal* representatives in Iran in a meeting with Ayatollah Hossein Ali Montazeri under the auspices of the *Office of Liberation Movements*, on November 23, 1984.[150] Despite alleged Iranian involvement with *Islamic Amal* in the hijacking, which explained the rapid conclusion of the incident as well as Iran's refusal to either prosecute or extradite any of the perpetrators, the next abduction of American Lawrence Jenco, on January 8, 1985, by the Hizb'allah was initiated not only as an effort to increase the pressure on Kuwait with respect to the *al-Da'wa* prisoners but also preceded an earlier effort by the Hizb'allah to abduct a French citizen. This was manifested by the mistaken abduction of Eric Wehrli, Swiss chargé d'affaires in Lebanon, who was released after only four days in capitivity on January 7. Apart from the close proximity of the Swiss embassy to the French embassy in Beirut, other evidence would suggest that Hizb'allah deliberately targeted Wehrli in order to obtain the release of Housein al-Talaat, a Hizb'allah member arrested at Zürich airport on December 18, 1984, with explosives in his possession intended for an attack on the American embassy in Rome.[151]

This phase of Hizb'allah abductions revealed the close connection between the hostage-takings and the fate of the 17 al-Da'wa prisoners in Kuwait. As these Lebanese *al-Da'wa* members, in cooperation with exiled elements from Iraq's *al-Da'wa al-Islamiyya*, were acting on behalf and with the support of Iran, the involvement of Iran was not only evident in some of these abductions but also converged with the individual interests of leading Hizb'allah security officials, most notably Imad Mughniya.

Third Phase: March 1985–June 1985

The third phase of Hizb'allah abductions of foreigners in Lebanon, between mid-March until the beginning of June 1985, was related to an accelerated effort by the movement to expel any remaining Western foreign influence or presence from Lebanon. Hizb'allah's release of an

official manifesto in February 1985, in conjunction with the first commemoration of the death of Sheikh Ragheb Harb (known among the
Hizb'allah rank and file as the "sheikh of the martyrs"), was symbolic of
the major accomplishments by the movement in forcing not only the
earlier departure of the MNF from Lebanon but also the gradual and unilateral retreat of Israel to the narrow security-zone in southern Lebanon.
While Hizb'allah's successful and relentless guerrilla activity bolstered
the movement's support and image, as an implacable foe of Israel and
other enemies of Islam, the kidnapping of Westerners by Hizb'allah were
directly related to issues surrounding the completion of Israel's retreat in
Lebanon, most notably the transfer of hundreds of imprisoned Shi'ites
from Ansar prison camp in Lebanon to Atlit in Israel. Apart from
Hizb'allah efforts to achieve the release of these imprisoned Shi'ites held
by Israel, the abduction of Westerners was initiated not only as a response
to the failure by Western governments to condemn Israel's military practices in occupied southern Lebanon, as manifested by the American veto
of a Lebanese-sponsored UN resolution to that end, but also to the unsuccessful assassination attempt on Sheikh Fadlallah, on March 8, 1985, in
the Bir al-'Abed quarter in the southern suburbs of Beirut.

The alleged involvement of Lebanese intelligence units, backed by the
CIA, in the car bomb explosion near the residence of Sheikh Fadlallah,
which killed at least 80 people and injured 200 others,[152] led to the Hizb'allah
retaliatory abductions of two British hostages, Geoffrey Nash and Brian
Levick. The early release of Nash and Levick, two weeks later, seems to
indicate that their abductions had been made on the mistaken assumption that
they were American citizens. However, the attempt on Sheikh Fadlallah's
life, in combination with the American veto of a Lebanese-sponsored resolution in the United Nations Security Council on March 12,[153] led to the abduction of American Terry Anderson on March 16, 1985.

As the Hizb'allah intensified its anti-Israeli operations, mirrored by
Shams al-Din's declaration of a defensive *jihad* against Israel, French con-
demnation of Israel's military practices in southern Lebanon failed to
prevent the abduction of three French embassy employees, on March 22,
1985. Although the decision by the Hizb'allah was motivated by considerations more aligned with Iran's foreign policy, most notably related to
France's continued arms shipments to Iraq and outstanding financial debt
to Iran (specifically repayment of a $1 billion loan made by the Shah to the
French Atomic Energy Commission in 1974), it was also taken as a
response to the presence of the French UNIFIL contingent in southern
Lebanon and its perceived practice of failing to provide adequate protection to the local Shi'ite population.[154]

Another reason for Hizb'allah's concentration on the abduction of French citizens, as became evident by the kidnapping of Jean-Paul Kaufmann and Michel Seurat on May 22, 1985, was an effort to obtain the release of Anis Naccache, imprisoned in France for the attempted assassination of the Shah's former Prime Minister Shapour Bakthiar in Paris in July 1980.[155] Apart from Bakhtiar's overall leadership status of the exile opposition movements to the Islamic Republic of Iran, the main interest by the Hizb'allah in the release of Anis Naccache stemmed from both his role as head of the Iranian assassination team and his close personal friendships with both Ahmad Khomeini, son of the Iranian revolutionary patriarch, and Mohsen Rafiqdust, IRGC commander in Lebanon.[156] Furthermore, factions within Hizb'allah's SSA had a close interest in achieving the release of Naccache as he was allegedly affiliated with Fatah Force 17, and as several key operational leaders of Hizb'allah's own intelligence network had longstanding experience within Force 17.[157] Due to Imad Mughniya's close personal friendship with Naccache, coupled with official Iranian interest in the case, the Hizb'allah focused its efforts to achieve his release through the abduction of these five French citizens.

Apart from the individual interest of leading Hizb'allah clergy in the release of the *al-Da'wa* prisoners in Kuwait and Anis Naccache in France, Hizb'allah focused its efforts on the release of 766 mainly Lebanese Shi'ites, transferred to *Israel* in conjunction with its *withdrawal* from Lebanon, through the abductions of mainly American citizens, as demonstrated by the further kidnapping of David Jacobsen and Thomas Sutherland. This was revealed most clearly by the Hizb'allah hijacking of TWA 847, which immediately followed the completion of Israel's departure from Lebanon, on June 14, 1985, the last and holiest Friday of Ramadan. While the release of the 766 imprisoned Shi'ites dominated Hizb'allah demands, Iranian involvement with the hijackers, both in the supervision and planning of the incident itself and as an active participant in the defusion and resolution of the hijacking through the intercession by Iran's Rafsanjani, overshadowed the competition between Amal and Hizb'allah in the incident. The TWA-hijacking was executed by leading Hizb'allah members, most notably by Hassan Izzeldine, who was also involved in the later hijacking of KU422 in 1988, and by Muhammad Ali Hamadi, whose brother was one of the heads of Hizb'allah's SSA. The incident itself was not only part of an effort to obtain the release of the 766 Shi'ite prisoners but also of a wider strategy by Hizb'allah to discredit Amal leader Nabih Berri in the Amal-Hizb'allah competition over southern Lebanon in the power-vacuum created by the withdrawal of Israel. This intra-Shi'ite feud intensified with Amal's attack on Palestinians in the "war of camps", under Syria's influence, and Hizb'allah's alliance with the PLO, supported by Iran, in order to keep the military option active against Israel in southern Lebanon. Consequently, the abduction campaign was related not only to the interests of individual Hizb'allah clergy, as evident in the case of the *al-Da'wa* prisoners and Anis Naccache, but also to the movement's broader efforts to confront Israel in southern Lebanon and assume the role of protector of the Shi'ite community at the expense of the Amal movement. Although the subsequent cessation in the abduction of Westerners by the Hizb'allah, which resumed in February 1986, has been explained by the secret dealings surrounding the Iran-Contra affair, Hizb'allah's concentration of resistance in southern Lebanon and its competition with Amal over the Shi'ite community eclipsed any need for the capture of other Westerners. As demonstrated by the revelation of the US-Iranian arms-for-hostages affair, Hizb'allah showed disillusionment regarding the prospects of any *rapprochement* between Iran and the United States.

Fourth Phase: February 1986–May 1986

The fourth phase of Hizb'allah abductions of Westerners, between February and May 1986, was directed mainly at French citizens and came as a response to the decision by France to expel two exiled members of *al-Da'wa al-Islamiyah* to Iraq and continued demands by the Shi'ite movement for the release of Naccache and other Shi'ite prisoners held in France. The abduction of seven French citizens was also initiated for the advancement of Iranian foreign policy in a range of outstanding disputes with France, which occurred in conjunction with a Hizb'allah bomb campaign in Paris in February and September 1986 and against the French UNIFIL contingent in southern Lebanon. Consequently, the concentration on the abduction of French citizens underlined the close cooperation between Hizb'allah's SSA and Iran. Apart from the French hostages, Hizb'allah also abducted two British citizens in reprisal for the American raid on Libya in April 1986.

Hizb'allah's decision to abduct Marcel Coudry and a French four-man Antenne-2 television crew, on March 3, was directly initiated in response to the expulsion of two pro-Iranian Iraqi dissidents to Iraq, Fawzy Harmza and Hassan Kheir al-Din, belonging to the Iraqi *al-Da'wa*.[158] Although the Hizb'allah abductions were a reaction to the expulsions of thirteen Muslims, including the two opponents of the Iraqi regime, coupled with the announcement by the Hizb'allah of the retaliatory execution of Michel Seurat, it underlined not only the continued close relationship between the

Shi'ite movement in Lebanon and the Iraqi *al-Da'wa al-Islamiyya* but also that the Hizb'allah was well-attuned to the political climate in France, as the abductions and the Paris bombing campaign occurred in conjunction with the French national elections in March 1986. This maximized the pressure on the French government to accede to Hizb'allah demands not only with respect to the fate of the expelled Iraqis and in the case of Naccache but also for the advancement of Iranian foreign policy in a range of outstanding issues with France.

Apart from the abduction of Marcel Coudry and the four Antenne-2 crew-men, the Hizb'allah applied additional pressure on the French government through its participation in a series of bomb attacks in Paris between February and September 1986. While a shadowy group, using the *nom de guerre* of the *"Comité de solidarité avec les prisonniers politiques arabes et du Moyen-Orient"* (C.S.P.P.A), demanded the release of FARL leader George Ibrahim Abdallah; Anis Naccache; and Varadjian Garbidjian, the direct involvement of the Hizb'allah became clear with the arrest of its presumed members in March 1987, most notably Mohammad Mouhajer, a nephew of Hizb'allah leader Sheikh al-Amin, and Fouad Ali Saleh, a leader of Hizb'allah's network in France.[159] As Hizb'allah's involvement in the Paris bombings had been revealed by the previous arrest of Mohammad Ali Hamadi in West Germany, evidence of complicity between Hizb'allah and Iran in the incident was clearly demonstrated by the involvement of high-ranking Hizb'allah intelligence officials, most notably Abd Al Hadi Hamadi and Ibrahim Aqil, in cooperation with Iranian embassy officials, Wahid Gordgy, and Pasdaran officials, most notably Mohammad Salek and Ahmad Kan'ani.[160] This close relationship between Hizb'allah operatives and Iranian officials revealed that the Paris bombing campaign and the abduction of French citizens in Lebanon were motivated by the converging interests between Hizb'allah's own agenda in seeking the freedom of its imprisoned members and Iran's own foreign policy agenda aimed at extracting political and financial concessions from the French government. This was confirmed by Sheikh Fadlallah, who explicitly linked the issue of the French hostages with French-Iranian relations.[161] Furthermore, Hizb'allah maximized efforts to pressure France by the abduction of another French citizen (Camille Sontag) in Lebanon on May 7, 1986, and, more importantly, through the initiation of an armed campaign against the French UNIFIL contingent in southern Lebanon. In the latter case, Hizb'allah's armed efforts were not only motivated by the desire to increase pressure on France to accede to its own and Iranian demands for the withdrawal of UNIFIL and abrogation of UN Security Council Resolution 425 but also mirrored the organisation's decision to actively confront Israel in southern Lebanon.

While Hizb'allah's decision to abduct these French hostages was in alignment with both Iran's and the movement's collective interest, the decision to kidnap two British citizens, John McCarthy and Brian Keenan, in April 1986 was less clear beyond its retaliatory nature in response to Britain's tacit participation in the American raid on Libya. However, the fate of the British hostages became intertwined with demands for the release by Israel of 260 Shi'ites held in al-Khiam prison in the security zone in South Lebanon and the release of the three Iranian hostages who disappeared in 1982.

Fifth Phase: September 1986–October 1986

A next short series of Hizb'allah abductions were directed against American citizens, beginning with the kidnappings of Frank Reed on September 9, 1986 and Joseph Ciccipio three days later, and reached its culmination with the seizure of Edward Tracy on October 21, 1986. While Hizb'allah's decision to resume the hostage-taking of Americans, after a fifteen-month period of cessation, must be viewed in the context of efforts to replace released American hostages within the framework of the so-called Iran-Contra Affair, evidence suggests Hizb'allah had at best only limited knowledge of the arms-for-hostages deals, as evident by the organisation's vehement opposition to any U.S.-Iranian rapproachement. It seems more likely, however, that the abduction of these three Americans reflected clerical factionalism in Iran as the incidents shortly preceded the revelation of the Iran-Contra Affair on November 3, 1986, by Ayatollah Montazeri's representative in Lebanon, Sheikh Ismail al-Khaliq, a leading Hizb'allah cleric.[162] In addition, information about Robert McFarlane's visit to Iran had been previously printed in a small newsletter published by Hizb'allah-followers of Montazeri in Ba'albek.[163] Although it may be the case that Hizb'allah abducted these American citizens in an effort to both replace previously released hostages and discredit Rafsanjani's position in Iran, the alleged involvement of Hizb'allah leader Imad Mughniya in these abductions suggests that concern over the 17 *al-Da'wa* prisoners in Kuwait was a strong motivation for the resumption of the kidnapping of American citizens.

These three anti-American abductions also signalled a growing rift between Hizb'allah and Iran, as evident by the reassignment of the *Office of Islamic Liberations Movements* to the Ministry of Foreign Affairs and the arrest of its commander Mehdi Hashemi.[164] This made Hizb'allah's leadership more susceptible to Iranian clerical factionalism and provided the opportunity for some leading Hizb'allah operatives to pursue a more independent agenda in the abductions of foreigners.

Sixth Phase: January 1987–January 1988

The decision by Hizb'allah leaders to abduct a number of Western citizens in January 1987 came directly in response to the arrest of three leading Hizb'allah members in Europe. While the abduction of Frenchman Roger Auque, on January 13, appears to be related to the previous day's arrest of Bashir al-Khodour in Milan by Italian authorities, other abductions of Western foreigners came directly in response to the arrest of Mohammad Ali Hamadi in Frankfurt by West-German authorities. Apart from his prominent role in the June 1985 TWA 847 hijacking, Mohammad Ali Hamadi's elevated position within the Hizb'allah was revealed not only by the retaliatory abductions of two West-German citizens, Rudolph Cordes and Alfred Schmidt, but also by the fact that his brother, Abdul Hadi, was the chief of security for Hizb'allah. The connection between the Hamadi clan's high-ranking position within Hizb'allah's SSA and the abduction campaign of foreigners in Lebanon was made even clearer with the arrest of Mohammad Ali Hamadi's younger brother, Abbas, in West Germany. The arrest of the two Hamadi brothers in January 1987, coupled with American extradition requests, led to the kidnapping of four American teachers in Beirut. While Hizb'allah's abduction campaign was motivated by individual interests of leading Hizb'allah clergy, it was also a reflection of clerical factionalism in Iran in the aftermath of the revelation of the U.S.-Iranian arms-for-hostages deal, as evident by the unprecedented number of abductions of foreigners by the organisation during January 1987. This clerical factionalism was evident by the separation of the *Islamic Liberation Movements* from the IRGC in Iran in December 1986, in an effort by Rafsanjani to strengthen Iran's control over Hizb'allah activity in Lebanon. Although the abduction of Terry Waite, an Anglican mediator negotiating independently in the hostage-crisis, by the Hizb'allah may have been caused by a perceived indirect association with the U.S.-Iran arms-for-hostages deal, (which he publicly denied prior to his kidnapping) it was mainly a consequence of his inability to affect the fate of the imprisoned 17 *al-Dawa* prisoners in Kuwait.

Hizb'allah's demand for the return of 400 Shi'ite and Palestinian imprisoned in Israel as a precondition for the release of these hostages also mirrored the movement's escalatory efforts to confront militarly IDF and SLA positions in southern Lebanon. The concentration of Hizb'allah efforts was underlined by the organisation's use of a hiterto unknown *nom de guerre*, the *Islamic Jihad for the Liberation of Palestine*, in claiming responsibilty for the abduction of Western foreigners. In response to these abductions, direct military intervention by Syria into the Muslim areas of Beirut in February 1987, in which 23 members of Hizb'allah were killed, demonstrated not only a rift with Syria over Hizb'allah's hostage-taking activity but also the increased hostility between the Hizb'allah and its competitor Amal. Apart from an isolated abduction of an American journalist, Charles Glass, in June 1987, the Syrian-imposed security plan in Beirut, coupled with Hizb'allah-Amal armed clashes in Beirut, the Biq'a and southern Lebanon, contributed to a reorientation of Hizb'allah's focus away from hostage-taking towards armed confrontation with both Amal, over the support of the Shi'a community, and Israel, in the struggle for the "liberation of Jerusalem". This was particularly evident by Hizb'allah's display of sophisticated armaments during its parades in southern Beirut, Ba'albek, Sidon and Tyre on 14 May (anti-Zionist day) and on 22 May, "Jerusalem Day".[165] While Hizb'allah's shift towards armed struggle was supported by Iran's allocation of $90 million to the organisation in late 1987 for its military enhancement,[166] it was also evident by the existence and display of regular Hizb'allah *Islamic Resistance* military units, equipped with anti-tank and anti-aircraft missiles. The recall of several regional operational leaders of Hizb'allah from southern Lebanon to Ba'albek for extensive retraining in the latter half of 1987 indicated the employment of new tactics which combined guerrilla warfare with regular military operations.

This phase of Hizb'allah abductions revealed a line of greater independence from Iran as the hostage-takings were aligned with the interests of individual high-ranking Hizb'allah SSA operatives over the fate of imprisoned relatives abroad and for the movement as a whole in its confrontation with both Amal and Israel. The lack of other additional abductions, with the exception of American Charles Glass, can be attributed to the Amal-Hizb'allah confrontation in Beirut and the South as well as the movement's concentration in the enhancement and projection of its military capability against Israel in southern Lebanon.

Seventh Phase: February 1988–January 1989

Hizb'allah's military and political confrontation with Amal over Beirut and southern Lebanon escalated with the abduction of Lt. Col. William Higgins, the American Chief of the UN Truce and Supervision Organisation's observer group in Lebanon (UNTSO) on February 17, 1988. Apart from the symbolic importance of the abduction, occurring on the fourth annual commemoration of the death of Hizb'allah leader Sheikh Ragheb Harb, Hizb'allah's decision to abduct Lt. Col. Higgins was not only directed against UNIFIL for impeding armed attacks against the Israeli occupation of the south but, more importantly, constituted a direct challenge to Amal's authority to maintain a stable security environment in southern Lebanon. This was seen as a direct challenge against Amal as Lt. Col. Higgins was abducted from his UN vechicle between Tyre and Nakara after a meeting with Abd al-Majid Salah, Amal's political leader of southern Lebanon. As the Amal launched a major campaign to eliminate the Hizb'allah presence in the South, it became clear that Sheikh al-Musawi, the commander of Hizb'allah's *Islamic Resistance*, had been personally responsible for the abduction of Lt. Col. Higgins in close cooperation with both Sheikh Abdul Karim Obeid, the local commander of Hizb'allah's military wing, and Mustafa al-Dirani, the former head of Amal's security service.[167] Although the abduction of Lt. Col. William Higgins remained an isolated incident, executed by Hizb'allah to challenge Amal's authority in the South and to obtain the release of Israeli-held Shi'ite prisoners, the decision by the movement to hijack Kuwaiti airliner KU422 on April 4, 1988, highlighted the continued importance of the fate of the 17 al-Da'wa prisoners in Kuwait for leading members of Hizb'allah. Apart from close Iranian involvement in the hijacking, the incident reflected a shift in Hizb'allah tactics as the movement's activity was constrained not only by Amal's control over Beirut but also through its armed confrontation with Amal in the South.

Although the abduction of Lt. Col. William Higgins served as a triggering mechanism for the armed confrontation between Amal and Hizb'allah, the intra-Shi'ite warfare in Beirut and southern Lebanon dominated Hizb'allah's agenda at the expense of any further abduction of Western foreigners. As Amal scored decisive military victories in the South against the Hizb'allah in the spring of 1988, leading to the expulsion of a number of Hizb'allah clergy to the Bi'qa, Hizb'allah itself reorganized its efforts towards armed confrontation with Amal in the southern suburbs of Beirut. For example, elements within Hizb'allah and the Iranian Pasdaran established a joint command to assassinate high-ranking Amal officials and carry out operations against Amal checkpoints and centres.[168] This led not only to the military defeat of Amal in Beirut in May, and to the infiltration within its ranks by Hizb'allah members and the defection of Amal members, but also to Syrian political and military intervention in June 1988, in order to rescue Amal from defeat and to influence the forthcoming presidential elections in September 1988.[169] After Iranian proposals for the insertion into Beirut of a joint Syrian-Iranian force were rejected by

both Syria and Amal, Hizb'allah leaders were assured that Syria would
not clamp down on the movement if it left the Western hostages
unharmed. As a result, Hizb'allah leader Sheikh al-Amin claimed that this
arrangement between Iran and Syria allowed Hizb'allah to resume activities in the south, the main objective by the movement for challenging
Amal in the suburbs of Beirut.[170] As Hizb'allah's position was weakened
in Beirut, it turned its attention to the challenge of confronting Amal's
supremacy in southern Lebanon. The protracted conflict between Amal
and Hizb'allah for the control of the major Shi'a areas in the South and
Beirut continued with ferocity until late January 1989, when Syria
and Iran intervened and announced an agreement between Amal and
Hizb'allah. Under this agreement, Amal's authority over the security of
southern Lebanon was recognized while Hizb'allah was permitted to
maintain only a nonmilitary presence through political, cultural, and
informational programmes.[171]

The intensification by the Hizb'allah, through its military wing, of
armed confrontation in southern Lebanon reflected not only the competition with Amal over military and political influence in the region but also
the substitution of Hizb'allah's grand pan-Islamic strategy from the failure
to achieve Islamic victory in adjacent territories, as demonstrated by the
announcement of a cease-fire between Iran and Iraq in July 1988, to solidarity with the revival of Islamic fundementalism within the Palestinian
intifada (uprising) in the Israeli-occupied territories. This was demonstrated not only by Hizb'allah's closer co-operation with local anti-Arafat
Palestinian elements for operational expediency in the resistance struggle
against Israel, but also through involvement with Islamic groups within
the Israeli-controlled occupied territories.

As shown by Hizb'allah's *rapprochement* with Amal in January 1989,
which was facilitated by Iranian-Syrian diplomacy, the change in
Hizb'allah's position came under the threat of Syrian military intervention as Syria moved to extend its hegemony over Lebanon. Apart from
Hizb'allah's disillusionment with Iran's reversal of policy towards Iraq, it
became clear that the Hizb'allah-Iranian relationship showed certain signs
of strain as Iran moved to extend its relationships with Amal and other less
militant Shi'ite organisations in Lebanon. Although Iran's attempt to minimise Amal-Hizb'allah differences was made in order to close ranks
against Iraq's accelerated injection of military support to militias in
Lebanon after the cease-fire in the Gulf war, it failed as Amal remained
the unconditional ally of Syria and Hizb'allah resumed its armed confrontation with Amal over the control of southern Lebanon. The expansion
of Hizb'allah's presence in the South proved important for both Iran and

the movement itself as despite having a well-entrenched position in Beirut, it was unable to significantly exert political influence beyond the suburbs and as the movement's stronghold in Ba'albek was encircled by Syrian military presence. Apart from providing Iran with a direct means to participate in the politics of the Arab-Israeli conflict, Hizb'allah's military option and political presence in the South would become increasingly significant, especially as Hizb'allah's position remained uncertain in the aftermath of the death of Ayatollah Khomeini in June 1989 and the conclusion of the Ta'if Accords for political reform in Lebanon in October 1989.

Eighth Phase: April 1989–April 1991

Hizb'allah's abduction of British citizen, Jack Mann, in May 1989, was in response to Iran's fatwa against Salman Rushdie for the publication of his book *The Satanic Verses* and, more specifically, for his refuge and protection in the United Kingdom. The incident itself was soon overshadowed for the Hizb'allah movement by the death of Ayatollah Khomeini on June 3, 1989, and the abduction of Sheikh Abd al-Karim Obeid, a senior Hizb'allah cleric and regional military commander of the *Islamic Resistance*, by élite Israeli military units on July 28, 1989.[172]

Apart from Hizb'allah's disagreement with Iran's clerical establishment over the devolution of Ayatollah Khomeini's spiritual and political authority, following the dismissal of the designated heir Montazeri in March 1989, the death of Ayatollah Khomeini left the movement in disarray over its future position in Lebanon. The ouster of Hizb'allah's most staunch ally within Iran's clerical hierarchy, Ali-Akbar Mohtashemi, by Iran's new president Rafsanjani, came at a time when Hizb'allah experienced Iranian moves to downgrade its support for the movement while it felt increased pressure from Syria to release the Western hostages. In Rafsanjani's inaugural speech to the Majlis, he warned that hardliners would have to forego their 'extremism' for new political and economical program.[173] In particular, Syria pressured the Hizb'allah through the limited prevention of additional or replacement IRGC from passing through Syria into Lebanon, while Iran's Rafsanjani attempted to replace the exisiting IRGC contingent with one more loyal to the political leadership in Iran.[174] In addition, Hizb'allah's position within Lebanon was directly threatened by the Saudi-brokered Ta'if Accord, concluded with Syrian support in October 1989, which the movement vehemently opposed. In response to the challenges facing the organisation inside Lebanon, the Hizb'allah assembled a major meeting to discuss the challenges the movement faced both within

Lebanon and beyond in its relationship with Iran and the revolutionist faction within the clerical establishment. While the meeting resulted in the ascendancy of Sheikh al-Tufayli as leader of Hizb'allah's command leadership, it also revealed deep splits within the organisation over the future direction of the movement in Lebanon.

While the movement remained divided over its future direction, the abduction of Sheikh Obeid, a leading figure within the *Islamic Resistance*, represented not only a major security problem for the organisation, as Jibshit was a key organisational center for *Islamic Resistance* in its attacks against IDF and SLA positions, but also a shift in tactics by Israel in its confrontation with Hizb'allah. As the Hizb'allah had previously not been immune from Israeli kidnappings of its operational members, as demonstrated by the abduction of Sheikh Jawad Kafsi and three of his colleagues from the south Lebanese village of Tibnin on December 15, 1988,[175] the abduction of Sheikh Obeid forced the organisation into negotiations with Israel over the return of six missing IDF soldiers held by the organisation. While the IDF kidnapping of Sheikh Kafsi failed to yield any prisoner exchange, due to the semi-independent status of the *Believers Resistance Movement* and his low-ranking position within this organisation, the decision to abduct Sheikh Obeid was not only due to his leading position as a regional commander within the *Islamic Resistance* but also for his personal involvement in the abductions of two IDF servicemen in February 1986 and Lt.Col. William Higgins in February 1988.[176] Although the fate of the Hizb'allah-held missing Israeli servicemen[177] remained conditional on any Israeli release gesture of Shi'ite Lebanese detainees from Atlit or al-Khiam prisons, Hizb'allah remained adamant over its refusal of both the release of any IDF soldiers as well as any Western hostages under the more militant leadership of Sheikh al-Tufayli.

Although the more radical elements within Hizb'allah's leadership had control over the movement's activity, it was clear that the organisation faced increased confrontation with both Iran and Syria over its position within a rapidly changing political and military environment in Lebanon. In particular, it became clear that the new Iranian leadership wanted to pursue a more controlled policy in its relationship with the Hizb'allah, as evident by Rafsanjani's appointment of his brother, Mahmud Hashemi, to head the Lebanon desk within the Ministry of Foreign Affairs.[178] However, it was also clear that Iran had great difficulty in restraining Hizb'allah in its clashes with Amal, despite the January 1989 agreement between the two militias and continued Iranian mediation efforts, and that the Pasdaran remained a staunch ally of Hizb'allah throughout its conflict with Amal and in its opposition for the release of foreign hostages, notwithstanding efforts by Iran to effect its withdrawal from Lebanon or assign more pragmatic Pasdaran units in order to make it more pliable and loyal to the political leadership in Iran. While Hizb'allah, in cooperation with Pasdaran and radical clergy, effectively managed to obstruct the release of hostages in many cases, its position within Lebanon was dependent on Iran's relationship with Syria. As a result, the hostage-issue for Hizb'allah became increasingly intertwined with insurance for its own survival in a post-militia phase of Lebanese politics under Syrian hegemony. In particular, this was evident by the Syrian-Iranian *rapprochement* between Hizb'allah and Amal in November 1990 and the reposition of Hizb'allah forces from Beirut to the Biq'a and the South.[179] As the foreign hostages were increasingly used by the Hizb'allah in negotiations with Iran and Syria to ensure its position within Lebanon, the mechanism for their release was facilitated by the resolution of the case of the 15 *al-Da'wa* prisoners in Kuwait, who escaped following Iraq's invasion of Kuwait on August 2, 1990. The 15 *al-Da'wa* prisoners were among 1,300 prisoners from Kuwait's Salidia central prison who escaped during the turmoil of Iraq's invasion of Kuwait. Iraqi officials took them into custody in Iraq and released them to Iran. A few of these prisoners obtained Iranian and Lebanese documents provided by Iranian embassies in Kuwait and other Gulf states, and made their way back to Lebanon.[180] While the release of the 15 *al-Da'wa* prisoners had eliminated one of Hizb'allah's principal demands, the foreign hostages were used to reach an agreement between Iran and Syria over the future of Hizb'allah in Lebanon, which was concluded on April 21, 1991.[181] Under this agreement, Hizb'allah was allowed to remain armed as a resistance movement. In turn, Hizb'allah would facilitate the release of all its foreign hostages within the framework of fulfillment of its own requirements as well as in alignment with Iranian and Syrian interests.[182] In order to ensure Hizb'allah's part of the agreement and in line with the movement's position, the command leadership of Hizb'allah decided to elect a new Secretary-General of the movement in May 1991.[183]

Ninth Phase: May 1991–December 1992

The election of Sheikh Abbas al-Musawi as Secretary-General of the Hizb'allah resulted in a new leadership not only closer to the position of Iran but, more importantly, more equipped to deal with both an escalation in the resistance activity against Israel, as he had commanded the movement's military wing, as well as facilitating the release of the hostages by Hizb'allah's SSA, as he had headed the movement's internal security

apparatus in Beirut. While Sheikh Abbas al-Musawi seemed more pragmatic and less militant than his predecessor, throughout the denouement of
the hostage-crisis under the auspices of the office of UN Secretary-General
Javier Perez de Cuellar, Hizb'allah under his command escalated its confrontation with Israel in southern Lebanon. Although Sheikh al-Musawi
managed to receive important concessions, most notably the release of
Hizb'allah members from al-Khiam in order to satisfy his followers in
southern Lebanon,[184] in the comprehensive hostage-negotiations, any sign
of pragmatism was matched by the movement's militancy in the struggle
for the "liberation of Jerusalem". While Hizb'allah's militancy reflected
the movement's new position within Lebanon, it was also a joint effort by
Iran to sabotage the scheduled Middle East peace process. The closer relations between Hizb'allah's command leadership and official Iran was also
revealed by substantial Iranian injection of financial resources in southern
Lebanon affected by retaliatory warfare between IDF and the *Islamic
Resistance*. For example, an Iranian delegation visited the western Bi'qa
region and southern Lebanon for the supervision of Iranian food assistance
and distribution. It distributed 380 tons of food and medicine to 5,000
families "who had suffered in the recent Israeli bombardments."[185]

The conclusion of the Western hostage-crisis, with the release of the
last American hostage Terry Anderson on December 4, 1991, revealed
the convergence of interest between Hizb'allah and Iran in response to the
transformed political climate in Lebanon and elsewhere in the Middle
East. Hizb'allah's *volteface* over the hostage-crisis, and its subsequent participation within Lebanon's democratic process, demonstrated not only an
ability by Hizb'allah's command leadership to adapt rapidly to shifts in its
environment and in its relationship with Iran, as long as hostage-taking
served its useful political purposes, but also that the hostage-crisis itself
was intimately dependent on the internal position of the movement in
Lebanon as well as its relationship within Iran's clerical establishment.
While Iranian hardliners had no real desire to block the release of Western
foreigners as their value had been reduced due to the course of political
events, the appointment of Hojjat al-Islam Mohtashemi as Chairman of
the Defense Committee of the Iranian *Majlis*, in August 1991, not only
increased his political power in Iran but also neutralized any reason for the
obstruction of the release of hostages.

Although Hizb'allah obtained substantial concessions from Israel, in the
form of the release of 77 imprisoned members from Israel in return for
providing information on the fate of missing IDF soldiers, the return of
Sheikh Obeid remained deadlocked as long as Hizb'allah refused to make
any progress in the case of missing IAF navigator, Ron Arad.[186] After the

return of the bodies of Americans, William Buckley and Lt.Col. William Higgins, in late December 1991, Israel's disappointment with the stalemate of negotiations on Israeli POWs and MIAs between Israel and Hizb'allah, through the offices of the UN's special hostage envoy, was expressed by the assassination of Hizb'allah Secretary-General Sheikh Abbas al-Musawi on February 17, 1992. While Hizb'allah had previously voiced concern over the possibility of any form of American-led military or legal retribution against its SSA members and guards involved in the abduction of foreigners,[187] the selection and timing of the assassination of Sheikh al-Musawi by Israel was symbolic in many ways of his previous responsibility in the kidnapping and death of missing IDF servicemen on February 16, 1986 and in the case of the abduction of American Lt. Col. William Higgins on February 16, 1988.

The immediate election of Sheikh Hassan Nasserallah, an unsuccessful candidate in the Hizb'allah elections in May 1991, signalled an attempt by the command leadership to unify the movement and control their reaction to the death of Sheikh Abbas al-Musawi. Although the death of Sheikh al-Musawi increased the militancy of Hizb'allah in its resistance attacks against Israel, the movement's retaliatory response, a car bomb outside Israel's Embassy in Buenos Aires on March 17, 1992, which caused 30 deaths and 252 injuries, was not only claimed by *Islamic Jihad* in the name of "the Martyr Child Hussein" (Sheikh al-Mussawi's son) and occurred symbolically on *al-Quds* day, but the subsequent investigation also revealed close Iranian involvement in the operation.[188] However, the Hizb'allah, under the helm of Sheikh Nasserallah, demonstrated a firm commitment to not jeopardize its own new position within Lebanon's political environment as well as Iran's foreign policy through hostage-taking and terrorism against the West; rather the movement pursued a carefully coordinated dual-track approach of participation within the democratic process while focusing its resistance activity towards the liberation of Jerusalem through armed attacks against Israel. Although Sheikh Nasserallah was more closely aligned with the line of Iran's radical hardliner Hojjat al-Islam Mohtashemi than his predecessor, the political necessity of close affiliation with Iran's official leadership for its survival in Lebanon took precedence over any other individual or collective agendas within the Hizb'allah as well as motivations by Iran's revolutionist faction.[189] Under the Ta'if agreement, Hizb'allah handed over the Sheikh Abdallah barracks to the Lebanese army in the summer of 1992 while it retained a base for training and weaponry storage in the eastern Biq'a.[190]

Under the leadership of Sheikh Nasserallah, Hizb'allah's decision to participate in the Lebanese parliamentary elections in August/September

1992 and its achievement of winning 12 seats out of a total 128 was not only the result of a necessary adaptation to a new military-security and political environment in Lebanon after a decade of civil war but also recognition that the path towards the pan-Islamic goal of an creating an Islamic state in Lebanon would be more easily achieved through the democratic process rather than simply through a militant revolutionary approach. Under the main slogan "faithfullness to Islamic Resistance", Hizb'allah's electoral victory was not only achieved by the increased popularity of the movement's vastly expanded infrastructure of social and financial services to the impoverished Lebanese Shi'ite community but also through a carefully calibrated strategy, in close cooperation with Iran, of using its massive electoral machine in the various districts by transporting voters located in remote areas and by assessment of chances for victory running either independently or in coalition with others.[191] The *Majlis al-Shura* also issued a *fatwa* urging members to vote for Hizb'allah candidates in the election.[192] While the Hizb'allah has pushed in the Lebanese parliament for improvement of the social conditions in the neglected Shi'ite areas of Lebanon, it has also concentrated on demands for the elimination of the confessional system and official recognition of the *Islamic Resistance*. Although Hizb'allah has shown a willingness to work within the political system rather than from the outside, the revolutionary forces within the movement are dependent on developments in Lebanon and subject to the relationship between Iran and Syria in terms of ties to the movement and strategies for the Middle Eastern arena.

CONCLUSION

Analysis of the hostage-crisis in Lebanon yields that Hizb'allah was undisputably responsible for the aforementioned abductions of Westerners despite attempts to shield its complicity through the employment of covernames. Its organisational framework was not only sophisticated and assimilated according to Iranian clerical designs but also closely integrated with several key Iranian institutions which provided it with both necessary weaponry and training to successfully confront self-proclaimed Islamic enemies and invaluable financial support for it to generate as well as sustain massive support and recruitment among the Shi'a community at the expense of other confessional groups. Hizb'allah's close working relationship with Iranian clergy and official institutions suffered also from major inherent constraints in the projection of Iranian clerical factionalism onto the organisation and in relation to the changing dynamics of Lebanon's civil war environment. These influences were most evidently manifest through Hizb'allah's practice of hostage-taking of Westerners, most notably in the release process rather than decisions to initiate these acts.

The initiation of abduction of Westerners has demonstrated a strong causal linkage between events (internal Lebanese, regional or international) and motivation for hostage-taking acts by the Hizb'allah and often on behalf of Iran. A close convergence of interests between Hizb'allah and Iran governed hostage-taking activity in Lebanon until the end of 1986 without any signs or impact of any clerical factionalism either within the organisation or from Iran in the process of abductions or releases of hostages. Subsequent Hizb'allah discord with Iran was a manifestation of rivalry within Iran's clerical establishment which affected the organisation directly as its closest Iranian allies were demoted from positions in institutions at work within the organisation in Lebanon. However, the imposition of Iranian clerical factionalism on the movement's activity has been most notable in the process of the release of Western hostages rather than in the actual abductions. Factional rivalry in Iran was also translated into clerical infighting within the Hizb'allah and disobedience towards Iran, governed by longstanding individual relationships stemming from the Najaf period in Iraq. While efforts to obstruct the release of Western hostages by Iranian opposition factions were designed to undermine more moderate Iranian foreign policy towards the West, the motivations to delay any releases by Hizb'allah were motivated by its preoccupation towards readjustment of its position within the Lebanese civil war and internal clerical rivalry within the movement over its present and future direction. As insurance of its position within Lebanon and against retribution by Western governments, the hostage-issue became increasingly dependent on guarantees of Hizb'allah's own survival in post-civil war Lebanon. Hizb'allah's *volte face* over the hostage issue in 1991 was largely the result of a *quid pro quo* arrangement with Iran and Syria that strengthened the organisation's position within Lebanon. A reduction of the influence of the more radical Iranian clergy in Iranian politics paralleled a demotion in positions of its closest allies within the Hizb'allah.

The influence of the internal Lebanese environment on any progress for the release of hostages underlines the dynamics of Hizb'allah's relationship with Syria, closely determined by the status of the Iranian-Syrian relations in the Lebanese, regional and international arena.

4 The Influence of the Iranian-Syrian Relationship On the Hizb'allah

INTRODUCTION

The close involvement by Iran and Syria in the hostage-taking of Western foreigners by the Hizb'allah has been evident in their roles as both active participants in some of the abductions and as facilitators in all negotiations for the release of hostages. Although the Iranian-Syrian partnership over Hizb'allah activity has been a useful foreign policy instrument in the extraction of political and economic concessions from Western governments whose citizens are held hostage, the relationship between Iran and Syria cannot be viewed as monolithic but rather marked by cooperation and friction, at times, projected onto the Lebanese arena. While Iran and Syria found some common ground for operational cooperation against common enemies, most notably against Iraq and Israel, the Iranian-Syrian alliance has also been marked by irreconcilable differences with respect to their interests and aspirations over the future of Lebanon. While Syria's ambition to gain local hegemony over Lebanese affairs stands opposed to Iran's and Hizb'allah's ideological vision of an Islamic Republic of Lebanon, any strain in their relationship also stems from the underlying and contradictory political ideologies of the two regimes.[1] Although the nature of the supranational pan-Islamic regime of Iran is inherently incompatible with the secular and socialist-oriented pan-Arabism espoused by the Alawite political leadership of Syria,[2] the Iranian-Syrian nexus has converged in a marriage of convenience against common enemies in an atmosphere of crisis and political isolation in the Middle East. As such, an understanding of the basis for and evolution of the Iranian-Syrian relationship over the last decade with reference to Lebanon is necessary as it is not only a direct determinant of the position of the Hizb'allah and its hostage-taking activity. It also influenced the process of the release of foreign hostages as well as the motivation of the two regimes in the resolution of the hostage-crisis in accordance with achievement of economic and political concessions from Western governments.

110

By admission from many leading Hizb'allah and Iranian clerical officials, the issue of the foreign hostages has not only been intertwined with the nature of the movement's relationship with its patrons over Lebanese issues but also deeply influenced by the dynamics of the Iranian-Syrian relationship either in alignment with, or opposition to, their regional and international agendas.

THE BASIS OF THE IRANIAN-SYRIAN RELATIONSHIP

In the post-revolutionary period of Iran, Syria has remained Iran's closest and only ally in the Arab world. While Syrian-Iranian relations were marked by animosity in the pre-revolutionary period, the basis for the newly-found relationship, which gradually developed into a full-fledged working alliance, was rooted in historical antecedents and regional political developments in the Middle East.

Prior to the 1979 Islamic Revolution in Iran, the hostility between Syria's Ba'ath regime and the Shah's Iran was primarily based on Iran's close relationship with Israel, Syria's self-proclaimed arch-enemy, within the context of the Arab-Israeli conflict, and the Shah's friendly relations with pro-Western Arab states hostile to Syria. It was, therefore, only natural for Syria to cultivate links with emerging Iranian Shi'a opposition movements led by Ayatollah Khomeini.[3] While Syria supported individual opponents of the Pahlavi regime, most notably Ibrahim Yazdi, Mustafa Chamran and Sadeq Qotbzadeh,[4] the challenge by the Syrian *Muslim Brotherhood* to the non-Islamic character of the al-Asad regime in 1973 forced the Alawite élite to consolidate links with emerging Shi'a individuals and movements outside Syria.[5] The cultivation of Syrian relations with the leader of the Shi'a community, Imam Musa al-Sadr, proved useful as it extended Syrian involvement with an emerging and important confessional group within Lebanon, a vital component of Syria's political ambitions. More importantly, Syria's amicable relations with Musa al-Sadr enhanced the religious credentials of the Syrian ruling regime as al-Sadr issued a fatwa in 1973 which conferred legitimacy on the Alawites as *bona fide* Shi'i Muslims.[6] Syria's relationship with Musa al-Sadr enhanced not only the positions of both the Alawite regime and the Lebanese Shi'a community but also provided Syria with an important Islamic ally in efforts to consolidate its influence over Lebanon. In fact, Syria's close affiliation with Musa al-Sadr and the training of Iranian oppositionists by the Amal movement facilitated and consolidated co-operation between Syria and the future Iranian clerical leadership.[7] As a result, the Amal movement became an important instrument for Syrian policy in Lebanon.[8] Syria's vital interests in Lebanon, extending from military and security needs to the political and economic realm, led to unrelenting moves by al-Asad to exploit the Lebanese civil war as a pretext to extend Syrian hegemony over Lebanon and as a means to promote broader aspirations on the inter-Arab scene and against its Zionist enemy, Israel. While Amal remained Asad's loyal proxy in Lebanon, Syrian moves to exploit the Lebanese civil war through continuous realignment with an array of Lebanese confessional factions, in order to maintain a Syrian-controlled military balance between the warring factions which served to preserve and enhance it's interests in Lebanon, was undermined by friction in Syria's inter-Arab relationships during the late 1970s. In particular, Syria felt increasingly isolated following the Egyptian-Israeli *rapprochement* with the conclusion of the Camp David accord in 1977 and its rapidly deteriorating relations with Jordan and Iraq. As a result, the Islamic Revolution in Iran in 1979 provided Syria with an ideal opportunity to redress the imbalances of its intra-Arab relations, to rejuvenate the rejectionist camp in the Arab-Israeli conflict, to contain Islamic opposition within Syria, as well as to forge and ensure closer ties and continued influence with the Lebanese Shi'a community.[9]

A common opposition against Iraq's ascendancy in inter-Arab politics served as the unifying axis for the newly-found alliance between Ba'athist Syria and Shi'ite Iran.[10] For Syria, an alliance with Iran provided it with a useful means to counter Iraqi subversive activity within both Lebanon and Syria while discrediting and weakening the militancy of the Syrian *Muslim Brotherhood*.[11] Also, Iraq's invasion of Iran in 1980 not only threatened the regional balance of power but also detracted from the Arab-Israeli conflict. For Iran, the problem of developing relations with Syria's secular regime quickly disappeared with the implications of Iraq's invasion, especially for strategic expediency in Teheran's foreign policy.[12] An alliance with Syria against Iraq eliminated the perception of the Iran-Iraq war as a conflict purely between the Arabs and the Persians. Syrian support against Iraq also provided Iran with invaluable political support and material assistance in its war with Iraq, especially in terms of providing a distraction for Iraq's armed forces for the defence of its other border with Syria and providing alternative channels for the supply of armaments.[13] Apart from the valuable role of Syria as mediator between Iran and the Persian Gulf states,[14] Syria joined Iran in anti-Iraqi economic warfare, most evidently displayed by the closure of the Syrian border to Iraq and cutting off the passage of Iraqi oil via Syria on April 8, 1982. Using Iraq's support of the Syrian *Muslim Brotherhood* as a pretext for the closure of Iraq's pipelines, Syria's action caused a major economic crisis in Iraq as it curtailed over \$5 billion per year in Iraq's foreign exchange earnings.[15] Due to Syrian dependence on Iraqi oil, this measure followed the conclusion of a formal economic agreement between Iran and Syria a month earlier, whereby Iran agreed to supply Syria with 8 million tons of free-bartered crude oil per year (in return for a reciprocal Syrian export of phosphate to Iran). In fact, the agreement was for Iran to supply 1 million tons of oil per annum free of charge and 5-7 million tons at a discount of one-third of posted prices.[16] Syria's action was also due to a significant reduction in its financial subventions from Arab regimes, originally amounting to \$1.8 million per year in recognition for its frontline status in the struggle against Israel pledged under the terms of the 1978 Baghdad summit, who were collectively hostile to Syria's pro-Iranian policy.[17] While the joint economic agreement between Iran and Syria as well as the closure of the Syrian pipeline transformed the Iranian-Syrian relationship into a full-fledged partnership, Syrian substitution of dependence on Iraqi oil for Iranian oil left it vulnerable to Iranian pressures.[18] As Syria's anti-Iraq policy led it to increased political and economic isolation in the Arab world, its economic dependency on Iran and its closely pledged allegiance to Teheran's foreign policy produced friction and tension in the Syrian-Iranian alliance as Syria had difficulty in balancing Iran's confrontational foreign policy and polemics within the framework of its own relations with the Arab world. Despite this difficulty, Syria has successfully managed to exploit its relationship with Iran by serving as a bridge between Iran and the Arab world, both in terms of providing valuable mediation between the two sides and in persuading Gulf states that Iran's relationship with Syria guarantees their own security especially to influence the Gulf states to increase their financial contributions to Syria.[19]

While Syria's *raison d'être* for its alliance with Iran against Iraq was based on the detraction of Iraq's defection from Arab ranks in their struggle against Israel, particularly as Iraq's military strength could not only be used against Israel but would also ensure "strategic parity" between the Arabs and Israel,[20] the Arab world remained passive and left Syria to its own devices to confront Israel's invasion of Lebanon in 1982. In fact, according to al-Asad: "The Iran of Khomeini is anti-Israel. Iran was the only country to send forces when Israel invaded Lebanon in 1982."[21] Syria's increased isolation in the Arab world, coupled with Iranian rhetorical calls for the transformation of the war in Lebanon into a total war against Israel, led to a military agreement between Iran and Syria which allowed the entry of Iranian Pasdaran contingents into Lebanon.[22]

The decision by Iran to dispatch a military contingent to Lebanon was a reflection of the success of Iran's massive military offensive in the Gulf war in which all Iraqi-occupied Iranian territory had been recovered while Iraq appeared weak as it used Israel's invasion of Lebanon as an excuse for suggesting an end to hostilities in order to confront the common enemy, Israel.[23] While the diversion of IRGC units from the Iraqi front to Lebanon was intended to reveal for domestic and foreign consumption that Iran's war with Iraq was successful and under control, it was also an opportunity for Iran to demonstrate practically its serious commitment to the "export of the revolution" and its support to all Islamic liberation movements worldwide.[24] As such, the anarchical environment of Lebanon's civil war, coupled with Iran's close relationships within the Shi'a community, provided Iran with an ideal opportunity to exert its influence and construct a Shi'ite power-base beyond its borders.[25] From Lebanon, Iran could transcend the Persian-Arab linguistic barriers through the Hizb'allah and reach out to a larger Arab audience in the preaching of Islamic ideology and government.[26] More significantly, the presence of an Islamic Pasdaran contingent in Lebanon provided Iran with a window of opportunity to not only actively participate militarily in the Arab-Israeli conflict via proxy but also to affect the Arab-Israeli and, consequently, wider Middle East conflicts and politics.[27] Iran's presence and influence would also be used to manipulate the behaviour and policies of regional and international actors in any way connected with Lebanese politics through acts of terrorism and hostage-taking.[28]

The establishment of an Iranian headquarters in the Syrian border village of Zebdani and the arrival of the first 800 Pasdaran, later reinforced by another 700 Pasdaran dispersed among villages in the Biq'a, came at the invitation of Syria.[29] For Syria, Iran's incursion into Lebanon provided invaluable support in its efforts to counter both the Western and Israeli presence and intervention in Lebanon. This became increasingly vital in order to oppose the American-endorsed Gemayel regime in Lebanon and to sabotage the Lebanon-Israel Agreement of May 17, 1983.[30] While neither Syria nor Iran wished to engage these enemies directly in Lebanon, the continous harassment by Hizb'allah against the Israeli and American military forces provided them with a valuable instrument to maintain and accomplish their strategic interests in Lebanon, most notably the expulsion of the West's political and military presence from Lebanese territory. The emergence of the Hizb'allah provided Iran and Syria with a viable alternative as well as a solution to its previous support of Fatah.[31] Although Iran's military presence supported Syria's strategic objectives in countering internal political developments contrary to its interests and foreign presence on Lebanese soil, Syria remained in firm control over Iran's access to Lebanon in terms of numbers and frequency of visits, as the Pasdaran was dependent on being inserted to the Biq'a via Syria.

The Iranian-Syrian alliance has been manifest in the Lebanese arena, through the Pasdaran's support of the Hizb'allah, as a fluctuation between close cooperation and friction determined by internal as well as regional developments while it has demonstrated the conflicting ideological positions of Iran and Syria and their vision for the future of Lebanon. In particular, the conflicts between Iran and Syria basically stemmed from threats to Syrian hegemony and designs over Lebanon in the form of Hizb'allah activity.[32] Apart from the fact that the Hizb'allah's vision of Lebanon stands against the ideological foundations of the Syrian regime, tension in the Syrian-Iranian axis has come from unpredictable Hizb'allah activity which has worsened Syria's image in the Arab world and in the West.[33] As a result, Syria has not only attempted to distance itself from involvement with, or control over, the Hizb'allah but has also kept the nature of its relationship with Iran low-profile. In some cases, Syria's political and economic relations have been seriously damaged by Hizb'allah hostage-taking activity as Syria has been closely identified with the movement and its patron. While Syria has been forced to crackdown against the Hizb'allah in order to limit its expansion and domination over the Shi'a community, it has also attempted to keep the Hizb'allah under control in order to avoid the possibility of a direct military confrontation with Israel, provoked by the movement's uncontrolled resistance attacks. In turn, friction between the Hizb'allah and Syria must also be measured against the nature of the Syrian-Iranian relationship over time and the impact of Hizb'allah activity on Iran's own geostrategic interests in Lebanon and elsewhere. While the strains between Iran and Syria naturally impacted on the issue of the release of Western hostages, periods of close cooperation have also led to the decision by Hizb'allah to abduct Western citizens in accordance with the advancement of specific foreign policy objectives by both Iran and Syria.[34] Apart from Hizb'allah's own agenda in the abduction of foreigners, the impact of the often troublesome Syrian-Iranian alliance and its superimposition on the internal Lebanese scene must be viewed in the context of individual motivations by these states to either intitiate hostage-taking or facilitate its resolution in order to advance a specific foreign policy objective within or external to the Lebanon.[35] While the Iranian-Syrian relationship within Lebanon can be characterized by close joint cooperation in the struggle against the Israeli and Western presence until their withdrawal in 1985 and subsequent increased friction due to Syria's attempt to exert its hegemony over Lebanon, it is necessary to balance their internal Lebanese agenda against the Syrian-Iranian requirements in the foreign policy arena on the regional and international level.[36]

PHASE I: IRANIAN-SYRIAN COOPERATION AGAINST WESTERN ENEMIES (1982–85)

The introduction of the Pasdaran contingent to Lebanon's Biq'a area was accomplished by the imminent threat posed by Israel's 1982 invasion to Syria and its interests in Lebanon. While the first Hizb'allah abduction of David Dodge came at the behest of the Pasdaran contingent as a result of the previous kidnapping of four Iranian officials of the Iranian Embassy in Beirut, most notably IRGC commander Ahmad Moteveselian, the major concern of Syria and Iran was joint cooperation against their external enemies within Lebanon in order to confront Israel and the regime of Amin Gemayel, perceived by Hizb'allah to be protected by the presence of the MNF.[37] The imminent conclusion of the American-sponsored peace treaty between Lebanon and Israel, the 17 May 1983 agreement, precipitated the first car bomb attack on the U.S. Embassy in Beirut on April 18, 1983, which clearly revealed the hallmarks of a jointly Iranian-Syrian supervised Hizb'allah operation.[38] While the Hizb'allah, with close Syrian cooperation, continued to confront the MNF in an effort to expel Western influence from Lebanon and to undermine the Gemayel regime, Iran had other foreign policy motivations related to its war with Iraq which accounted for its close involvement in the October 1983 Hizb'allah twin-suicide attacks against the American and French MNF contingents in Lebanon.[39] Although Iran's hostility towards the U.S. administration stemmed from its support for Israel in attacking Lebanon and its direct political and military involvement within the civil war, Iranian concerns over American and French support for Iraq, mainly through the supply of arms, contributed to the decision to strike at these enemies through proxy in Lebanon. In particular, the main point of friction was over French arms deliveries to Iraq of Super-Etendard aircraft equipped with Exocet missiles which Iran viewed as the main reason for the survival of the Ba'athist regime and the prolongation of the war.[40] In fact, Iraq owed $7 billion to France and absorbed almost 40 percent of all French arms export.[41] Between 1977 and 1985, France sold more than $11.8 billion of high-technology weaponry to Iraq, including 113 Mirage F1 fighter aircrafts and three quarters of French total exports of Exocet missiles.[42] At the same time, Iran was particularly angered over the refusal by the French government to pay between $1–1.5 billion owed from the days of the Shah and supply Iran with military-related equipment.[43] Iranian hostility was also due to the decision by the American administration to launch *Operation Staunch* in 1983, halting all shipments of arms to Iran, while it extended $2 billion in trade credit to Iraq.[44] Prior to the suicide operations by Hizb'allah in Lebanon against the American and French MNF contingents, Iran warned that the provision of armaments to Iran's enemies would provoke retaliatory punishment.[45] In particular, Iran charged France to be a co-belligerent in the war after France leased five Super-Etendard aircraft with Exocet missiles to Iraq in October 1983.

While the American and French MNF contingents in Lebanon provided Iran with the ideal targets for retaliation through proxy, Iran also used combined elements from Iraq's *al-Da'wa al-Islamiyya* and the Lebanese *Islamic Amal* to strike at U.S. and French targets in Kuwait, among the most loyal Arab-monarchies extending substantial military and financial support to Iraq, in December 1983.[46] This subversion by Iran was also intended to persuade Arab Persian Gulf states not to provide financial assistance to the Iraqi war effort.[47] While the arrest and conviction of the seventeen *al-Da'wa* terrorists motivated Hizb'allah to abduct five American citizens and one Frenchman, as evident by the connections of the abductions with the progress of the trial in Kuwait, the nature of the targets mirrored also close alignment with Iranian foreign policy in its confrontation with the American and French administrations over support to Iraq. In particular, the close convergence between Hizb'allah abductions and Iranian foreign policy was not only revealed by the abduction of William Buckley, the CIA-station chief in Beirut, but also by the kidnappings of two Kuwaitis and a Saudi citizen in 1984.[48]

In Lebanon, Iranian-Syrian cooperation in Hizb'allah's attacks against the MNF was rewarded by their withdrawal in February 1984 and the Gemayel regime's abrogation, under heavy Syrian pressure, of the 17 May 1983 accord between Lebanon and Israel.[49] The close bilateral relations between Iran and Syria were evident by the frequency of high-level visits between the two states and by Iran's promised delivery of one million tons of oil free of charge to Syria in 1984.[50] Having accomplished a major victory with the expulsion of the MNF contingent, Hizb'allah concentrated on confrontation with the Israeli presence in southern Lebanon, with the active support of both Iran and Syria. While the Hizb'allah held three American hostages, as an American and a French citizen had been rescued and released by Amal in April 1984, the movement's respite in the abduction of foreigners reflected its concentration in the resistance against Israel while Syria and Iran remained pre-occupied with Lebanon and the war effort with Iraq respectively.

At the end of 1984, Iran's involvement with the hijacking of a Kuwaiti airliner by *Islamic Amal* and the abduction of two American hostages in December 1984 and in January 1985 reflected solidarity with Hizb'allah's concern over the fate of the 17 al-Da'wa prisoners held in Kuwait. While Iran's relations with Kuwait continued to be tense due to the treatment and expulsion of Iranian citizens in Kuwait and over its cooperation with Iraq, the concentration on American citizens as targets reflected the influential position of the U.S. over Kuwait in an effort to pressure for the release of the *al-Da'wa* prisoners. It may have also been due to the formal U.S. resumption of diplomatic relations with Iraq on November 26, 1988.[51] While these subversive efforts failed, Hizb'allah emerged victorious with the announcement of Israel's decision of a three-phase unilateral withdrawal from Lebanon, between January 20 and June 6, 1985. Accordingly, the Hizb'allah escalated its abduction campaign of Western foreigners while it accelerated its confrontation with Israel. Although the escalatory Hizb'allah's attacks on Israel suited the strategic designs of both Syria and Iran, a few signs of tension emerged in the Iranian-Syrian relationship. Apart from Syrian differences with Iran over the continuation of the Gulf war and Iran's persistant attacks on Ba'athist ideology, a source of tension stemmed from Syria's rejection of Iranian offers of both sending more IRGC units to Lebanon and allowing those present an active combat role against Israel.[52] However, any tension in their relationship was temporarily overshadowed by the Iranian *Majlis*' approval in 1985 to supply Syria yearly with one million tons of crude oil, free of charge, and five million tons at the discount of $2.5 per barrel over a ten-year period to lessen the impact of reduced Arab support.[53] This tension would heighten again in 1986 when Iran cut the supply of oil to pressure Syria to honour its debt repayment to Iran.

Apart from Hizb'allah's own reasons for the abduction of Western foreigners, it coordinated the kidnappings with Iran as a leverage in its patron's foreign policy disputes with both the American and French administrations. The abduction of five American citizens by the Hizb'allah was not only in response to the continued imprisonment of the *al-Da'wa* members in Kuwait but also to U.S. support for Iraq, in terms of the renewal of diplomatic ties and continued military and financial assistance, and the U.S. refusal to recognize Iranian compensation's claims before the Hague Joint Committee.[54] Furthermore, tensions between Iran and the U.S. were exacerbated by the American administration's claims of Iran's role in the sponsoring of terrorism. While the abduction of American citizens represented a mixture of interests by both Hizb'allah and Iran, the case of the abduction of five French citizens was clearly aligned with Iranian foreign policy motivations. Apart from Iranian demands on repayment of the $1 billion loan, made by the Shah's government in 1974 to the French Atomic Energy Commission for a uranium separation plant (Eurodiff project),[55] the abduction of French citizens was connected with France's continued arms shipments to Iraq and Arab Persian Gulf states, most notably the supply of Mirage 2000 aircraft to Saudi Arabia and Iraq, and the harbouring of exiled Iranian opposition groups in France.[56] It also represented an effort by Iran to obtain the release of Anis Naccache from France due to his longstanding friendship with Ahmad Khomeini and Mohsen Rafiqdust as well as with leading Hizb'allah members. In order to increase the pressure on France to concede to Iranian demands, the Hizb'allah attacked the French UNIFIL contingent in southern Lebanon.[57]

After the completion of the American and Israeli withdrawals from Lebanon, which culminated with Hizb'allah's hijacking of TWA-847 in June 1985, Iranian-Syrian differences became apparent over Syria's attempt to impose political hegemony over Lebanon. In an effort to derail Syria's attempt to end the civil war and transform Lebanon into a Syrian satellite, through the so-called Tripartite Agreement, Iran urged the Muslims in Lebanon to rise and establish an Islamic Republic.[58] This marked the beginning of tacit rivalry between Syria and Iranian efforts to expand their influence over Lebanon through Hizb'allah activity. As a result, while Syria moved to confront and crackdown on Hizb'allah activity in order to advance its own political agenda in Lebanon, the movement became increasingly dependent on Iranian support and, more importantly, its ability to influence Syria's policy and position *vis-à-vis* the Hizb'allah.

PHASE II: INCREASED IRANIAN-SYRIAN RIVALRY OVER HIZB'ALLAH (1985–92)

While the American administration pursued a confrontational policy towards Iran, the initiation of a clandestine policy of providing armaments to Iran via Israel in August 1985 led to a cessation in the abduction of American hostages by Hizb'allah in cooperation with Iran. Instead, Iran focused on its confrontation with France as it had failed to meet any of its previously stated foreign policy demands for the release of French hostages. This became manifest in an Iranian-Hizb'allah orchestrated terrorist campaign in France between December 1985 and September 1986, which led to 13 deaths and 303 injuries. This was motivated by

Hizb'allah's own organisational requirements and, more significantly, by Iran in an effort to alter French foreign policy. While the abduction of eight French citizens, between February and May 1986, was initiated by Hizb'allah in response to the expulsion of two Iraqi *al-Da'wa* members from France to Iraq, the timing of Iran's escalation of terrorism against France occurred within the framework of the general elections in the country in an effort to force concessions in terms of repayment of the French outstanding debt to Iran and in order to block French arms shipments to Iraq. As Iran also demanded a complete *volte face* in French foreign policy in the Middle East, it placed additional pressure on France through Hizb'allah attacks against its UNIFIL contingent in southern Lebanon.[59] The abduction campaign of French citizens was also motivated by an accelerated effort to gain the release of Anis Naccache as well as to force the expulsion of leading exiled Iranian opposition leaders living in France.

Iranian relations with the member-states of the so-called *Steadfastness Front*, especially Syria and Libya, were brought even closer as a result of the accusations by the West against these three states for their support of terrorism, especially in the aftermath of both the American raid on Libya and the imposition of political and economic sanctions against Syria for its involvement in the Nizar Hindawi affair, of April 1986. Due to the central role of Great Britain in these operations, the Hizb'allah abducted two British citizens with the active support of both Syria and Iran while Syria continuously emphasized the restoration of diplomatic relations as a prerequisite for any attempt to facilitate the release of British hostages. While the West's accusations of Syrian and Iranian involvement in terrorism increased their isolation and strengthened their bilateral relations, areas of disagreement surfaced from Syria with Iran, especially over Hizb'allah activity in Lebanon. Apart from an Iranian-Syrian dispute over oil prices and Syria's inability for repayments, which at the time amounted to over $2 billion[60] and led to a reduction in Iran's supply of oil to Syria in mid-1986, Syrian disagreement with Iran came as a response to the escalation in Hizb'allah activity in southern Lebanon which highlighted the lack of control Syria exercised over Lebanon while it directly threatened to bring Israel into an all-out confrontation with Syria.[61] Furthermore, Hizb'allah's abduction of Westerners, with the active support of Iran, also undermined the internal and external perception of Syria's firm control over Lebanese affairs while it damaged its international image in Syrian efforts to rehabilitate its relations with Western governments. As a result, it is not surprising that tension in the Syrian-Iranian relationship surfaced publicly with the leak of the U.S.-Iranian arms-for-hostages deal in the pro-Syrian weekly *al-Shira* in Lebanon. Consequently, while Iran and Syria maintained good relations on the strategic level, ensured by Syria's dependence on Iranian oil which was resupplied after Syrian veiled signals of a possible *rapprochement* with Iraq,[62] they differed increasingly on the ground in Lebanon over Hizb'allah's activity and designs for the future of Lebanon. This was exacerbated by Syrian disillusionment with Iranian dealings with the U.S. through secret arms-for-hostages deals as well as Iran's significant extension of financial and military support to the Hizb'allah and its rapid expansion of recruitment within the Lebanese Shi'a community at the expense of pro-Syrian Amal.

Although the *al-Shira* revelation of the U.S.-Iranian arms-for-hostages signified tension in the Iranian-Syrian relationship, it also revealed the imposition of Iranian clerical factionalism over Hizb'allah activity in Lebanon. Apart from the three anti-American abductions by Hizb'allah in September-October 1986, which undermined any U.S.-Iranian *rapprochement*, Hizb'allah's unprecedented campaign of abductions in January 1987 led to a direct Syrian military intervention and clashes with Hizb'allah fighters in Beirut. In particular, the actual level of confrontation was revealed by Hizb'allah's abduction of 14 Syrian soldiers in the Beirut suburb of al-Basta. While the abductions of four Americans, a Frenchman, and a British citizen were motivated as a response to the arrest of leading SSA operatives in Europe, which coincided with a series of Iranian attempts to undermine Kuwait's hosting of the Islamic Conference Organization,[63] Syria's action against the movement, without prior discussions with Iran, signalled an effort to restore its relations with Western governments by acting to resolve the hostage-problem as well as to reassert its authority over Lebanon by limiting the movement's activity in Beirut. These tensions assumed the form of protracted Amal-Hizb'allah warfare in Beirut and in southern Lebanon and retaliatory attacks between Hizb'allah and Syrian military units. The restrictions on the Hizb'allah's freedom of movement and activity led it to a reorientation from hostage-taking activity to armed confrontation against Israel, as evident by the substantial military and financial support from Iran for the movement's shift from clandestine guerrilla operations to semi-regular military units. In particular, as a conciliatory measure to Iran, Syria promised support to Hizb'allah in its war with Israel in the South by supplying weaponry to the movement, to allow Hizb'allah fighters to be deployed in the South and allow Iranian Pasdaran to establish command posts in the South[64] As evident by the abduction of an American citizen in June 1987, Syria opposed any challenges to its control of Beirut and mounted extensive searches for the hostages while placing pressure on the Pasdaran

122 Hizb'allah in Lebanon

contingent by confining it to the Biq'a area. While the abduction was considered to be a reaction by Iran to the U.S. expanded role in the Gulf (protecting reflagged Kuwaiti tankers) it signified that Hizb'allah abduction of Western foreigners was directly incompatible with Syrian efforts to consolidate its hegemony over Lebanon. As a result, Hizb'allah could no longer count on Syrian tacit cooperation in the abduction of Western foreigners as Syria threatened direct military action against the movement while it made gestures to improve its relationships with Western governments and pressure Iran in negotiations over oil supply.[65] The friction between Iran and Syria over the limitation on Hizb'allah activity and Syrian efforts to break its own isolation, not only towards the West but also Arab states,[66] was clearly evident by Iranian requests for assurances that any hostage release would circumvent the possibility of Syrian custody and credit for their release.[67] It also led to the establishment of a Hizb'allah unit in Beirut to challenge Syria through direct military operations. Consequently, due to the tight Syrian security over Beirut, the Hizb'allah was forced to abstain from any new abduction of Western foreigners; rather, it used previously kidnapped hostages as a useful leverage against Iran's enemies, especially in the case of it's intensified dispute with France in June 1987 over French arrests of a Hizb'allah network and siege of the Iranian Embassy in Paris, which led to the rupture of their diplomatic relations on July 17, 1987. Although the diplomatic confrontation between Iran and France was ostensibly over the release of Wahid Gordji and arrested Hizb'allah members, it also concerned demands by Iran for the repayment of a $1.5 billion Eurodiff loan, the halt of future French arms shipments to Iraq, especially the delay in delivery of twenty Mirage fighter aircraft due in Iraq in 1988, as well as an end to the French oil embargo with Iran.[68] Furthermore, Iran also requested a reduction in the French naval presence in the Persian Gulf as well as the expulsion of a number of anti-Khomeini activists and Iranian opposition leaders living in France.[69] The Iranian-French "embassy war" was defused after the exhange of Wahid Gordji for the retaliatory detention of French consul, Paul Torri, in Iran in November 1987.[70]

While the Hizb'allah abduction of British citizen, Terry Waite, in January 1987 had occurred in response to the intermediary's inability to make any progress in the case of the al-Da'wa prisoners in Kuwait, it resulted in serious friction between Syria and Iran, most notably through threats of Syrian military action against Iran's Embassy in Beirut where Waite was allegedly held before presumably transferred to the Biq'a (infact, Waite was always held in Beirut). Although Syria attempted to obtain the release of Terry Waite in an effort to restore its relations with

Great Britain (Anglo-Iranian relations deteriorated with a diplomatic crisis in May 1987), it became clear that the fate of all British hostages was intertwined with Iranian demands for the release of the four Iranians missing since 1982 as well as the withdrawal of British warships from the Persian Gulf and the resumption of normal and full diplomatic relations. As Iranian hostility towards Britain's participation in U.S. naval Gulf operations in August 1987 resulted in the closure of Iranian arms procurement offices in London,[71] Iran focused on the issue of the four missing Iranians as a means of leverage to restore Anglo-Iranian diplomatic relations.

While Syria also linked efforts to release the British hostages with resumption of diplomatic relations, it concentrated on pressuring the Hizb'allah on the issue of the American hostages through coercion as a means of normalising relations with the American administration as well as containing Hizb'allah's continued expansion and incompatible activity with Syrian interests in Lebanon. In the case of the abduction of four American hostages in January 1987, it would appear that the Hizb'allah initiated these kidnappings for its own organisational reasons, which was marked by its close solidarity with the Palestinian uprising in the occupied territories as shown by the nature of the demands as well as by the emergence of a new *nom de guerre*. Rather than in alignment with Iranian motivations, especially as the movement's most loyal radical allies within Iran's clerical establishment were relegated to the background at a time when Iran attempted to exert more control over the Hizb'alllah while it was engaged in negotiations with the American administration over the release of Iranian assets. As these abductions were clearly incompatible with Syrian efforts to extend its hegemony over Lebanon, leading to tension and friction in the Iranian-Syrian alliance, the Hizb'allah's newfound solidarity with the Palestinian uprising, by connecting Israel to the hostage-issue, suited Iranian interests as leverage in the economic and political realm against the American administration's refusal to release frozen Iranian assets and to limit its military intervention in the Persian Gulf.

Notwithstanding the convergence of motivations between Hizb'allah and Iran in these abductions, the movement's hostage-taking activity was not only a direct challenge to Syrian efforts to consolidate control over Lebanon but also served to highlight the underlying friction between Syria and Iran, especially in terms of using Lebanon in their own individual foreign policy agendas. Iran's diplomatic intervention in the "war of the camps" in late 1986 and its support for anti-Syrian Sunni movements in Lebanon, most notably the *Tawhid* movement in Tripoli,[72] reinforced the fact that Iran and Syria often worked without consideration for each other's individual agendas in Lebanon.[73] While tension between Iran and Syria over Lebanon was highlighted by requests from Syria to Iran of the handing over of Imad Mughniyya, Iran's challenge to Syrian hegemony was most evident by the protracted warfare between Amal and Hizb'allah, which was initiated with the abduction of Lt. Col. William Higgins by the Hizb'allah in February 1988. While the Amal-Hizb'allah warfare surfaced the tensions between Iran and Syria in the challenge by their proxies for control over Beirut and southern Lebanon, Iranian control over the movement was increasingly difficult to maintain as revealed by Hizb'allah's continued confrontation with Amal despite Iranian efforts to mediate a solution between the warring Shi'a factions. Apart from being a direct affront to Amal's security position, this was clear from the fact that Hizb'allah concentrated on internal Lebanese issues directed against Israel, most notably the withdrawal of Israel's military from Lebanon and the release of all Lebanese and Palestinians held by Israel and SLA in the detention camps in south Lebanon, and to undermine the possibility of any Syrian participation in a U.S.-led Middle East peace initiative. In particular, Hizb'allah members protested against the tour of U.S. envoys to Syria and Lebanon by marching in the streets while calling for the execution of kidnapped Lt.Col. William Higgins.[74] The kidnapping of the American hostage seems to have been initiated by the movement itself in order to confront Amal's hegemony in southern Lebanon and the presence of UNIFIL. Apart from obstructing Hizb'allah's resistance against Israel, UNIFIL was accused of serving as a front for Western intelligence agencies. In particular, Sheikh Fadlallah claimed the French UNIFIL team was conducting large-scale surveys on the political and sectarian affiliations of the inhabitants of south Lebanon.[75] The kidnapping of Higgins was also used by Hizb'allah and Iran in an attempt to sabotage the *rapprochement* between Syria and the American administration, as evidenced by the visit of Richard Murphy, the U.S. undersecretary for the Near East, to Syria in February-March 1988. Furthermore, the concentration in use of American hostages by Iran was also a reflection of the release of France's last hostages in May 1988, on the eve of the French presidential elections, after agreement between Iran and France to settle certain outstanding differences, most notably clear with the immediate French agreement to repay over $300 million in a second tranche of the outstanding Eurodiff loan.[76]

While the abduction of Lt. Col. William Higgins served as a pretext for a Syrian effort to crackdown on the Hizb'allah through its proxy Amal in the South, in order to advance its designs in Lebanon by demonstrating to the American administration that it was firmly committed to confronting Shi'a extremism in the form of Hizb'allah abductions of foreigners and uncontrolled attacks against Israel, Syria was forced to intervene militarily in order to rescue Amal from defeat in Beirut. Despite the fact that Syria rejected Iranian offers of the insertion of a joint Iranian-Syrian security force in Beirut, Syria had to pursue a conciliatory policy towards the Hizb'allah in order to avoid an escalation of tension in the Iranian-Syrian relationship, evidenced by the Syrian-sponsored May 1988 agreement which implicitly allowed the Hizb'allah to resume its activities in southern Lebanon. The Amal-Hizb'allah ceasefire agreement, sponsored by Syria and Iran, came after the conclusion of a renewed one-year oil agreement in April 1988, in which Iran agreed to supply one million tons of oil free of charge to Syria.[77] However, the continued intra-Shi'ite warfare between Hizb'allah and Amal over the control of southern Lebanon revealed that the movement displayed a greater degree of autonomy from previosuly exerted Iranian influence as Iranian attempts to mediate between the two warring factions proved unsuccessful. Apart from the continued importance of Iran's supply of oil to Syria for the Iranian-Syrian alliance,[78] any differences between Iran and Syria were reduced by a common agenda to confront Iraq's involvement with various militias in Lebanon, in the aftermath of Iran's acceptance of UN Resolution 598 for a ceasefire in the Iran-Iraq war, by unifying Amal-Hizb'allah differences against a common enemy.[79] While the Iranian *volte face* over its war with Iraq and elsewhere, under the consolidated leadership of Rafsanjani, created disillusionment within the ranks of the Hizb'allah over the achievement of its broader pan-Islamic goals, Iran's more moderate officials had difficulty in restraining Hizb'allah against Amal in order to avoid tension in its relationship with Syria. Rafsanjani himself admitted the difficulty of restraining Hizb'allah and the movement's greater loyalty to Mohtashemi.[80] In addition, Iranian pressure on Syria through earlier dependence on oil had lost most of its effect as Syria had received no deliveries of free oil from Iran since the end of 1988 and intended no additional purchases of Iranian oil at preferential OPEC prices, a reflection of increased Syrian self-sufficiency from the Deir ez-Zor oil production fields.[81]

The common interests between Iran, which desperately needed to attract foreign investment and improve relations with the West in order to repair its war-ravaged economy, and Syria, which also needed to compensate for the reduction of Soviet support by better relations with the U.S. administration and for the consolidation of its hegemony over Lebanon, led to a united front against the Hizb'allah, under the threat of Syrian military intervention which forced the movement to accept a political and military agreement with Amal in January 1989.[82] Under the accord, Hizb'allah was hindered in any planned future abduction of any more Western foreign hostages as it would directly contravene the clauses granting security control in Beirut to Syria and in the South of Lebanon to Amal. It would also appear that Syria pressed the Hizb'allah for the prevention of any release of British hostages as long as Britain was unwilling to restore full diplomatic relations with Syria. At the same time Iran had moved to broaden its relations with other Shi'ite movements in Lebanon in an effort to unity forces against Iraq's involvement in Lebanon, while it also attempted to exploit internal divisions within the Hizb'allah in an effort to achieve the release of some Western hostages as a leverage to advance its more moderate foreign policy.[83] However, both strategies proved difficult to accomplish for the Iranian political leadership as other Shi'ite movements were less susceptible than Hizb'allah to Iranian influence and as the then current Hizb'allah leadership under the command of Sheikh Subhi al-Tufayli was more inclined to take orders from the Iranian revolutionist faction than from Rafsanjani.

Iran's problem of excerting pressure on the Hizb'allah to release a few of its Western hostages for foreign policy gains in the international arena was overshadowed by more important developments in Lebanon, most notably by challenges to Syrian hegemony and the conclusion of the Syrian-sponsored Ta'if agreement, and within Iran itself, most importantly by the death of Ayatollah Khomeini and the ascendancy of Rafsanjani to the political leadership at the expense of the revolutionist faction. Although the issue of the Western hostages was briefly elevated by Israel's kidnapping of Sheikh Obeid in the summer of 1989, it was also relegated against the background of Syria's preoccupation with the challenges presented by General Aoun's "war of liberation" against the Syrian presence in Lebanon and the changes in Iran's political leadership as well as by the Salman Rushdie affair. While a closer Iranian-Syrian alliance emerged in Lebanon to counter Iraq and support for the regime of Aoun, a common rejection of the Ta'if agreement unified the positions of Iran and the Hizb'allah in Lebanon, especially as the movement would become the main casualty of the Syrian-sponsored agreement and Iran would lose most of its influence in Lebanon.

On the ground, however, Iranian-Hizb'allah relations diverged over the issue of continued intra-Shi'ite warfare between the movement and Amal in southern Lebanon as well as over refusals by the Hizb'allah's to release any foreign hostages. As a result, tension between the Hizb'allah and Iran was heightened by the decision of Rafsanjani to both downgrade financial support for the movement while ousting radical Iranian elements advocating the export of the revolution, most notably Hizb'allah's mentor Ali

Akhbar Mohtashemi who lost his position as interior minister in 1989.[84] However, the clerical factionalism within Iran was projected not only onto the issue of the foreign hostages in Lebanon but was also mirrored in Hizb'allah's clerical leadership, divided by the position and future direction of the movement in a post-civil war phase of Lebanon's political and military environment under stricter Syrian control.

Hizb'allah's opposition to the Ta'if agreement was not only based on the creation of a barrier to the establishment of an Islamic state in Lebanon but also on the plan for comprehensive disarmament of all militias. While the Hizb'allah came under pressure from Syria, through military intervention against the movement in search for the hostages while it blocked the movement of the IRGC units in the Biq'a, and from Iran, through the reduction of financial and military support and the attempt to control the IRGC by assignment of loyal units to Rafsanjani,[85] it became apparent that Syria was staunchly committed to the implementation of the Ta'if agreement to the extent that it would be willing to sacrifice Hizb'allah's political and military presence in the process.[86] At the same time, it was equally clear that Iran was unwilling to abandon the Hizb'allah to the wolves of Lebanese politics, mainly because of its enormous financial investments in the movement for the expansion of the Shi'a base and as it represented the only means to participate effectively in the Arab-Israeli conflict. Although this prevented Syria from any immediate attempts to eliminate the Hizb'allah, the hostage issue became increasingly subject to Iranian clerical factionalism while vital as a bargaining instrument for the movement to ensure its position within Lebanon, especially as Syria gradually moved towards full implementation of the Ta'if accord. This became evident by the renewed efforts to enforce an agreement by Syria and Iran in the intra-Shi'ite conflict between Hizb'allah and Amal on November 5, 1990, which reaffirmed the earlier principles and agreements reached in 1988 and 1989.[87] However, the dramatic shifts in the regional political context following Iraq's invasion of Kuwait in August 1990, coupled with the extension of Syrian hegemony in Lebanon, overshadowed temporarily any urgency for either Iran and Syria to force the Hizb'allah to hand over its Western hostages.

Apart from providing the Hizb'allah with a detraction from the hostage-issue in Lebanon while it displayed strong solidarity with the fate of Iraqi Shi'ites, the Gulf crisis also provided Iran and Syria with a window of opportunity to break their isolation by repairing relations with Arab states and improve their image and position in the West. While Syria had previously moved to improve relations with U.S. regional allies, most notably Egypt, it exploited the Gulf crisis to gain recognition of its suzerainty over

Lebanon and to extract financial aid and support from the Persian Gulf states by joining the U.S.-led coalition against Iraq and by using its influence over Iran to ensure either neutrality or, at least, non-cooperation between Iran and Iraq. In exchange, Syria facilitated mediation for Iran in an effort to improve the latter's relations with Saudi Arabia and Egypt.[88] Iran managed also to benefit economically from Iraq's invasion of Kuwait, as evident by the removal of sanctions by the E.C. in October 1990 and increased trade activity with Western governments. Although Iran and Syria managed to exploit the Gulf crisis for their own ends, a new source of increased tension in the Iranian-Syrian alliance was revealed by Iran's criticism of the continuous improvement in the U.S.-Syrian relationship, while the U.S.-Iranian remained frozen, and by Syrian flexibility towards Israel as well as its willingness to participate in the U.S.-initiated Middle East peace process. In particular, Iran was fully aware that any improvement in Iranian-U.S. relations, even gestures of reconciliation towards Iran, depended on obtaining the release of American hostages in Lebanon. As a result, Syria decided to permit the Hizb'allah to remain armed as a resistance movement, while it completed the disarmament of all other Lebanese militias in April 1991, in an agreement with both Iran, to reduce Iranian-Syrian tensions,[89] and the Hizb'allah, as a means to find a resolution to the hostage crisis and to suit its strategic designs in Lebanon as well as within the framework of the Arab-Israeli peace conferences. The convergence of interest between Iran and Syria was also evident by Syria's permission to allow the continued presence of Pasdaran units in Lebanon contrary to the Ta'if agreement.

As Hizb'allah's denouement of the hostage affair reflected the movement's readjustment within Lebanon's post-war environment, by substituting hostage-taking and terrorism for armed resistance and a willingness to participate within the democratic process, the comprehensive nature of the settlement of the hostage problem revealed close cooperation between Syria and Iran, albeit for their own individual interests. Although Syria's decision to allow the Hizb'allah to remain armed coincided with the formal recognition of Syrian hegemony over Lebanon, through the conclusion of the Treaty of Brotherhood, Cooperation and Coordination in May 1991,[90] Syria had a natural interest in securing a resolution to the foreign hostage problem, mainly in order to assure its role in the new regional order within the Arab-Israeli peace conferences as well as to attract Western economic relations and assistance. In particular, this commitment was revealed by the unprecedented Syrian security moves in Beirut in search for a kidnapped French citizen, abducted by a dissident Hizb'allah faction after the initial release of an American and a British hostage in early August 1991.

While Iran's vehement opposition, in concert with the Hizb'allah, to Syrian endorsement of the U.S.-sponsored Middle East peace negotiations, was manifest by a marked escalation in Hizb'allah attacks against Israel, Iranian interests in seeking a comprehensive resolution to the foreign hostage crisis was aligned with a carefully calibrated policy in the foreign policy arena. In an effort to achieve *rapprochement* with the West, Iran's decision to involve the good offices of the UN Secretary-General, Javier Perez de Cuellar, was not only chosen as the only available face-saving instrument for all parties involved in an overt process but also served to detract from both Iranian and Hizb'allah subversive activity elsewhere as well as to advance Iran's own position *vis-à-vis* Iraq in disputes over the terms of UN Resolution 598.[91] While the involvement of the United Nations in the hostage negotiations provided the Hizb'allah with a useful shield, in the form of international attention, against unrestrained Israeli reprisals to the movement's resistance activity, it also provided Iran with a diversion from its assassination campaign of political opponents abroad, as clearly evident by the killing of the Shah's last prime minister, Shapour Bakhtiar, in Paris which coincided with the initiation of the hostage release process in Lebanon. Apart from also providing its proxy in Lebanon with tangible achievements, in the form of the exhange of Western hostages for Lebanese Shi'ites through pressure on Israel,[92] Iran involved not only the United Nations from its previous successful mediation in the Gulf war between Iran and Iraq but also, more importantly, as a measure to bolster its position with the UN Secretary-General regarding the findings of UN Resolution 598, in particular the question of responsibility for starting the Iran-Iraq war, prior to his departure from the post at the end of 1991.[93] Both Iran and Hizb'allah had a vested interest in exploiting the linkage between these two issues before Perez dé Cuellar's term as Secretary-General expired at the end of 1991 as they had distrust for the new UN Secretary-General, Boutros Ghali, because of his close relation-ship with Egypt's Anwar Sadat and his involvement with the Camp David peace process. The fruits of this concerted drive became evident by the final report by the UN Secretary-General, on December 10, 1991, which found Iraq responsible for starting the Iran-Iraq war and made it legally responsible for claims by Iran for damages incurred during the eight-year war.[94]

Although Iran failed to achieve assurances from the American administration of non-retaliatory measures against the Hizb'allah once it relinquished all foreign hostages, acting on behalf of Hizb'allah's command leadership through the offices of the UN, Iran's consolidated strong influence over the movement became apparent after the Israeli assassination of Secretary-General Sheikh Abbas al-Musawi in February 1992. In particular, this was revealed by Iranian exerted moves in the appointment of al-Musawi's successor and restraining Hizb'allah retaliatory measures against Israel in southern Lebanon. While Iran's greater control over the Hizb'allah was a reflection of the movement's readjustment within a post-civil war Lebanese environment, particularly by the movement's decision to participate in the parliamentary elections, it was equally clear that Syrian hegemony took precedence over any Iranian or Hizb'allah plans which would threaten Syria's designs within Lebanon and elsewhere in the region.

CONCLUSIONS

The comprehensive conclusion of the hostage-crisis in Lebanon revealed the common interests of Hizb'allah, Iran, and Syria which converged from the advancement of their own individual agendas in Lebanon, in the region, and in relations with Western governments. While monumental changes in the internal Lebanese and regional environment in the Middle East served to contribute to the complete denouement of the hostage affair, in a manner conducive and expedient for all parties concerned, it also clearly underlined the nature and importance of the triangular Hizb'allah-Iran-Syria relationship in order to discern the influences and mechanisms exerted by Iran and Syria, both individually and collectively, over the process of abduction and releases of foreign hostages by the Hizb'allah. As demonstrated, this process was subject to the continuous changing relationship and alliance between Iran and Syria over a decade, itself subjected to either confluence or conflict in individual political and economic agendas in the Middle East and affected by a wide variety of internal Lebanese, regional, and international events. Although the Iranian-Syrian alliance was born out of mutual tactical convenience to confront common enemies in the Middle East, cemented by Syrian economic dependence upon Iran in a hostile Arab environment, the relationship between Iran and Syria has experienced serious tension in conjunction with shifting political and economic conditions in the region. While the larger problems in the Iranian-Syrian nexus highlighted their contradictory political ideologies, they have also been superimposed on the ground in Lebanon over Hizb'allah activity. An understanding of the basis for the Iranian-Syrian alliance, and its subsequent evolution in Lebanon, is necessary not only in terms of examining the way in which the Iranian-Syrian relationship has affected the position and activity of the Hizb'allah in Lebanon but also in the provision of a useful framework for the application of crisis-management principles and techniques by Western governments to the hostage-crisis, outlining opportunities and constraints in their application in accordance with tension and coordination in the alliance between Iran and Syria over Hizb'allah activity.

The status of the political and economic dimensions of the Iranian-Syrian alliance was closely mirrored in all aspects of Hizb'allah activity in Lebanon. While both Iran and Syria were adept at exploiting the relationship for their own benefit in Lebanon and elsewhere in the region, the collusion between Iran and Syria remained uniform in Lebanon in the confrontation against common foreign enemies, coupled with the complete obedience by the Hizb'allah to Iranian orders. This was particularly evident in Syrian and Iranian rejection of the agreement of 17 May 1983 between Lebanon and Israel as well as by their close involvement with Hizb'allah's efforts to strike at the Western and Israeli military presence in Lebanon. After the departure of the MNF in 1984 and, more importantly, Israel in 1985 from Lebanon, the incompatibility of the aims of Iran, seeking to establish an Islamic republic on Iranian lines, and Syria, seeking to consolidate hegemony over Lebanese affairs, came to the surface through intense competition by their clients, Hizb'allah and Amal, over the hearts and minds of the Shi'ite community. The friction between Iranian and Syrian attempts to seek political and military dominance in Lebanon, as manifest through armed clashes between Amal and Hizb'allah, intensified with an array of other difficulties in their relationship both internal and external to Lebanon. In particular, the underlying economic bond between Syria and Iran, especially Syrian dependence on Iranian oil supplies, experienced several rifts over Syrian refusals to settle outstanding debts over oil payments to Iran between 1986 to 1988 and over subsequent Syrian efforts to lessen its economic dependency on Iran through development of internal Syrian oil production. Although Syria proved adept at exploiting the economic difficulties with Iran to its own advantage, as it positioned itself as a bridge between a politically isolated Iran and the rest of the Arab world, other differences between the two regimes over Lebanon stemmed from incompatibility between Syrian attempts to consolidate its control over Lebanon while seeking a political and economic *rapprochement* with Western governments after accusations of Syrian involvement in terrorism, and Iranian exploitation of Hizb'allah abductions in the pursuit of specific foreign policy objectives and in the expansion of the movement at the expense of Amal. While both Syria and Iran had an interest in defusing any serious conflict in Lebanon in order to preserve their relationship, the pursuit by the Hizb'allah of a greater

independent line from Iran, in the aftermath of Iranian clerical factionalism in late 1986, compounded the problems in any attempts to make the
movement answerable to either Iran or Syria for both the control over and
the limitation of its activities. Although Syria has avoided a complete
crackdown on the Iranian proxy, whenever the Hizb'allah has seriously
challenged Syrian authority, the Syrian regime has moved to exercise
control over the activity of the Hizb'allah through a blockade of the transfer of Iranian Pasdaran in the Biq'a area and the control of movement of
the Hizb'allah in the Biq'a and Beirut areas. However, Syrian restraint in
the elimination of the military and political presence of the Hizb'allah was
based on its nonexpendable relationship with Iran. Neither Syria nor Iran
were willing to sacrifice their alliance on account of any Hizb'allah activity, rather both regimes have been forced to exercise restraint in their relations with Hizb'allah at various times as to not offend each other. When
Hizb'allah activity was harmful to the Iranian-Syrian alliance, as evident
by Amal-Hizb'allah armed clashes and certain hostage-taking incidents,
both Iran and Syria acted in concert to enforce agreements between their
two proxies as well as to place limitations on the abduction of foreigners.
While the former was revealed by the three enforced agreements between
Amal and Hizb'allah by Iran and Syria (1988–1990), the latter became
apparent by the Syrian-Iranian imposed cessation of any abductions by the
movement after the January 1987 wave of kidnappings by the Hizb'allah.
However, the Iranian-Syrian alliance experienced particular problems in
conjunction with the projection of Iranian clerical factionalism onto the
Hizb'allah command leadership in attempts by Iran and Syria to use
extraction from the hostage-crisis as an instrument in the foreign policy
arena.

The unequivocal support for the Hizb'allah from Iran and, to a lesser
extent acceptance by Syria, changed concurrently with the changes in the
Iranian leadership, following the death of Ayatollah Khomeini, and with
Syrian efforts to consolidate its control over a post civil-war Lebanon with
the Ta'if agreement in 1989. While the defeat of the revolutionist faction
in control over the political authority in Iran translated into diminished
possibility for a radical leadership of the Hizb'allah to be able to confront
Syrian efforts to establish political and military hegemony in Lebanon, it
also became clear that Syrian designs within Lebanese territory took
precedence over any official Iranian interests. Syrian concessions to
Hizb'allah and Iran, in the form of allowing the movement to remain
armed and for the continued presence of the Pasdaran contingent on
Lebanese territory, meant not only that the movement was forced to
submit to a reorientation in activity in alignment with Syrian interests in

order to survive within Lebanon's post civil-war environment but also underlined the increasingly asymmetrical nature of the Iranian-Syrian relationship both within and external to Lebanon.

The identification of the individual and the collective motivations as well as an understanding of the process of the triangular Hizb'allah-Iranian-Syrian relationship behind the abduction and the release of Western foreign citizens had profound significance in the application of crisis-management principles and techniques. Apart from deciphering the underlying motivations in incidents involving the abduction of foreigners by the movement, either for internal organisational requirements or in alignment with Syrian and Iranian interests, comprehension of the process of the changing interaction between Hizb'allah and the Iranian-Syrian relationship becomes necessary in order to determine not only the direction but also the timing of the application of certain crisis-management principles and techniques.

5 Western Responses to the Hostage-Crisis and Crisis-Management

"Government is about crisis-management.
Governments do not think."[1]

INTRODUCTION

The responses by the American, French, and British governments to the abduction of its citizens in Lebanon have underlined the inherent difficulty in striking a balance between their moral obligation towards providing safety and protection for their citizens abroad without having to sacrifice national interests in the conduct of foreign policy. While all three states have pursued a firmly held and coordinated public position of no-negotiations with terrorists and no-concessions to their demands in the Lebanese hostage-crisis, the reality of actual conduct behind this facade has revealed not only the conduct of secret negotiations, either directly with the Hizb'allah, Iran, and Syria or indirectly through third party inter-mediaries, over the release of hostages, at times resulting in complex and murky deals, but also that the hostage-issue was intimately influenced by the conduct of foreign policies by these Western states in the Middle East.[2] Although the two Western European states and the United States have shared similar types of problems and challenges in efforts to manage and secure the extraction of its citizens from captivity in Lebanon, each individual state has pursued its own overt and covert policies to accom-plish this task. Apart from their almost equal standing in Hizb'allah's anti-Western demonology, largely due to their colonial past and present involvement in the Middle East, the divergence of approach to the hostage-crisis reflected not only the individual experiences of these Western states in confronting terrorism within their own borders, but also the nature and status of their relationships with both Iran and Syria as well as their policies in the Middle East, driven by different sets of political motivations as well as economic considerations. The differences from state to state in the frequency, time periods, and number of its citizens

134

abducted by the Hizb'allah, coupled with the specific nature of demands, also contributed to the way in which the Western governments have crafted individual or concerted strategies to the problem of obtaining the release of their citizens from captivity. As a consequence, any examination of the pendular responses by the United States and the two West European states to the hostage-crisis in Lebanon within the framework of crisis-management must not only take into account the broader environment of Western foreign policy towards the region but also the specific dynamics of the triangular relationships between Hizb'allah and Iran as well as Syria as a key component in the application of successful crisis-management. Apart from the evaluation of the performance of Western governments according to the previously outlined requirements for effective crisis-management, these will also serve as the framework of this analysis. The underlying *criteria* for the "successful" application of crisis-management is not only *close adherence to the seven essential requirements* of effective crisis-management balanced against inherent constraints for Western governments in the conduct of domestic and foreign policy but also the *performance* of their approach in the hostage-crisis based on the previous case-study on the dynamics of the relationships at work between Hizb'allah, Iran and Syria.

CRISIS-MANAGEMENT: THE LIMITATION OF POLITICAL OBJECTIVES

The responses by the United States and the two West European states to the hostage-crisis in Lebanon have been governed by a uniform policy of refusal to negotiate or make concessions to terrorists under any guise. This policy of no-negotiations and no-concessions to terrorists has been embodied in a series of unilateral or joint declarations of principles which reflects not only the previous experience of liberal democracies in countering terrorism at home, based on the principled position that hostage-taking constitutes an unforgivable act that must not be rewarded through concessions and that a readiness to negotiate as well as a willingness to concede to demands only encourages further terrorist acts, but also that state support for terrorism in any form constitutes unacceptable international behaviour subject to punishment. While principles of U.S. no-concessions policy have been unilaterally proclaimed by policymakers on countless occasions in response to new hostage-takings of American citizens, as outlined by public policy statements and documents, the European states have adopted not only unilateral policies in

alignment with the uniform principles of no-concessions but also a concerted European approach to the hostage-problem, as evident by their
solemn promise to make "no concessions under duress to terrorists or
their sponsors" at the 1986 European Community (E.C.) summit in
London.[3] The inconsistency between the declaratory policy of not negotiating or conceding to any demands and the actual conduct by Western
governments in dealing with the hostage-crisis in Lebanon can be attributed to the often incompatible nature of firmly held counterterrorism
principles as an integral component of foreign policy in the Middle East
towards Iran and Syria, who exercise any degree of control over the
Hizb'allah movement. Despite the fact that both Iran and Syria have con-
cealed the exact nature of their close relationship with the Hizb'allah,
the recognition of Iran and Syria as intermediaries for Western governments in dealing with the Hizb'allah posed problems in upholding a
nonflexible no-concessions policy as these states benefited indirectly
from concessions made to influence the movement despite their own
complicity in some of the movement's terrorist acts. While most Iranian
or Syrian demands of concessions for any intercession with Hizb'allah
centered on specific outstanding disputes or a shift in foreign policy
behaviour by Western governments towards these states, the issue of any
deviation from the principles of a no-concessions policy became dependent on the conduct of conciliatory foreign policy by Western states
towards either Iran or Syria in alignment with shifts in the regional environment creating opportunities and constraints in the pursuit of wider
foreign policy interests. Any perceived breach of the no-negotiations and
no-concessions policies must be related to the desire by Western
governments to extract its citizens from captivity, heavily influenced by
domestic political pressures, and its unwillingness to maintain a non-
conciliatory position at the expense of the pursuit of wider foreign policy
opportunities in the region. As such, the shifts in the elevation of the
political objective to secure the release of hostages must not only be
related to the importance of the hostage-issue on the political agenda at
home and its impact on the conduct of foreign policy but also in alignment with changes in the Middle East regional environment which determines whether Western governments can afford to discard other foreign
policy interests with Iran and Syria over principles of counterterrorism.
In turn, this evaluation must also be placed within the context of the
opportunities and constraints in the environment which governs the relationship between Hizb'allah and Iran as well as Syria in order to evaluate
the effectiveness of policy initiatives on efforts to secure the release of
hostages.

The importance of the hostage-issue on the domestic political agenda and in the conduct of foreign policy has varied between Western states and over specific time periods. This has been subject to the legacy of previous national experience and success of countering internal political violence as well as state-sponsored international terrorism with Middle Eastern origin as well as to the public perception of the adversary and the fate of the hostages as projected through political pressure on decision-makers to act or abstain from any action for the resolution of the hostage-crisis. The relative absence of Middle East terrorism on American soil has reflected the great impact of the Lebanese hostage-crisis on the U.S. domestic and foreign policy agendas. Yet the calmer treatment of the hostage-crisis by West European public opinion was not only a reflection of past occurrences and treatment of indigenous and international terrorism within their borders but also to awareness of the necessity for a more restrained response by their governments to the hostage-crisis in light of the fear of retribution to any overreactions given the geographical proximity of the Middle East as well as to careful consideration of any responses in view of their effectiveness and potential consequences for the conduct of overall foreign policy towards the region.

American Hostages

Apart from the impact of the previous hostage-crisis in Iran which resulted in paralysis of the Carter administration for 444-days, the issue of American hostages in Lebanon was elevated on the U.S. domestic and foreign policy agenda against the backdrop of both the Hizb'allah suicide-attack on the U.S. Marine barracks in October 1983, which inflicted the single worst number of casualties for the U.S. military since the Vietnam war, and exacerbated by the media spectacle surrounding the TWA-hijacking in June 1985. The multiple abduction of four American citizens in early 1984 highlighted not only the impotence of any U.S. efforts to confront the threat of Islamic militancy but also was elevated as a major national security issue as one of the hostages was the CIA station-chief in Beirut, William Buckley.[4] While the media exacerbated the pressure on the Reagan administration to act with resolve to secure the release of all American hostages, as manifest through the modification of U.S. counter-terrorism policy in April 1984 through National Security Directive (NSDD) 138 authorizing pre-emptive strikes and reprisal raids against terrorists abroad, the U.S. government assigned extraordinary priority to extract William Buckley from captivity as evident from the influence of his case for the initiation of the secret efforts pursued through contacts within Iran's clerical establishment which later culminated in the U.S.-Iranian arms-for-hostages scandal. However, the issue of the U.S. hostages was successfully downplayed by the Reagan administration in the 1984 presidential election campaign.[5] Although the U.S. government resisted pressure from the individual campaigns by hostages' families in the media, even with the addition of more abductions of American citizens in early 1985, it was forced to respond to the June 1985 TWA-hijacking which not only highlighted the inaction of efforts on behalf of the U.S. hostages in Lebanon but also marked the beginning of a clandestine policy shift towards a willingness to negotiate with Iranian clergy in a wider effort to improve its relationship with a post-Khomeini Iran. As the increased pressure from hostage's families exacerbated the problems for the Reagan administration to secure the release of U.S. captives, especially as the U.S.-Iranian arms-for-hostages deals failed to yield the return of hostages as others were captured to replace those released, the revelation of the affair in November 1986 undermined not only the political credibility of the Reagan presidency and its hardline posture against international terrorism at home and with its allies abroad, but also the total viability of any efforts to secure the release of hostages as it was relegated to a more subordinate position in relation to efforts by the Reagan administration to survive politically. The *de facto* departure from U.S. publicly stated policy led not only to the most serious domestic challenge and political turmoil facing the Reagan presidency for its continued survival but also created confusion and anger among its European allies, which had received repeated U.S. pleas not to negotiate with terrorists and not to breach a U.S. sponsored worldwide arms embargo on Iran. Apart from raising questions about U.S. credibility abroad, the coherence of its foreign policy and the management of its intelligence operations, the revelation of the U.S.-Iranian arms-for-hostages deals also created serious tensions in American relations with more moderate Arab states.[6] As a consequence, the hostage-issue was effectively abandoned for the remainder of the Reagan administration's tenure in office and confined to token shows of military force against the movement with the spate of abductions of U.S. citizens in January 1987 despite continued pressure from the hostage's families and the media.

The ascendancy of Bush to the U.S. presidency inherited the previous legacy of political constraints to enter into negotiations that would resemble any deal-making. While the Bush administration showed a more conciliatory attitude towards Iran in the aftermath of Ayatollah Khomeini's death, it downplayed the hostage-issue in order to advance its wider foreign policy objectives in the region in the vacuum created by the end of the Iran-Iraq war.[7] Although the kidnapping of Lt. Col. William Higgins became the first test for the Bush presidency, the response was confined to the show of military force as the hostage-issue became increasingly more dependent on the shifting political environment of the Middle East and elsewhere than to any concerted effort to secure their release in response to media and public campaign pressures. The devaluation of the hostage-issue in the foreign policy agenda reduced the political vulnerability of the Bush administration as it adjusted to the Middle East environment during and after the Gulf-war of 1990/91. Any pressure to act for the release of the U.S. hostages diminished completely as an issue with the UN involvement which resulted in the comprehensive denounement of the hostage-crisis by December 1992.[8]

The high-priority assigned by two successive Republican administrations to secure the release of its citizens in Lebanon was symptomatic not only of a desire to limit the effects of hostage-taking on the U.S. presidency, as epitomized by the downfall of President Carter over the Iranian hostage-crisis, but was also the result of an overexpectation of U.S. ability to achieve the rapid release of its citizens through reliance on coercion without any special consideration for the constraints and opportunities of the political environment in the Middle East which was regulated by its conduct of foreign policy in the region, specifically U.S. policy towards Iran and Syria, and governed by the dynamics of Iran's and Syria's ability to intervene with the Hizb'allah as well as their willingness to intervene in return for tangible rewards. Apart from the strong influence of the media and pressure groups on U.S. policy towards the hostage-crisis, the discrepancy between raised public expectations of the ability by the government to resolve the hostage-incidents rapidly and effectively, created partly by U.S. official hardline policies, and the actual reality of the extremely limited maneuverability of the U.S. government, given the constraints, and by the failure to pursue a consistent and coherent Middle East policy and by the political consequences of the disastrous U.S.-Iranian arms-for-hostages deals, contributed to the failure of any success in the achievement of U.S. political objectives. These problems were exacerbated by the U.S. approach to link the hostage-issue as a precondition for wider normalization of its relationship with Iran while it pursued a policy of containment towards Iran and without consideration for Iran's actual ability to coerce the Hizb'allah to release its hostages, compounded by an unwillingness to make any concessions of a substantial nature in return.[9]

French Hostages

The issue of the French hostages assumed a highly elevated position on the
domestic and foreign policy agenda as evident by its exploitation by political parties in the 1986/1988 national elections as well as by its integral role
in the conduct of foreign policy towards the region and specifically with
Iran and Syria. The abduction of a number of French journalists, most
notably Jean-Paul Kauffman in May 1985 and four TV crew-members of
Antenne-2 in March 1986, increased the pressure on the French government to act on behalf of the hostages as their fate was highlighted by a
highly visible campaign in the media. The French TV channel *Antenne-2*,
inspired by the American news coverage of the 444-day captivity of U.S.
hostages in Iran, broadcasted daily the pictures of the French hostages and
the number of days they had been held by kidnappers.[10] This pressure was
exacerbated by the Hizb'allah bomb campaign in Paris which occurred in
conjunction with the March 1986 French national elections. While the
hostage-issue was used as an instrument in the election campaign by the
respective presidential candidates to discredit the opponent in efforts to
obstruct or secure the release of the hostages prior to the dual elections in
France for the presidency and the National Assembly, the French hostages
assumed increasing importance after the elections with the rivalry between
President Mitterrand and Prime Minister Chirac within the French
cohabitation government.[11] For example, Chirac condemned President
Mitterrand's Socialist government, during the election campaign, for
turning France into a "weakened and worried" nation and the conservative
candidates pledged that they would adopt a stronger and tougher attitude
towards dealing with terrorism.[12] The intensity of this political rivalry
between Chirac and Mitterand was apparent by the employment of various
emissaries in individual efforts to secure the release of hostages.[13]

   The French hostage-issue was also symptomatic of its conduct of
foreign policy in the Middle East, most notably in relation to its close
support for Iraq and in any outstanding disputes with Iran. As a major
issue in the conduct of French foreign policy in the Middle East, the
importance of the hostage-crisis was clearly evident in the decision of the
Chirac government to abandon its traditional support and close cooperation with Iraq, crafted by his socialist predecessors, in favour of improved
relations with Iran, most notably in order to limit the impact of French
public fears of Iran as a major threat.[14] It was also revealed by the reluctance of the French government to impose any sanctions on Syria and Iran
despite appeals from its European allies and the United States. As French
policy towards Iran vacilliated between accommodation and confrontation

in response to the conflicting positions of various political representatives with different institutional responsibilities and approaches to the hostage-affair, its impact on the French political climate was also evident by the exploitation of the hostage-issue in the build-up to the French presidential elections in May 1988.[15] This was particularly demonstrated by Chirac's last-minute attempt to boost his chances of electoral victory, trailing in the French presidential race, by interrupting a campaign speech in Strasbourg on May 4, 1988, announcing his government achieved the dramatic double releases of French hostages in Beirut and New Caledonia.[16] However, as aptly observed by Berry:

> "[t]he French press has focused quite heavily on this issue, and not without justification. Only a few days before the election, it seemed possible that the hostage release would give Chirac the boost he needed to defeat Francois Mitterrand...[t]he French were initially jubilant, and Chirac happily accepted public plaudits. But uneasiness about the terms of the release soon turned into a political liability."[17]

The elevated importance of the French hostage-issue on the political agenda has been largely the result of the rivalry between Chirac and Mitterrand for political expediency in the battle for the presidency as well as by Iranian willingness to exact punishment on French soil for its support to Iraq in the Iran-Iraq war. This institutional rivalry between French political factions as manifest through the exploitation of the hostage-issue for their own political advantages made any hostage release dependent not only on the ability of different political emissaries to exert their influence over the kidnappers and its patrons through offers of concessions but also on the nature of their political agendas as to whether any release would occur in return for concessions either before or after French national elections.[18] Apart from the dependence of the political objective to secure the release of hostages on French institutional and political rivalry, the hostage-issue was assisted by the subordination of the French judiciary to political authorities in alignment with the traditional sanctuary doctrine and by the unique French approach to Middle East politics and to international terrorism with a proven ability to resist outside pressures from allies while the only serious challenge to any action came from media pressures.

British Hostages

The issue of the British hostages was never of any high priority for the British government: they were effectively abandoned to their own fate bound by the constraints in the Middle East environment, by the official refusal to either conduct any negotiations with Hizb'allah or its patrons and to concede to any demands. While this hardline position was accept-able to most strands within the government and in the public arena, it was symptomatic of the British experience with, and tough attitudes towards, terrorism on its own soil by the Provisional Irish Republican Army (PIRA) over the last two decades. The hostages in Lebanon also received low-priority as an issue not only because of Britain's limited involvement in Middle East politics but also as the government operated without any real pressure from either the media or hostages' families, the latter urged by government officials to remain silent to allow progress through quiet diplomacy.[19]

The abandonment of silence with the formation of "Friends of John McCarthy" in January 1988, with no progress in achieving any releases through an official policy of quiet diplomacy, contributed to some public pressure on the British government, most notably after the release of the remaining French hostages in May 1988. After the release of the French hostages in May 1988, the French hostage, Jean-Paul Kaufmann criticized openly the U.S. and British government policy by stating in interviews: "I don't understand the Americans and the British. The hostages must be rescued as soon as possible. The theory that keeping quiet about hostages will speed their release is sterile, even grotesque."[20] While this visible and public media campaign kept the issue of the hostages in the public domain, and highlighted what it claimed to be the inadequacy of any official efforts to extract its citizens from captivity, it failed to yield sub-stantial pressure for a re-evaluation of its hostage-policy as the British government, under the helm of Mrs Thatcher, refused to seek *rap-prochment* with either Iran or Syria. As a consequence, the low-priority assigned to secure the release of hostages by the British government, coupled with its refusal to negotiate with intermediaries connected with the Hizb'allah, was consistently applied until the ascendancy of Douglas Hurd to the post of Foreign Secretary and, ultimately, with the resignation of Prime Minister Margaret Thatcher in 1990.[21] While the change from Howe to Hurd as Foreign Secretary was significant in the new approach to British relations in the Middle East, it was due more to the opportunities created by a changed Middle East environment in 1990–91 than to any change of ministerial office-holders. Although the new leadership under PM John Major devalued the hostage-issue, it accelerated the necessary process of reconciliation and *rapprochment* with Iran and Syria in the changed Middle East environment with Iraq's invasion of Kuwait which created a window of opportunity for the resolution of the British hostage-crisis. As in the case of American hostages, any pressure on the British government to act on behalf of its citizens in captivity disappeared with the UN involvement providing a comprehensive resolution to the hostage-crisis in 1991.

The complete devaluation of the British hostage-crisis by its government was a reflection not only of previous national experience in effectively countering terrorism at home and abroad which reinforced the public acceptability of the no-negotiations and no-concessions policy, embodied by the hardline policies under Mrs Thatcher, but also of the tacit acceptance by the British government that the fate of the hostages could only be affected by its ability to offer concessions, as evident by the nature of demands, in order to compensate for its reduced influence in the Middle East. Although the British government upheld its publicly stated principles of counterterrorism successfully without entering into any deal-making, it achieved this at the expense of prolonging the confinement of the hostages without any major benefits in the foreign policy arena. However, this can be attributed to the fact that Britain faced unforeseen insuperable obstacles beyond its power to control, most notably the row with the U.S. government over the Iran-Contra debacle and the consequences of the Rushdie-affair. As a consequence, any criticism for the lack of progress in the release of British hostages must not only account for the approach of British policy but also, more importantly, the constraints imposed by the political environment in the Middle East, creating obstacles for any British government efforts.

CRISIS-MANAGEMENT: LIMITATION OF MEANS IN PURSUIT OF POLITICAL OBJECTIVES

The use of the military option by Western governments has been confined to efforts to either punish the Hizb'allah for previous terrorist actions through retaliatory strikes, as a deterrent to prevent the execution of hostages through demonstration of military power or in attempts to rescue hostages from captivity. While both the United States and France have used military actions against known Hizb'allah bases in the Biq'a area as punishment for the October 1983 twin suicide attacks against their MNF contingents, these actions have revealed the major weakness of applying military force as an instrument to extract retribution for terrorist acts in a manner which would seriously undermine the operational activity of the movement.[22] This was demonstrated by the failure of the French raid against a Hizb'allah training camp, the Sheikh Abdallah barracks, south of

Ba'albek on November 17, 1983, and the shelling by American naval aircrafts against Syrian and Hizb'allah positions in the Biq'a area in
December 1983.[23] The identification of the Sheikh Abdallah barracks as a
main center for coordination between Hizb'allah and Iranian Pasdaran was
accurate, but a major failure for these military operations stemmed from
the inherent difficulties in the conduct of military actions within an
extremely hostile civil-war environment. This was admitted by President
Reagan in that he: "wholeheartedly agree[d] with the Long Commission's
finding that the military is not adequately equipped to fight state-sponsored
terrorists. The U.S. needs to systematically redevelop our approach to the
problem."[24]

The Utility of Military Force

Apart from the lack of precise intelligence on the location of Hizb'allah
command centers, this was compounded by the need to employ only
limited levels of military violence against the movement in order to avoid
a wider confrontation with Syria in and over Lebanon. The utility of using
retaliatory military actions against the Hizb'allah had diminished in conjunction with extreme measure of operational secrecy adopted by the
Hizb'allah, the nature of the organisational structure of the Hizb'allah,
and, more importantly, with the abduction of foreigners by the movement,
held at several different locations as a shield against military retribution by
Western governments. As explained by PLO's Salah Khalef, the
Hizb'allah maintained the foreign hostages as insurance against retaliation
by the U.S., Syria or any other force.[25] Although Israel was successful in
the abduction of senior Hizb'allah leaders and members in southern
Lebanon in December 1988 and in July 1989 and in the assassination of its
Secretary-General in February 1992, the increased militancy of the
Hizb'allah in response to these IDF operations demonstrated not only that
the military approach failed to yield any of the underlying political objectives but also that it contributed to a spiral of escalation. According to
Sheikh Abbas al-Musawi: "America should think a million times before
carrying out any foolish action: There will be no limits whatsoever to our
reprisals."[26] Infact, uncoordinated military action against any Hizb'allah
base or member, especially through a third state, may have severe adverse
consequences for the fate of Western hostages, as revealed by the murder
of Lt. Col. William Higgins following the IDF kidnapping of Sheikh
Obeid in southern Lebanon. The case of the assassination of Sheikh
Raghib Harb in February 1984 demonstrated early that the death of any
Hizb'allah leader exacerbates the Shi'ite sense of martyrdom and the

willingness by Hizb'allah fighters to sacrifice their own lives in the struggle against Israel and the West.[27] The extreme operational security adopted by Hizb'allah SSA members and its institutional position within the organisational structure of the movement, coupled with the decentralized nature of Hizb'allah's command leadership, have contributed to the difficulty in the selection of available targets as well as the limited effectiveness of military strikes against individual leaders or command centers to undermine the actual operations of the movement. For example, the abduction of Sheikh Abdul Karim Obeid failed to reduce any of the movement's military activity against Israel. This was also clearly demonstrated by the IDF assassination of Sheikh Abbas al-Musawi in 1992, which strengthened the radicalism of Hizb'allah's command leadership and contributed to increased operational security of the Islamic Resistance, its military wing, in the conduct of anti-Israeli attacks, and in due course led to the major bombing attack on the Israeli Embassy in Buenos Aires.[28]

Apart from the failed retaliatory response to the twin-suicide attacks against the American and French MNF contingents in 1983, the reluctance by Western governments to use military force in retribution has not only been based on inadequate access to good intelligence on the location of Hizb'allah leaders and command centers but also closely linked to the political restraints of avoiding any military involvement in a civil war environment at the expense of their political agenda towards Lebanon and Syria as well as Iran. As a consequence, the emphasis by the American administration on the use of military means to preempt and counter terrorism, embodied by U.S. National Security Directive 138, was not only ill-suited to the actual environment of the hostage-takings in Lebanon and to the actual military as well as intelligence capabilities in support for such operations but also served to erode the credibility of the Reagan administration in conjunction with unfulfilled threats of U.S. military actions against the kidnappers despite continuous hostage-taking acts of American citizens by the Hizb'allah.

The demonstration of military force as a deterrent measure to the abduction of foreigners was only used by the United States in response to the multiple kidnappings of American citizens in January 1987 and in response to threats against the lives of hostages after Israel's kidnapping of Sheikh Obeid in July 1989. While the United States signalled a military threat to the Hizb'allah in 1987, through the position of the Sixth Fleet off the Lebanese coastline, it led to a serious escalation of the hostage-crisis whereby the movement threatened the execution of Western hostages in the event of the employment of American military force in Lebanon. Unwillingness to use the show of military force against unknown targets and for unknown political objectives again undermined the credibility of the American administration and its overall response to the hostage-crisis in Lebanon. In contrast, any French fleet presence in the area has been coupled with assurances to the Muslim community that they had no plans to intervene militarily in Lebanon.[29] Although U.S. officials claimed that its show of military force against the Hizb'allah in 1989 actually prevented the execution of American hostages, its main effectiveness must be placed within the context of an overall reluctance by the movement to execute its hostages,[30] and can be attributed to veiled threats of using U.S. military force against Iran in order to control the movement's actions in Lebanon.[31] However, the effectiveness of use of military force against Iran to prevent the execution of foreign hostages in Lebanon is questionable as Hizb'allah's murder of Lt. Col. Higgins allegedly occurred from orders issued by Iranian radicals, most notably Mohtashemi, in an effort to derail any improvement in the U.S.-Iranian relationship. Although Iran's Rafsanjani cannot control the exact activity of the Hizb'allah, the absence of further executions of foreign hostages can be attributed to Iranian threats to cut financial and military assistance if the movement took any actions without prior consultation from Iran.

Military Rescue Operations

The use of military rescue operations by the Western governments for the release of foreigners have also suffered from the constraints of the complex civil war environment in Lebanon. A major problem for Western intelligence agencies was the identification of the exact locations where the hostages were being held, compounded by the fact that many hostages were dispersed in the three regional areas of Lebanon and continously moved by the Hizb'allah for security reasons. Although information about the possible location of the Western captives emerged with the release of each hostage or through escapes, problems of rapidly confirming and acting on the information undermined any opportunity or desire by Western governments to launch any rescue operations in which failure would almost certainly guarantee the death of hostages. As a number of Western hostages were held in the Biq'a area, any rescue operation was constrained by a logistical difficulty of gaining access to an area both firmly controlled by Hizb'allah militiamen and an Iranian Pasdaran contingent as well as surrounded by the Syrian military. This problem led to the direct or indirect employment of local militias by Western governments in efforts to search for the hostages in Beirut and in southern Lebanon, as evident by the successful rescue of two hostages in 1984 by Amal and the same movement's search for the abducted American military officer in February 1988.[32] However, Amal's ability to locate hostages and mount any rescue operations diminished early in conjunction with the expansion of the Hizb'allah at the expense of the Amal movement and with the endemic Amal-Hizb'allah warfare between 1987 until 1990. Equally, the employment of the Druze militia in the search for Terry Waite in 1987 demonstrated the limited ability of local militias on the ground in Lebanon to gain access to reliable intelligence on the location of the Western hostages.[33]

Apart from the lack of available information on any plans or attempts by the French or British government to rescue its citizens from captivity in Lebanon, the only admission was made by Captain Paul Barril, former head of GIGN (French counterterrorism force) that the French military considered a military intervention to rescue its hostages in 1986 but soon concluded that it was not only too risky but also impossible.[34] On the contrary, all efforts by the American administration were channelled through the Hostage Location Task Force, firmly established in December 1985.[35] While a number of unsuccessful and unconventional attempts were made to identify the location of American captives (leading to defined hostage-rescue plans between 1985–87), most notably through the purchase of information from local informants and in the establishment of a counter-terrorism programme for the Lebanese intelligence, the failure of these methods underlined not only the immense security precautions adopted by Hizb'allah's Special Security Apparatus (SSA) but also that the military approach was inadequate in dealing with and in resolving these types of hostage-taking situations. As revealed by the concealment of Lt. Col. Higgins despite a massive search operation by Amal and the arrest warrants against Imad Mughniya, it is alleged that even Syrian military intelligence was unable to locate the whereabouts of hostages and wanted terrorists. While the application of military pressure through proxy, most notably by Syrian military, has been a successful means to prevent additional abductions of foreigners and to prevent the execution of hostages, it has been limited to the political environment in Lebanon and in relation to the status of Syria's relationship with Iran as well as with Western governments. As demonstrated by Syrian consolidation of its hegemony in Lebanon, which prevented the abduction of foreigners by the Hizb'allah after 1987 through the deployment of the Syrian military in Beirut, any Syrian willingness to apply military pressure on the Shi'ite movement has been always governed by a desire not to jeopardize its wider relationship with Iran and in conjunction with opportunities to safeguard its interests in Lebanon as well as with an improvement of its relations with Western governments. Despite the fact that Syrian military intelligence know the identity of main officials within Hizb'allah's SSA, this has meant that Syrian moves towards Hizb'allah must be considered mainly gestures towards the West, in alignment with its wider interests in Lebanon of preventing Hizb'allah to become too strong at the expense of other militias, rather than any real willingness to offend its partner Iran. Apart from the continued presence of the IRGC contingent in Lebanon, a clear indication of this is the lack of Syrian efforts to control the activities of the Hizb'allah and Iranian Pasdaran in the Bi'qa area, as it could effectively isolate their movement beyond this area as well as their resistance activity against Israel since the overall military command center of the Islamic Resistance is situated near Ba'albek.[36]

The restrictions in the application of military force to the hostage-crisis in Lebanon must also be viewed in a broader context. While it can be argued that a military approach should only be adopted as a last resort when non-military means are exhausted, it is important to recognize that the application of military force against the Hizb'allah has not only fuelled the militancy of the movement and provided it with many new members and recruits among the Shi'ite community but also strengthened the allegiance of Hizb'allah's command leadership to the more radical clergy within Iran's clerical establishment.[37] While retaliatory strikes may seem morally justifiable in response to terrorist atrocities, the questionable legality of any type of unilateral military response not only causes strain for regional or international cooperation against terrorism but also will result in a high probability of collateral damage against civilian targets given the limited qualitity of intelligence on the Hizb'allah. This was clearly demonstrated in the failed assassination attempt of Hizb'allah's spiritual leader, Sheikh Muhammad Fadlallah, at his residence in the Bir al'Abed quarter in the southern suburbs of Beirut, in which at least 80 civilians were killed and 200 injured. The reluctance by the U.S. government to execute any type of rescue operation must also be viewed within the context of previously failed attempts, most notably the failure of the 1980 Iranian hostage-rescue attempt.

Apart from its limited effectiveness in the reduction of terrorism, another main limitation of using the military approach to the hostage-crisis in Lebanon relates to the constraints in the political environment within which it is applied. In order to avoid a military confrontation with other state actors, applying military force to the hostage-crisis by Western governments has been constrained by the political and military risks of Syrian involvement and response to any action. For example, in response to the 1987 U.S. naval deployment, Syria accused the American administration of using the hostage-situation as an excuse for a possible attack against Lebanon. As a consequence, the military option by Western governments for the resolution of the hostage-crisis has not been a viable and realistic option given the intelligence constraints in identifying responsible Hizb'allah individuals and bases in the civil war environment as well as the political constraints in avoiding an escalation or a wider confrontation with either Syria or Iran.

The Political, Economic and Legal Options

In the absence of an effective military option, Western governments have utilized other instruments of statecraft in the political, economic and legal realm in pursuit of political objectives to secure the release of its citizens from captivity in Lebanon. The political options used by Western governments have been geared towards forcing Iran and Syria to intercede with the Hizb'allah for the release of hostages through a combination of either sanctions or conciliatory diplomatic and political measures. While the underlying political objective has been to make it clear to Iran and Syria that support for terrorism in any form constitutes unacceptable international behaviour, the employment of political sanctions as punishment, through the withdrawal of diplomatic relations and increased political pressure in the regional and international context, has rested on the assumption that it would generate a change in the behaviour of Iran and Syria to abstain from its close support of the Hizb'allah and to force these states to influence the movement to intercede on their behalf for the release of Western captives. However, the disruption or absence of relations between Western governments and Iran as well as Syria have neither been the result of any Iranian or Syrian involvement with Hizb'allah nor yielded the release of any foreign captives, rather it has been in response to specific diplomatic incidents and in the wider context of the conduct of foreign policy. This was evidently displayed by the French decision to maintain relations with both Iran and Syria despite their complicity in the 1983 suicide attack against the French MNF contingent in Lebanon. The reluctance of the French government to sever ties with Syria in 1986, despite E.C. efforts to impose comprehensive sanctions, out of political expediency in the conduct of foreign policy demonstrated also the weakness of using punitive measures without the mechanism to enforce a uniform approach. Apart from the permanence of U.S. policy of diplomatic isolation towards Iran, the absence of relations with Iran and Syria by other Western governments has more often hindered the pursuit of foreign policy interests towards the region and prevented a direct dialogue with these states over the hostage-issue rather than assisted in the reduction of terrorism or procured the release of the foreign captives.[38]

The effectiveness of the diplomatic option of punishing Iran and Syria through the withdrawal of diplomatic relations is closely dependent on using conciliatory political measures as a complement, through offers for their restoration in the event Syria and Iran use their influence with the Hizb'allah to secure the release of foreigners from captivity. In the case of U.S.-Syrian diplomatic relations, the U.S. government has consistently applied a pragmatic approach towards Syria in the absence of any relations with Iran and as it has been the main channel used for intercession with the Hizb'allah over the hostage-issue. Despite the fact that Syria has remained on the U.S. State Department list of state-sponsors of terrorism, the reluctance by the U.S. government to punish Syrian involvement with the Hizb'allah or pressure it to exert its influence over the movement was evidently displayed by the brief application of sanctions between mid-1986 until the autumn of the following year (Syria has remained on the U.S. State Department's list of state-sponsors between 1986–1995). Although Syria has occupied the role as the main channel for U.S. efforts to release its hostages, despite Syria's limited ability to intervene with the Hizb'allah, the desire to disrupt U.S.-Syrian relations has decreased with the elevated role of Syria in the region and within Lebanon as well as with its key participatory role within the Middle East peace process. In contrast to Syria, the U.S. government has persistently refused to remove sanctions towards Iran as it has pursued a subversive and aggressive foreign policy in the region. Although the dichotomy of full U.S. diplomatic relations with Syria and their absence *vis-à-vis* Iran has been guided by other foreign policy considerations in the region, the unwillingness by the U.S. government to punish Syria for its involvement and, at the same time, be conciliatory towards Iran have undermined not only the utility of placing pressure on these states, through sanctions and conciliatory moves, to intervene more forcefully with Hizb'allah in Lebanon for the release of hostages, but also blocked any overall progress in negotiations over the hostage-crisis.[39]

The French approach to political sanctions and conciliatory gestures has been uniformly one-sided as France has maintained diplomatic relations with both Iran and Syria despite efforts by the E.C. to impose sanctions on Syria in late-1986.[40] Unlike its European allies, the French government has accommodated Syria in the region despite its clear involvement in terrorism against French interests, and has maintained relations with Iran, with the exception of a brief period over diplomatic incidents from July until November 1987. While the French refusal to disrupt relations has been based on its wider foreign policy interests in the Middle East (especially as

Prime Minister Chirac argued that Syria played a key role in any solution to the chaos in Lebanon and would retain relations with Syria), it has also closely mirrored the French approach to negotiations with Iran and Syria over the hostage-crisis. In the French case, the use of sanctions against Iran and Syria could be seen as unnecessary as its negotiation position was assumed to have warranted the exploitation of Syrian and Iranian influence over the movement, and this was coupled with an overall willingness to make concessions to Iranian and Hizb'allah demands.

While French unwillingness to sever relations with Syria in alignment with other E.C. states has undermined the effectiveness of sanctions, the British approach to the employment of sanctions and conciliatory measures has been contrary to the approach adopted by the U.S. government, as it has applied uncompromising sanctions against Syria between mid-1986 until November 1990 while its relations with Iran have been limited and relations temporarily severed over specific issues and incidents. As British-Syrian relations were permanently disrupted by the 1986 Nizar Hindawi affair, the British government adamantly refused to restore relations with Syria until it fulfilled certain preconditions and distanced itself from sponsoring terrorism.[41] The refusal by the British government to restore relations until November 1990, despite assurances by Syria that it had fulfilled these necessary preconditions, demonstrated the concentration on Iran as a limited channel for influencing the Hizb'allah to release its citizens from captivity. The policy also ignored the fact that the absence of relations obstructed any Syrian efforts or willingness to facilitate their release, while the policies of PM Thatcher, which overruled requests by the Foreign Office to renew ties with Syria, derailed any opportunity to secure the freedom of its hostages.[42] This was clearly evident by the *volte face* in the restoration of British relations with Syria immediately after the resignation of PM Thatcher in the autumn of 1990. Although the British government has concentrated on Iran as the key to the release of its hostages, the Anglo-Iranian relationship suffered a series of diplomatic incidents in mid-1987. The improvement in Anglo-Iranian relations, culminating in the formal reopening of Britain's embassy in Teheran in December 1988, was shortlived as Iran severed diplomatic relations in March 1989 after Ayatollah Khomeini's *fatwa* against Salman Rushdie. Following the ascendancy of Douglas Hurd as foreign secretary there were negotiations with Iran over the restoration of relations. Iraq's invasion of Kuwait contributed to the British urgency of resolving outstanding differences with Iran through diplomatic representation.

The varied individual approach by these three Western governments to the use of sanctions and conciliatory political measures as instruments to pressure both Iran and Syria to intercede with the Hizb'allah have been governed not only by their wider foreign policy interests in the region but also by differences in the approach to negotiations adopted by these states in terms of the selection of certain channels to influence the movement in Lebanon to release foreign hostages. Apart from the French approach to maintain diplomatic relations with both Iran and Syria, the absence of Anglo-Syrian and U.S.-Iranian diplomatic relations without a willingness to use conciliatory measures served not only to undermine any possibility for progress in securing the release of their citizens in captivity, but also demonstrated disregard for the opportunities and constraints in the fluctuating relationship between Syria and Iran as well as the political environment within Lebanon in which the Hizb'allah operates and exists. This has been evident by the failure to rely on either Iran or Syria as the only channel in negotiations over hostages without reference to their individual ability to exert its influence over the movement in accordance with shifts in their ties to Hizb'allah's command leadership between 1987–1991 and, more importantly, to the status of the Iranian-Syrian relationship over time, as evidently displayed by the increased friction between 1986 and 1988.

A major weakness in the Anglo-American approach has been the uncoordinated employment of opposite channels through either Iran or Syria in efforts to secure the release of hostages in Lebanon and the varied approach as well as consistency in applying santions or making conciliatory gestures. This problem was evidently displayed by the indiscriminate approach to comprehensive sanctions on Syria by the European allies and the United States. The lack of comprehensiveness of these sanctions, as displayed by French refusal to join a concerted E.C.-effort and by the decision of the U.S. government to abandon them the following year, rendered any pressure on Syria useless to forcefully intervene and limit the activities of the Hizb'allah, notwithstanding its already limited ability to avoid offending Iran.

The use of the economic option by Western governments has also assumed the form of the combined use of sanctions and conciliatory gestures towards Iran and Syria. While the status of economic relations between the U.S. and Iran has been governed and regulated by any progress in negotiations at the U.S.-Iranian Claims Tribunal in the Hague under the 1980 Algiers agreement, any impairment of economic relations with Iran by either the French or British governments has been avoided due to their alleged neutrality in the Iran-Iraq war and, more importantly, to the advancement of wider commercial interests in the Middle East. This was evident by the continued position of Iran as the second most important Middle East market in 1988 for the United Kingdom, and by France to a limited degree despite its close role as arms supplier to Iraq. Despite official observance by Britain of the arms embargo on Iran, it allowed the continuation of Iranian arms purchasing activity in London until September 1987.[43] France also placed an embargo against the purchase of Iranian oil after its relations with Iran were severed over the Gordji-affair in mid-1987. A resolution of the U.S.-Iranian financial disputes has been a central issue to Iran as emphasized by the conditional linkage between any efforts to intercede with the Hizb'allah preceded by the release of Iranian assets frozen in American banks.[44] While in some cases the release of U.S. hostages has occurred in conjunction with the payment of assets, the slow mechanism of adjudication in the U.S.-Iranian financial disputes, coupled with a delay in the release of frozen Iranian assets by the U.S. government, served to obstruct the release of any American hostages. However, any U.S. unwillingness for a speedy resolution to the financial disputes with Iran must be viewed within the context of the Iran-Iraq war and its economic consequences for internal Iranian politics as well as regional developments affecting other U.S. national interests.

The case of economic sanctions and conciliatory gestures towards Syria has been used by Western governments in alignment with the imposed political sanctions after Syrian involvement in the Hindawi-affair in mid-November 1986. While French reservations about E.C.-sanctions against Syria coincided with the release of two French hostages in November 1986, the effectiveness of using economic sanctions was undermined not only by the re-establishment of E.C. and U.S. relations with Syria in mid-1987, due to Syria's role in any negotiations in the Middle East peace process and the closure of Abu Nidal's offices in Damascus, but also by the continued close support provided to Syria by the Soviet Union and the Persian Gulf states as well as by Iran. Although any E.C. financial aid to Syria was blocked by a British veto until September 1990, any Syrian financial difficulties in the interim were circumvented by the Assad regime through adept exploitation of its relationship with Iran as well as within the Arab world and with its patron the Soviet Union.[45] This was particularly evident by Syrian moves towards a *rapprochment* with Iraq within the context of Syrian-Iranian rivalry over debt repayments from supplied oil to Syria. While Western governments failed to utilize Syria's dependency on Soviet or Arab financing as a leverage over Syria, through pressure on these states, the vulnerability of Syria was reinforced by the gradual reduction in aid from the Soviet Union and the Persian Gulf states in conjunction with their own economic difficulties in and after 1989. Yet, Syrian moves towards strengthening its position within Lebanon, through the Ta'if accord, its key role in leading the Arab forces within the UN-coalition during the Gulf war, and its participation in the American-sponsored Middle East peace process led to an economic *rapprochment with* Western governments. The elevated political role of Syria within the Arab world in the aftermath of the Gulf war facilitated Syrian willingness to intercede with Hizb'allah to persuade the movement to release the foreign hostages in close cooperation with Iran.

The Legal Approach

The legal approach by the Western governments has been related to the active apprehension and prosecution of Hizb'allah members and the extradition of arrested suspects. While the U.S. government actively encouraged the apprehension of leading Hizb'allah members after the TWA-incident in 1985, through rewards leading to the location and apprehension of terrorist suspects as well as through increased proactive legislation, the absence of any Hizb'allah actions on U.S. soil and and any case of apprehension or prosecution of Hizb'allah members by U.S. law enforcement agencies has led to a concentration of efforts to pressure its allies in Europe to apprehend Hizb'allah suspects and to request the extradition of those members responsible for terrorist activity involving U.S. citizens and property. This was clearly evident in U.S. efforts for the extradition of Muhammad Hamadi, who was responsible for the hijacking of TWA-847 following his arrest in West Germany in January 1987. Despite unsuccessful efforts by U.S. officials to persuade the Bonn government to extradite Hamadi, it actively assisted in preparation of the prosecution case, leading to the conviction which sentenced Muhammad Hamadi to life-imprisonment.[46] While unsuccessful efforts were made by Hizb'allah SSA officials to influence the legal process in the Hamadi-case through threats and abductions of West German citizens in Lebanon, the U.S. government has received less cooperation from other states in efforts to apprehend, prosecute or extradite Hizb'allah members, mostly for the fear of retribution by the movement and for political expediency. This was demonstrated by Algeria's refusal to apprehend and extradite Izzeldine for his involvement in the TWA-847 hijacking in their handling of the resolution of the KU422-hijacking in 1988.[47] It was also clearly revealed by the French failure to apprehend Imad Mughniya during his known visit to Paris on November 10–16, 1985, despite U.S. requests for his arrest.[48]

Although French law enforcement has been successful in the apprehension of a number of other Hizb'allah members, most notably a whole network in March 1987, it has been simultaneously undermined by a French willingness to circumvent the legal process in certain cases for political expediency in relation to the hostage-crisis in Lebanon.[49] Apart from the Gordji affair, a main case was the arrest of Sheikh Ibrahim al-Amin's nephew, Mohammed Mouhajer, who occupied a senior position as coordinator of the French pro-Iranian network and Hizb'allah in Lebanon, and his subsequent release in March 1988 prior to the complete resolution of the French hostage-crisis.[50] While French political interference in the judicial process was also evident in the release of Anis Naccache and his three accomplices in July 1990,[51] it has underlined the French application of the sanctuary doctrine in order to avert violence on its own soil through the expulsion of terrorist suspects rather than allowing the legal process to take its full course.[52] Although the French has pursued a tough policy of capturing and punishing terrorists at home, as evident by the arrests of a pro-Iranian network in 1987 and by its cooperation with Spanish authorities in 1989, it has avoided the arrest and prosecution of any leading Lebanese Hizb'allah member in alignment with the sanctuary principle and to agreements entered with Iran. This has been evident, for example, by the presence and activity of the *Ahl al-Beit* center in Paris headed by Muhammad Bakir Fadlallah, the brother of Hizb'allah's spiritual leader, Sheikh Muhammad Fadlallah.[53] Although a French magistrate issued arrest warrants against seven Hizb'allah members in Lebanon in April 1989 for involvement in the 1986 Paris bombings, there is limited ability as well as probability for French authorities to apprehend these suspects.

The absence of overt Hizb'allah members or activity on British soil has prevented the apprehension and prosecution of any Hizb'allah-affiliated individuals which has led to a concentration by British authorities on the expulsion of any Iranian and Syrian diplomats using their embassies as a cover for activities connected with terrorism and on pressure against states for the extradition of any Hizb'allah members. While British authorities have continued to expel a significant number of Iranian diplomats and individuals, they have strongly condemned other states, most notably France and Algeria, for their decisions to release several key Hizb'allah suspects. This was evident in British official protests to the Quai d'Orsay after every French concession and by the attempts of the British government to organize a boycott against Algeria for its decision to allow the hijackers free passage out of the country after the KU422-hijacking incident in 1988.

ACCURATE AND TIMELY INTELLIGENCE ON ADVERSARY AND CRISIS

The lack of available intelligence on Hizb'allah and its activities can be attributed not only to the chaotic environment of Lebanon's civil war, but also to the extreme operational security of the Hizb'allah governing its own operations and its relationship with Iran and Syria. As stated by U.S. President Bush: "[w]e are dealing with less than a full deck of information. Its very hard...to get all the information that you need to make a decision."[54] While the U.S. intelligence capability had been almost completely stymied by the Hizb'allah car bomb attack against the U.S. embassy in Beirut on April 18, 1983, and by the kidnapping of William Buckley on March 16, 1984, any subsequent collection of intelligence on the Hizb'allah was almost solely confined to signal and photo intelligence efforts by U.S. embassies in Tel Aviv and Cairo in the absence of human intelligence resources on the ground in Lebanon.[55] Although these methods were successful in monitoring the activities of the Iranian Pasdaran contingent in Ba'albek and the interaction between the Iranian embassies in Beirut and Damascus, they failed to yield accurate intelligence on the Hizb'allah or to predict any terrorist attacks against U.S. citizens and property in Lebanon. This is compounded by the fact that for security reasons, the Iranian embassy in Syria liaised with Hizb'allah due to Iranian fears of intelligence surveillance of satellite and other communications by U.S. against the Iranian embassy in Beirut.[56] Apart from protection through increased physical security for any remaining U.S. facilities in Lebanon and provision of counterterrorism training for the Lebanese intelligence, U.S. intelligence efforts focused on finding the location of hostages and available Hizb'allah targets in the event of a rescue operation or retaliatory strikes. These intelligence efforts were assisted by limited cooperation from Israel's military intelligence in pinpointing specific Hizb'allah command centers. However, the inability of even the IDF to penetrate the Hizb'allah through human intelligence underlined the inherent constraints of efforts to track down not only Western hostages but also missing IDF soldiers held by the Hizb'allah or to predict its modus operandi, as evident by Hizb'allah's suicide-bombing of IDF headquarters in Tyre in 1984. Despite successful IDF abductions of leading Hizb'allah members in southern Lebanon, most notably Sheikh Obeid, it failed to yield any new or useful information about the organisation due to its compartmentalized structure and obsession with security.[57] As American and Israeli intelligence efforts to collect high-quality information on Hizb'allah remained unsuccessful, the efforts by the French Direction

Générale de la Sécurité Extérieure (DSGE) within Lebanon were limited to close liaison with the Lebanese intelligence community while the British GCHQ in Cyprus assumed responsibility for signal intelligence collection.[58] These intelligence collecting activities were not only a reflection of individual capability through actual physical presence within Lebanon but also of the way in which the individual states approached negotiations with the Hizb'allah in accordance with their strategies.

In the absence of accurate information on the exact location of foreign hostages, it was possible to discern certain weaknesses in a number of areas of Hizb'allah activity, vulnerabilities which made the movement susceptible to pressures and offers of accommodation as an instrument of leverage by Western governments to maximise the utility of the application of crisis-management techniques and the possibility for a resolution to the hostage-crisis. It is also possible to identify weaknesses in the Iranian-Syrian relationship as superimposed over the movement's activity in Lebanon in order to evaluate the utility of crisis-management to the hostage-crisis in accordance with opportunities and constraints within the context of the Lebanese political environment and, more importantly, within the multi-dimensional and triangular relations between Hizb'allah, Iran and Syria.

While the collective and centralized nature of Hizb'allah's command leadership made the movement's decision-making process towards the hostage-issue strictly the affair of the highest authority within the movement, most notably by the most senior and powerful cleric who occupied the position of Secretary-General at the time, it was also closely influenced by the personal allegiance of the Hizb'allah leader and other influential members with individual factions within the clerical establishment in Iran. This meant that increased intensity in Iranian clerical factionalism manifested itself through Hizb'allah activity, most notably visible with the diminished power of the Iranian radical cleric Mohtashemi as the movement has pursued a more independent line from official Iran since 1987. While the projection of Iranian clerical factionalism onto the Hizb'allah was clearly evident in efforts by Iranian radicals to obstruct efforts to release Western hostages in alignment with pressures from its rival clerical colleagues after the ascendancy of President Rafsanjani in 1989, it was also displayed by the downgrading of official Iran's financial support to the movement. Previously Iran had also maintained close supervision of most Hizb'allah activity through the presence of two Iranian members within Hizb'allah's main *Majlis al-Shura*, whose presence was gradually reduced with Iranian pressures. As a consequence, the status of Iranian clerical factionalism and its manifestations through the Hizb'allah, as well as the nature of personal allegiances of its leaders manifested through its own clerical factionalism, have been vital to gauge in order to determine the exact ability of Iran to pressure the movement to release foreign captives. This must be balanced against the constraint of Iran's inherent reluctance to pressure the Hizb'allah beyond a certain point, given Iran's enormous financial investments to the movement and the fact that it constitutes the most successful example of Iran's ability to export the revolution. The intensity of clerical factionalism either within Iran or the Hizb'allah translated effectively into a limited ability of official Iran to exert its influence over the Hizb'allah than at any other times. Although Iranian pressure on the Hizb'allah led to a closer allegiance by the movement's command leadership to Iran's radical clergy, it was dependent on the vulnerability of the position of the movement within the context of militia warfare and in a post-civil war environment of Lebanon.

As the Hizb'allah strengthened and consolidated its position within Lebanon in conjunction with the withdrawal of Western MNF contingents in 1984 and Israel in 1985, a main source of vulnerability for the movement was its frictional relationship with Syria, which has been most manifest through its protracted warfare with Amal between 1987–1990. While Syria was forced to crackdown on the Hizb'allah to maintain its control over Lebanon, it exercised considerable restraint in its relationship with the movement in order to safeguard its relationship with Iran. However, strains in the Iranian-Syrian relationship have also been clearly manifest by the degree of Syrian crackdown on Hizb'allah activity, most notably displayed in 1987. The occurrence of this friction provided a window of opportunity for Western governments to exert maximum amount of pressure on Syria to intervene with the Hizb'allah to procure the release of the foreign hostages and undermine the Syrian-Iranian alliance through economic and political offers to substitute Syria's dependence, most notably of oil supply, from Iran.

A major source of potential pressure on the Hizb'allah relates to the presence of the Iranian Pasdaran contingent in Lebanon as it has been crucial to the movement in supplying training and weaponry as well as in the extension of ideological indoctrination and moral support. While the Hizb'allah has been dependent on the interaction with the Pasdaran for the rapid transformation of the movement into a well-organized militia and for its ability to recruit new members, any early efforts to isolate or remove the Pasdaran presence would have disabled the extent to which the Hizb'allah has been able to expand and carry out its operational activity. This has been underlined by the role of the Biq'a as the transit point for not only the infusion of Iranian financial assistance and massive weaponry to the movement but also as it serves as the major command and control center for the movement's resistance activity against Israel in southern Lebanon. The closeness of the relationship between Hizb'allah and the Iranian Pasdaran was also evident by the unsuccessful efforts of President Rafsanjani to reassign Pasdaran members more loyal to his clerical faction in order to influence progress in securing the release of Western hostages. Any limitation to the 2,000-man strong IRGC presence in the Biq'a has always been dependent on Syrian ability and willingness to intercede at the expense of its wider relationship with Iran. While a major opportunity was presented to Syria with the implementation of the Ta'if agreement in early 1991, Syrian reluctance to offend its ally Iran was clearly revealed by its agreement to allow the continued presence of the Pasdaran contingent within Lebanon.

Another pre-emptive measure to limit the early expansion and the militancy of the Hizb'allah relates to finding means and ways to both block the financial channels from Iran to the movement in Lebanon as well as providing economic substitution to the Shi'ite community through any third party or militia to undermine the purely economic attractiveness of Hizb'allah's recruitment for potential members.[59] As seen by the massive defections from other confessional movements to Hizb'allah, most notably by Amal members, the ability to provide economic assistance in the absence of a functioning state has been a key component for popularity of the movement and of Hizb'allah's electoral victory, when it gained the largest single block of seats in Lebanon's post-war parliamentary elections.

Despite the absence of precise intelligence on the Hizb'allah, it is possible to provide an analysis of the environment in which the movement is confined as well as an assessment of the reactions by the movement to pressure on the movement and to changes in its position within Lebanon. It is also essential in the determination of the vulnerability of the adversaries in the employment of crisis-management techniques with an objective of securing the release of its citizens in captivity. While the weaknesses of the movement usually correspond to the shifts in the relationship between Iran and Syria and their own vulnerability to pressures and offers of accommodation, it is vital to accurately assess the weak links in the triangular relationship between Hizb'allah and its patrons through exploitation of crisis-management within not only the framework of the regional environment but also the boundaries of the ability and willingness of these states to intercede on behalf of the Western governments. A measurement of Western governments' understanding of the dynamics of this

triangular relationship can be viewed in terms of their selection of negotiation channels and the direction of pressure on either Iran and Syria to force
the movement to relinquish its foreign captives.

MAINTENANCE OF COMMUNICATION CHANNELS WITH ADVERSARY

The effectiveness of crisis-management in negotiations with the adversary
is not only directly dependent on the selection of communication channels with the adversary through either direct dialogue or the employment
of intermediaries as well as on decisions to conduct negotiations in public
or secret, but also on their employment in relation to the opportunities and
constraints in the political environment which governs the possibility for
either success or failure in the resolution of the hostage-crisis. While the
actual types of communication channels have been bound by the constraints of the political environment and selected on the basis of being successful in influencing the dynamics of the hostage-crisis for its resolution,
their effectiveness have also been closely influenced by the willingness to
enter into negotiations backed by the ability to grant at least minimum
concessions. The employment of vastly different channels by the French,
American, and British governments in their approach to negotiations has
changed in accordance with the status of their relationships with Iran and
Syria as well as with the actual willingness and ability of these states to
intercede with the Hizb'allah for the release of foreign hostages. This has
been closely influenced by the level of willingness and ability of Western
governments to grant specific concessions to these states measured against
the political acceptability and expediency of caving in or holding out to
any demands.

   Unlike Britiain's adamant refusals to negotiate with the Hizb'allah or
with those states closely identified with the movement in Lebanon, both
the French and the American experience with negotiations in the hostage-
crisis have revealed a shared willingness to explore almost all channels
available to them while they have significantly differed in approach to the
negotiations, the selection of intermediaries and the willingness to concede
to any demands for the release of their citizens. The effectiveness of these
different approaches to negotiations must be evaluated in terms of the suit-
ability of intermediaries in relation to the opportunities and constraints of
the political environment in which they have been applied to as well as the
actual mechanics of the process of individual negotiations by Western
governments.

French Negotiations

The approach to negotiations by the French government in response to the multiple abductions in 1985 assumed several simultaneous strategies directed towards direct discussions with Iran and Syria as well as towards the establishment of indirect contacts with individual members of the Hizb'allah.[60] After the discovery of Amal's limited influence to act as an intermediary despite its close involvement in negotiations over the TWA 847-incident, Mitterrand's government dispatched Dr. Raza Raad, a Shi'ite French medical doctor with close contacts within the Lebanese Shi'a community, to establish channels with the Hizb'allah in November 1985 in response to the earlier kidnappings of four French citizens.[61] These negotiations lasted until early 1986 and were led by: Lt. Col. Jean-Louis Esquivier (head of antiterrorism unit at the Champs-Elysées); d'Hubert Védrine, an aide to Mitterrand; and Jean-Claude Cousseran (later head of DGSE). While negotiations failed to yield any positive results,[62] as evident by Hizb'allah's terrorist campaign in Paris (initiated to pressure the French government during national elections in order to gain the release of Anis Naccache and halt French arms shipments to Iraq), the subsequent efforts by French intermediaries towards indirect negotiations with the kidnappers reflected political rivalry between President Francois Mitterrand and the newly elected Prime Minister Jacques Chirac, as evident by their dual independent efforts through personal envoys.[63] While Mitterrand employed Syrian businessman Omran Adham as its new intermediary after the abduction of four more French citizens in Lebanon,[64] the Chirac government intensified its own efforts through Dr. Raza Raad and, more importantly, through the employment of Jean-Charles Marchiani, alias Alexandre Stefani,[65] a personal envoy of the Interior Minister Charles Pasqua. The central role of Marchiani as the main French emissary in the negotiations with representatives of the Hizb'allah reflected not only the lead effort by the Chirac government in securing the release of its citizens through mainly Iran as a channel, in contrast to Mitterrand's efforts via Syria through Omran Adham, but also that French institutional responsibility for the hostage-issue was increasingly delegated through the Prime Minister's Office and the Ministry of Interior rather than through the Ministry of Foreign Affairs.[66] The lead role of the Ministry of Interior in the process of negotiations for the release of its citizens from Hizb'allah captivity was also revealed by certain actions which undermined efforts to normalize relations with Iran by the Ministry of Foreign Affairs. This was evident by the expulsion of Iraqi *al-Da'wa al-Islamiyya* members to Iraq, the arrest of a number of leading pro-Iranian Hizb'allah members in

France and, more significantly, by the Gordji affair which led to the rupture of diplomatic relations between France and Iran. While Wahid Gordji had occupied a central role in negotiations between the French Ministry of Foreign Affairs and Iran towards normalized relations, efforts by the Ministry of Interior to arrest him also revealed the intense rivalry between the various ministries controlled by either Chirac and Mitterrand linked in some ways to the hostage-affair. In particular, the rivalry between the Ministry of Foreign Affairs and Ministry of Interior was revealed by the claims by Gordji that French foreign ministry officials had warned him to go into hiding prior to attempts by the police to arrest him.[67] The elevated role of the Ministry of the Interior was also displayed in exploiting these actions in negotiations with Iran and the Hizb'allah over the hostage-issue, as evidently displayed by the expulsion of political opponents of the Khomeini regime, most notably the leader of *Mujahidin al-Khalq* organisation, and its interference in and control over the French judicial process which led to the release of several key Iranian and Hizb'allah terrorist suspects.[68] While the expulsion of Mahmoud Rajavi led to the release of two French hostages in June 1986, the release by France of $330 million of the $1 billion loan to Iran in November 1986 contributed to the release of three other French hostages.

The negotiating efforts by Marchiani, aided by the enlistment of Iskandar Safa in July 1987,[69] progressed with the release of several French hostages in conjunction with a number of concessions to Iran. While Marchiani received a *carte blanche* by Chirac to pursue the complete resolution of the hostage-crisis prior to the May 1988 national elections, as evident by the release of Mohammad Mouhajer in March 1988, rivalry between the two French political factions was manifest through the expulsion of Mitterrand's envoy, Omar Adham, by Interior Minister Charles Pasqua from both any participatory role in French negotiations with Hizb'allah on the hostages and from France itself on May 3, 1988.[70] Although Marchiani managed to secure the release of the last French hostage on May 5, 1988, three days before the final round of the French presidential elections, Jacques Chirac lost the election to the incumbent, Francois Mitterrand. The Interior Minister Pasqua insisted that no deals had been entered into with Iran, though acknowledging that France had agreed to repay a second instalment of $330 related to its outstanding Eurodif loan (it also included a deal for financial compensation to captors and to families of the IRGC killed in the French retaliatory raid on Ba'albek in 1983).[71] However, Mitterrand's electoral victory created problems in the implementation of any prior deals made by Marchiani, most notably the release of Anis Naccache as evident from denials by Prime

Minister Michel Rochard that he had any record of such deals, despite Iranian insistance.[72] The Iranian dispute with the French government continued over the case of Anis Naccache was resolved in July 1990 when he was pardoned by President Mitterand,[73] while the last tranche of $330 million to Iran was settled by France in December 1991.[74]

The unique French approach to negotiations over the hostage-issue concentrated on the employment of unofficial intermediaries in direct contact with leading Hizb'allah members rather than through formal and high-level representatives of the French government in talks with Iran and Syria. This posture towards negotiations was greatly assisted by the rivalry between Chirac and Mitterand through their individual emissaries, who were able to exploit initiatives with either Iran and Syria to the advantage for a resolution of the French hostage-crisis. While it is clear that Hizb'allah and Iran preferred to deal with unofficial French emissaries to ensure deniability in their responsibility in the hostage-affair, the French government also used the offices of a third state, Algeria, to guarantee the terms of any agreement with Iran. The acceptable role of Algeria for the kidnappers had been highlighted by their previous involvement as interlocuter in the resolution of 1980 U.S. embassy siege in Iran as well as Hizb'allah's hijacking of KU422 in April 1988 in which it guaranteed the security of the hijackers and their free passage out of the country.

The effectiveness of French negotiation efforts have not only been related to an expressed willingness to grant major concessions in order to secure the release of its citizens from captivity but also to the approach of direct negotiations with Hizb'allah officials assisted by the maintenance of diplomatic relations with Syria and Iran, which was exploited by the rivalry between the various French emissaries. Although these emissaries were able to use their close influence with either Iran or Syria to place simultaneous pressure on the Hizb'allah for the release of French citizens, it also fuelled the competition between Iran and Syria in efforts to receive benefits from any release of hostages. This was revealed by Syrian warnings against the execution of French hostages by the Hizb'allah, while Iran attempted to circumvent Syria in the release process in order to receive the credit for the release of French hostages for political advantage in negotiations with other states whose nationals were held hostage in Lebanon. The employment of individual emissaries with close contacts with either Iran and Syria benefited from the tension and rivalry in the wider Iranian-Syrian relationship and on the ground in Lebanon between 1986 and 1988. However, the political rivalry between the emissaries was also exploited by the Hizb'allah and Iran as they were able to raise the level of concessions in conjunction with the political expediency in having French

citizens released before or after the presidential elections. Although
Charles Pasqua claimed that France had refrained from paying any price
for the release of French hostages, the admission by Sheikh Fadlallah that
France had made concessions to secure the release of its citizens from captivity also predicted that the movement would be equally successful in its
negotiations with the U.S. government.[75]

American Negotiations

In contrast to the French approach to the negotiations with the Hizb'allah,
the strategy employed by the United States to the hostage-crisis was based
on a refusal to deal directly with the Hizb'allah on the ground in Lebanon.
While the the U.S. refusal to negotiate directly with the kidnappers was a
direct reflection of a major weakness to cultivate and employ useful local
contacts within the Shi'a community, it can also be attributed to limitations of direct negotiations given the extremely hostile attitude of the
Hizb'allah, to the manner in which American officials viewed the relationship between the Hizb'allah and its patrons Iran and Syria, as well as to
the limited ability to grant concessions to any demands given the constraints of political accountability both at home and abroad. Although the
American administration had successfully resolved the earlier abduction of
U.S. citizens through mainly negotiations with Syria, and rescue operations by its proxy Amal,[76] the handling of the TWA 847-hijacking became
a landmark event in which the personal intervention by Iran's Hashemi
Rafsanjani with Hizb'allah fostered the initiative by U.S. officials to
exploit Iranian clerical factionalism through an exchange of arms-for-
hostages as a key component in an wider effort to re-establish relations
with "moderate" officials in Iran for a more pro-Western policy after the
death of Khomeini. Apart from Iranian intervention for the resolution of
the TWA-847 incident and the close involvement of Syria and Amal in the
negotiations,[77] the release of 766 Shi'ite prisoners in exchange for
American passengers also revealed a willingness by the U.S. government
to employ Israel as a conduit and shield for any direct concessions to the
Hizb'allah.

  While the U.S.-Iranian arms-for-hostages deal between August 1985
until its disclosure in the pro-Syrian Lebanese weekly, *al-Shira*, in
November 1986 yielded the release of three American hostages, the failure
of this initiative demonstrated not only a severely flawed analysis by U.S.
officials of Hizb'allah's closer allegiance to the more radical clergy within
Iran's clerical establishment, but also exposed the dangers associated
with reliance on Iran as the only channel at the expense of any Syrian

involvement. The failure of the arms-for-hostages affair highlighted also the major problems of efforts to use the comprehensive solution of the hostage-issue as a key component in U.S. attempts to normalize relations with Iran without a willingness to make any concessions. While the previous option of using Syria as a vechicle for negotiations by the Reagan administration had been curtailed by the imposition of sanctions due to Syria's close involvement in the Hindawi-affair in mid-1986, the U.S. government was forced to renew its dialogue with Syria over the hostage-issue in the absence of ties with Iran and in the absence of other negotiation channels with the Hizb'allah after the exposure of the U.S.-Iranian arms-for-hostages deals. The decision by the Reagan administration to devalue the issue of the hostages in January 1987, accompanied by an official decree barring travel to Lebanon by American citizens, came not only as a direct response to efforts to limit the hostage issue on the political agenda, following the revelation of the Iran-Contra affair and the abduction of four American citizens during that month, but also reflected the lack of available negotiation channels for the U.S. government, especially as the British independent envoy Terry Waite was abducted by the Hizb'allah, and an unwillingness to offer any kind of concessions to either the Hizb'allah or Iran. Although the PLO had offered to act as an intermediary with the Hizb'allah over the hostages in 1986, especially as Imad Mughniyya of the Hizb'allah SSA had been a member of Fatah Force 17, all efforts failed as PLO's contacts within the movement were in no position to act independently as Hizb'allah's main leadership rejected any PLO overtures.[78] In addition, the option of using Israel as a third party, through the release of imprisoned Lebanese Shi'ites in a similar exchange surrounding the TWA-847 incident, was also curtailed as Israel linked any release of prisoners with the return of its missing IDF servicemen held by Hizb'allah and as any reciprocal moves towards a hostage-release process would exacerbate the political damage created by the Iran-Contra affair.

Apart from an array of unofficial and independent mediation attempts by private individuals and businesses,[79] the only available channel towards Iran used by the U.S. government in relation to the hostage-issue was through the financial negotiations at the U.S.-Iranian Claims Tribunal in the Hague, which was initiated in December 1986 and lasted until mid-1987. However, the official American rejection to link the issue of the release of U.S. citizens in Lebanon with the return of frozen Iranian assets, while it also publicly disavowed any efforts by private mediators, left limited scope for manoeuver in any negotiations for the resolution of the hostage-crisis. Although the concentration on Syria for negotiations by the Reagan administration yielded progress in the cessation of abduction of

American citizens, as revealed by the Syrian intervention in response to the kidnapping of Charles Glass in June 1987, it is important to recognize that these results can mainly be attributed to Syrian efforts to consolidate its hegemony over Lebanon rather than to any American success in persuading Syria to act for the resolution of the hostage-crisis. The reliance on Syria as a main channel for negotiations resulted in limited progress for the release of any hostages given the increased tension between Iran and Syria as well as by the Hizb'allah-Amal warfare in Lebanon.

The succession of Bush to the U.S. presidency in 1989 represented an opportunity and a major shift in the way in which the American administration approached channels of negotiations and the issue of concessions to the hostage-crisis. This shift was first revealed in October 1988 by overt U.S. signals towards Iran of a willingness to open a dialogue on the hostage-issue through a third party. While the U.S. government used Algerian, Swiss, and Pakistani officials as channels to pass messages to the Iranian regime, the Bush administration overtly signalled the Iranian regime that to use its influence with the Hizb'allah for the release of American hostages would be rewarded in some way, especially with the ascendancy of Rafsanjani in the aftermath of the death of Ayatollah Khomeini. In an effort to facilitate this process through goodwill gestures, the U.S. government agreed to return $567 million to Iran, in an agreement under the auspices of the U.S.-Iranian Claims Tribunal in November 1989, coupled with a willingness to compensate the families of the victims of the Iranian airbus mistakenly shot down by U.S.S. Vincennes in July 1988. While Hizb'allah clerical rivalry and efforts by Iran's Rafsanjani to consolidate the Iranian revolution at home prevented the release of any U.S. hostages, Iranian signals that 1990 would be the last year for foreigners in captivity led to the release of two American hostages in April 1990, through Swiss mediation, prior to scheduled talks at the U.S.-Iranian Claims Tribunal in the Hague. Yet, U.S. officials adopted the position that it would withhold tangible incentives or rewards until the remaining American hostages were released. However, the changes in the strategic environment in the Middle East following Iraq's invasion of Kuwait, which led to the freedom of the *al-Da'wa* prisoners in Kuwait, blocked any significant progress in the hostage-crisis as it increasingly became dependent on Middle Eastern politics rather than on individual initiatives by Western governments.

The personal involvement of UN Secretary-General Javier Perez de Cuellar and his personal envoy, Giandomenico Picco, in efforts to find a comprehensive resolution to the hostage-crisis through a triangular hostage-release process in which the Hizb'allah would release Western hostages and missing IDF servicemen in return for Israel's release of imprisoned Shi'ites,[80] came at the invitation of Iran and provided the necessary face-saving solution for all involved parties as well as a shield for any indirect involvement by the Bush administration. Apart from the removal of a major impediment to hostage-negotiations in the form of the release of the *al-Da'wa* prisoners in Kuwait, the success of the negotiation efforts by the UN envoy was rooted in not only the personal efforts by Giandomenico Picco to find a satisfactory overall solution to demands of all parties through secretive dialogue,[81] but also, more importantly, that his negotiation efforts were backed by assurances to Iran that the UN Secretary-General would release the findings with regard to UN Resolution 598 prior to the expiry of his term of office on December 31, 1991. While the Bush administration rejected demands by the Hizb'allah, via the UN envoy, that the U.S. government would refrain from retributions with the release of the last American hostage, it was privately agreed to in communications with Iran and Syria.[82] A major contribution to the release of the American hostages was the settlement of outstanding financial disputes between the U.S. government and Iran under the ten-year old Algiers agreement most notably in December 1991 and February 1992.

The American approach to negotiations over the hostage-issue has been characterized by the employment of an array of official and unofficial intermediaries without a clear consideration for opportunities and constraints created by the political environment within Lebanon and in the region. This has been evident in the continous and erratic shifts in the direction of any U.S. dialogue with Iran and Syria as well as through the nature and employment of intermediaries. While the limited achievements by U.S. negotiation efforts can be attributed to the absence of diplomatic relations with Iran and to its refusal to deal directly with the Hizb'allah in Lebanon, it can also be explained by the reliance on Syria as the only vehicle for intercession with the movement in light of the limited ability and willingness by the Syrian regime to intervene at the expense of its wider relationship with Iran. Any Syrian intercession with the Hizb'allah from 1984 to the TWA-847 incident in 1985 had been possible with the active support and knowledge of both Hizb'allah and Iran to position itself as a useful intermediary in an effort to exploit the hostage-crisis for political purposes and to distance itself from the activity of the movement despite complicity in these Hizb'allah operations. The use of Syrian influence over the Hizb'allah had been limited by its revelation of the U.S.-Iranian arms-for-hostages deal and by intensified Iranian-Syrian rivalry over Syria's unwillingness to settle its outstanding payments for oil to Iran. As a consequence, Syrian inability to effect the release of Western hostages was increasingly weakened in conjunction with the Amal-Hizb'allah warfare in Lebanon and by the increased standing of the Hizb'allah as a movement at the expense of Amal as well as by the over-riding interests to maintain its useful relationship with Iran as a leverage in the wider inter-Arab politics. This tendency for overestimation of the ability by certain intermediaries to persuade or intervene with Hizb'allah's command leadership for the release of American hostages was also evident in the approach adopted by U.S. officials in the efforts to use rivalry within Iran's clerical establishment to its advantage in the U.S.-Iranian arms-for-hostages initiative. The exclusion of Hizb'allah officials from any negotiations also ignored the effects of clerical rivalry within the movement itself as well as its allegiance with more radical Iranian clergy. This was clearly demonstrated by the obstruction of any progress in the release of U.S. hostages by the Hizb'allah command leadership with the active support of the radical Iranian clerical faction between 1988 and 1990.

Another major drawback of U.S. negotiation efforts has been related to the non-secretive nature of dialogue conducted through intermediaries with Iran and Syria which has undermined the willingness by American administrations to grant any concessions for progress in negotiations which resemble any dealmaking. In many cases, the negotiation efforts by the U.S. government have been not only severely weakened by the employment of nonconciliatory rhetoric and posturing towards Iran and the Hizb'allah, exacerbated by the announcement of new and hardline counterterrorist policies, but also undermined by negotiation efforts through intermediaries without the actual ability or mandate to make any concessions. As a consequence, U.S. negotiation efforts have sent mixed signals to the Hizb'allah and Iran through the contradiction between pri-vately conciliatory positions and publicly stated hardline positions. As noted by Amir Taheri: "[t]o them any concession given is a sign of weak-ness and automatically invites further aggression on their part. The wield-ing of the stick by the West, on the other hand, is considered to be perfectly normal and a temporary hardship which has to be endured."[83]

British Negotiations

The British approach to negotiations has been characterized by a firm and uncompromising refusal to negotiate not only with the Hizb'allah but also with either Iran or Syria over the hostage-crisis. On October 21, 1986, the British Foreign Office advised its nationals in Lebanon to take maximum

security precautions or leave the country. Although never officially sanc-
tioned by the British government, the independent mediatory role of Terry
Waite, a special envoy to the Archbishop of Canterbury, was the only
available option for the release of the two British citizens abducted by the
Hizb'allah in April 1986. The British government has repeatedly distanced
itself from Waite and made it clear that his missions to Beirut were
unofficial and that it could provide no assistance in the event of trouble for
Waite.[84] While the negotiation efforts by Terry Waite in Lebanon had
been formally initiated on November 14, 1985, ostensibly by American
requests and on behalf of a humanitarian effort to secure U.S. hostages,[85]
the issue of the British hostages was linked by default in his efforts to find
a comprehensive solution to the Western hostage-problem. As the case of
the *al-Da'wa* prisoners in Kuwait remained a central demand for the kidnappers in Lebanon, Waite concentrated on this issue in secret face-to-
face meetings with Hizb'allah officials in Beirut and through repeated
requests to the Kuwaiti government to allow him entry and permission to
visit the *al-Da'wa* prisoners. While his two missions to Lebanon, in
November and December 1985, failed, as the Kuwaiti government firmly
refused to grant him an entry visa, it underlined the difficulty of the
conduct of clandestine negotiations with any Hizb'allah officials privately
and, at the same time, maintaining a highly visible outward profile and
spearheading a humanitarian mission without the ability to make any concessions in efforts to influence the Kuwaiti government over the fate of the
al-Da'wa prisoners.[86] Due to Waite's own discredited position, being
falsely perceived to be associated with U.S. officials involved in the Iran-
Contra affair in the aftermath of its revelation in November 1986 coupled
with his inability to affect any progress in the case of the *al-Da'wa* prisoners despite numerous efforts, Waite's return for a direct dialogue with the
Hizb'allah in Lebanon in the true spirit of a *humanitarian* effort resulted in
his own captivity in January 1987. As revealed by a declassified document, the principal architect of the Iran-Contra affair, Oliver North, jeop-
ardized Waite's mission as an independent negotiator by informing
Iranians that he was in close contact with Waite and could be used as a
shield for the U.S. and Iranians.[87]

   An unsuccessful attempt was made by the Irish Republican Army (IRA)
to persuade the Hizb'allah to release Brian Keenan through the visit of a
two-man IRA delegation to Beirut in December 1987. The pro-Syrian *al-
Shira* reported that the IRA-delegation consisted of Joe Austin and Denis
Donaldson, who arrived in West-Beirut and attempted to establish contacts
with Hizb'allah's SSA. Apart from holding a meeting with Sheikh
Fadlallah, the IRA representatives offered false Irish passports in return for

the release of Brian Keenan, which would grant the movement a major propaganda coup. However, Hizb'allah were more interested in establishing a working relationship with the IRA through the supply of weapons, safe-houses, and other assistance for its terrorist networks in Britain. This offer was rejected by the IRA.[88] However, any real mediation attempts on behalf of the British hostages were confined to independent humanitarian efforts towards Iran by representatives of the Archbishop of Canterbury in the absence of British diplomatic relations with Syria and with the limitation of dialogue with Iran after diplomatic incidents in late 1987. The involvement of John Lyttle in efforts to conduct a dialogue with Iran and Hizb'allah over the hostage-issue was useful as he served as a conduit between the British Foreign Office and Iran. Although the British government pursued a dialogue with Iran over improvement of relations and over the hostage-issue, these efforts were interrupted by Iran's *fatwa* against Salman Rushdie in 1989. In the absence of British relations with either Iran or Syria, the Republic of Ireland used the issue of the dual nationality of hostage Brian Keenan for its own political advantage in direct negotiations with the Hizb'allah, Syria and Iran. While the release of Keenan in August 1990 represented a diplomatic triumph for Irish diplomacy in contrast to the British failure to negotiate with anyone over their hostages, it was achieved by Iranian willingness to use the Irish hosting of the E.C. presidency as a vechicle to improve its relations with the E.C. member states and as a means to induce improved relations with the Thatcher government, which had indicated a shift in approach to relations with Iran with the ascendancy of Douglas Hurd as the Foreign Minister in late 1989. In a similar fashion to the resolution of the American hostage-crisis, the shifts in the Middle East by the impact of Iraq's invasion of Kuwait facilitated the normalisation of relations between the UK government and Iran as well as Syria while any limited British efforts for the release of its citizens was overtaken by the UN mediation of the comprehensive denouement of the hostage-crisis in Lebanon in 1991.

The British approach to the hostage-crisis, characterized by a strict observance of a no-negotiations and no-concessions policy as it has refused to deal with the Hizb'allah or even those states who have influence over the movement, has been closely influenced by the absence of any friendly diplomatic relations with Iran and Syria. Apart from the unsuccessful efforts by independent negotiators, any British official contacts over the hostage-issue have been veiled behind larger issues of improvement of UK-Iranian diplomatic relations while it has also concentrated solely on Iran as the channel for their release at the expense of Syrian involvement or any contacts with the kidnappers themselves. Unlike the

French or American hostage-cases, the British government has been exempt from any outstanding financial disputes in demands for the release of its citizens. Any progress for their release has been completely dependent on the willingness by British officials to grant Iran and Syria limited political concessions. Although Britain has chosen to maintain an uncompromising lead role in adhering to its publicly stated counterterrorism principles, it also faced unseparable and unavoidable barriers, most notably the Rushdie affair, which prevented any volte face in its position and to any negotiated solution to the British hostage-crisis. Apart from the selection of various negotiation channels to communicate with the adversaries, the success of these efforts are dependent on the functions of the existing crisis-management machinery in limiting the effects of the crisis on the policymakers in Western governments.

FUNCTIONING MACHINERY TO LIMIT EFFECTS OF CRISIS

All three Western governments have instituted and developed sophisticated crisis-management machinery specificially designated to deal and counter incidents of terrorism within and beyond their own borders. While the type and function of this crisis-management machinery reflect the individual governmental structures and varying threats of terrorism, they all share a common purpose of providing essential support mechanisms for both reducing the effect of terrorism on the agenda for poliymakers as an advisory and policy directing body as well as coordinating any response as an operational body. Despite the diversity of exisiting machinery, measurement of success lies in their ability to shield the effects of pressure from terrorism on the higher echelons of decision-makers and to provide a coordinated response to the specific terrorist situations. Unlike other types of terrorism, the prolonged duration of the hostage-crisis in Lebanon has placed special burdens on the machinery to operate effectively over a sustained period. In most cases, the crucial role of crisis-management machinery has been evident in the acute and periodic short-term pressures created by Hizb'allah's threats of execution of hostages unless Western governments meet certain ultimatums.[89]

The role of the media and its impact on the effective functioning of Western government decision-making in such short-term pressure situations has undoubtedly played an instrumental role in exacerbating the acceleration and type of any responses to the hostage-crisis. This has been clearly displayed by the American media's coverage of hijackings and abduction of U.S. citizens by the Hizb'allah, most notably the TWA-847 hijacking in 1985 and in response to the unprecedented number of abductions in January 1987 during the *furor* surrounding the revelation of the Iran-Contra debacle at home and abroad. While U.S. media coverage of the Lebanese hostage-crisis has failed by itself to precipitate any government response, as shown by the restraints in using military force, it has significantly served to elevate the hostage-issue on the U.S. foreign and domestic agendas. The inability of U.S. administrations to deal with and limit the effects of media coverage on the fate of American hostages has acted as a major constraint for any effective response as any action or inaction towards the crisis has either been scrutinized for any resemblance of concessions or underlined the impotence of government response to terrorism, reaffirming the failure to deal effectively with the 1980 U.S. embassy siege in Iran. Although the subsequent U.S. administrations have been constrained by Carter's legacy and the critical role of the media in shaping U.S. foreign policy, the ineffective role of crisis-management machinery as an operational body was also underlined by the political crisis caused by the covert U.S.-Iranian arms-for-hostages deals. The revelation of the so-called Iran-Contra affair became a pivotal event as it not only completely discredited the U.S.-led campaign against international terrorism, undermining previous and current efforts by its allies, but also caused a severe political crisis for the Reagan presidency which his administration never completely recovered from, as the truth about the Iran-Contra scandal remains to be resolved. The political fall-out of the U.S.-Iranian arms-for-hostages deals severely curtailed any official U.S. efforts to procure the release of its citizens from captivity as it also had severe political consequences in Iran. As a result, any subsequent ability of the U.S. government to act *vis-à-vis* the American hostages was severely limited by the political environment in the Middle East, tarnished by the Iran-Contra affair, despite the existence of a well-delineated machinery for dealing with terrorism.

In the French case, the role of the media has not only elevated the importance of the hostage-crisis on the French domestic and foreign policy agendas but has also been exploited by the various political parties for expediency in the two elections in 1986 and 1988. While the circumvention of any coordination between existing and responsible crisis-management bodies was a reflection of the nature of the French "cohabitation" government, the absence of any overall response, facilitated by the political rivalry between Chirac and Mitterrand, contributed to severe friction and cross-purpose activity between responsible French ministries and agencies, most notably in relations with Iran. Although this rivalry worked to the advantage for a speedy resolution of the French hostage-crisis in conjunction with elections, the role of the media exacerbated the search for accommodation with Hizb'allah and Iranian demands in which French foreign policy became bound by the urgency for solutions to the hostage-crisis for political expediency. It also served to give the impression that the French judiciary was subservient to the political masters, most notably in relation to the Gordji-affair.

The British experience with countering domestic terrorism has led to the development and existence of a well-defined crisis-management structure, minimizing interagency rivalry, as well as a reduction in media pressure on the decision-making process. Apart from the moral leadership of the British government in its crusade against terrorism, these functions contributed to a complete devaluation of the hostage-crisis as an issue for poliymakers, facilitated by broad cross-party support, until the 1988 emergence of hostage-pressure groups and political observers questioning government policy in the aftermath of apparent French concessions assisting in the complete resolution of its own hostage-crisis in Lebanon. The British Ministry of Defence and Foreign Office require its employees to sign disclaimers that neither any official extraordinary measures will be taken beyond the normal conduct of foreign policy nor will the British government alter its policy for concerns of individual welfare.[90] While the inflexibility of PM Thatcher deflected criticism from within and from the public for its refusal to conduct any dialogue at all despite Britain's longstanding position and contacts in the Middle East, any real pressures from critics were kept at bay by the inner sanctum of British policymaking and overshadowed by the imposition of the Iranian *fatwa* on Rushdie and developments in the region eminating from Iraq's invasion of Kuwait which limited the government's manoeuverability and urgency to resolve the crisis.

Despite the existence of fully functional crisis-management machinery in all these three Western governments, the inability to shield policymakers from the effect of the hostage-crisis in Lebanon demonstrates not only the vulnerability of Western democratic states with a free press to this form of crisis, aptly exploited by these terrorist groups and their patrons, but also the inadequate functioning of the crisis-management devices in educating the public and pressure groups on the constraints and opportunities of the complex environment under which they operate under in efforts to extract its fellow citizens from captivity. As stated by Ambassador Robert Oakley:

"[t]he highest officials are torn between maintaining a national and governmental posture of strength, based on antiterrorist principles, and a policy more in keeping with their humanitarian and domestic political concerns. Public opinion and media pressures are similarily schizo-phrenic, one day calling for toughness and no concessions to terrorists, but the next day moved by the plight of the hostages and the appeals of their families."[91]

The revelation of the Iran-Contra affair had an enourmous impact not only on the ability by the U.S. presidency to function but also made any British and even French responses to their own hostage-crisis in Lebanon look relatively less damaging or at least more politically defensible in compari-son. Efforts to limit media impact must form the first line of defense in the search for better adaptability of exisiting crisis-management machinery to the hostage-crisis as these incidents exhibit unique features, distinguishing them from other forms of terrorism in longevity and in the complexity of the environment.

BROAD PLATFORM OF SUPPORT FOR MEASURES

The options of response selected by Western governments are not only a reflection of their capability to adapt its crisis-management techniques and machinery to the dynamics of the hostage-crisis environment, but also mirror the urgency created by domestic pressures as well as the political acceptability of any response both at home and abroad. While the number and frequency of hostage-takings differ among various governments, the degree to which Western governments are willing to bend an uncompro-mising no-concessions policy depends on elevated public expectations of the perceived ability by their governments to deliver the freedom of citi-zens held in captivity in accordance with made promises without a visible sacrifice of any principled positions against terrorism.[92]

The support by the public for any military reply to terrorism has been strongest in the United States as evident by the domestic popular support for the retaliatory raid on Libya in 1986 and the military interception of the aircraft carrying the Achille Lauro perpetrators in 1985. Notwithstanding the questionable legality of these actions and the strains caused in alliances with friendly states, the creation of false expectations for the American public in the utility of using military force in the response to the hostage-crisis in Lebanon undermined the credibility of the U.S. government in its resolve to exact swift and effective retribution and exacerbated the pressures on the policymakers to find alternative ways to extracticate the U.S. from previously made guarantees to return its citi-zens home safely.[93]

The issue of negotiations with the Hizb'allah and its patrons over the hostages has also to be seen in the context of a switch from support of hardline policies to more conciliatory tones in conjunction with the duration of the crises. While the revelation of the U.S.-Iranian arms-for-hostages deals totally discredited U.S. hardline rhetoric against state sponsored terrorism, the U.S. public increasingly recognized the value of negotiation with the ascendancy of the Bush administration and, at the same time, the limits of military response in retaliation or rescue attempts in the event of deaths of hostages. In a poll conducted by TIME/CNN in August 1989, over 58 percent of respondents favoured negotiations with the terrorist groups for the hostages' release.[94] The Iran-Contra affair certainly had a very adverse effect on Reagan's standing with the U.S. public, as evident in opinion polls which found Reagan's approval rating plummeting drastically as the largest single drop for any U.S. president in history. A New York Times/CBS News poll recorded a drop in Reagan's approval rating from 67 percent to 46 percent in November 1986.[95] Another New York Times/CBS News poll found that 53 percent of the public believed that the president was lying about the Iran-Contra affair, while only 34 percent believed he was telling the truth.[96] Although Western governments moved to limit their responsibility towards citizens by either issuing, in the case of Britain, warnings to nationals to adopt extreme security precautions or leave Lebanon, or barring travel to and staying in Lebanon, in the case of the U.S. government, an overwhelming majority of Western public consider it still a duty for their governments to do whatever they can to free its citizens taken hostage. This trend was echoed by the British public who overwhelmingly supported negotiations for the hostages' release, after the 1990 release of two American hostages without any apparent sacrifice of principle.[97] The French case underlined the acceptability of conducting negotiations and entering into concessions, shielded by tough visible hardline policies, for the public as long as these in the end yielded the freedom of the all the hostages.

While entering into deals with the Hizb'allah and Iran received limited degree of acceptability in the domestic arena for Western governments with the return of released hostages, it created serious friction in friendly alliances as decisions to deviate from commonly agreed principles seriously undermined the position of those Western governments, most notably Britain, who chose to adhere to a rigid refusal to either negotiate or conduct behind-the-scenes deals for the release of its citizens. This was evidently displayed by the British outcry against the U.S. covert policy with Iran, trading arms for hostages. It was also a serious source of tension in Anglo-French relations with public and private condemnations after every release of French hostages. This became clear by the decision of Chirac to request the French parliament for a surprise vote of confidence, on the eve of the December 1987 Copenhagen E.C. summit, in order to provide extra protection against criticism from British PM Thatcher.[98] These unilateral actions by Western governments may have served their immediate national interests and alleviated public pressures, yet it seriously impaired the collective political will and credibility of any closer international cooperation between states in the field of counterterrorism. It also rendered the effectiveness of coercive instruments of crisis-management in pressuring state-sponsors of terrorism useless as Western states often circumvented collective action for short-term political expediency in pursuit of their own individual national interests in the Middle East and elsewhere.

CRISIS-MANAGEMENT: CONSIDERATION OF PRECEDENT EFFECT OF CRISIS-BEHAVIOUR

A major underlying assumption of adhering to the principles of no-negotiation and no-concession for Western governments to the hostage-crisis is that terrorism must not be rewarded and that appeasement through concessions will only encourage further acts of terrorism. As outlined by President Reagan:

> "concessions to terrorists only serve to encourage them to resort to more terror to obtain their political objectives, thereby endangering still more innocent lives. If terrorists understand that a government steadfastly refuses to give in to their demands...this will serve as a strong deterrent."[99]

These concerns were even echoed by the French Prime Minister Chirac:

> "[w]hen you negotiate with people who take hostages you are obliged, in the negotiation, to give something. It may be just a little, it may be a lot, but you have to give something. Once you have given something, the kidnapper gains from his action. So what is his normal and spontaneous reaction? He does it again, thinking that is a way of obtaining what he cannot obtain by other means. So you get caught in a process. Naturally you can get maybe two, three or four hostages freed. But you immediately give the kidnapper an inducement to seize another three, four, five or six. So it is an extraordinarily dangerous and irresponsible process. That is why I don't negotiate."[100]

While the underpinnings of these principled assumptions are based on absolute standards in alignment with common moral values in the West, their transformation from theory into practice *vis-à-vis* the Western hostage-crisis in Lebanon revealed inconsistency and hypocrisy as these standards were gradually discarded for other overriding concerns in the foreign and domestic arenas. The difficulty of applying these principles consistently in practice underlines the inseparable nature of responses to terrorism and the conduct of Western foreign policy in the Middle East. In short, there are other factors at work here. As such, Western government dealings with hostage-taking incidents became dependent on each government's own foreign policy behaviour towards those states, most notably Iran and Syria, with influence over the Hizb'allah as well as constrained by events in the overall political environment in the Middle East. The commonly accepted assertion, providing the foundation for the principles of no-negotiations and no-concessions, that softening the tough line through dealing with, and providing concessions to, the Hizb'allah only rewards and encourages more hostage-taking must be examined within the framework of the dynamics of Middle East politics rather than in isolation. While U.S. experience with hostage-takings in Lebanon supports the assertion that conceding to Hizb'allah demands leads to further kidnappings, the experience of the French and the British governments in their approach to the hostage-crisis provide ample contradictory evidence. Despite major French concessions to the Hizb'allah and its patrons, no new French hostages were abducted after January 1987. Although most of these French concessions related to the settlement of legitimate outstanding foreign policy disputes with Iran, a number of French concessions, most notably the expulsion of anti-Iranian opposition leaders and the release of imprisoned terrorists were serious breaches of the highly principled moral position of Western governments. Equally, British policy towards negotiation and concessions failed to provoke either new hostage-takings or any resolution to existing hostage-incidents.

The virtuous principles of no-negotiation and no-concession can neither be applied in a vacuum nor in absolute terms. As the announcement of setting these rigid principles on one's own conduct frequently fail to conform to the realities of pursuing foreign policy in highly dynamic hostage-situations, as other interests in the Middle East take precedence over the hostage-crisis, it is bound to invite charges of hypocrisy and double-standards at home and by allies. As aptly observed by Ronald Crelinsten: "[l]ike a child clamoring for forbidden toys, the public expects the government simultaneously to give in and to hold fast."[101]

6 Conclusions

"To release a hostage, it is necessary to identify the group and the country that supports that group. There is no single country in the region that alone can wield pressure on all the groups: indeed, different political groups of the same country have been known to patronise differing Beirut groups. These groups, interact with each other and exchange information: but each has its own hierarchy, its own allegiance and each guards its hostages dearly...[I]n their war against the outside enemy, these groups will do with their hostages what best serves their interests: whether it be demands for political moderation in the Arab-Israeli conflict, the release of fighters from Israeli prisons, the purchase of arms and spare parts, or the freeing of assets in Western banks. It is a war without arms."[1]

INTRODUCTION

The interaction between the dynamics of the foreign hostage-crisis in Lebanon and the responses by the American, French, and British governments, in efforts to secure the release of their citizens from Hizb'allah captivity, has demonstrated the difficulty for Western states in reconciling their firmly-held principles of no-negotiations and no-concessions in dealing with either the Hizb'allah or its patrons with the actual and practical realities governing any resolution to the foreign hostage-situations in Lebanon. This difficulty has been not only based on the uniqueness and complexity of the triangular and multi-dimensional interactions between Hizb'allah, Iran, and Syria that governed motivations for any release of foreign captives but also on the manner in which these Western governments actually responded to the hostage-crisis itself, given the framework of opportunities and constraints in the crisis-environment. This study has provided a methodological approach which not only evaluates the inner dynamics of Hizb'allah and its continous interaction with the Lebanese environment as well as with Iran and Syria but also provides a framework, integrating the principles of crisis-management, which makes it possible to assess the effectiveness of Western government responses to the hostage-crisis in Lebanon. This combined analysis has yielded new and valuable insights on the individual level through the case-study into the mechanisms that govern the behaviour of one of the most dangerous and militant

Middle Eastern terrorist organisations (the Hizb'allah) within its environment in Lebanon, as well as its relationship with those states providing direct or indirect support (Iran and Syria). The study also provided a new analytical framework in the study of terrorism for the evaluation of the performance and effectiveness of Western government responses to the foreign hostage-crisis, using traditional crisis-management techniques, which were evaluated against the actual crisis-environment. This chapter will discuss the most important findings of the case-study of Hizb'allah and its patrons, Iran and Syria, and whether the American, British, and French governments were effective in their approach to the hostage-crisis using crisis-management techniques in terms of their adherence to previously delineated requirements as well as to the dynamics of the crisis-environment itself. It will also briefly discuss the applicability and lessons of crisis-management techniques based on these findings for Western governments and the international system as a whole, most notably in order to more closely resolve the dilemma of fulfilment of the duty by these states to protect their citizens taken hostage abroad, without any major sacrifice in the conduct of foreign policy.

THE CASE-STUDY ON HIZB'ALLAH

This case-study demonstrated, contrary to the longstanding conventional wisdom of most academic scholars, analysts, and policymakers, that an indepth analysis of one of the most complex and secretive terrorist organisations in the Middle East cannot only be accomplished despite the subject's complexity but also yield predictable patterns and conclusions for a fuller comprehension of the inner dynamics of the hostage-crisis in Lebanon. Moreover, the case-study achieved these results through the linkage of the findings throughout the analysis into an aggregate whole, which provided a new mechanism for understanding the behaviour of the Hizb'allah and its interaction with Iran and Syria with special reference to the process of hostage-taking of Westerners.

A main task of this case-study was to answer the underlying questions of why the Hizb'allah resorted to hostage-taking and what mechanisms governed the initiation and resolution of the hostage-incidents. An essential starting point to find answers to these questions was to discard the prevalent assumptions in the West that the Hizb'allah movement emerged on the Lebanese scene in 1982 as a mere creation of Iran and acted to a large extent as an Iranian autonom, principally as it ignored the importance of the historical antecedents to the formation of the Hizb'allah, which fundamentally shaped its ideological outlook as well as its current behaviour. In particular, it was argued that the shared theological experience between future Hizb'allah and Iranian clergy in Najaf, Iraq, provided the basis for close personal friendships which have been instrumental in governing the Lebanese movement's ideological deference to the Islamic Republic of Iran and provided the basis for the evolution of a series of complex clerical networks which governed previous and present activity. While this Najaf-experience has been traditionally overlooked, despite its major importance in explaining the origins and depth of the continued close personal relationships which extended between a number of Iranian and Hizb'allah clerics, it also explained the movement's ready assimilation of, and close adherence to, Islamic Iran's ideological doctrines, especially as most of Hizb'allah's clerical élite were influenced by Ayatollah Khomeini during his exile in Najaf between 1964 and 1978.

This contextual approach, stressing the importance of the shared theological experience in Najaf between leading Hizb'allah clergy and members of Iran's clerical establishment, was a necessary prelude for a fuller understanding of the Hizb'allah as a militant Shi'ite organisation and for the underlying mechanisms that governed its hostage-taking activity. Firstly, it explained the nature and scope of the underlying personal relationships between Hizb'allah and Iranian clerics, which fundamentally served to regulate and govern the movement's previous and present activity. Secondly, it was used also to explain the Hizb'allah's ideological and spiritual deference to Islamic Iran's pan-Islamic vision and authority within the context of the way in which it has influenced and translated into the movement's own revolutionary struggle and activity in Lebanon.

In what way did the shared theological experience in Najaf between leading Hizb'allah clergy and members of Iran's clerical establishment influence and govern the previous and present activity of the movement? It was demonstrated that the collective Najaf-experience played a pivotal role in the actual formation of the Hizb'allah in 1982 and the subsequent guidance provided by its former Iranian Najaf-educated clerical colleagues, most notably from Ali Akhbar Mohtashemi. The strengths of these ties were evident in the pre-Hizb'allah period not only through the close assistance provided by Lebanese Shi'ites to its Iranian clerical colleagues in their anti-Shah revolutionary activity but also within the parallel activities of the Lebanese *al-Da'wa* party and Shi'ite educational institutions, led by Najaf-educated Lebanese clerics. These clerics became a natural and conducive source for Iranian clergy to spread the revolutionary Islamic ideology in Lebanon as defined and led by Imam Khomeini through increased political activism of the Lebanese *al-Da'wa* party and challenges by its more radical and loyal followers within Amal to the movement's moderate and secular orientation. It was demonstrated that these ties between Lebanese Shi'ites and Iranian clergy consolidated with Israel's 1982 invasion, influenced by an array of other key preceding events which accelerated the political radicalization of the Shi'ite community in Lebanon, and translated into the formation of the Hizb'allah under the active supervision and guidance of leading Iranian clergy, closely assisted by the presence of an Iranian Pasdaran contingent in the Biq'a area. Apart from the strong influence of Najaf-educated Iranian clergy over its Lebanese counterparts in the actual creation of Hizb'allah, it was demonstrated that these ties increasingly assumed importance as Najaf-schooled Iranian clergy, most notably members of the so-called revolutionist faction within Iran's clerical establishment, were appointed to head the major official Iranian institutions at work within Hizb'allah and to act as main official liaison with the Lebanese movement. This meant that the Hizb'allah was not only closely dependent on its Iranian allies for material support for the survival and rapid expansion of the movement but also most closely attuned to the uncompromising radical ideology of the Iranian revolutionist faction and, consequently, very susceptible to clerical factionalism in Iran. It was shown that the dismissal and appointment of Iran's radical clergy within these Iranian institutions at work within the Hizb'allah determined the degree of obedience displayed by the movement to Islamic Iran's official leadership and orders, most notably revealed by Hizb'allah's willingness to release its Western hostages. The close influence of the Iranian revolutionist faction over members of Hizb'allah's command leadership was used, at times, as an instrument by these Iranian clergy to both sabotage moderate and pragmatic overtures by the Iranian official leadership in the foreign policy arena as well as to bolster the faction's own positions within Iranian clerical power-struggles. This faction was assisted by the Iranian Pasdaran's active and close involvement with the Hizb'allah, as it often acted in opposition to the policy directions and goals of its civilian superiors, in order to further its own hardline revolutionary principles. It was demonstrated that the dismissal of Hizb'allah's closest Iranian allies from Iranian institutional positions at work within the movement strongly affected the behaviour of the movement towards official Iran, beginning in late 1986 and intensifying after the death of Ayatollah Khomeini in 1989.

While the collective Najaf-experience was useful in explaining the strong personal relationships between the Hizb'allah leadership and Iranian clerics, which fundamentally governed and regulated the hostage-taking activity of the Lebanese Shi'ite movement, it was also used to explain the way in which Hizb'allah's ideological and spiritual deference to Islamic Iran's pan-Islamic vision and authority influenced and translated into the movement's own revolutionary struggle and activity in Lebanon. It was clearly shown that Hizb'allah's rapid growth and popularity within Lebanon was achieved not only by a successful combination of ideological indoctrination and material inducement by the movement through Iranian assistance, but also by the ability of Hizb'allah leaders to mobilize and unite the Lebanese Shi'ite community within the framework of an organisation with clearly defined and articulated political objectives. While Hizb'allah's ideological deference to Ayatollah Khomeini's pan-Islamic vision and authority was instrumental in shaping the nature of the movement's organisational structure and the manner in which the movement sought to implement its pan-Islamic strategy of overthrowing the confessional system and establishing an Islamic state in Lebanon governed by Islamic law, Hizb'allah's mastery of political violence became an essential component in the pursuit of its pan-Islamic goals as it projected itself as the spearhead of the struggle against the enemies of Islam, namely the United States and Israel. In turn, this pan-Islamic premise provided the ideological *raison d'être* for most of the movement's political and military activity in Lebanon and acts as a defining characteristic of the movement's symbiotic relationship with Iran, which underlines their close cooperation and converging interests.

While it was demonstrated that these pan-Islamic goals have provided the Hizb'allah with a sense of purpose and mission as a revolutionary movement and that its activity closely converges with Iranian foreign policy interests, the Iranian-Hizb'allah relationship experienced tension and friction when Islamic Iran's ruling clergy was forced to subordinate the radical philosophy of the revolution for the pragmatic interests of the state. This reinforced the close allegiance between Hizb'allah leaders and members of Iran's revolutionist faction. Despite the fact that Hizb'allah veils its revolutionary struggle in uncompromising pan-Islamic motifs, the movement has demonstrated greater flexibility in readjusting to the realities of constraints imposed by Lebanon's multiconfessional civil war environment and by Syria's wider ambition to establish hegemony over Lebanon.

While Hizb'allah's leading clergy adhere to Iran's pan-Islamic vision and profess absolute allegiance to the authority and guidance of Ayatollah Khomeini, it was established that the rank and file of the movement are far from monolithic but rather bound by their own complex allegiances and subject to frequent disagreements within the movement. Intra-Hizb'allah disagreements have been most evidently focused on the degree to which the movement should conform to Iranian and Syrian foreign policy interests in Lebanon, especially any quest for the resolution of the Western hostage-issue at the expense of compromising the movement's own agenda. In particular, Hizb'allah's "democratization process", whereby elections were held every two years for senior positions in the Consultative and Executive Shura, was not merely a rotation of responsibility among a core group of senior Hizb'allah clergy but also reflected the internal dynamics of the power struggle for the leadership between the more moderate and radical factions within the organisations. As such, any election that either maintains the *status quo* or yields significant changes within the Hizb'allah hierarchy reveals not only the degree of radicalism of a Hizb'allah leader, which subsequently will influence the direction of the organisation, but also where the allegiance of that leader lies within Iran's clerical establishment. At another level, the Hizb'allah elections were not merely a useful guide to monitor Hizb'allah's relationship with Iran but also indications of challenges confronting the organisation inside Lebanon. This was clear from the ascendancy of both Sheikh Abbas al-Musawi in May 1991, which allowed a resolution to the Western hostage-crisis in return for Hizb'allah's permission to remain the only armed movement in Lebanon's post-civil war environment, and Sheikh Hassan Nasserallah in February 1992, which led to Hizb'allah's decision to participate in the Lebanese parliamentary elections in the autumn of that year. This illustrates that an understanding of the behaviour of the Hizb'allah movement depends on the depth and allegiance of closely forged relationships between individual Hizb'allah leaders and Iranian clergy as well as the adaptability of a particular Hizb'allah leader to suit the movement's activity to the political requirements of the environment within which it operates. As a result, it was demonstrated that any analysis of Hizb'allah requires not only an understanding of the movement itself but also its interaction with elements within Iran's clerical establishment as well as with Iranian institutions. Furthermore, Hizb'allah is far from a unified body, as displayed by continous clerical factionalism between its leading members over the direction of the movement and its constant readjustments within Lebanon.

Any analysis of Hizb'allah's involvement in the process of hostage-taking of Westerners must not only take into account these mechanisms of relationships that control and govern the movement's activities but also the influences of the multilayered Lebanese, regional, and international politics. These influences affect the process of the hostage-crisis as Westerners are abducted and released for individual Hizb'allah motives or in convergence with Iranian, and to a lesser extent, Syrian interests.

This involves examination of the nature and dynamics of Hizb'allah's command leadership and its decision-making process, which must be balanced against the dynamics of Hizb'allah's institutional relationships with Iran and Syria in Lebanon in accordance with internal Lebanese factors and external developments, creating opportunities and constraints in the practice of hostage-taking.

It was demonstrated that the use of different cover names by the Hizb'allah, when engaged in hostage-takings and other covert operations, is a remnant of the Shi'a tradition of concealment as practised when religiously persecuted in ancient times in order to confuse the enemy. Apart from providing a shield against persecution or reprisals, Hizb'allah's use of cover names has also signified the different currents and concerns within the movement at specific periods, reflecting the movement's political and military orientation. While the involvement of a specific and small number of Hizb'allah clans in the actual hostage-takings underlined that clan-loyalty and individual clerical relationships provided the basis for the movement, it also showed that it functioned under a centralized and well-organized leadership structure, governed by a supreme politico-religious board of authority, composed of a small and select group of Najaf-educated uluma. The absolute nature of the supreme religious authority of Hizb'allah's command leadership debunked the idea that any of Hizb'allah's hostage-taking activity was pursued independently by individual Hizb'allah clans. This was reinforced by Hizb'allah's institutionalized cooperation and coordination with Iran and Syria in some of these operations. This has meant that Hizb'allah initiated its hostage-taking activity within the context of the collective interests of the organisation as a whole. As a consequence, it was necessary to analyze the nature of Hizb'allah's command leadership, its decision-making structure as well as policy with specific reference to the movement's hostage-taking activity. This made it also necessary to examine the role and influence of Iranian clergy and institutions at work within the movement as well as Syria's influence within and over Hizb'allah activity.

While the highest authority within Hizb'allah's command leadership reflected the individual Shi'ite clergy that assisted in the foundation of the movement in July 1982, it was also detailed that the main clergymen who exercise control over the movement are the ones responsible for a specific committee or portfolio, especially since the 1989 restructuring of the movement with the addition of two new organs, the Executive Shura, and a Politbureau, leading to greater decentralization of decision-making as well as increased factionalism over specific portfolios. It was established that Hizb'allah's hostage-taking activity was executed by a separate

Hizb'allah body, the so-called Special Security Apparatus (SSA), whose members maintained close liaison with Iranian diplomatic representatives in Beirut and Damascus as well as with Iranian Pasdaran officials and Syrian military intelligence. The relations between Hizb'allah's SSA and Syrian military intelligence have been characterized by periods of conflict and cooperation, dictated by the shifting internal situation in Lebanon. Syria has pursued a calibrated policy of tacit cooperation with Hizb'allah and support for its abductions of foreigners, as long as they were in accordance with Syrian strategic interest in Lebanon.

Apart from the Hizb'allah decision-making apparatus and the institutionalized relationship with Iran and Syria through military and civilian channels at work in Lebanon, it was shown that Hizb'allah's mechanism for hostage-taking was also subject to influence from clerical factionalism within the organisation itself and to a web of clerical relationships extending from members of the national *Majlis al-Shura* to various clergy within Iran's civilian and military establishment. It demonstrated that the degree of divergence between Hizb'allah's subordination, in principle, to the supreme religious and political authority of Ayatollah Khomeini, and the disobedience and disagreements displayed within Hizb'allah ranks towards Iran's official leadership, was dependent on Hizb'allah's and individual clergymen's interaction with official Iranian institutions as well as on clerical factionalism in Iran. In turn, any friction in Hizb'allah's relationship with Iran was influenced by the impact of Iranian clerical factionalism on the institutions at work in Hizb'allah.

It has been shown that the Hizb'allah, as a revolutionary movement, was most closely attuned to the revolutionist faction within Iran's clerical establishment, stemming from the involvement of these Iranian clergy prior to and in the actual formation and development of Hizb'allah, which translated into the appointment of these Iranian clergy to the official Iranian institutions at work in Hizb'allah, ranging from the Pasdaran contingent and personal Iranian representatives in Damascus and Beirut to Iran's Ministry of Foreign Affairs and the Martyrs' Foundation. As a result, the Hizb'allah became gradually susceptible to clerical factionalism in Iran, as evident by the dismissal and appointment of Iran's radical clergy within these institutions after 1986. It was demonstrated that the Hizb'allah has been affected by the availability of Iranian financial and material resources to sustain its massive services and project for the Shi'a community, while the Iranian Pasdaran has remained the most reliable and loyal ally of the Hizb'allah.

Hizb'allah's abduction of Western citizens was initiated in specific and limited time periods, or phases, which indicated they were directly influenced by a number of factors and events affecting the organisation within Lebanon, either for the purposes of survival or for the advancement of its pan-Islamic goals. It was also recognized that Hizb'allah activity was directly related to the collective as well as individual interests of high-ranking Hizb'allah clergy. This was examined also through the influence and involvement of Iranian clergy and institutions at work on Hizb'allah's hostage-taking activity, which was governed by the array of official and unofficial interaction between the Hizb'allah and Iran as manifest through hostage-taking, either in alignment with the motivations of official Iran or as a manifestation of clerical factionalism. This assessment was balanced against Hizb'allah's own requirements for its position within the internal Lebanese environment, especially in terms of Syrian influence over its activity.

The initiation of abductions of Westerners demonstrated a strong causal linkage between events (internal Lebanese, regional or international) and motivation for hostage-taking acts by the Hizb'allah, often on behalf of Iran. This was clearly highlighted by Hizb'allah's first four abduction campaigns of American, French, and British citizens, lasting until the autumn of 1986, in which the movement's activity was closely coordinated with Iran and Syria. Apart from Hizb'allah's cooperation with Iran and Syria in a wider attempt to rid Lebanon of all foreign presence through suicide-attacks, the kidnappings of Westerners were motivated by the movement's support for Iran in the Iran-Iraq war and in an attempt to free imprisoned members held in Europe and the Middle East, most notably in Kuwait and Israel. This phase also underlined the heavy influence of certain Iranian revolutionary clergy within and over Hizb'allah's decision-making process.

The close convergence of interests between Hizb'allah and Iran governed hostage-taking activity in Lebanon until the end of 1986 without major signs or impact of any clerical factionalism either within the organisation or from Iran in the process of abductions or releases of hostages. The following phases revealed discord between Hizb'allah and Iran which was largely the result of rivalry within Iran's clerical establishment which affected the organisation directly as its closest Iranian allies were demoted from positions in institutions at work within the organisation in Lebanon. It was demonstrated that the imposition of Iranian clerical factionalism on the movement's activity was most notable in the process of the release of Western hostages rather than in the actual abductions. This Iranian factional rivalry was also translated into clerical infighting within the Hizb'allah. Although efforts to obstruct the release of Western hostages by the Iranian revolutionist factions were designed to undermine more moderate Iranian foreign policy towards the West, this phase revealed that efforts to delay any releases by Hizb'allah were also motivated by its pre-occupation towards readjustment of its position within the Lebanese civil war and internal rivalry within the movement over its present and future direction. As such, the Western hostages were not only abducted for causal motivations but also kept as insurance of its position within Lebanon and against retribution by Western governments.

While the January 1987 spate of kidnappings of Westerners was motiv-ated by the arrest of leading Hizb'allah members in Europe as well as reflected clerical factionalism in Iran in the aftermath of the revelation of the U.S.-Iranian arms-for-hostages deals, it also underlined Hizb'allah's escalatory efforts to confront IDF and SLA militarily in southern Lebanon and its competion with Amal, supported by Syria, over the control of the Shi'a community and territory. The protracted Amal-Hizb'allah warfare between 1987 until 1989 produced friction with Syria, as it threatened mil-itary intervention against the movement with the extension of its hege-mony in Lebanon, which prevented the abduction of any further Westerners. While the Hizb'allah used the Western captives as leverage against Syria and the West, it increasingly concentrated on the expansion of its political and military influence and presence in southern Lebanon, especially after the death of Ayatollah Khomeini and the conclusion of the Ta'if accord in 1989.

It was demonstrated that the devolution of Ayatollah Khomeini's spiri-tual and political authority, coupled with the ouster of the movement's staunchest allies within Iran's clerical hierarchy, led to a crisis within Hizb'allah's command leadership and increased clerical factionalism over the direction of the movement, especially as Iran downgraded its support while the movement felt increased pressure from Syria to release its hostages. Although the Hizb'allah, in co-operation with the Pasdaran, managed to obstruct the release of hostages, the movement's position was increasingly dependent on Iran's relationship with Syria and the hostage-issue became closely connected to its own survival in a post-militia phase of Lebanese politics under Syrian hegemony. Ultimately, the hostage-issue was used by the Hizb'allah to reach an agreement between Iran and Syria over its future in Lebanon, under which the movement was allowed to remain armed as an resistance movement in return for the release of its foreign hostages within the framework of fulfilment of its own requirements as well as in alignment with Iranian and Syrian interests. It was demonstrated that the ascendancy of a new Secretary-General of the movement, which led to both the comprehensive conclusion of the Western hostage-crisis under UN-auspices in 1991 as well as its participation in the 1992 Lebanese parliamentary elections, underlined that ultimately the political necessity of close affiliation with Iran's official leadership for its survival in Lebanon took precedence over any individual or collective agendas within the Hizb'allah as well as motivations by Iran's revolutionist faction. It was underlined that a reduction of the influence of the more Iranian clergy in Iranian politics paralleled a demotion in positions of its closest allies within the Hizb'allah.

The understanding of the influences exerted for the process of release of hostages depended not only on the impact of the relationship between Hizb'allah and Iran at various levels as well as the internal Lebanese environment but also on the movement's relationship with Syria, closely determined by the status of the Iranian-Syrian relations in the Lebanese, regional and international arena.

THE INFLUENCE OF IRANIAN-SYRIAN RELATIONS ON HIZB'ALLAH

The nature and dynamics of the triangular Hizb'allah-Iran-Syria relationship have been vital in order to discern the influences and mechanisms exerted by Iran and Syria, both individually and collectively, over the process of abduction and, more importantly, releases of foreign hostages by the Hizb'allah. It was shown that this process was subordinate to a continuous changing relationship and alliance between Iran and Syria over a decade, itself subjected to either confluence or conflict in their own individual political and economic agendas in the Middle East affected by a wide variety of internal Lebanese, regional, and international events. In particular, the Iranian-Syrian relationship was shown to experience serious tension in conjunction with shifting political and economic conditions in the region, especially marked by irreconcilable differences with respect to their interests and aspirations over the future of Lebanon. Apart from underlining their contradictory political ideologies, the larger problems between the two states were also superimposed on the ground in Lebanon over Hizb'allah activity. It was argued that the way in which the Iranian-Syrian relationship affected the position and activity of the movement in Lebanon fundamentally shaped the application of Western crisis-management techniques with the opportunities and constraints in their application in accordance with tension and coordination in the alliance between Iran and Syria over Hizb'allah activity, especially as these two states acted as facilitators in all negotiations for the release of hostages.

It was clearly demonstrated that any friction or cooperation in the political and economic relationship between Iran and Syria affected all aspects of Hizb'allah activity in Lebanon. While both Iran and Syria were adept at exploiting the relationship for their own benefit in Lebanon or elsewhere in the region, their close collusion remained uniform in Lebanon in the confrontation against common foreign enemies, coupled with complete obedience by the Hizb'allah to Iranian wishes and orders. However, after the success of Hizb'allah's activity in ridding Lebanon of foreign influence, the incompatible aims by Iran, seeking the establishment of an Islamic republic on Iranian lines, and by Syria, seeking consolidation of its hegemony over Lebanese affairs, became visible through intense competion by their clients, Amal and Hizb'allah, over the hearts and minds of the Shi'ite community. The underlying friction between Iranian and Syrian attempts to seek political and military dominance in Lebanon, as manifest through Amal-Hizb'allah warfare, was exacerbated by other difficulties in their alliance both internal and external to Lebanon. Specifically, the underlying economic bond between Syria and Iran, especially Syrian dependence on Iranian oil supplies, demonstrated several rifts over Syrian refusals to settle outstanding debts over oil payments to Iran between 1986 and 1988 and over subsequent Syrian efforts to lessen its economic dependency on Iran through internal Syrian oil production. While Syria exploited the economic disputes with Iran to its own advantage, it was demonstrated that other differences over Lebanon stemmed from the incompatibility between Syrian attempts to consolidate its control over Lebanon while seeking a political and economic *rapprochement* with Western governments after accusations of Syrian involvement in terrorism, and Iranian exploitation of Hizb'allah's abductions in the pursuit of specific foreign policy objectives and in the expansion of the movement at the expense of Amal.

Both Syria and Iran have shown an interest in defusing serious conflict in Lebanon in order to preserve their relationship. However, Hizb'allah's pursuit of a greater independent line from Iran, in the aftermath of clerical factionalism in late 1986, compounded the problems in any attempts to make the movement answerable to either Iran or Syria for both the control over and the limitation of its activities. Although Syria avoided a complete crackdown on the Iranian proxy, whenever the Hizb'allah seriously challenged Syrian authority, the Syrian regime moved to exercise control over the activity of the Hizb'allah through a blockade of the transfer of Iranian Pasdaran in the Biq'a area and control of movement of the Hizb'allah in the Biq'a and Beirut areas. However, the underlying factor for any Syrian restraint in the elimination of the military and political presence of the Hizb'allah was based on its nonexpendable relationship with Iran. It was clearly shown that neither Syria nor Iran have been willing to sacrifice their alliance on account of any Hizb'allah activity, rather both regimes have been forced to exercise restraint in their relations with Hizb'allah at various times as to not offend each other. When Hizb'allah activity was harmful to the Iranian-Syrian alliance, as evident by Amal-Hizb'allah armed clashes and certain hostage-taking incidents, both Iran and Syria acted in concert to enforce agreements between their two proxies as well as to place limitations on the abduction of foreigners. However, the Iranian-Syrian alliance experienced particular problems in conjunction with the projection of Iranian clerical factionalism onto the Hizb'allah command leadership in attempts by Iran and Syria to use extraction from the hostage-crisis as an instrument in the foreign policy arena in their dealings with Western governments.

It was demonstrated that the support for the Hizb'allah from Iran and, to a lesser extent acceptance by Syria, changed concurrently with the changes in the Iranian leadership, following the death of Ayatollah Khomeini, and with Syrian efforts to consolidate its control over a post civil-war Lebanon with the Ta'if agreement in 1989. While the defeat of the revolutionist faction in control over the political authority in Iran translated into diminished possibility for a radical leadership of the Hizb'allah to be able to confront Syrian efforts to establish political and military hegemony in Lebanon, it also became clear that Syrian designs within Lebanese territory took precedence over any official Iranian interests. Syrian concessions to Hizb'allah and Iran, in the form of allowing the movement to remain armed and for the continued presence of the Pasdaran contingent on Lebanese territory, meant that the movement was forced to submit to a reorientation in activity in alignment with Syrian interests in order to survive within Lebanon's post-civil war environment.

CONCLUSION

In a larger context, the unravelling of these complex mechanisms of the Hizb'allah-Iranian-Syrian relationship that governed the movement's hostage-taking activity have been essential in providing answers to why the Western hostage-crisis occurred and what mechanisms governed the initiation and resolution of these hostage-incidents. However, it is also essential to address the reasons why the hostage-crisis ultimately became resolvable; what the hostage-crisis achieved for the Hizb'allah, for the Iranian regime, as well as for the Lebanese Shi'a community; and, ultimately, what the future course is for the Hizb'allah, especially whether its transformation over a decade from a revolutionary movement to a political party has meant the abandonment of political violence as a principal means to achieve its pan-Islamic goals.

While the abduction of foreigners by the Hizb'allah almost always converged with the interests of Iran and, to a lesser extent, Syria, the process of releasing Western hostages became a source of frequent disagreement within the Hizb'allah movement itself and in its relationship with Iran and Syria as well as a source of constant friction in the Iranian-Syrian alliance. The complete closure of the Western hostage-file in 1991, under the auspices of the United Nations, was explained by many analysts as a result of the fact that Western hostages had outlived their usefulness to Hizb'allah, Iran, and Syria. However, the breakthrough in the comprehensive release of Western hostages was not merely a way to resolve an issue which had become a liability question for those involved but rather the combined result of the dynamics at work of the Hizb'allah-Iranian-Syrian relationship, which had been profoundly influenced by a confluence of regional and international events. Apart from the profound changes and influences in the Middle East, following Iraq's invasion of Kuwait which facilitated the release of the 15 *al-Da'wa* prisoners, Hizb'allah's responsiveness to close the hostage-file was based on its own threatened position in a post-civil war Lebanon and a convergence of interests with Iran, who needed to resolve the hostage-issue in order to rehabilitate itself economically and politically with the West, and Syria, who had lost its traditional support from the Soviet Union when it had an opportunity to expand its influence over Lebanon and participate in regional political processes. As the Western hostages constituted an asset for the Hizb'allah in its relations with Iran and Syria, the movement agreed to release the hostages as a *quid pro quo* for Syrian guarantees that the movement was permitted to remain armed, when all other militias were disarmed, in order to confront Israeli occupation of southern Lebanon. Syrian aquiescence to Hizb'allah's armed struggle also served its interests in both pressuring Israel in the Arab-Israeli peace talks as well as waging a proxy war against Israel which ensured Syrian deniability. Hizb'allah's own initiative of inviting the UN Secretary-General as the mediator in the hostage-release process highlighted the movement's continued close consideration for Iranian interests, most notably as a means to pursue Iran's outstanding disputes with Iraq under UN Resolution 598. The denouement of the Western hostage-crisis in 1991 demonstrated not only the importance of understanding the mechanics of the Hizb'allah-Iranian-Syrian relationship but also that they were all extremely adept at using the hostage-crisis to their own advantage.

While the Hizb'allah and Iran have demonstrated skillful adaptation to changes in their environment, they have equally been skilled at exploiting the hostage-issue to extract political and economic concessions. However, what did the hostage-crisis actually achieve for the Hizb'allah, and Iran, as well as the Lebanese Shi'a community? Hizb'allah's practice of hostage-taking has meant different levels of achievement for the organisation itself, for varying factions within Iran's clerical establishment and for the Lebanese Shi'a community as a whole. For the Hizb'allah movement itself, the hostage-taking activity has served many important functions which reinforced the movement's ideological and political *raison d'être*, assisted in the expansion of its influence within the Lebanese Shi'ite community as well as defined and forged the movement's ties to Iran's clerical establishment. In many ways, Hizb'allah's hostage-taking activity has been a total success for the movement in the advancement of its pan-Islamic cause on the strategic level and as an instrument to achieve practical and tactical goals for the organisation itself. As a practical instrument, the hostage-issue was used to accomplish specific organisational requirements for the movement, most notably to force the release of imprisoned Shi'ites in Europe and Israel while it shielded the movement from retaliation when waging its relentless armed warfare against foreign presence in Lebanon. In many ways, the hostage-issue also insured the movement against any serious confrontation with Syria and, in the end, translated into ensuring and consolidating the very survival of the movement in a post-civil war Lebanon. As the movement used the hostage-issue in close convergence with Iranian foreign policy interests *vis-à-vis* the West, its hostage-taking activity served to ensure continued close Iranian support and material assistance for the movement, which was essential for its expansion within the Shi'a community. In a wider sense, Hizb'allah's hostage-taking activity also served to enhance its revolutionary credence and image as the true defender of the Lebanese Shi'a community against the enemies of Islam, especially as it played an instrumental role in expelling foreign forces out of Lebanon and through its tireless armed campaign against Israel. In this revolutionary struggle, the Hizb'allah was very successful in achieving not only its practical goals but also in accomplishing a psychological athmosphere of fear in the West of the actual threat and capability of the movement which served to enhance the status of the movement within Lebanon and beyond as a major nemesis of Western governments.

As the most successful example of Iran's export of the revolution, the Hizb'allah and its hostage-taking have also greatly benefited Iran as an instrument of proxy in the foreign policy arena towards the West. While the Hizb'allah served a vital role for Iran in providing it with a translator and conduit to spread Iran's Islamic revolutionary message to the Islamic masses of the Arab world and the possibility to actively participate in the Arab-Israeli conflict, the movement's hostage-taking activity provided Iran with a means to force the gradual improvement of economic and, to a lesser extent, political relations with Western governments. During the Iran-Iraq war, Hizb'allah's hostage-taking activity was used to pressure Western governments to concede military and economic assistance to Iran vital to its continued war efforts, as evidenced by the U.S.-Iranian arms-for-hostages deal and by French financial concessions. While Hizb'allah's hostage-taking failed to influence the West's Middle East policies to any great extent, as any arms sales to Iran were equally matched by military and financial support to Iraq, the hostage-issue was increasingly used by various factions within Iran's clerical establishment for any array of political purposes. For the revolutionist faction, which enjoyed close ties to Hizb'allah's leadership, the movement's hostage-taking activity was used as an instrument to sabotage pragmatic moves by the official Iranian leadership towards the West by blocking the release of hostages. The increasing difficulty for Iran's official leadership to control the movement to release Western hostages has had serious consequences for Iran in accordance with its need to rehabilitate its war-ravaged economy through improved relations with the West. This often served to enhance the position of the radical clergy in Iran and to undermine any more moderate signs of *rapprochement* between Iran and the West.

For Lebanon's Shi'a community, the Hizb'allah and its hostage-taking activity have served to propel a traditionally impoverished and passive community into political action and militancy within Lebanon's civil war and at the forefront of Lebanese politics. While Hizb'allah activity served to consolidate Iran's material assistance to the movement, its rapid transformation from a rag-tag militia into a tightly organised movement with an impressive military and extensive social services programme for the Shi'a community meant that the Hizb'allah positioned itself as a true political, ideological, and economic defender of the Shi'a community, filling the vacuum in place of the scant protection and assistance provided by the Lebanese government and other militias. In this process, Hizb'allah's hostage-taking activity ensured financial backing from Iran, as it suited the patron's interests, which it used for the expansion of the movement's popularity and influence over the Shi'a community through a skilful combination of material inducement and ideological indoctrination. While Hizb'allah's terrorism stereotyped the image of Lebanon's Shi'ites as religious fanatics bent on martyrdom in the Western world, the profound role

and service of the Hizb'allah movement, fighting and buying its way into
the hearts and minds of the Shi'ite community, far outweighed the consequences of any non-Islamic moral constraints imposed by Western public
opinion. Apart from the fact that Hizb'allah veiled its justifications of
violent activity solely to Muslim believers and according to Islamic law,
the movement also provided the dispossessed Shi'ite community within a
lawless civil war environment with a divine Islamic purpose and mission,
which transformed from revolutionary struggle to a political vechicle
aimed at addressing Shi'ite grievances and enhance its wider agenda in
Lebanon.

The transformation of the Hizb'allah from a revolutionary movement to
a political party in Lebanon's post-civil war environment raises the question of whether the movement has abandoned the use of political violence,
especially hostage-taking, to achieve its pan-Islamic goals. While the
Hizb'allah has demonstrated a mastery of political violence in its quest for
enhancement of its position and agenda within Lebanon and beyond, the
movement also demonstrated it was very susceptible of, and adaptable to,
changes within its own environment. However, every sign indicates that it
has retained the same degree of its pan-Islamic zeal and militancy. While
Hizb'allah's reorientation in activity, substituting hostage-taking for participation within the political process, occurred to suit the realities of a
post-civil war Lebanon, the movement has also escalated its commitment
and struggle to confront Israel and achieve its pan-Islamic goal of liberating Jerusalem both within Lebanon and beyond. The intensification of the
movement's attacks against Israel in southern Lebanon can be attributed
to efforts to sabotage any prospect for any Arab-Israeli peace, which
would *de facto* jeopardize its very existence and its accomplishments hith-
erto within Lebanon. While the Hizb'allah has increased its Islamic
extremism by continuing its guerrilla attacks against Israel in southern
Lebanon, the movement also launched a new form of terrorism, car bomb
attacks, specifically aimed against Israeli high-profile targets outside the
region since March 1992, most notably in South America and possibly in
Europe, both in revenge for Israeli actions against the Hizb'allah as well
as to sabotage any emerging signs of Arab-Israeli peace. Although the
Hizb'allah discovered that it can subvert the system from within through
its participation within Lebanese electoral politics, its vanguard position
of Islamic extremism with its messianic aspirations for the establishment
of an Islamic republic in Lebanon and the eradication of Israel, means
that the movement for the moment will intensify its concentration of
attacks against Israel through bombs to avert any emerging Arab-Israeli
rapproachement rather than on hostage-taking against the West.

Ultimately, the degree to which the movement's position is threatened, coupled with the ability of Iran to sustain its revolutionary pan-Islamic zeal at home and abroad, will determine the means and levels of political violence employed by the Hizb'allah in the future. This case-study laid the foundation for understanding and predicting these mechanisms which governed Hizb'allah's employment of terrorism in the past and for the future.

WESTERN RESPONSES TO THE HOSTAGE-CRISIS IN LEBANON: EFFECTIVENESS OF CRISIS-MANAGEMENT TECHNIQUES

In view of the complexity of the preceding case-study of the Hizb'allah and its interaction with Iran and Syria, the balance-sheet for Western responses to the hostage-crisis in Lebanon has not surprisingly reinforced the fact that these states have experienced difficulty in not only adapting to the crisis-environment itself but also in balancing their individual responsibility towards their citizens taken hostage abroad with their requirements to safeguard the maintanence of other collective national interests. This recognition that the hostage-crisis in Lebanon constituted a unique form of foreign policy crisis for Western governments, in which the Western policy of no-negotiations and no-concessions severely restricted the maneuverability in the selection of response to the hostage-crisis, led to the employment of traditional principles and techniques of crisis-management as useful instruments for the evaluation of the crisis itself as well as a guideline in order to cope and manage this complex form of crisis more effectively and successfully.

The highly context-dependent nature of crisis-management necessitated the delineation of seven political and operational requirements for its effective application to terrorist crisis-situations, especially within the framework of the hostage-crisis in Lebanon. An underlying common feature of these crisis-management requirements was close considerations of the crisis-environment, most notably as it determined the effectiveness in the selection, direction, and timing of crisis-management techniques. The underlying criteria for the successful application of crisis-management was determined to be not only close *adherence* to the seven essential requirements of effective crisis-management balanced against the inherent constraints for Western governments in the conduct of domestic and foreign policy but also the *performance* of their approach in the hostage-crisis based on the previous case-study on the dynamics of the relationship at work between Hizb'allah, Iran, and Syria.

The evaluation of Western government performance in accordance with the employment of specific crisis-management techniques in alignment with opportunities and constraints in the crisis-environment cannot be adequately judged solely on the ability of these states to achieve the rapid release of its citizens from captivity. As all three Western governments eventually achieved the release of their hostages in Lebanon, a complete balance-sheet of Western response must also account for the gains and losses incurred individually and collectively by the behaviour of these governments in their efforts to extract their citizens from captivity. As a consequence, what are the lessons and insights from Western responses, using crisis-management techniques, to the hostage-crisis in Lebanon? What is the balance-sheet of Western responses in terms of gains and losses in the selection of their individual and collective approaches to the hostage-crisis? And finally, what are the general lessons of the hostage-crisis in Lebanon for Western governments and for the international system as a whole?

A main problem for the inconsistency between the West's declaratory policy of not negotiating or conceding to any demands and the actual conduct by these governments in dealing with the hostage-crisis in Lebanon can be explained by the often incompatible nature of firmly held counterterrorism principles as an integral component of foreign policy in the Middle East towards Iran and Syria, who exercise any degree of control over the Hizb'allah movement. The fact that Iran and Syria acted as intermediaries for Western governments in dealing with the Hizb'allah posed problems in upholding a non-flexible no-concessions policy as these states benefited indirectly from concessions made to influence the movement despite their own complicity in some of these terrorist acts. While most Iranian and Syrian demands of concessions for any intercession with the Lebanese movement focused on specific outstanding disputes in the foreign policy behaviour by Western governments towards these states, it was shown that any deviation from the principles of a no-concessions policy was dependent on the conduct of conciliatory foreign policy by Western states towards Iran or Syria in alignment with shifts in the regional environment creating opportunities and constraints in the pursuit of wider foreign policy interests. In turn, this had to be balanced against the desire by Western governments to extract its citizens from captivity, closely influenced by domestic political pressures and its unwillingness to maintain a non-conciliatory position at the expense of the pursuit of wider foreign policy opportunities in the region. The balance-sheet for the American, British, and French efforts to limit their political objectives towards the hostage-crisis and their means employed in pursuit of those objectives demonstrated not only the urgency of the crisis on the political agenda and the expected ability by these states to secure the release of its citizens from captivity but also the way in which these governments adapted to the crisis-environment through the selection and employment of crisis-management techniques.

The lessons from the U.S. experience in responding to the hostage-crisis are multifold. Firstly, the American approach to the hostage-crisis has been a complete failure in terms of deviating from the principle of limited objectives in the crisis and limited means in pursuit of these objectives. While the hostage-issue was elevated on the U.S. political agenda, mainly as the result of its previous traumatic experience with the 1979 Iranian hostage-crisis, the problems for the U.S. policymakers were exacerbated by its own creation of unrealistic expectations of what could be achieved given the restrictions imposed by the crisis-environment. Despite the fact that the Lebanese hostage-crisis differed fundamentally from the previous Iranian hostage-situation, the U.S. government approached the Lebanese hostage-crisis from the same vantage point, as any U.S. manoeuverability was curtailed by its non-flexible public policy of no-negotiations and no-consessions while it assumed a lead-role in the West's containment of Iran, which U.S. policymakers viewed as the main culprit behind these acts of terrorism. Contrary to limited political objectives in the hostage-crisis, the U.S. government assured its domestic constituency of the rapid release of its citizens from captivity without any negotiation with, or concessions to, either Iran or Hizb'allah, a policy pursued only through the means of coercion and force. A major problem with this approach was that the release of American hostages could not be achieved through the reliance of force and coercion, especially as this only strengthened the militancy and popularity of the movement itself and the strength of Iranian radical clergy within Iran's official leadership.

Secondly, the U.S. response to the hostage-crisis demonstrated a failure to adequately understand the dynamics and mechanisms of the hostage-crisis and the configuration between the Hizb'allah, Iran, and Syria, which ultimately governed the release of American citizens from captivity. This was revealed by its reliance on force and coercion as the main crisis-management technique employed against the Hizb'allah as well as Iran and, more importantly, in the flawed selection of communication channels with the adversaries. This was most clearly demonstrated by the behaviour of certain policymakers behind the clandestine U.S.-Iranian arms-for-hostages initiative, which attempted to use the hostage-issue to open a new strategic relationship with Iran. This flawed unidimensional approach, which demonstrated both a lacking knowledge of the configuration of the

Hizb'allah-Iranian relationship and the psychology behind Iranian moves, led not only to the most serious crisis for the political survival of the Reagan administration and the credibility of its counter-terrorism posture among its allies but also set back any prospects for a U.S.-Iranian *rapprochement* for many years. It also totally undermined any propects for progress on the U.S. hostage-front, as the issue was devalued immediately after the revelation of the Iran-Contra affair in President Reagan's battle for political survival at home. Although his presidential successor treated the hostage-issue with extreme caution, the failure of U.S. reliance on military force to coerce the Hizb'allah and Iran, coupled with the disarray of channels pursued in the crisis, revealed the continued inability of U.S. leaders to recogize ways to limit the hostage-issue on the political agenda and of their own limited manoeuverability in responding as well as resolving the hostage-crisis. However, any criticism of the way in which the U.S. administration tackled the hostage-issue in the period following the revelation of the U.S.-Iranian arms-for-hostages deals must also recognize that any maneuverability or avenues for negotiation or resolution of the American hostage-crisis in Lebanon were completely closed, especially given the public scrutiny of any U.S. moves which even slightly resembled concessions and given the fervent anti-U.S. hostility displayed by both Iran and the Hizb'allah. It was demonstrated throughout the case-study that limited intelligence on the behaviour of the Hizb'allah and its allies does not translate into limited knowledge of how the movement operates and interacts with Iran and Syria, rather it can be determined by examining the boundaries of the dynamics governing this complex triangular relationship, yielding opportunities and constraints in the crisis-environment which should serve as the basis for the selection of crisis-management techniques and the evaluation of their likely effect in eliciting a favourable response from either Iran or Hizb'allah. A main problem with the U.S. response was this disregard for the opportunities and constraints in the fluctuating relationship between Syria and Iran as well as the political environment within Lebanon in which the Hizb'allah operates and exists. This became clear by the failure to rely on either Iran or Syria as the only channel in negotiations over hostages without reference to their individual ability to exert its influence over the movement in accordance with shifts in their ties to Hizb'allah's command leadership between 1987–1991 and, more importantly, to the status of the Iranian-Syrian relationship over time, as evidently displayed by the increased friction between 1986 and 1988.

Thirdly, the U.S. response to the hostage-crisis also demonstrated that the release of Americans from captivity could only be achieved in exchange for U.S. direct or indirect concessions to Iran and, to a lesser extent, Syria. While it was demonstrated that a causal relationship existed between Hizb'allah's abduction of American citizens and internal as well as external Lebanese events, it was also clear that their release were contingent on the removal of underlying points of friction in the U.S.-Iranian relationship, most notably the U.S. return of Iranian frozen assets and a change in U.S. foreign policy towards the region, and in the wider U.S.-Syrian relationship, especially U.S. willingness to recognize Syrian hegemony over Lebanon. Despite the fact that the U.S.-Iranian arms-for-hostages deal in real terms only achieved a temporary cessation in the abduction of Americans, as more hostages were taken to replace those released, Hizb'allah's willingness to release its hostages seemed to occur in conjunction with U.S. conciliatory measures, especially with the release of Iranian assets, and, more importantly, with the changes in the regional environment which made the refusal to release U.S. hostages more of a liability than an asset for Iran and Hizb'allah in the advancement of their own agendas. This has meant that the fate of the U.S. hostages was more bound by U.S. flexibility in resolving its foreign policy disputes with Iran rather than by non-conciliatory positions and reliance on coercion. It was also underlined that Syria's ability to pressure the release of the U.S. hostages remained limited and was governed by its wider relationship with Iran. However, any Syrian pressure on Hizb'allah to release U.S. hostages increased with the American approval of the Ta'if agreement which confered recognition of Syria's role over Lebanese affairs.

Fourthly, the U.S. response to the hostage-crisis showed also that the existing crisis-management machinery remains unable to shield U.S. policymakers from the effects exerted by the mass media as they continue to exacerbate the pressures of any type of response. It was argued that a major effort must be made by U.S. policymakers to educate the mass media and the public of the complex dynamics which governs the Lebanese hostage-crisis and any subsequent response by the U.S. government. Furthermore, it is important to discuss publicly the consequences of any U.S. government response not only to highlight the limitations imposed by the crisis-environment in securing the release of U.S. hostages but also to safeguard broad support for any measures at home and abroad among allies. The inability of U.S. policymakers to conduct their dealings over the hostage-crisis in the open contributed to the need for initiating clandestine operations to meet the demands of public expectations and to resort to short-term coercive measures rather than a more calculated long-term foreign policy approach in the region.

The lessons of the French experience in dealing with the hostage-crisis have been unique to the nature of political rivalries within France's cohabitation period between 1986 and 1988 as well as to its individualistic style and manner in dealing with Middle East terrorism in the past. The French political objectives in the hostage-crisis were contingent on the political rivalry between Mitterrand and Chirac for political expediency in the battle for the French presidency, and on whether the delay or immediate release of French hostages benefited the political agenda of respective candidate, in the 1986/1988 national elections. This political rivalry between the two candidates was also manifest through institutional rivalry between specific French ministries in some way in charge of issues connected with the hostage-crisis. It was determined that the achievement of the individual political objectives in the hostage-crisis and the means employed in pursuit of these were directly dependent on the strategy of the two political candidates in negotiations with Hizb'allah, Iran, and Syria. This strategy was directly manifest through the dispatch of individual emissaries to conduct negotiations directly with the Hizb'allah and with either Iran or Syria. Although the French political and institutional rivalry over the hostage-issue constituted an asset in its efforts to limit Iranian retribution over French support for Iraq in the Iran-Iraq war, through the process of individual offers to grant concessions in outstanding disputes with Iran, it also became a liability as Iran and the Hizb'allah were able to use this political rivalry to achieve maximum concessions to their own advantage and as the difficulties in meeting already agreed concessions to Iran continued long after the release of the last French hostage.

Clearly the French response to the hostage-crisis demonstrated not only a very sharp understanding of the mechanisms that governed the behaviour of the Hizb'allah, Iran, and Syria but also adept ability to utilize the dynamics of the crisis-environment for its own advantage in securing the rapid release of French hostages prior to the May 1988 elections. It is beyond doubt that the degree to which the French government was able to exploit this configuration for the advancement of foreign policy in the region and to secure the release of French hostages was directly related to the nature of the anomaly of "cohabitation" in the French political system. While the success of the French approach was related to the unique exploitation of the crisis-environment, which translated into the employment of unofficial intermediaries in direct contact with the Hizb'allah rather than through formal and highlevel contacts with Iran or Syria, it can also be attributed to the fact that the French pursued its own policy in the Middle East without any close consideration of its allies or any substantial pressure from the domestic media. The former was clear by the use of individual emissaries with close ties to either Iran or Syria, who benefited from the tension and rivalry in the wider Iranian-Syrian relationship and on the ground in Lebanon between 1986 and 1988. The latter was demonstrated by the French ability and willingness to grant major concessions while withstanding criticism from its allies and the mass media, a task assisted by the subordination of the judiciary to political expediency.

The French handling of the hostage-issue also showed the value of using crisis-management techniques through a mixture of accommodation and coercion. Although French reluctance to impose sanctions on Iran and Syria reflected the underlying political strategy to the hostage-crisis and the uniqueness of its foreign policy in the region, any tension in the French-Iranian relationship was equally manifest of, and exploited by, the French political rivalry. However, the French approach underlined the advantages of a mixture of coercion and accommodation in relations with Iran and Syria rather than strict reliance on punishment through the rupture of diplomatic ties or through sanctions, as exemplified by the U.S. and British approach. The latter approach only served to contribute to limiting the options available for Western governments.

The lessons of the British response to the hostage-crisis are related to its uncompromising policy of refusal to conduct any negotiations with the Hizb'allah and Iran as well as Syria or concede to any demands, coupled with its successful ability to limit the hostage-issue on the political agenda. The British government managed to successfully subordinate and limit its political objectives by relegating the issue of the British hostages on the foreign policy agenda. This devaluation of the British hostage-issue reflected not only its previous experience in countering terrorism at home and abroad, which was reinforced by a public acceptability of a hardline policy, but also a wider recognition that the hostage-issue was bound by wider constraints of the Middle East environment, most notably restricted initially by the U.S.-Iranian arms-for-hostages debacle and later by the Rushdie-affair. The adamant policy of the British government that there would be no deals with terrorists and no ransom paid under any guise from the outset of the hostage-crisis, reinforced by public support, contributed to consistency and effectiveness in subordinating the hostage-issue on the political agenda. A contributing factor to this success was the relatively limited number of British citizens in captivity compared to the American and French hostage-problem. It was also recognized that the British hostage-takings occurred in conjunction with major events in the Middle East, many of which affected the hostage-issue, which directly led to a limited degree of maneuverability for the British government in employing crisis-management techniques.

The British response to the hostage-crisis showed also limited comprehension of the mechanisms that governed any release of British hostages. Apart from the fact that the British government faced insuperable obstacles in the Middle East which hampered any response to the hostage-crisis, the limited efforts of using indirect negotiation channels and its almost permanent imposition of diplomatic and economic sanctions against Iran and Syria demonstrated clearly that its behaviour was not attuned to the realities of the crisis environment. This was clearly evident by its individual insistence on maintaining sanctions against Syria long after its allies removed them while it also concentrated on using Iran as the only limited vechicle towards the resolution of the British hostage-crisis. While it may be argued that Britain and its policy towards the hostage-crisis could afford to neglect a close understanding of the crisis dynamics, most notably as it refused to alter its counterterrorism policy and was faced with huge obstacles in the conduct of foreign policy towards the Middle East, it also created problems for the British government when faced with increasing criticism at home after the release of other hostages of different nationality and for unnecessarily prolonging the agony of its citizens in captivity due to its inflexible and principled stand against terrorism. Despite the fact that the mass media increasingly raised the profile of the hostages on the political agenda, the British government never faced a serious problem in limiting the effects of publicity critical of its approach and the way it met its responsibility towards securing the release of its citizens.

These individual lessons of the American, French, and British responses to the hostage-crisis in Lebanon have shown that crisis-management can be used as an instrument to better understand why Western governments have experienced difficulty or success in efforts to secure the release of their citizens from captivity. More importantly, the context-dependent nature of crisis-management and its application to the dynamics of the crisis-environment made it possible to bridge the diversity of circumstances surrounding the hostage-crisis for each individual Western government with a means to evaluate the effectiveness of their individual response. However, adaptability to the crisis-environment constitutes only a facet of judging the effectiveness of Western government response to the hostage-crisis as it cannot only be measured by the speed of which the freedom of Western hostages was secured. It also requires the provision of a balance-sheet of Western responses in terms of gains and losses in the selection of their individual and collective approaches to the hostage-crisis.

The previous lessons of the Western hostage-crisis demonstrated the difficulty for Western states in adapting crisis-management techniques to the crisis-environment while also balancing their individual responsibility towards their citizens taken hostage abroad with their requirements to safeguard the maintenance of other collective national interests. How serious were the setbacks and reverberations of Western responses to the hostage-crisis both individually and collectively, and what was ultimately lost and gained in this process?

The overall American response to the hostage-crisis in Lebanon clearly demonstrated its continued vulnerability to this form of terrorism and that it was slow in learning from previous lessons and in adapting to the crisis-environment. The U.S. policymakers' preoccupation with the safety and well-being of American hostages in Lebanon, elevated to the status of a major national security concern in response to the grave damages caused by the Hizb'allah's suicide- and abduction campaigns as well as to its own public's fear and alarm of Iranian-inspired Shi'ite terrorism, contributed to the disastrous U.S.-Iranian arms-for-hostages deal which had serious consequences not only for its domestic credibility but also in its inability to conduct foreign policy in the Middle East and justify its actions to its allies. The misperception of the dynamics of the crisis-situation and its own ability to resolve the crisis quickly and with coercion which led to the Iran-Contra affair contributed to one of the most serious crises in constitutional U.S. government in recent history. It also totally undermined the credibility of the U.S.-led effort in counterterrorism and cooperation among its allies, whose steadfastness in refusing to concede to terrorist demands seriously damaged its own and its allies' prospects of securing the release of its citizens from captivity. U.S. willingness to engage in concessions with Iran and the Hizb'allah not only signalled to its adversaries that hostage-taking was an extremely useful instrument in extracting political and financial concessions from the West but also undermined any credibility of U.S. criticism of other states' deviation from the principles of no-negotiation and no-concession to terrorists and their demands. It also exacerbated the problems for the U.S. in the conduct of its foreign policy in the Middle East, most notably in the Iran-Iraq war and its involvement in Lebanon, as the hostage-issue became a pressure-point used by Iran for its own regional interests and designs. As the political fall-out reverberated within the U.S. and among its allies for a very long time, the restricted manoeuverability of any U.S. response led to the overreliance on the use of force to respond to the hostage-crisis. Apart from the limited utility of the U.S. military option given the intelligence constraints in identifying responsible Hizb'allah individuals and bases within a civil war environment and the political constraints in avoiding a wider confrontation with either Iran and Syria, it also undermined the process of negotiation by other Western states as coercion strengthened the militancy of the movement and the position of the more radical Iranian leaders within Iran's clerical establishment. The legacy of the U.S.-Iranian arms-for-hostages deal restricted the options available for U.S. policymakers, which devalued the hostage-issue from a prominent position on the political agenda and placed its resolution in the fate of the underlying shifting currents of Middle East politics.

The overall French response to the hostage-crisis in Lebanon showed that it firmly understood the dynamics of the hostage-crisis in Lebanon and the requirements for successfully conducting business in the Middle East, most notably with Iran and Syria. While the inner dynamics of the French response were bound by internal political rivalry between Chirac and Mitterand, the salience of the hostage-issue was clearly felt as an electoral issue in 1986 and 1988 as well as with an increase in retaliatory Iranian measures against French policy in the Middle East. While the French political rivalry skilfully dictated the fate of its hostages in Lebanon and exploited the crisis-dynamics through complex negotiations, the reverberations of the French conduct of granting political and financial concessions to Iran and the release of imprisoned Hizb'allah members to the movement in Lebanon were largely felt abroad rather than at home. The French subordination of the judiciary to the political authorities through the release of suspected Hizb'allah members not only seriously impaired the success and collective will of the West's wider efforts to apprehend and prosecute terrorists but also gravely dented the reputation of French counterterrorism and cooperation with its allied agencies. It also totally undermined any progress by the efforts of those Western states which continued to adhere to a no-negotiations and no-concessions policy out of principle. Unlike other Western states that refused or were slow to adapt to changing conditions, the French government managed to master the art of manoeuvering between Iran, the Hizb'allah, and Syria. However, French willingness to readily concede to demands for political expediency for its domestic constituency and in the foreign arena had also a price. This was manifest with the bombing campaign in Paris which aimed to force the French government to give into the demands of Iran and the Hizb'allah. It must also be recognized that the consequences of French behaviour did not cease with the release of its last citizen from captivity, most notably as the difficulty in fulfilling outstanding concessions to Iran created tension and friction in France's wider conduct of foreign policy in the Middle East over an extended period. This was clearly revealed by the anger displayed by Iran over the difficulty for, and unwillingness of, Mitterrand to fulfill promises made by his predecessor.

The overall British response to the hostage-crisis managed successfully to minimize any damage to its reputation as the unsurpassed champion of hardline counterterrorist policy. While the British approach was unable to use the crisis-dynamics to its own advantage in attempts to resolve the hostage-crisis, it was clearly recognized that the British government faced insuperable problems in the foreign policy arena beyond its power to control, most notably as its options towards the hostage-issue were restricted by its adversarial relationship with both Iran and Syria as well as by the disclosure of deals by its allies with the hostage-takers themselves. However, increased domestic political criticism focused on the applicability of this type of hardline counterterrorist policy in conjunction with the clandestine deals made by Britain's allies with the release of hostages with different nationalities. In particular, a major source of criticism focused on the perceived limited efforts made by British officials in utilizing their contacts in the Middle East to explore possible avenues for securing the release of its citizens from captivity. Nothwithstanding the validity of this criticism, it raises the question of whether negotiating or conceding to terrorist demands actually encourages or leads to further kidnappings. While the French and the British behaviour towards the hostage-crisis provide evidence that this is not necessarily the case, it underlines the problem of applying firmly established counterterrorism principles in a vacuum without consideration for the dynamics of the crisis-environment. This is at the heart of the dilemma for Western governments in attempting to balance its individual responsibility towards its citizens while maintaining its overall national interests.

What are the general lessons of the hostage-crisis for Western governments and for the international system as a whole? Unlike any other previous studies of the hostage-crisis in Lebanon or the way in which Western states have responded to it, this study has merged the dynamics of the crisis-environment surrounding the hostage-incidents with the instruments and techniques of crisis-management in order to more closely reconcile the underlying policy dilemma for Western governments and to improve the success and effectiveness of any response. While this case-study provided an indepth understanding of the mechanisms that governed the hostage-crisis in Lebanon, the employment of crisis-management offered a uniform manner in which to judge the different individual Western responses. The Hizb'allah and its hostage-taking activity represented an isolated phenomenon of unparalleled sophistication in the use of terrorism for political purposes in the Middle East in the 1980s, which served to paralyze the capability of many Western governments to function in the domestic and foreign policy arena. Yet the nature of the post-Cold war

Hizb'allah in Lebanon

environment in the Middle East with the rise of militant Shi'ite movements and with the possibility of these groups abducting Western hostages within civil war environments necessitates this type of approach not only to understand Islamic movements and their use of terrorism within a political context but also to begin a move away from applying generalized counter-terrorism guidelines to context-specific problems.

NOTES FOR CHAPTER 1

1. *The Holy Qur'an*, Ch.7:60. Some Hizb'allah leaders cite this verse from the Qur'an to justify the organisation's terrorist activity against the enemies of Islam.

2. *The Holy Qur'an*, Ch.47:4. As laid down by the laws of *Sharí'ah*, once the taking of "prisoners of war" brings the enemy under control: either generosity (i.e. the release of prisoners without ransom) or ransom is the only ordained conduct under Islamic law. Also see: Abdur Rahman I. Doi, *Sharí'ah: The Islamic Law* (London: Ta Ha Publishers, 1984).

3. *Public Papers of the President*, 28 November 1979.

4. For a useful overview, see: Maskit Burgin, Ariel Merari, and Anat Kurz, *Foreign Hostages in Lebanon*, JCSS Memorandum no.25–August 1988 (Tel Aviv: Jaffee Center for Strategic Studies): pp.42–50; and Brian Michael Jenkins and Robin Wright, "The Kidnappings in Lebanon", *TVI Report*, Vol.7, No.4 (Fall, 1986): pp.2–11.

5. *Public Report of the Vice-President's Task Force on Terrorism* (Washington, DC.: U.S. Government Printing Office, February 1986): p.7.

6. Gilbert Guillaume, "France and the Fight Against Terrorism", *Terrorism and Political Violence*, Vol.4, No.4 (Winter 1992): p.134.

7. For example, see: Theodore Draper, *A Very Thin Line: The Iran-Contra Affairs* (New York, NY.: Simon and Schuster, 1991); and L. Chauvin, "French Diplomacy and the Hostage-Crises", in B. Rubin (ed.) *The Politics of Counter-Terrorism: The Ordeal of Democratic States* (Washington, DC.: The Johns Hopkins Foreign Policy Institute, 1990): pp.91–104.

8. W. David Clinton, "The National Interest: Normative Foundations", *Review of Politics*, Vol.48, No.4 (1986): p.506.

9. International Convention Against the Taking of Hostages, [Article 1(1)], annexed to GA Res 34/146 of 17 December 1979, *UN GAOR*, 34th Sess., Supp.46, pp.245–47, UN Doc A/34/46 (1980). As of August 1989, the Convention had 56 signatories. Neither Lebanon, nor Iran and Syria, are parties to the Convention.

10. While there is still disagreement within academia over definitions of terrorism, the most comprehensive has been provided by Alex Schmidt: "terrorism is an anxiety-inspiring method of repeated violent action, employed by a (semi)clandestine individual, group or state actors, for idiosyncratic, criminal or political reasons, whereby–in contrast to assassination–the direct targets of violence are not the main targets. The immediate human victims of violence are generally chosen randomly (targets of opportunity) or selectively (representative or symbolic targets) from a target population, and serve as message generators. Threat- and violence-based communication processes between terrorist (organisation), (imperiled) victims, and main targets are used to manipulate the main target (audience(s)), turning it into a target of terror, a target of demands, or a target of attention, depending on whether intimidation, coercion, or propaganda is primarily sought", see: Alex P. Schmidt, Albert Jongman, *et al.*, *Political Terrorism: A New Guide to Actors, Authors, Concepts, Data Bases, Theories, and Literature* (Amsterdam: North Holland Publishing, 1988): p.28.

11.   Paul Wilkinson, *Terrorism and the Liberal State* (London: Macmillan, 1977): p.174.
12.   Clive C. Aston, "Political Hostage-Taking in Western Europe", in William Gutteridge (ed.) *The New Terrorism* (London: Mansell Publishing Ltd, 1986): p.59.
13.   Kent L. Oots, "Bargaining with Terrorists: Organizational Considerations", *Terrorism*, Vol.13, No.2 (March-April 1990): pp.146.
14.   R. Reuben Miller, "Negotiating with Terrorists: A Comparative Analysis of Three Cases", *Terrorism and Political Violence*, Vol.5, No.3 (Autumn 1993): p.103.
15.   Thomas Schelling, *Arms and Influences* (New Haven, CN.: Yale University Press, 1966): p.6.
16.   Martha Crenshaw, "The Logic of Terrorism: Terrorist Behavior as A Product of Strategic Choice", in Walter Reich (ed.) *Origins of Terrorism* (Cambridge: Cambridge University Press, 1990): p.21.
17.   Bruce D. Fitzgerald, "The Analytical Foundations of Extortionate Terrorism", in *Terrorism*, Vol.1, No.3–4 (1978): p.350.
18.   S.E. Atkinson, T. Sandler, and J. Tschirhart, (1987), *op. cit.*: p.3; and Nehemia Friedland, "Hostage negotiations: types, processes, outcomes", *Journal of Negotiation*, Vol.2, No.1 (January 1986): pp.57–72.
19.   A comparison between the data-bases of Mickolus A (1968–1980) and Mickolus B (1968–1987) reveals that hostage-taking incidents with a con-cealed·nature increased only three percent from 6 percent to 9 percent of the total number of types of terrorist events, see: Edward F. Mickolus, *Transnational Terrorism, A Chronology of Events, 1968–1979* (London: Aldwych Press, 1980); and Edward F. Mickolus, *Transnational Terrorism, A Chronology of Events, 1980–1987* (London: Aldwych Press, 1989).
20.   *Weekly Compilation of Presidential Documents* 21 (1985): p.859; and *Le Monde*, 6 May 1988.
21.   For the etymology of the word crisis, see: André Béjin and Edgar Morin, "Introduction", *Communications*, No.25 (1976): pp.1–3. For general agree-ment that crisis involves a turning-point or decision-point, see: Oran Young, *Politics of Force: Bargaining During International Crisis* (Princeton, NJ.: Princeton University Press, 1968): pp.6–15.
22.   See: Edgar Morin, "Pour une crisologie", *Communications*, No.25 (1976): p.149–63; and James A. Robinson, "Crisis", in D.L. Sills (ed.) *International Encyclopedia for Social Sciences*, Vol.3 (New York, NY.: Macmillan, 1968): pp.510–14.
23.   For the context-dependency of crisis-management, see: Alexander George, "A Provisional Theory of Crisis Management", in Alexander L. George (ed.) *Avoiding War: Problems of Crisis Management* (Boulder, CO.: Westview Press, 1991): p.23.
24.   See: Randolf Starn, "Métamorphose d'une notion. Les historiens et la 'crise'", *Communications*, No.25 (1976): pp.4–18. Also see the twelve general attributes of crisis formulated by Anthony J. Wiener and Herman Kahn cited in: Charles F. Hermann, "Some issues in the study of interna-tional crisis", in C.F. Hermann (ed.), *International Crises: Insights from Behavioral Research* (New York, NY.: The Free Press): p.21.

25. Alexander F. George, David K. Hall, and William R. Simons, *The Limits of Coercive Diplomacy* (Boston, MA.: Little-Brown, 1971): p.217.

26. Charles F. Hermann (ed.), (1972), *op. cit.*: p.13.

27. A.J.R. Groom, "Crisis management in long range perspective", in Daniel Frei (ed.), *International Crisis and Crisis Management* (London: Saxon House, 1978): p.102. Charles Hermann recognized himself the limitation of surprise and later dropped it as a necessary condition of crisis, see: Jonathan Wilkenfeld, *et al.*, *Crises in the Twentieth Century, Vol.II* (Oxford: Pergamon, 1988): p.3.

28. See: Ole R. Holsti, "Foreign Policy Decision Makers Viewed Psychologically: 'Cognitive Process' Approaches", in J.N. Rosenau (ed.) *In Search of Global Patterns* (New York, NY.: Free Press, 1976).

29. See: Hedley Bull, *The Anarchical Society: A Study of Order in World Politics* (London: Macmillan, 1977): pp.4–5.

30. Paul Wilkinson, Terrorism and the Liberal State (London: Macmillan, 1977): p.124.

31. See: M. Sassoli, "International Humanitarian Law and Terrorism", in Paul Wilkinson and A.M. Stewart (eds.) *Contemporary Research on Terrorism* (Aberdeen: Aberdeen University Press, 1987): p.466. Also see: George F. Kennan, "Morality and Foreign Policy", *Foreign Affairs* (Winter 1985/6): p.206.

32. See: Martin Kramer, "Redeeming Jerusalem: The Pan-Islamic Premise of Hizballah", in David Menashri (ed.) *The Iranian Revolution and the Muslim World* (Boulder, CO.: Westview Press, 1990): p.111–2.

33. Jane Mayer and Doyle McManus, *Landslide: The Unmaking of the President* (Boston, MA.: Houghton-Mifflin, 1988): p.292.

34. See: Doris A. Graber, *Verbal Behavior and Politics* (Urbana, IL.: University of Illinois Press, 1976): pp.66–7. Also see: Martha Crenshaw, "The Psychology of Political Terrorism", in Margaret G. Hermann (ed.) *Political Psychology* (San Francisco, CA.: Jossey-Bass, 1986); and O. Rosenthal, P.T. Hart, and M. Charles, *Coping with Crisis: The Management of Disasters, Riots, and Terrorism* (Springfield, IL.: Charles Thomas Books, 1989).

35. For a very useful overview of these influences, see: Gary Sick, "Taking Vows: The Domestication of Policymaking in Hostage Incidents", in Walter Reich (ed.), *op. cit.*: pp.230–44. Also see: Ariel Merari, "Government Policy in Incidents Involving Hostages", in Ariel Merari (ed.) *On Terrorism and Combatting Terrorism* (Frederick, MD.: University Publication of America, 1985): p.166.

36. Ronald Reagan, *An American Life* (New York, NY.: Simon & Schuster, 1990): p.510.

37. See: John Tower, *et al.*, *The Tower Commission Report* (New York, NY: Bantam Books, 1987): p.96.

38. For the moral justification of the seizure of hostages by the Hizb'allah, see: Martin Kramer, "The Moral Logic of Hizballah", in Walter Reich (ed.) Origins of Terrorism, *op. cit.*: pp.131–160.

39. The obligation to protect "the lives, liberty and property of the people composing it, whether abroad or at home" in the United States is legally

210   *Notes*

enshrined in: *Durand v. Hollins*, 4 Blatch. 451, 454, 8 Fed. Cas. 111 (no.4186) (C.C.S.D.N.Y. 1860).

40. See: Coral Bell, "Decision-Making by Governments in Crisis Situations", in Daniel Frei (ed.), (1978), *op. cit.*: p.51.

41. Alexander L. George, "Crisis Management: The Interaction of Political and Military Considerations," *Survival* (September/October, 1984): p.224.

42. The term "crisis-management" was an American concept which developed from the Cold War years in the 1950s in the use of coercive bargaining between the two superpowers in competitions short of war. The faith in the concept increased significantly in stature by the 1962 Cuban Missile Crisis, as demonstrated by Robert McNamara's statement that there was no longer any such thing as strategy only crisis-management, see: Coral Bell, *The Conventions of Crisis: A Study in Diplomatic Management* (London: Oxford University Press, 1971): p.2.

43. Phil Williams, *Crisis Management: Confrontation and Diplomacy in the Nuclear Age* (New York, NY.: Wiley, 1972): p.30.

44. Glenn H. Snyder and Paul Diesing (eds.), *Conflict Among Nations: Bargaining, Decision-Making, and System Structure in International Crises* (Princeton, CT.: Princeton University Press, 1977): p.196.

45. See: Robert L. Pfalzgraff, Jr. "Crisis Management", in Werner Kaltefleiter and Ulrike Schumacher (eds.) *Conflicts, Options, Strategies in a Threatened World* (Kiel: Institute of Political Science, Christian-Albrechts-University, 1987): p.29–30.

46. Coral Bell, (1971), *op. cit.*: pp.73.

47. For a typology of crisis-management instruments and techniques, see: Jonathan Wilkenfeld, *et al.* (1988), *op. cit.*: pp.70–3.

48. See: North Atlantic Assembly Political Committee Working Group on Terrorism, *Interim Report*, November 1986: p.39.

49. Brian M. Jenkins, "The U.S. Response to Terrorism: A Policy Dilemma", *TVI Journal* (1985): p.34.

50. Paul Wilkinson, *The Fight Against Terrorism*, Mackenzie Paper No.14 (Toronto: The Mackenzie Institute, 1989): p.15.

51. Alexander George, (1984), *op. cit.*: p.225.

52. Bell distinguishes between techniques and instruments of crisis-management: a technique indicates how an instruments is used, see: Coral Bell, (1971), *op. cit.*: p.73.

53. This astute observation was made by Alexander George in a crisis-situation involving armed conflicts between two states and can be invariably related to all other types of crisis, see: Alexander George, "A Provisional Theory of Crisis Management", in Alexander George, (1991), *op. cit.*: pp.23–4.

54. See: Thomas Schelling, *The Strategy of Conflict* (Cambridge, MA.: Harvard University Press, 1960).

55. See: Alexander George, "Crisis Management: The Interaction of Political and Military Considerations", *op. cit.*: pp.225–6.

56. These requirements of crisis-management were adapted from a wide variety of sources as recurrent components without the elements of war, see: Richard Clutterbuck, *International Crisis and Conflict* (London: Macmillan, 1993); Daniel Frei (ed.), (1978), *op. cit.*; Harlan Cleveland, "Crisis Diplomacy", *Foreign Affairs*, Vol.41 (July 1962/63); U. Rosenthal, *et al.*,

(1989), *op. cit.*; Alastair Buchanan, *Crisis Management* (Boulogne sur Seine: Atlantic Institute, 1966); Alexander George (ed.), (1991), *op. cit.*; and Hilliard Roderick, *Avoiding Inadvertent War: Crisis Management* (Austin, TX.: L.B. Johnson School of Public Affairs, 1983).

57. J. Philip Rogers, "Crisis Bargaining Codes and Crisis Management", in Alexander George (ed.), (1991), *op. cit.*: p.415.
58. *Ibid.*: pp.23–4.
59. Coral Bell, "Decision-Making by Governments in Crisis Situations", in Daniel Frei (ed.), (1978), *op. cit.*: p.54.
60. See: Charles F. Hermann, "Types of Crisis Actors and Their Implications for Crisis Management", in Daniel Frei (ed.), (1978), *op. cit.*: pp.29–30.
61. Robert Jervis, *Perception and Misperceptions in International Politics* (Princeton, CT.: Princeton University Press, 1976): p.58.
62. See: Coral Bell, "Decision-Making by Governments in Crisis Situations", Daniel Frei (ed.), (1978), *op. cit.*: p.55. For a useful overview of the importance of this in the Middle East, see: Xavier Raufer, "Middle East Terrorism: Rules of the Game", *Political Warfare*, No.18 (Fall 1991): pp.1 and 11–13.
63. See: Uriel Rosenthal, Paul 't Hart and Alexander Kouzmin, "The Bureau-Politics of Crisis Management", *Public Administration*, Vol.69 (Summer 1991): pp.211–33.
64. Paul Wilkinson, (1977), *op. cit.*: p.129.
65. Alexander George, "A Provisional Theory of Crisis Management", in Alexander George (ed.), (1991), *op. cit.*: p.23.
66. Michael Brecher and Hemda Ben Yehuda, "System and Crisis in International Politics", *Review of International Studies*, Vol.11 (1985): p.29.
67. As aptly observed by North: "[a]s research scholars and would-be theorists in international relations we might all derive at least three useful lessons from the old fable about the blind men and the elephant. The first is that the elephant [crisis] presumably existed; the second is that each of the groping investigators at the unit and system levels, despite sensory and conceptual limitations, had his fingers on a part of reality; and the third is that if they had quieted the uproar and begun making comparisons, the blind men might–all of them–have moved considerably closer to the truth", see: R.C. North, "Research Pluralism and the International Elephant", *International Studies Quarterly*, Vol.11 (December 1967): p.394.
68. For definition of system analysis, see: Anatol Rapoport, "Foreword", in Walter Buckley (ed.) *Modern Systems Research for the Behavioral Scientists* (Chicago, IL.: Aldine, 1968): p.xvii.
69. Morton A. Kaplan, "Systems Analysis: International Systems", in *International Encyclopedia of Social Sciences* (New York, NY.: The Macmillan Co. & The Free Press, 1968): p.481.
70. See: James E. Docherty and Robert J. Pfalzgraff, Jr. *Contending Theories of International Relations: A Comprehensive Survey* (London: Harper & Row, 1990): pp.172–5.
71. See: Stanley Hoffman, "Theory as a Set of Questions", in Stanley Hoffmann (ed.) *Contemporary Theory of International Relations* (Englewood Cliffs, NJ.: Prentice-Hall, 1960); and *idem*, "International Relations: The Long

Road to Theory", in James N. Rosenau (ed.) *International Politics and Foreign Policy* (New York, NY.: The Free Press, 1961).
72. Robert Jervis, Richard Ned Lebow, and Janice Gross Stein, *Psychology and Deterrence* (Baltimore, MD.: Johns Hopkins University Press, 1985): p.183.
73. For remarks by William J. Casey, CIA director, *"International Terrorism: Potent Challenge to American Intelligence"*, Fletcher School of Law and Diplomacy, Tufts University, April 17, 1985. Also see: James A. Bill, "The U.S. Overture to Iran 1985–1986: An Analysis", in Nikki R. Keddie and Mark J. Gasiorowski (eds.), *Neither East Nor West: Iran, the Soviet Union, and the United States* (London: Yale University Press, 1990): p.176
74. See: Paul Wilkinson, "Fighting the Hydra: Terrorism and the Rule of Law", *Harvard International Review*, Vol.7 (1985): pp.11–15.
75. George Andreopoulos, "Studying American Grand Strategy; Facets in an Exceptionist Tradition", *Diplomacy and Statecraft*, Vol.42, No.7 (July 1991): p.226.
76. As Uri Bar-Joseph has aptly described the problem: "[t]hat the best methodology is no substitute for common sense, and that basic errors in selecting propositions and in testing them through inappropriate case-studies will yield erroneous conclusions", see: Uri-Bar-Joseph, "Methodological Magic", *Journal of Intelligence and National Security* (October 1988): p.134.
77. This can be considered in alignment with the ideas for theory formation advanced by Schmid and Jongman through case-studies to make any theoretical progress, see: Alex P. Schmid and Albert J. Jongman, (1988), *op. cit.*: pp.61–130.
78. See: John Lewis Gaddis, *The United States and the End of the Cold War* (Oxford: Oxford University Press, 1992): p.192. For example, in a memorandum for the U.S. President, entitled "Covert Action finding Regarding Iran" (January 17, 1986), John Poindexter advocated that the approach through Iran was the *only* way to achieve the release of the American hostages, see: Peter Kornbluh and Malcolm Byrne (eds.) *The Iran-Contra Scandal: The Declassified Story* (New York, NY.: The New Press, 1993): p.233.
79. Charles W. Kegley, Jr.: *International Terrorism: Characteristics, Causes, Controls* (London: Macmillan, 1990): p.98.
80. See: Robert Jervis, "Models and Cases in the Study of International Conflict", *Journal of International Affairs*, Vol.44, No.1 (Spring-Summer 1990): pp.81–101.
81. John L. Esposito, "Presidential Address 1989–The Study of Islam: Challenges and Prospects", *Middle East Studies Association Bulletin*, Vol.24–5 (1990–1): p.5.

NOTES FOR CHAPTER 2

1. See: Augustus Richard Norton, "Changing Actors and Leadership Among the Shiites of Lebanon", *The Annals of the American Academy of Political Sciences*, Vol.482 (November 1985: pp.109–121).

2. The Amal movement (Harakat AMAL–Movement for the Dispossessed) was formed by Imam Musa al-Sadr, the president of the Higher Shi'i Islamic Council from 1969 until his disappearence in Libya in August 1978. See: Marius Deeb, "Lebanon: Prospects for National Reconciliation in the mid-1980's", *The Middle East Journal*, Vol.38 (1984): pp.268–9. Also see: Shimon Shapira, "The Imam Musa al-Sadr: Father of the Shiite Resurgence in Lebanon", *Jerusalem Quarterly*, No.44 (Fall 1987): pp.121–44.
3. Augustus Richard Norton, (1990), *op. cit.*: p.121.
4. See: Hanna Batatu, "Shi'i Organizations in Iraq: al-Da'wah al-Islamiyya and al-Mujahidin", in Juan R.I. Cole and Nikki R. Keddie (eds.), Shi'ism and Social Protest (New Haven, CT.: Yale University, 1986): p.191; and *Le Monde Diplomatique*, April 1984.
5. See: Hanna Batatu, "Iraq's Underground Shi'a Movements: Characteristics, Causes and Prospects", *Middle East Studies*, Vol.35, No.4 (Autumn 1981).
6. Amazia Baram, *Culture, History and Ideology in the Formation of Ba'athist Iraq: 1968–89* (New York, NY.: St. Martins Press, 1991): p.138.
7. Shimon Shapira, "The Origins of Hizballah", *The Jerusalem Quarterly*, Vol.46 (Spring 1988): p.130. Also see: *The Times*, 3 April 1986; *al-Nahar*, 19 January 1989; *al-Nahar*, 21 March 1989; and Xavier Raufer, *La Nebuleuse: Le Terrorisme du Moyen-Orient* (Paris: Libraire Artheme Fuyard, 1987): pp.160–1.
8. *al-Shira*, 15 March 1986.
9. Sheikh Fadlallah was born in 1934 in Najaf. A descendant of a family of clergymen, Sheikh Fadlallah hails from Aynata, a southern Lebanese town near the Shi'ite center of Bint Jbail. For a full biographical account of Sheikh Fadlallah, see: Martin Kramer, "Muhammad Husayn Fadlallah", *Orient: German Journal for Politics and Economics of the Middle East*, Vol.26, No.2 (June 1985): pp.147–49; and "Leadership Profile: Sheikh Muhammad Husayn Fadlallah", *Defense & Foreign Affairs Weekly* (June 23–29, 1986): p.7
10. See: Fouad Ajami, *The Vanished Imam: Musa al Sadr & the Shia of Lebanon* (Ithaca, NY.: Cornell University Press, 1986); and Majed Halawi, *A Lebanon Defied: Musa al-Sadr and the Shi'a Community* (Oxford: Westview Press, 1992).
11. See: Fouad Ajami, "Lebanon and Its Inheritors", *Foreign Affairs*, Vol.63 (Summer 1985): pp.778–99.
12. For many Shi'ites, the event was reminiscent of the Shi'i doctrine of the Hidden Iman, the occultation of the twelfth Imam who would return to restore a just order and it elevated Musa al-Sadr as a national hero. For Musa al-Sadr's disappearence, see: Augustus Richard Norton, "Political Violence and Shi'a Factionalism in Lebanon", *Middle East Insight,* Vol.3, No.2 (1983): pp.9–16; and Salim Nasr, "Roots of the Shi'i Movement", *MERIP Reports* (June 1985).
13. For the attitude of the southern Shi'i population following Israel's invasion, see: Augustus Richard Norton, "Making Enemies in South Lebanon: Harakat Amal, the IDF, and South Lebanon", *Middle East Insight*, Vol.3, No.3 (January-February 1984): pp.1–19.
14. See: Nassif Hitti, "Lebanon in Iran's Foreign Policy: Opportunities and Constraints", in Hooshang Amirahmadi and Nader Entessar (eds.), *Iran and*

214 *Notes*

the *Arab World* (London: Macmillan, 1993): pp.182–3; and *al-Watan al-Arabi*, 11 December 1987.

15.   Marius Deeb, *Militant Islamic Movements in Lebanon: Origins, Social Basis, and Ideology*, Occasional Paper Series (Washington, DC.: Georgetown University, 1986): p.12.

16.   *al-Safir*, 10 June 1982; and *al-Nahar al-Arabi wa-al-duwali*, 10–16 June 1985.

17.   As'ad AbuKhalil, "Ideology and Practice of Hizballah in Lebanon: Islamization of Leninist Organizational Principles" *Middle Eastern Studies*, Vol.27 (July 1991): p.391.

18.   Augustus Richard Norton, *Amal and the Shi'a: Struggle for the Soul of Lebanon* (Austin, TX.: University of Texas Press, 1987): p.88.

19.   Robin Wright, "Lebanon", in Shireen T. Hunter (ed.), *The Politics of Islamic Revivalism* (Indianapolis, IN.: Indiana University Press, 1988): p.63.

20.   *The Times*, 3 April 1986.

21.   See: *Middle East Reporter*, 14 September 1982.

22.   *al-Majallah*, 15 August 1993.

23.   Nassif Hitti, "Lebanon in Iran's Foreign Policy: Opportunities and Constraints", in Hooshang Amirahmadi and Nader Entessar (eds.), (1993), *op. cit.* p.183.

24.   *al-Shira*, 17 March 1986; *al-Watan al-Arabi*, 11 December 1987; and As'ad AbuKhalil, (1991), *op. cit.*: p.392.

25.   *Le Point*, 11 May 1987; *Daily Telegraph*, 6 June 1980; and *Teheran Domestic Service*, February 13, 1984.

26.   Hussein J. Agha and Ahmad S. Khalidi, *Syria and Iran: Rivalry and Cooperation* (London: Pinter, 1995): p.38.

27.   See: Nader Entessar, "The Military and Politics in the Islamic Republic of Iran", Hooshang Amirahmadi & Manoucher Parvin (eds.) *Post-Revolutionary Iran* (Boulder, CO.: Westview Press, 1988): pp.69–70.

28.   See: John L. Esposito, (1992), *op. cit.*: pp.146–51; *Independent*, 23 October 1991; and Roger Faligot & Rémi Kauffer, *Les Maîtres Espions* (Paris: Robert Laffont, 1994): pp.412–3.

29.   R.K. Ramazani, *Revolutionary Iran: Challenge and Response in the Middle East* (Baltimore, MD.: Johns Hopkins University Press, 1986): p.156.

30.   *al-Nahar*, 23 May 1986. Also see: *Le Point*, 11 May 1987; and *Liberation*, 19 March 1985. In the terms for the 1982 accord between Iran-Syria, Iran agreed to supply Syria with 9 million tons of free bartered discounted crude oil per year, see: *The Economist*, 30 April 1983.

31.   The Zebdani headquarters was the Pasdaran's single largest base outside Iran, see: *New York Times*, 4 October 1984; and *Le Point*, 11 May 1987.

32.   Robin Wright, *In the Name of God: the Khomeini Decade* (New York, NY.: Simon & Schultz, 1989): pp.108–9; *Radio Free Lebanon*, 23 November 1982; and *Voice of Lebanon*, 10 December 1982.

33.   Shimon Shapira, (1988), *op. cit.*: p.123; *Washington Post*, 19 January 1994; and *al-Dustur*, 6 November 1989. The importance of the Iranian clergy within the Pasdaran in the process of ideological indoctrination for the Hizb'allah was discussed in an interview between the author and Martin Kramer at the Jaffee Center for Strategic Studies, Tel Aviv University, September 1, 1991.

34. See: Robin Wright, "Lebanon", in Shireen T. Hunter (ed.), (1988), *op. cit.*: p.68. Also see: *L'Orient le Jour*, 25 November 1982.

35. Voice of Lebanon, 0615 gmt 10 April 91–BBC/*Summary of World Broadcasts* (hereinafter SWB)/ME/1043, 11 April 1991.

36. *al-Wasat*, 2–8 May 1994.

37. The base of the Iranian Pasdaran for indoctrination was the Imam Muntazar School, east of Ba'albek, see: *International Herald Tribune*, 10 January 1984. Also see: Robin Wright, "A Reporter at Large", *The New Yorker*, 5 September 1988.

38. See: *Politique International*, April 1984; *al-Dustur*, 6 November 1989; *al-Watan al-Arabi*, 11 December 1987; and *Liberation*, 29 March 1985.

39. *Ma'aretz*, 14 June 1984; *al-Shira*, 17 March 1986; *Washington Post*, 14 February 1986; *Ha'aretz*, 10 January 1984; and *al-Nashra*, 5 December 1983.

40. See: William Harris, "The View from Zahle: Security and Economic Conditions in the Central Bekaa 1980–1985", *Middle East Journal*, Vol.39, No.3 (Summer 1985): pp.270–86; *Time*, 15 August 1984; and *AP*, 24 April 1984.

41. *Ha'aretz*, 4 June 1984; and *al-Nahar*, 20 February 1989.

42. For Shi'a opposition, see: *al-Nahar*, 6 December 1982; and *Radio Free Lebanon*, 23 November 1982.

43. *Beirut Domestic Service*, November 25, 1983.

44. See: *Middle East International*, 19 December 1987; and Augustus Richard Norton, "Lebanon: The Internal Conflict and the Iranian Connection", in John L. Esposito (ed.), *The Iranian Revolution: Its Global Impact* (Miami, fl.: florida University International Press, 1990): pp.126–27. Also see: *Middle East Reporter*, 22 March 1986; *Financial Times*, 25 July 1987; *al-Dustur*, 14 October 1985; and *Jerusalem Post*, 22 July 1987.

45. *Ha'aretz*, 21 June 1987.

46. *The Times*, 14 November 1987; and *Independent*, 3 August 1989.

47. Martin Kramer, "The Pan-Islamic Premise of Hizb'allah", in David Menashri (ed.), (1990), *op. cit.*: p.122

48. For Sheikh Fadlallah's position as the spiritual guide, see: Martin Kramer, "Muhammad Husayn Fadlallah", *op. cit.*: pp.147–49; *al-Shira*, 4 August 1986; and "Leadership Profile: Sheikh Muhammad Husayn Fadlallah", *Defense & Foreign Affairs Weekly* (June 23–29, 1986): p.7.

49. Shimon Shapira, (1988), *op. cit.*: p.127.

50. *Ibid.*: p.127. Also see: *al-Nahar*, 6 February 1989; *al-Hayat*, 27 November 1989; and *Independent*, 30 August 1989.

51. See: *Ma'aretz*, 11 January 1984; and *Ha'aretz*, 3 June 1986; *Foreign Report*, 27 September 1984.

52. See: *Israeli Defence Forces Spokesman* (IDFS), 18 February 1986; and *International Herald Tribune*, 1 January 1984.

53. *FBIS*, August 1994.

54. *al-Shira*, 19 September 1988; and *Jeune Afrique*, 25 January 1984.

55. Prominent among the local leaders were: Sheikh Rageb Harb of Jibshit; Abd al-Karim Shams al-Din of Arab Salim; and Sa'id Ali Mahdi Ibrahim of Adlun, see: Augustus Richard Norton, (1987), *op. cit.*: p.112; Shimon Shapira, (1988), *op. cit.*: p.128. Other local leaders are: A'bd al-Karim Abid

Mohamad and Afif Nabalsi, see: *Israeli Defense Force Spokesman*, 19 February 1986.

56. See: Martin Kramer, "The Pan-Islamic Premise of Hizballah", in David Menashri (ed.), (1990), *op. cit.*: p.128; Shimon Shapira, (1988), *op. cit.*: pp.128–29; and *Liberation*, 19 March 1985.

57. See: *Ettela'at*, 21 December 1983; and *The Times*, 23 February 1984.

58. On the Nabatiya incident, see: Augustus Richard Norton, *External Intervention and the Politics of Lebanon* (Washington, DC.: Washington Institute for Values in Public Policy, 1984): pp.12–3.

59. For Hizb'allah's claim of credit, see: *Nass al-risla al-maftuha allati wajjaha hizb allah ila al-mustad áfin fi lubnan wa al-alam* (Text of Open Letter Addressed by Hizb'allah to the Downtrodden in Lebanon and in the World), February 16, 1985, reprinted in Augustus Richard Norton (1987), *op. cit.*: pp.171–73. For interview with Sheikh Fadlallah, see: *al-Nahar al-arabi wa-al-duwali*, 18–24 March 1985.

60. For the centrality of the *Ashura* for Hizb'allah, see: *al-Nahar*, 5 October 1984; and *Libération*, 26 September 1985.

61. *al-Nahar*, 5 June 1985.

62. For further explanation of the Arabic term Hizb'allah, see: Bernard Lewis, *The Political Language of Islam* (Chicago, Ill.: The University of Chicago Press, 1988): p.123.

63. See: Muhammad Husayn Fadlallah, *Al-islam wa-mantiq al-quwwa* (Beirut: 1981 (2nd ed.)): p.246.

64. See: *al-Nahar al-arabi wal-duwali*, 10–16 June 1985; and *La Revue du Liban*, 27 July-3 August 1985.

65. See: *Independent*, 30 August 1989; and As'ad AbuKhalil, (1991), *op. cit.*: p.394.

66. Ali al-Kurani, *al-Harakat al-Islamiyya fi Lubnan* (Beirut, 1984). This information was confirmed in an unattributable interview with a former Israeli military intelligence officer, Tel Aviv, 28 August 1991.

67. See: Marius Deeb, (1986), *op. cit.*: p.16.

68. See: "An Open Letter: The Hizb'allah Program", *Jerusalem Quarterly*, No.48 (Fall 1988): pp.111–16.

69. *Al-Ahd*, September 30, 1988.

70. For a useful discussion of these problems, see: Martin Kramer, "La Morale du Hizballah et sa Logique", *Maghreb-Machrek*, No.119 (January-March, 1988): pp.39–59.

71. *Middle East Insight*, June-July 1985; *Monday Morning*, 16 December 1985; and *La Revue du Liban*, 27 July 1985.

72. *al-Nahar al-Arabi wal-Duwali*, 20–26 August 1984.

73. *al-Diyar*, 19 December 1993.

74. *al-Shira*, 27 September 1993.

75. Al-Ahd, 25 February 1994.

76. See: "Hizballah", in *Terrorist Group Profiles*, US Department of Defense (DOD), Washington DC. (November 1988): p.15; *Independent*, 25 August 1989; *The Jerusalem Report*, 1 August 1991; *al-Shira*, 16 March 1986; *al-Anba*, 11 November 1989; and *Independent*, 30 August 1989.

77. Unattributable interview with high-ranking Israeli military official, 28 August 1991.

78. As'ad AbuKhalil, (1991), *op. cit.*: p.397. Also see: *Da'var*, 11 January 1987.
79. Marius Deeb, (1988), *op. cit.*: p.693. Also see: *IGPO*, 5 July 1985.
80. Most prominent of Iranian diplomatic representatives on the Majlis al-Shura have been: Ali Akhbar Mohtashemi (Iran's Ambassador to Syria between 1981–85); Muhammad Nurani (Iranian charge d'affair in Beirut); Ali Akbar Rahimi and Mohammed Javad (diplomatic staff at Iran's embassy in Beirut), see: *Foreign Report*, 30 July 1987; *al-Shira*, 19 September 1988; *Independent*, 7 March 1990; and *Israeli Defence Force Spokesman*, 19 February 1986.
81. Amir Taheri, *Holy Terror: The Inside Story of Islamic Terrorism* (London: Sphere Books, 1987): p.125. For meetings of Hizb'allah's Majlis al-Shura, see: *al-Watan al-Arabi*, 11 December 1987.
82. Augustus Richard Norton, "Lebanon: The Internal Conflict and the Iranian Connection", in John L. Esposito (ed.), (1990), *op. cit.*: p.125; and Martin Kramer, "The Moral Logic of Hizballah", in Walter Reich (ed.), (1990), *op. cit.*: p.134–35.
83. See: *Ma'aretz*, 14 June 1984; *al-Shira*, 17 March 1986; and *Ha'aretz*, 10 January 1984.
84. For Hizb'allah's adherence to the principle of *al-wali al-faqih*, see: Augustus Richard Norton, (1987), *op. cit.*: pp.167–87.
85. Marius Deeb, (1988), *op. cit.*: p.694; and *al-Shira*, December 5, 1983.
86. *New York Times*, 22 March 1987.
87. *Washington Post*, 4 June 1986.
88. *al-Hayah*, 18 April 1992.
89. See: James Piscatori, *Islam in a World of Nation-States* (Cambridge: Cambridge University Press, 1986): pp.114–15; and Martin Kramer, "Redeeming Jerusalem: The Pan-Islamic Premise of Hizballah", David Menashri (ed.), (1990), *op. cit.*: pp.105–30.
90. *Voice of the Oppressed*, 25 October 1989.
91. *Independent*, 9 October 1991.
92. See: *al-Harakat al-Islamiyya fi Lubnan* (Beirut, 1984).
93. Martin Kramer, "Redeeming Jerusalem: The Pan-Islamic Premise of Hizballah", David Menashri (ed.), (1990), *op. cit.*: pp.105–30.
94. *Ibid*: p.127.
95. *Ibid.*: p.119.
96. *Ettela'at*, 13 February 1993.
97. *Independent*, 15 June 1992.
98. *Al-Haqiqa*, 3 November 1987.
99. See: *Voice of the Oppressed* 1430 gmt 9 Sept 91–BBC/SWB/ME/1176, 13 September 1991.
100. *Keyhan International*, 22 December 1990.
101. For Iran's and Hizb'allah's opposition to the Ta'if agreement, see: Augustus Richard Norton, "Lebanon After Ta'if: Is the Civil War Over?", *Middle East Journal*, Vol.45, No.3 (Summer 1991): pp.457–473.
102. For agreement between Iran and Syria, see: *Financial Times*, 17 February 1992; and *Voice of the Oppressed* 0630 gmt 30 Apr 91–BBC/SWB ME/1061, 2 May 1991.
103. See: Chibli Mallat, *Shii Thought from the South of Lebanon*. Papers on Lebanon, no.7 (Oxford: Centre for Lebanese Studies, 1988): pp.36–7.

218 Notes

104. See: *Middle East Insight*, June-July 1985.
105. See: *Voice of the Oppressed* 0630 gmt 3 Jan 92–BBC/SWB ME/1269, 4 January 1992; and *AFP*, 8 January 1992.
106. See Hizb'allah's manifesto reprinted in Augustus Richard Norton, Amal and the Shi'a: Struggle for the Soul of Lebanon, *op. cit.*: pp.167–87.
107. See: John L. Esposito, *Islam and Politics* (Syracuse, NY.: Syracuse University Press, 1991): p.252.
108. For the agreement between Hizb'allah and Amal, see: *Radio Free Lebanon* 0545 gmt 15 Jan 89–BBC/*SWB*/ME/0360, 17 January 1989; *Voice of the Oppressed* 0630 gmt 28 Jan 89–BBC/*SWB*/ME/0371, 30 January 1989.
109. See: *al-Nahar al-Arabi wal-Duwali*, 10–16 June 1985.
110. See: Mohssen Massarrat, "The Ideological Context of the Iran-Iraq War: Pan-Islamism versus Pan-Arabism", in Hooshang Amirahmadi & Nader Entessar (eds.), (1993), *op. cit.*: pp.28–41; and *al-Ahd*, 29 August 1985.
111. *Teheran home service* 1030 gmt 29 Jan 88–BBC/SWB ME/0063, 1 February 1988.
112. See: Shireen T. Hunter, "Islamic Iran and the Arab World", *Middle East Insight*, Vol.5, No.3 (1987); and idem, "After the Ayatollah", *Foreign Policy*, Vol.66 (Spring 1987): pp.741–2.
113. Martin Kramer, "The Pan-Islamic Premise of Hizballah", in David Menashri (ed.), (1990), *op. cit.*: p.118.
114. See: Chibli Mallat, (1988), *op. cit.*; and *al-Shira*, 28 September 1987.
115. For Hizb'allah resistance activity as a means to the establishment of an Islamic state, see: Chibli Mallat, (1988), *op. cit.*: 35–37.
116. *Voice of the Oppressed*, 0630 gmt 19 Feb 92–SWB ME/1309, 20 February 1992.
117. *L'Orient du Jour*, 30 July 1994.
118. *Ettela'at*, 13 February 1993.
119. Interview with Sheikh Nasserallah by *IRNA*, 1745 gmt 13 Oct 92–*SWB* ME/1512, 15 October 1992.
120. *AFP*, 24 February 1994.
121. Martin Kramer, "The Moral Logic of Hizb'allah", in Walter Reich (ed.), (1990), *op. cit.*: p.134; and Ali al-Kurani, *Tariqat Hizballah fil-Amal al-Islami* (Beirut, 1986).

NOTES FOR CHAPTER 3

1. See: Ariel Merari and Yosefa (Daiksel) Braunstein, "Shiite Terrorism: Operational Capabilities and the Suicide Factor", *TVI Journal*, Vol.5, No.2 (Fall 1984): pp.7–10; and Con Coughlin, *Hostage* (London: Little and Brown, 1992).
2. John Calabrese, "Iran II: The Damascus Connection", *World Today* (October 1990): p.189.
3. Graham E. Fuller, *The "Center of the Universe": The Geopolitics of Iran* (Boulder, CO.: Westview Press, 1991): p.20.
4. See: *Le Matin*, 29 January 1987; and *Keyhan*, 12 February 1987. For the practice of *taqiyah*, see: Juan R.I. Cole and Nikki R. Keddie (eds.), (1986),

op. cit.: pp.28–29. For a useful exposition of concealment in Shi'ism, refer to lecture by Prof. Etan Kohlberg, Hebrew University, delivered at the Tel Aviv University, 23 May 1993.

5. See: *al-Dustur*, 6 November 1989; and *al-Dustur*, 11 September 1989.
6. Marius Deeb, (1986), *op. cit.*: p.19; *al-Nahar*, 7 September 1985; and *La Revue du Liban*, 27 July –3 August 1985.
7. *al-Nahar al-Arabi*, 10 June 1985; *Ma'aretz*, 16 December 1983; *Le Point*, 30 July 1987; *al-Shira*, 28 August 1988; and *Nouveau Magazine*, 23 July 1988.
8. See: *Davar*, 11 January 1987; and *New York Times*, 18 December 1986.
9. See: *Ma'ariv*, 3 November 1987; *Richochets*, Israel Defence Forces Spokesman, July 1990; and *al-Diyar*, 4 December 1989.
10. See: *International Herald Tribune*, 20 February 1988.
11. Hizb'allah's radio station, *Radio of Islam – Voice of the Oppressed*, is broadcasted from the Biq'a valley and was first monitored on 14 January 1986. Another radio station, Voice of Faith, which appeared in November 1987, is supportive of Hizb'allah, see: BBC/*SWB*/ME/0024, 12 December 1987. For information on Hizb'allah's TV-station al-Manar (the Beacon), see: *Sunday Times*, 19 July 1992.
12. See: Maskit Burgin, Ariel Merari and Anat Kurz, (1988), *op. cit.*: pp.11–12.
13. See: *Los Angeles Times*, 26 November 1989; *Independent*, 9 October 1991; and *Le Figaro*, 4 December 1989.
14. Samuel M. Katz, *Soldier Spies: Israeli Military Intelligence* (Novato, CA.: Presidio Press, 1992): p.319; and *Newsweek*, 27 February 1989.
15. Unattributable interview with senior Israeli official in Ministry of Foreign Affairs, Jerusalem, Israel, August 1991. Also see: *al-Sharq al-Awsat*, 18 April 1989; and *al-Shira*, 17 March 1986.
16. *Le Matin*, 29 January 1987
17. This section was previously published in a revised form in "Terrorism & Political Violence", Vol.6, No.3 (Autumn 1994).
18. Gilles Delafon, *Beyrouth: Les Soldats de l'Islam* (Paris: Stock, 1989): p.90.
19. *Ha'aretz*, 4 June 1984; and *al-Nashra*, 5 December 1983.
20. See: *al-Dustur*, 31 March 1985; *al-Ittihad*, 4 December 1986; *Ma'aretz*, 14 June 1987; *Ha'aretz*, 29 November 1987; and *La Revue du Liban*, 30 January 1988.
21. *International Herald Tribune*, 27 March 1987; *Ha'aretz*, 29 November 1987; *Ma'aretz*, 14 June 1987; and *Ha'aretz*, 22 February 1988.
22. *Foreign Report*, 30 July 1987; *Ha'aretz*, 2 October 1987; *al-Hayat*, 27 November 1989; and *Independent*, 7 March 1990.
23. *Ha'aretz*, 20 March 1987; and *al-Anba*, 18 February 1984. The military leader of Islamic Amal is Abu Yahia, see: *AP*, 18 November 1983; *Israeli Defense Forces Spokesman*, 3 February 1984.
24. See: *Ha'aretz*, June 21, 1987.
25. *al-Watan al-Arabi*, 11 December 1987; *al-Hayat*, 27 November 1989; *al-Shira*, 17 March 1986; *Ma'aretz*, 14 June 1986; and *Independent*, 15 June 1992.
26. *Independent*, 7 March 1990; *al-Shira*, 17 March 1986; *Foreign Report*, 30 July 1987 and *al-Shira*, 19 September 1988.
27. *al-Nahar*, 6 February 1989.

28. *Politique International*, April 1984; and *Liberation*, 19 March 1985.
29. See: *al-Shira*, 17 March 1986; *Israeli Government Press Office*, 5 July 1985; *Israeli Defense Forces Spokesman*, 19 February 1986; and *al-Nahar*, 16 June 1985. Also see: Marius Deeb, (1986), *op. cit.*: pp.18–19.
30. *Ha'aretz*, 13 May 1987; and *Foreign Report*, 5 December 1991.
31. See: *Ha'aretz*, 21 June 1987; *Foreign Report*, 13 August 1988; and *Foreign Report*, 13 May 1993.
32. *Intelligence Newsletter*, No.260, 16 March 1995.
33. *al-Watan al-Arabi*, 11 December 1987
34. As'ad AbuKhalil, (1991), *op. cit.*: p.397; and *Davar*, 11 January 1987.
35. See: Marius Deeb, "Shia movements in Lebanon: their formation, ideology, social basis, and links with Iran and Syria", *Third World Quarterly*, Vol.10, No.2 (April 1988): p.693. Also see: "Hizballah", in US Department of Defense (DOD), *Terrorist Group Profiles*, November 1988: p.15.
36. Private communication with Dr Yossi Olmert, Director, Government Press Office, Israel, 30 December 1991. Also see: *Da'var*, 11 January 1987.
37. *The Lebanon Report*, Vol.4, No.3 (March 1993): p.6.
38. For information concerning Hizb'allah's SSA, see: Rolf Tophoven, "Der Tod eines Terroristen – Hintergründe und Konsequenzen", *Terrorismus*, Nr.3 (March 1992): pp.1–4; *al-Hayat*, 27 November 1989; *Wall Street Journal*, 16 August 1989; *Washington Post*, 15 May 1990; *Le Figaro*, 4 December 1989; *Independent*, 26 April 1988; and *Ha'aretz*, 29 January 1988. In addition, information on the Hizb'allah SSA was collected by the author during interviews with high-ranking Israeli officials in the Ministry of Defense and Ministry of Foreign Affairs, Tel Aviv, 25 August–10 September 1991.
39. Private communication with Dr Yossi Olmert, Director, Government Press Office, Israel, 30 December 1991. This was also confirmed in unattributable interviews with senior IDF officials in Israel (August/September 1991) and a senior counter-terrorism official at the Department of State, Washington DC, 4 September 1993.
40. Roger Faligot and Remi Kauffer, (1994), *op. cit.*: p.485.
41. See: *Independent*, 7 March 1990; *al-Watan al-Arabi*, 11 December 1987; *Independent*, 9 October 1991; *Le Figaro*, 4 December 1989; *Yediot Aharanot*, 24 June 1988; *Independent*, 26 April 1988; and *al-Nahar al-Arabi wal-Duwali*, 16 January 1989.
42. *Davar*, 8 February 1989; *Independent*, 30 August 1989; *al-Anba*, 27 November 1989; and *Ha'aretz*, 17 December 1989. Also see: Roger Faligot and Rémi Kauffer, (1994), *op. cit.*: p.485.
43. See: *BBC*, 13 April 1988; and *Ha'aretz*, 4 December 1988.
44. *Radio Free Lebanon*, 9 September 1986; and *al-Watan al-Arabi wal-Duwali*, 11 December 1987.
45. *Le Point*, 1 June 1987; *al-Sharq al-Awsat*, 21 November 1991; *Yediot Aharanot*, 1 July 1987; *Defense & Armament Heracles*, November 1989; and *Independent*, 7 March 1990.
46. *Le Point*, 3 August 1987.
47. *Foreign Report*, 22 August 1991; *Ma'ariv*, 11 October 1991; and *Reuters*, 4 October 1991.
48. See: *Wall Street Journal*, 16 August 1989; *Ha'aretz*, 29 January 1988; and *Jerusalem Post*, 14 April 1988 This was also confirmed in an unattributable

interview with a former senior Fatah advisor in Cairo, Egypt, who had personally known Imad Mughniya until his defection to Hizb'allah (Cairo, Egypt, April 1994).

49. For Imad Mughniya's position, see: *Los Angeles Times*, 26 November 1988; *Davar*, 6 May 1988; *Le Point*, 3 August 1987; *Da'var*, 6 May 1988; *Independent*, 26 April 1988; Also see: Neil C. Livingstone and David Halevy, *Inside the PLO* (London: Robert Hale Ltd, 1990): pp.262–70. For Hizb'allah's relationship with Force 17, see: *Ma'ariv*, 17 October 1986; *Le Matin*, 29 January 1987; and *Ma'aretz*, 31 March 1987.

50. Unattributable interview with senior official in Israel's Ministry of Defense, 27 August 1991, Tel Aviv, Israel.

51. Unattributable interview with senior official in US Department of State, Washington DC, 4 October 1993.

52. See: Roger Faligot and Remi Kauffer, (1994), *op. cit.*: p.485.

53. *Yediot Aharonot*, 24 June 1988; *Le Quotidien de Paris*, 27–28 January 1990; and *Ma'aretz*, 8 July 1987.

54. *Independent*, 7 March 1990; and *Foreign Report*, 30 July 1987.

55. See: Maskit Burgin, Anat Kurz and Ariel Merari, (1988), *op. cit.*: p.14 n.4.

56. *al-Shira*, 17 March 1986; *Independent*, 7 March 1990; and *Da'var*, 11 January 1987.

57. *Middle East Reporter*, 1 September 1984; *Jeune Afrique*, 25 January 1984; *al-Sharq al-Awsat*, 18 April 1989; *AFP*, 16 May 1988; *al-Majallah*, 19–25 April 1989; and *New York Times*, 23 April 1990.

58. See: *Washington Post*, 8 January 1990; and *The Echo of Iran*, No.26 (February 1990): p.12.

59. *Middle East Defense News*, 16 May 1988; *Independent*, 22 June 1988; *al-Anba*, 7 April 1990; and *Foreign Report*, 27 October 1983.

60. See: Yosef Olmert, "Iranian-Syrian Relations: Between Islam and Realpolitik", in David Menashri (ed.), (1990), *op. cit.*: pp.171–188.

61. *Ma'aretz*, 10 March 1985; and *Ma'aretz*, 19 March 1985.

62. *al-Dustur*, 5 March 1990; and *Le Nouvel Observateur*, 28 March-3 April 1986.

63. Mustafa Dirani defected from Amal after the February 1988 kidnapping of US Marine Corps officer Lieutenant Colonel William Higgins. For information of Dirani's role, see: *Ma'aretz*, 24 February 1989; *Davar*, 28 February 1988; and *Yediot Aharanot*, 25 February 1988.

64. *Hadashot*, 10 May 1991; *Middle East Defense News*, 16 May 1988. Also see: *Le Point*, 11 September 1989; *al-Shira*, 5 February 1990; and U.S. Department of State, *International Narcotics Control Strategy Report* (Washington, DC.: Bureau of International Narcotics Matter, March 1988): pp.218–20.

65. *Foreign Report*, 11 October 1990; and *Wall Street Journal*, 24 March 1988.

66. *al-Shira*, 14 June 1987; and *Ma'aretz*, 15 June 1987.

67. *La Revue du Liban*, 30 January 1988; *Ha'aretz*, 22 February 1988; and *Ha'aretz*, 29 November 1987.

68. See: *al-Shira*, 2 August 1992. For rivalry over the post of Secretary-General of the movement, see: *Foreign Report*, 30 April 1992. For efforts by Sheikh al-Tufayli of undermining the position of Sheikh Nasserallah, see: *Foreign Report*, 5 November 1992.

222	*Notes*

69.	See: *The Lebanon Report*, Vol.4, No.3 (March 1993): p.6.
70.	*Foreign Report*, 13 June 1991.
71.	See: *al-Hayat*, 27 November 1989; and *Ha'aretz*, 17 December 1989.
72.	Private communication with Dr Yossi Olmert, Director, Government Press Office, Israel, 30 December 1991. Also see: *The Lebanon Report*, Vol.4, No.3 (March 1993): p.6.
73.	See: *Foreign Report*, 13 June 1991; and *The Lebanon Report*, Vol.4, No.3 (March 1993): p.6.
74.	For Hizb'allah factionalism at the meetings, see: *al-Anba*, 27 November 1989; *al-Ahd*, 27 October 1989; *al-Hayat*, 27 October 1989; and *Ha'aretz*, 17 December 1989. This was also confirmed in an unattributable interview with senior IDF official, Tel Aviv, September 1991.
75.	Assaf Kfoury, *Arabies*, December 1992.
76.	See: *Voice of Lebanon*, Beirut 1015 gmt 21 May 91–BBC/*SWB*/ME/1079 23 May 1991. For Hizb'allah's "democratization process", see: *Jerusalem Report*, 1 August 1991. Also see: *The Lebanon Report*, Vol.4, No.3 (March 1993): p.7.
77.	For insights on Hizb'allah's concern over disarmament, see: *Voice of the Oppressed* 0630 gmt 24 Mar 91–BBC/*SWB*/ME/1030, 26 March 1991. See also interview with Sheikh Subhi al-Tufayli, *Voice of the Oppressed* 0530 gmt 8 May 91–BBC/*SWB*/ME/1068, 10 May 1991.
78.	For agreement, see: *Financial Times*, 17 February 1992; and *Voice of the Oppressed*, 0630 gmt 30 Apr 91–BBC/*SWB*/ME/1061, 2 May 1991.
79.	Unattributable interviews with high-ranking counter-terrorism officials at Israel's Ministry of Defense, Tel Aviv, Israel, August 1991, and Office for Counterterrorism, US Department of State, October 1993. Also see: *Foreign Report*, 13 June 1991.
80.	See: *Terrorismus*, No.1, March 1992; and *Foreign Report*, 30 April 1992.
81.	See: *Foreign Report*, 30 April 1992; and *Foreign Report*, 8 October 1992.
82.	For Sheikh Nasserallah's strengthened position under the tenure of Sheikh al-Musawi, see: *al-Hayat*, 21 May 1991. At the end of 1989, Nasserallah had bolstered his position with Iran, who wanted him to fulfill a senior role in the next stage of Iranian policy in Lebanon, see: *al-Qabas*, 20 July 1989.
83.	Unattributable interview with official in Israel's Ministry of Foreign Affairs, 3 September 1992. In an interview with Sheikh Hassan Nasserallah, he is asked to elaborate on his links with Ayatollah Mohtashemi, see: *Voice of the People* in Arabic to Lebanon 1239 gmt 28 Feb 92–BBC/*SWB*/ME/1318, 2 March 1992.
84.	See: *Foreign Report*, 30 April 1992; *Foreign Report*, 8 October 1992; and *Foreign Report*, 5 November 1992.
85.	See: *Foreign Report*, 8 October 1992; *Foreign Report*, 13 May 1993; *al-Shira*, 13 July 1992; and *al-Shira*, 2 August 1992.
86.	*al-Shira*, 2 August 1992.
87.	For the Hizb'allah operation, initiated by Sheikh al-Tufayli, near the village of Kaoukaba which killed five IDF soldiers and wounded five others on October 25, 1992, see: *Foreign Report*, 5 November 1992.
88.	*Foreign Report*, 7 October 1993.
89.	See: *Foreign Report*, 30 April 1992; and *The Lebanon Report*, Vol.4, No.3 (March 1993).

90. See: *Foreign Report*, 13 May 1993.
91. *L'Orient-Le Jour*, 30 July 1994.
92. See: Martin Kramer, (1990), *op. cit.*: pp.105–31.
93. See: David Menashri, "Khomeini's Vision: Nationalism or World Order", in David Menashri (ed.), (1990), *op. cit.*: p.48.
94. See: Xavier Raufer, *Atlas Mondial de L'Islam Activiste* (Paris: La Table Ronde, 1991): pp.132–3; *al-Majallah*, 5–11 November 1983; and *Jeune Afrique*, 7 May 1986.
95. See: *Keyhan*, 18 September 1986; and *Le Monde*, 25 October 1986.
96. See: *Washington Post*, 8 January 1990; *al-Shira*, 19 September 1988; and *Independent*, 23 October 1991.
97. See: *Voice of the People* in Arabic to Lebanon 1239 gmt 28 Feb 92–BBC/SWB/ME/1318, 2 March 1992.
98. *al-Anba*, 29 November 1989.
99. For a debate within the Iranian Majlis on Mohtashemi's independent efforts, see: *FBIS*, 23 September 1988; and *Ha'aretz*, 17 December 1989.
100. For Hizb'allah's ties with Montazeri, see: *Ha'aretz*, 30 September 1984; *al-Dustur*, 22 December 1986; *al-Ahd*, 31 November 1986; *Foreign Report*, 13 December 1984; and *International Herald Tribune*, 8–9 December 1984.
101. See: *Paris Lettre Persane*, No.46 (June 1986): pp.6–10. Also see: Shireen T. Hunter, (1988), *op. cit.*: pp.743–4; and Dilip Hiro, *Between Marx and Muhammad* (New York, NY.: Harper Collins, 1994): p.284.
102. *FBIS*, 5 November 1986. Also see: Roger Faligot and Rémi Kauffer, (1994), *op. cit.*: p.412; Hazhir Teimourian, "The Mullah Goes Back to the Mosque", *The Middle East* (May 1989): pp.20–1; and *New York Times*, 18 March 1987.
103. See: George Joffe, "Iran, the Southern Mediterranean and Europe: Terrorism and Hostages", in Anoushiravan Ehteshami and Manshour Varasteh (eds.), *Iran and the International Community* (London: Routledge, 1991): p.85.
104. *IRNA*, 18 March 1987. Also see: Bruce Hoffman, *Recent Trends and Future Prospects of Iranian Sponsored International Terrorism* (Santa Monica, CA.: Rand Corporation, 1990): p.26; and *Foreign Report*, 18 December 1986.
105. See: Pierre Pean, *La Menace* (Paris: Fayard, 1987): p.262; and *al-Dustur*, June 11, 1990.
106. *al-Watan al-Arabi*, 12 February 1993.
107. See: Shireen T. Hunter, (1988), *op. cit.*: pp.743–4.
108. See: *US News & World Report*, 6 March 1989; *Independent*, 1 July 1987; *Keyhan*, 5 December 1985; *Le Nouvel Observateur*, 30 October 1983; and *Le Monde*, 6–7 November 1983. For the close relationship between Sheikh-ol-Islam and Mohtashemi, see: *IRNA*, 7 November 1982; and *Radio Damascus*, 9 November 1982.
109. See: *al-Dustur*, October 16, 1990; Kenneth Katzman, *The Warriors of Islam* (Boulder, CO.: Westview Press, 1993): pp.125–6; and *al-Dustur*, February 12, 1990.
110. Private communication with Dr Yossi Olmert, Director, Government Press Office, Israel, 30 December 1991.
111. See: Xavier Raufer, (1987), *op. cit.*: pp.180–2. Also see: *Times*, 1 June 1985.

224 *Notes*

112. See: *Middle East International*, 19 December 1987); *Financial Times*, 25 July 1987; *al-Dustur*, 14 October 1985; *al-Shira*, 19 September 1988; *Jerusalem Post*, 22 July 1987; and *al-Musawwar*, 17 September 1987. Also see: Augustus Richard Norton, "Lebanon: The Internal Conflict and the Iranian Connection", in John L. Esposito (ed.), (1990), *op. cit.*. In 1994, it was estimated that Hizb'allah received £40 million annually from Iran, see: *Independent*, 8 May 1994.
113. See: *al-Nahar al-Arabi wal-Duwali*, 19 September 1989.
114. For a useful overview, see: A Nizar Hamzeh, "Lebanon's Hizbullah: From Islamic Revolution to Parliamentary Accommodation", *Third World Quarterly*, Vol.14, No.2 (1993): pp.327–8. Also see: *The Lebanon Report*, Vol.4, No.3 (March 1993): p.7.
115. *al-Ahd*, 1 August 1989.
116. See: "Details about 'Hizballah' and Its Leaders", *Middle East Reporter*, 22 March 1986. For a lower figure to martyr's families, see: *Times*, 14 November 1987.
117. For details, see: Augustus Richard Norton, "Lebanon: The Internal Conflict and the Iranian Connection", in John L. Esposito (ed.), (1990), *op. cit.*: p.127.
118. See: *al-Shira*, 31 August 1992.
119. See: *al-Dustur*, 14 October 1985.
120. See: *Middle East Defense News*, May 1, 1988; and John L. Esposito, *The Islamic Threat: Myth or Reality?* (Oxford: Oxford University Press, 1992): p.147.
121. See: *al-Sharq al-Awsat*, 18 April 1989; and *Washington Post*, 22 September 1988.
122. See: *FBIS*, 3 June 1985; and *New York Times*, 18 March 1987.
123. See: *Teheran Domestic Service*, 6 September 1989; *Washington Post*, 22 September 1988; and *al-Sharq al-Awsat*, 18 April 1989.
124. See: Robin Wright, "Islam's New Political Face", *Current History*, Vol.90, No.552 (January 1991): p.28.
125. See: Radio Monte Carlo 1700 gmt 7 Apr 1994–BBC/*SWB*/ME/1967, 9 April 1994.
126. See: *al-Sharq al-Awsat*, 18 April 1989; *al-Majallah*, 19–25 April 1989; and *New York Times*, 23 April 1990.
127. See: *Washington Post*, 21 November 1991; *Jane's Defence Weekly*, 16 November 1991; *al-Majallah*, 19–25 April 1989; and *al-Sharq al-Awsat*, 18 April 1989.
128. See: *Independent*, 1 July 1987; *Wall Street Journal*, 16 August 1989; and *Washington Post*, 15 May 1990.
129. See: *Washington Post*, 23 August 1987; and Sean K. Anderson, "Iranian State-Sponsored Terrorism", *Conflict Quarterly* (Fall 1991): p.29.
130. See: *al-Shira*, 15 March 1986; and *Middle East Reporter*, 22 March 1986.
131. See: *IRNA*, 18 March 1987; *Foreign Report*, 18 December 1986; and Pierre Pean, (1987), *op. cit.*: p.262.
132. See: *al-Ittihad*, 31 January 1988; *Da'var*, 1 February 1988; and *Ha'aretz*, 29 January 1988.
133. See: *Le Figaro*, 4 December 1989; *Independent*, 26 April 1988; *al-Ittihad*, 15 January 1988; and *Radio Free Lebanon*, 5 July 1990.

134. *Jerusalem Post*, 13 November 1987.
135. *Intelligence Newsletter*, No.256, 19 January 1995.
136. See: Maskit Burgin, Ariel Merari & Anat Kurz, (1988), *op. cit.*: pp.7–11.
137. See: *Middle East Reporter*, 22 July 1983; and *Middle East Reporter*, 14 November 1990. The other two Iranians were Akhaven Kazem and Taqi Rastegar Moqaddam. Also see: Farhang Jahanpour, "The Roots of the Hostage Crisis", *The World Today* (February 1992): p.33.
138. *Middle East Reporter*, 22 July 1983.
139. *Israeli Defense Forces Spokesman* (IDFS), 18 February 1986; and *International Herald Tribune*, 1 January 1984.
140. See: Con Coughlin, (1993), *op. cit.*: pp.27–39.
141. See: *Israeli Defence Forces Spokesman* (IDFS), 18 February 1986; *International Herald Tribune*, 1 January 1984; and *Ha'aretz*, 3 June 1984.
142. *Foreign Report*, 20 June 1985; *New York Times*, 2 November 1983; and *New York Times*, 5 October 1984.
143. See: George Nader, "Interview with Sheikh Fadl Allah", *Middle East Insight* (June-July 1985); and John L. Esposito, (1991), *op. cit.*: p.252. For Shi'i hostility towards the MNF in Lebanon, see: US DOD Commission Report on Beirut, *Intelligence*, 20 December 1983, Part 4.
144. For a detailed overview of the competition between Hizb'allah and Amal, see: Martin Kramer, "Sacrifice and Fratricide in Shiite Lebanon", *Terrorism and Political Violence*, Vol.3, No.3 (Autumn 1991): pp.23–46.
145. Saab was specifically charged with setting timers and detonators for the explosives while al-Musawi and Azam Khalil were charged with planting the bombs at the American offices and residential buildings, see: *Kuwait Times*, January 25, 1984; and *Kuwait Times*, March 28, 1984. Apart from the three Lebanese suspects, Kuwaiti authorities arrested 17 Iraqis, 3 Kuwaitis and two stateless persons.
146. See: *Los Angeles Times*, 26 November 1988; *Le Point*, 3 August 1987; *Ma'aretz*, 27 February 1986; *Ma'aretz*, 14 April 1988; and *International Herald Tribune*, 7–8 January 1984.
147. See: *al-Qabas*, 28 March 1985; and US Congress. Joint Committee. The Iran-Contra Affair. *Report of the Congressional Committees Investigating the Iran-Contra Affair*, 100th Cong., 1st sess. 1987.
148. See: *Arab Times*, March 28, 1984.
149. Robin Wright, *Sacred Rage: The Wrath of Militant Islam* (London: Deutsch, 1986): p.110.
150. *Foreign Report*, 13 December 1984; and *Observer*, 9 December 1984.
151. See: *Jerusalem Post*, 8 January 1985; and E. Büchler, "Terrorismus in der Schweiz: Waffen- und Sprengstoffbeschaffung für den Internationalen Terrorismus?", *Seminararbeit MS II/86*, Zurich, 1986: p.24–5.
152. For CIA co-operation with Lebanese intelligence in the attack, see: *Middle East Reporter*, 17 May 1985; and *Wall Street Journal*, 20 May 1985.
153. Great Britain abstained from voting. For interview with Sheikh Fadlallah condemning British voting in the UN, see: *Middle East Reporter*, 2 April 1985.
154. *al-Watan*, 27 April 1985; *Jerusalem Post*, 7 October 1986; and *Middle East Reporter*, 28 March 1985.
155. See: *Liberation*, 5 June 1985; *Le Matin*, 29 January 1987; *Ha'aretz*, 30 January 1987; and *Ma'aretz*, 8 May 1988. Apart from Anis Naccache,

his four other accomplices were: Iranians Mehdi Nejad Tabrizzi and Mohamad Jawat Jeneb; Palestinian Fauozi Muhamad el Satari; and Lebanese Salaheddine el Kaara, see: *Kayhan*, 28 July 1990.

156. See: *L'Express*, 13 July 1984; *Le Nouvel Observateur*, 28 March-3 April 1986; and *International Herald Tribune*, 28–29 July 1990.

157. *Independent*, 27 October 1991. For Mughniya's affiliation within Force 17, see: *Da'var*, 6 May 1988; *Los Angeles* Times, 26 November 1988; and *Ma'aretz*, April 14, 1988.

158. See: *Guardian*, March 13, 1986; and *Ha'aretz*, March 10, 1986.

159. For Mohammad Mouhajer's relationship with Sheikh Ibrahim al-Amin, see: Steve M. Berry, "The Release of France's Last Hostages in Lebanon: An Analysis", *TVI Report*, Vol.8, No.3 (1989): p.21; *Liberation*, 26–27 March 1988; *Le Nouvel Observateur*, 3–10 April 1987; and *Le Figaro*, 28–29 October 1989. Mouhajer, who played a prominent role in Association islamique en France (AIF), was released on 24 March 1988, due to insufficient evidence, see: *Washington Post*, 6 April 1988; and Xavier Raufer, (1991), *op. cit.*: p.102. Fouad Ali Saleh, a Tunisian-born French citizen and Hizb'allah member, was the on-site commander of Hizb'allah's operations in France and was arrested together with Mohammad Muhajer. He was convicted of involvement in the 1985–6 bombings in Paris on 9 March 1990, and sentenced to a maximum of 20 years in prison. For information on Saleh, see: *al-Watan al-Arabi*, 12 November 1989; *Le Monde*, 27 April 1987; *Le Point*, 15 June 1987; *Le Nouvel Observateur*, 12–18 June 1987; *Le Figaro*, 28–29 October 1989; and *International Herald Tribune*, 10 March 1990.

160. In connection with the arrest of Hamadi, West-German authorities discovered a series of phone numbers leading to the arrested Hizb'allah suspects in Paris. See: *Le Monde*, 27 April 1987; *Le Nouvel Observateur*, 12–18 June 1987; and *al-Watan al-Arabi*, 12 November 1989. For the involvement of Mohammad Salek, deputy head of IRGC, and Ahmad Kan'ani, former IRGC commander in Lebanon, see: *al-Watan al-Arabi*, 27 November 1992; *Le Nouvel Observateur*, 12–18 June 1987; and *Jeune Afrique*, 30 November 1988.

161. See: *al-Nahar*, 24 March 1986; and *al-Mustaqbal*, 23 March 1986.

162. The US-Iranian arms-for-hostages deal was revealed by the Beirut-based al-Shira magazine. For the role of al-Khaliq, see: *al-Dustur*, 22 December 1986; and *Arab News*, 6 December 1986.

163. See: U.S. Congress, *Committes Investigating the Iran-Contra Affair*, 1987.

164. See: Bruce Hoffman, (1990), *op. cit.*: p.24.

165. See: Dilip Hiro, (1993), *op. cit.*: p.129–30.

166. *Jerusalem Post*, 13 November 1987; and Xavier Raufer, (1991), *op. cit.*: p.147.

167. For al-Musawi's involvement in the kidnapping, see: *Jerusalem Post*, 21 February 1988; and *Ha'aretz*, 28 February 1989. For involvement of Sheikh Obeid, see: *Foreign Report*, 17 March 1988; and *International Herald Tribune*, 3 August, 1988.

168. See: *Voice of Lebanon*, 0615 gmt 18 Apr 88–BBC/*SWB*/ME/0131, 21 April 1988; and *Ha'aretz*, 18 April 1988.

Notes 227

169. For infiltration of Amal by Hizb'allah members, see: *FBIS*, 28 February 1988. For Amal defections, see: *Da'var*, 10 November 1987; and *Ha'aretz*, 29 February 1988 For a useful discussion, see: Yossi Olmert, "Iranian-Syrian Relations: Between Islam and Realpolitik", in Martin Kramer (ed.), (1990), *op. cit.*: p.184.

170. *Voice of the Oppressed* 0545 gmt 27 May 88–BBC/*SWB*/ME/0163, 28 May 1988.

171. For a full text of the Amal-Hizb'allah Accord, see: *SANA* in Arabic 1435 gmt 30 Jan 89–BBC/*SWB*/ME/0373, 1 February 1989.

172. For details, see: Samuel M. Katz, *Soldier Spies: Israeli Military Intelligence* (Novato, CA.: Presidio Press, 1992): pp.344.

173. See: *Washington Post*, 18 August 1989.

174. See: *al-Majallah*, 19–25 April 1989; and *New York Times*, January 23, 1990.

175. For details, see: *The Times*, 1 August 1989. Also see: Samuel M. Katz, *The Elite* (London: Pocket Books, 1992): pp.270–2; and R. Reuben Miller, "Political Kidnapping: A Case Study of Israeli Practice", *Low-Intensity Conflict and Law Enforcement*, Vol.2 (1993).

176. The two IDF soldiers, Joseph Fink and Rahamim Levi Alsheikh, had been kidnapped on February 17, 1986, while patrolling the security area between Bint Jbeil and Beit Yahun, see: *Ma'aretz*, 26 February 1986; *Middle East Reporter*, 18 February 1986.

177. The other three IDF soldiers listed as missing-in-action were: Zvi Feldman, Zachary Baumel, and Yehuda Katz, who were captured during a battle in the Sultan Yakoub of the Biq'a valley on June 11, 1982. For information concerning their abductions, see: *Free Our Sons*: document published by the families of the soldiers missing-in-action, February 1989.

178. See: Nassif Hitti, "Lebanon in Iran's Foreign Policy: Opportunities and Constraints", in Hosshang Amirahmadi and Nader Entessar (eds.), (1993), *op. cit.*: p.188.

179. See: Dilip Hiro, (1993), *op. cit.*: p.183. Also see: *Ha'aretz*, 16 July 1991.

180. See: *Keyhan*, 23 August 1990; *Independent*, 5 August 1990; *Radio Monte Carlo*, 5 August 1990; *MENA*, 6 August 1990; and *Time*, 16 December 1991.

181. For Hizb'allah concerns over disarmament in accordance with Ta'if agreement, see: *Voice of the Oppressed* 0630 gmt 24 Mar 91–*BBC*/SWB/ME/1030, 26 March 1991. For agreement see: *Voice of the Oppressed*, 0630 gmt 30 Apr 91–*BBC*/SWB ME/1061, 2 May 1991.

182. See: *al-Hayat*, 25 May 1991. This was confirmed in interviews by the author with unattributable PLO sources close to the Hizb'allah leadership, Cairo, Egypt, 5 April 1994. Also see: Malise Ruthven, "Islamic Politics in the Middle East and North Africa", in *The Middle East and North Africa 1993* (London: Europa Publications Ltd, 1992): pp.121–2.

183. See: *Voice of Lebanon*, Beirut 1015 gmt 21 May 91–BBC/*SWB*/ME/1079, 23 May 1991; and *al-Hayah*, 25 May 1991.

184. The importance of the Lebanese Shi'ite detainees held by Israel for the Hizb'allah was discussed during an interview by the author with Uri Lubrani, Co-ordinator of IDF activity in Lebanon, Ministry of Defense, Tel Aviv, Israel, 28 August 1991. In total, Israel released 77 prisoners and nine

Hizb'allah bodies after receiving confirmed information that two IDF soldiers, missing since February 17, 1986, were dead.

185. See: *Radio Free Lebanon*, 13 November 1991.
186. While there has been contention whether Ron Arad is held under the control
      of Hizb'allah and the IRGC in the Bi'qa valley or in Iran, Israel hold Iran
      solely responsible for his safety, see: *IDF Radio*, Tel Aviv, 1500gmt
      17 Feb–BBC/*SWB* ME/1308, 19 February 1992.
187. For moves by US authorities of legal indictements of hostage-takers, see·
      Independent, 11 December 1991. For Hizb'allah concerns of retribution,
      see: *Independent*, 21 November 1991; and *Radio Lebanon*, Beirut 1030 gmt
      15 Oct 91–BBC/*SWB*/ME/1205, 17 October 1991.
188. *Ha'aretz*, 20 March 1992; *Ha'aretz*, 1 May 1992; *Yediot Aharanot*,
      27 March 1992; and *New York Times*, 9 May 1992.
189. For example, see: *Voice of the People* in Arabic to Lebanon 1239 gmt
      28 Feb 92–BBC/*SWB*/ME/1318, 2 March 1992.
190. See: *al-Nahar*, 31 July 1992. More than 100 Pasdaran guards act as advisors
      in 1994, see: *Independent*, 8 May 1994.
191. For a comprehensive overview of Hizb'allah's strategy and electoral results,
      see: A Nizar Hamzeh, (1993), *op. cit.*: pp.321–37. For claims of Hizb'allah
      tampering of election, see: Farid El Khazen, "Lebanon's first Postwar
      Parliamentary Elections, 1993", *Middle East Policy*, Vol.3, No.1 (1994).
192. See: *Al-Ahd*, 14 August 1992.

NOTES FOR CHAPTER 4

1. See: Yair Hirschfeld, "The Odd Couple: Ba'athist Syria and Khomeini's
    Iran", in Moshe Ma'oz and Avner Yaniv (eds.) *Syria under Assad:
    Domestic Constraints and Regional Risks* (London: Croom Helm, 1986):
    pp.105–24.
2. For a useful discussion of pan-Islam versus pan-Arabism, see: Mohseen
    Massarrat, "The Ideological Context of the Iran-Iraq War: Pan-Islamism
    versus Pan-Arabism", in Hooshang Amirahmadi and Nader Entessar (ed.),
    (1993), *op. cit.*: pp.28–41.
3. See: Joseph Alpher, "The Khomeini International", *The Washington
    Quarterly*, Vol.3 (1980): pp.58–63.
4. John Calabrese, (1990), *op. cit.*: p.188; and Patrick Seale, *Asad of Syria:
    The Struggle for the Middle East* (London: I.B. Tauris, 1988): p.352.
5. For discussions on the Syrian *Muslim Brotherhood*, see: R. Hinnebush,
    "The Islamic Movement in Syria: Sectarian Conflict and Urban Rebellion in
    an Authoritarian Populist Regime", in A.E. Hillal Dessouki (ed.) *Islamic
    Resurgence in the Arab World* (New York, NY.:): pp.138–69; and Hans
    Günter Lobmeyer, "Islamic Ideology annd Secular Discourse: the Islamists
    of Syria", *Orient*, Vol.32, No.3 (September 1991): pp.395–418.
6. Fouad Ajami, (1986), *op. cit.*: pp.174–5.
7. See: Salim Nasr, "Mobilisation Communautaire et Symbolique Religieuse:
    Imam Sadr et les chi'ite du Liban (1970–75) in Olivier Carré et Paul
    Dumond (eds.) *Radicalismes Islamiques: Iran, Liban, Turquie* (Paris:

Editions L'Harmattan, 1985); and Sobhani Sohrab, *The Pragmatic Entente: Israeli-Iranian Relations, 1948–1988* (New York, NY.: Praeger, 1989): p.106.

8. For a comprehensive overview of Syria's relationship with the Shi'a movements in Lebanon, see: Asad AbuKhalil, (1990), *op. cit.*: pp.1–20.

9. Shireen T. Hunter, Iran and Syria: From Limited Hostility to Limited Alliance", in Hooshang Amirahmadi & Nader Entessar (eds.), (1993), *op. cit.*: p.208–9.

10. Asad AbuKhalil, (1990, *op. cit.*: p.16. Also see: Mohammad-Reza Djalili, "Téhéran-Damas: une alliance équivoque", *Politique internationale*, Vol.24 (1984): pp.261–69; and *New York Times*, 14 May 1984.

11. For the intense Syrian-Iraqi rivalry in Lebanon, see: Marius Deeb, (1986), *op. cit.*: p.3. For Syria's reasons to discredit the Syrian *Muslim Brotherhood* through alliance with Iran, see: Umar F. Abdallah, *The Islamic Struggle in Syria* (Berkeley, CA.: University of California Press, 1983); and Martin Kramer, "Syria's Alawis and Shi'ism", in Martin Kramer (ed.), *Shi'ism, Resistance and Revolution* (London: Mansell, 1987): p.251.

12. Graham E. Fuller, *The "Center of the Universe": The Geopolitics of Iran* (Boulder, CO.: Westview Press, 1991): pp.125–28.

13. Syria also provided Iran with Soviet arms, see: *al-Majallah*, 27 March 1982. For Syria's contribution to Iraq's military insecurity, see: Yair Hirschfeld, "The Odd Couple: Ba'athist Syria and Khomeini's Iran", in Moshe Ma'oz and Avner Yaniv (eds.) Syria under Assad: Domestic Constraints and Regional Risks, *op. cit.*: p.107.

14. For an overview, see: Yosef Olmert, "Iranian-Syrian Relations: Between Islam and Realpolitik", in David Menashri (ed.), (1990), *op. cit.*: pp.176–78.

15. Dilip Hiro, *The Longest War: The Iran-Iraq Military Conflict* (London: Paladin, 1990): pp.57–58; and Dilip Hiro, The Iran-Iraq War, in Hooshang Amirahmadi and Nader Entessar (eds.) Iran and the Arab World, *op. cit.*: p.48. Also see: *Arab World Weekly* (17 April 1982).

16. David Menashri, *Iran: A Decade of War and Revolution* (London: Holmes & Meier, 1990): p.253; and R.K. Ramazani, (1986), *op. cit.*: p.81. Also see: *Middle East Economic Digest*, 13 March 1982; *Middle East Economic Digest*, 20 April 1984; *The Economist*, 30 April 1983; and *Middle East Economic Survey*, 7 May 1984.

17. *Middle East Economic Digest*, 8 September 1989; and *The Middle East Review 1988*: p.162.

18. For example, disputes over prices and payment led to a reduction in Iran's supply of oil to Syria, see: Derek Hopwood, *Syria, 1945–86: Politics and Society* (London: Unwin Hyman, 1988): p.109; and *Foreign Report*, 19 June 1986. Also see: *Middle East Economic Digest*, 20 April 1984.

19. Shahram Chubin and Charles Tripp, *Iran and Iraq at War* (London: I.B. Tauris, 1988): p.183. Also see: Moshe Ma'oz, *Syria and Israel: From War to Peace-Making* (Oxford: Oxford University Press, 1995): p.188.

20 See: Yosef Olmert, "Iranian-Syrian Relations: Between Islam and Realpolitik", in David Menashri (ed.) (1990), *op. cit.*: p.176.

21. *al-Qabas*, 24 January 1987. Also see: *Financial Times*, 8 July 1982; and Husseiyn Sirriyeh, *Lebanon: Dimensions of Conflict*, Adelphi Papers No.243 (Oxford: Brassey's, Autumn 1989): p.45.

22. David Menashri, (1990b), *op. cit.*: p.253; and *FBIS*, 16 June 1982. For Syrian-Iranian military agreement, see: *al-Nahar*, 26 May 1986. Also see: Marius Deeb, (1988), *op. cit.*: pp.697. Also see: *Le Point*, 11 May 1987; and *L'Orient le Jour*, 25 November 1982.

23. Dilip Hiro, "The Iran-Iraq War", in Hooshang Amirahmadi and Nader Entessar (eds.), (1993), *op. cit.*: p.47.

24. David Menashri, (1990b), *op. cit.*: p.295. Also see: R.K. Ramazani, "Iran's Export of the Revolution: Politics, Ends, and Means", in John L, Esposito (ed.), (1990), *op. cit.*: pp.40–6?; and *Iran Press Digest*, 19 April 1983.

25. See: Martin Kramer, (1988), *op. cit.*: pp.39–59; and Shimon Shapira, (1988), op. cit.: pp.115–30. *Politique International*, April 1984; *al-Nahar*, 27 November 1982; and *Iran Press Digest*, 3 May 1983.

26. Shireen T. Hunter, "Iran and the Spread of Revolutionary Islam", Third World Quarterly, *op. cit.*: p.741–42; and *Middle East Economic Digest*, (September 1987): pp.12–18.

27. Nassif Hitti, "Lebanon in Iran's Foreign Policy: Opportunities and Constraints", in Hooshang Amirahmadi and Nader Entessar (eds.), (1993), *op. cit.*: p.186.

28. See: John L. Esposito, (1991), *op. cit.*: p.250; and John L. Esposito, (1992), *op. cit.*: pp.150–1.

29. R.K. Ramazani, Revolutionary Iran: Challenge and Response in the Middle East, *op. cit.*: p.156. Also see: Robin Wright, (1990), *op. cit.*: pp.108–9; and *Le Point*, 11 May 1987.

30. *Middle East International* (22 March 1985): pp.6–7.

31. For Syria's relationship with Fatah, see: Reuven Avi-Ran, "The Syrian-Palestinian Conflict in Lebanon", *Jerusalem Quarterly*, No.42 (Spring 1987): pp.57–82.

32. Augustus Richard Norton, "Religious Resurgence and Political Mobilization of the Shi'a in Lebanon", in Emile Sahliyeh (ed.) *Religious Resurgence and Politics in the Contemporary World* (New York, NY.: State University of New York Press, 1990): pp.239–40.

33. Asad AbuKhalil, (1990), *op. cit.*: p.15. Also see: *New York Times*, 27 June 1987.

34. See: Maskit Burgin, Ariel Merari, and Anat Kurz (1988), *op. cit.*: 20–35.

35. See: Maskit Burgin, "Foreign Hostages in Lebanon–An Update", in *Inter: International Terrorism in 1988* (Jerusalem: Jaffee Center for Strategic Studies, 1989); and Maskit Burgin, "Shi'ite International Terrorism", in *Inter: International Terrorism in 1989* (Jerusalem: Jaffee Center for Strategic Studies, 1990): pp.36–60.

36. Discussions in the panel group on the Middle East during: *Dialogue Europe Occidentale–Union Soviétique en Matière de Terrorisme et de Lutte Anti-Terroriste*, Paris, 10 June 1991.

37. This was clearly revealed in Hizb'allah's manifesto, see: "An Open Letter: Hizballah program", *Jerusalem Quarterly*, No.48 (Fall 1988): pp.111–16.

38. For details of Iranian-Syrian complicity in the operation, see: *Jeune Afrique*, 24 January 1984; *Jerusalem Post*, 27 October 1983; *Le Monde*, 6–7 November 1983; and *Liberation*, 19 March 1985.

39. For details, see: *al-Watan al-Arabi*, 14–20 December 1984; and *Le Nouvel Observateur*, October 30, 1983.

40. For Iranian opposition, see: *Kayhan*, October 13, 1983. Also see: Walter de Bock and Jean-Charles Deniau, *Des Armes Pour L'Iran: L'Irangate Européen* (Paris: Gallimard, 1988).

41. See: *Wall Street Journal*, 19 August 1983; and *Economist*, 23 February 1983.

42. *Wall Street Journal*, 21 May 1987.

43. For Iranian claims, see: *Kayhan*, 12 March 1983; and *Ettela'at*, 23 August 1983.

44. Anthony H. Cordesman, *The Iran-Iraq War and Western Security 1984–1987: Strategic Implications and Policy Options* (London: Jane's Publishing Company, 1987): p.79; and Eric Hooglund, "The Policy of the Reagan Administration Toward Iran", in Nikki Keddie and Mark Gasiorowski (eds.), (1990), *op. cit.*: pp.269–93. Also see: *MERIP Reports* (July-September 1984): p.45.

45. For Iran's threat of retalitory measures, see: *Ettela'at*, 17 September 1983; *Kayhan*, 13 October 1983; and *Kayhan*, 26 October 1983.

46. For Iran's subversive activities in the Persian Gulf-states, see: Joseph Kostiner, "Shi'i Unrest in the Gulf", in Martin Kramer (ed.), (1987), *op. cit.*: pp.173–86; and R.K. Ramazani, "Iran's Islamic Revolution and the Persian Gulf", *Current History*, Vol.84 (January 1985): pp.1–41. Between 1983–84, Kuwait provided $7 billion in financial assistance and was second to Saudi Arabia in aiding Iraq, see: Bahman Baktiari, "Revolutionary Iran's Persian Gulf Policy: The Quest for Regional Supremacy", in Hooshang Amirahmadi and Nader Entessar (eds.), (1993), *op. cit.*: p.77. In 1985, Persian Gulf states provided Iraq with financial contributions in the range of US$ 40–50 billion, see: *Iran and Iraq: The Next five Years* (London: The Economist Intelligence Unit (EIU), 1987): p.20.

47. Shireen T. Hunter, *Iran and the World: Continuity in a Revolutionary Decade* (Bloomington, IN.: Indiana University Press, 1990): p.117. Also see: Ariel Merari and Yosefa (Daiksel) Braunstein, (1984), *op. cit.*: p.8.

48. *Yediot Aharanot*, 9 July 1985; and *International Herald Tribune*, 16 April 1984.

49. See: Helena Cobban, "The Growth of Shi'i Power in Lebanon", in Juan R.I. Cole and Nikki R. Keddie (eds.), (1986), *op. cit.*: p.151.

50. David Menashri, (1990b), *op. cit.*: p.334; *Middle East Economic Digest*, 20 April 1984; and *Ettela'at*, 24 May 1984.

51. For US-Iraqi rapproachement, see: Dilip Hiro, (1990), *op. cit.*: pp.159–63.

52. Robin Wright, "Lebanon", in Shireen T. Hunter, (1988), *op. cit.*: p.68; *US News & World Report*, 6 March 1989; and *al-Nahar*, 9 November 1987.

53. *Iran Press Digest*, 12 August 12, 1985; and Dilip Hiro, (1990), *op. cit.*: p.157.

54. See: *MERIP Reports*, Nos.125–26 (July-September, 1984): pp.44–48.

55. *al-Watan al-Arabi*, 27 April 1985; *Jerusalem Post*, 7 October 1986; *Ha'aretz*, 24 March 1985; and *Middle East Reporter*, 28 March 1985.

56. *Le Monde*, 6 May 1988; and *Yediot Aharanot*, 5 May 1988.

57. See: Alan James, (1988), *op. cit.*: pp.21–24.

58. *Davar*, 11 November 1987; and *Ha'aretz*, 22 February 1988.

59. *Ha'aretz*, 30 October 1986; *al-Shira*, 28 September 1987.

60. The dispute came over Syrian objections to Iran's high prices of discounted oil and Iran's complaints over Syrian non-payment of a $2.3 billion oil debt.

See: *Foreign Report*, 19 June 1986; *Middle East International*, 27 June 1986; and *AP* 25 April 1988. For U.S. intelligence on Iranian-Syrian dispute, see: Peter Kornbluh and Malcolm Byrne, (1993), *op. cit.*: p.293. For a useful overview of the dynamics of Syrian-Iranian relations, see: Hissein J. Agha and Ahmad S. Khalidi, *Syria and Iran: Rivalry and Cooperation* (London: Pinter Publishers, 1995): pp. 9–32.

61. Yosef Olmert, "Iranian-Syrian Relations: Between Islam and Realpolitik", in David Menashri (ed.) (1990), *op. cit.*: p.183.

62. After Syria's veiled threat, Iran supplied Syria with 2.5 million tons to cover a period of six months until March 1987, see: BBC/*SWB*, 22 July 1986; and *Middle East International*, 27 June 1986. However, Syria's threat of *rapprochement* with Iraq led also to the kidnapping of Mahmud Ayat, the Syrian charge d'affairs in Iran, see: *Middle East*, April 1987.

63. *New York Times*, 1 February 1987; *Arab News*, 5 April 1987; *Yediot Aharanot*, 14 January 1987; and *International Herald Tribune*, 19 March 1987.

64. *Jerusalem Post*, 13 November 1987; *Ha'aretz*, 21 June 1987; *Newsweek*, 24 August 1987; and *Ma'aretz*, 15 June 1987.

65. While Iran's agreement with Syria over oil supply was due for negotiation and renewal in March 1987, Syria and Iran had disagreements over Syria's failure to repay its oil debt to Iran, see: *Economist*, 14 March 1987; and *Financial Times*, 5 May 1987. In April 1987, a one-year agreement was reached for the supply of one million tons of oil free of charge to the Syrian army and two million tons at OPEC prices on a cash-payment basis, see: *OPEC Bulletin*, June 1987; and *New York Times*, 5 May 1987.

66. For Syria's exploitation of its relationship with Iran through economic inducements from the Arab world, see: *International Herald Tribune*, 18–19 July 1987. As a result, Iran extended Syria's debt payments and agreed to supply 20,000 barrels/day of free oil, see: *Observer*, 1 November 1987; *The Times*, 5 November 1987; and *Economist*, 26 September 1987.

67. *al-Watan al-Arabi*, 11 December 1987.

68. Jerusalem Post, 1 December 1987; and *New York Times*, 12 December 1987.

69. *Washington Post*, 8 December 1987.

70. *Washington Post*, 30 November 1987; and *Arab News*, 1 December 1987.

71. George Joffe, "Iran, the Southern Mediterranean and Europe: Terrorism and Hostages", in Anoushiravan Ehteshami and Manshour Varasteh (eds.), (1991), *op. cit.*: p.80. For Iranian demands for the renewal of British weapons supplies, see: *Ma'aretz*, 6 December 1987.

72. See: Marius Deeb, (1988), *op. cit.*: pp.7–10.

73. See: Asad AbuKhalil, (1990), *op. cit.*: pp.14–6.

74. *Washington Times*, 25 February 1988.

75. *Voice of Hope*, 27 February 1988.

76. *Ma'ariv*, 8 May 1988; *Newsweek*, 16 May 1988; Steve M. Berry, "The Release of France's Last Hostages in Lebanon: An Analysis", *TVI Report*, Volume 8, No.3 (1989): pp.19–22.

77. *AP*, 25 April 1988.

78. Economist Intelligence Unit, *Syria Country Profile, 1989–90*: p.32; and Volker Perthes, "The Syrian Economy in the 1980s", *Middle East Studies*, Vol.46, No.1 (Winter 1992): p.57.

79. On Iraq's involvement in Lebanon, see: *Middle East Report*, 28 July 1988; *The Guardian*, 19 October 1988; Asad AbuKhalil, (1991), *op. cit.*: p.400.

80. *Washington Post*, 7 January 1990.

81. *Middle East International*, 31 March 1989; and *Financial Times*, 6 June 1989. For Syrian-Iranian relations and oil, see: *Middle East International*, 17 November 1989.

82. Shireen T. Hunter, "Iran and Syria: From Hostility to Limited Alliance", in Hooshang Amirahmadi and Nader Entessar (eds.), (1993), *op. cit.*: p.210; John L. Esposito, (1991), *op. cit.*: 1991): p.256; and *Middle East International*, 3 February 1989. For the agreement, see: *SANA* in Arabic 1435 gmt 30 Jan 89–SWB ME/0373, 1 February 1989.

83. For Iranian efforts for intra-Shi'a unity, see: *Middle East International*, 20 October 1989. Also see: Nassif Hitti, "Lebanon in Iran's Foreign Policy: Opportunities and Constraints", in Hooshang Amirahmadi and Nader Entessar, (1993), *op. cit.*: pp.188–9; and *Ma'aretz*, 23 August 1988.

84. According to reports, Iran reduced its financial support to Hizb'allah from $5 million a month to $1 million a month, see: *Washington Post*, 1 January 1990.

85. *Washington Post*, 22 September 1988; *The Echo of Iran*, February 1990; *al-Majallah*, 19–25 April 1989; *New York Times*, 23 January 1990; and *Middle East International*, 16 March 1990.

86. See: Augustus Richard Norton, (1991), *op. cit.*: pp.470–3.

87. For a text of the agreement, see: *Syrian Arab TV*, Damascus 1840 gmt 5 Nov 90–BBC/*SWB*/ME/0915, 7 November 1990. For Amal-Hizb'allah agreement, see: *Middle East International*, 9 November 1990.

88. *Middle East International*, 3 April 1992; and *Middle East International*, 12 June 1992.

89. Shireen T. Hunter, "Iran and Syria: From Hostility to Limited Alliance", in Hooshang Amirahmadi and Nader Entessar (eds.), (1993), *op. cit.*: p.210.

90. *Middle East International*, 31 May 1991. For Hizb'allah's praise of the agreement between Syria and Lebanon, see: *Voice of the Oppressed* 0530 gmt 23 May 91–BBC/*SWB*/ME/1082, 27 May 1991.

91. See: *Middle East International*, 16 August 1991; *Independent*, 22 October 1991; *The Times*, 12 September 1991; and *The Echo of Iran*, August/ September 1991.

92. The text of a commentary entitled "Hostages: Message Received" by Hizb'allah radio provides an overview of the movement's own sense of achivement by holding hostages, see: *Voice of the Oppressed* 0550 gmt 16 Aug 91–BBC/*SWB*/ME/1153, 17 August 1991.

93. Under UN Resolution 598 (paragraph 6), the UN Secretary-General had been asked to explore, in consultation with Iran and Iraq, the question of entrusting an impartial body with inquiring into the responsibility for the Iran-Iraq war. When Giandomenico Picco, the UN Secretary-General's representative on the hostage issue, met with Iranian officials in Teheran, the issue of UN Resolution 598 was frequently discussed and it was clearly a high priority for Iran, see: *Voice of the Islamic Republic of Iran*, Teheran 1445 gmt 12 Sep 91–SWB ME/1177, 14 September 1991. For Iran's demands that UN Secretary-General must enforce resolutions against Iraq, see: *Voice of the Islamic Republic of Iran*, Teheran 1004 gmt 11 Sep

91–SWB/1176, 13 September 1991. Apart from Picco's involvement in the hostage negotiations, he had successfully mediated an end to the Iran-Iraq war in 1988, see: *The Times*, 19 November 1991. See: *The Independent*, 20 December 1991.

94. See: *Independent*, 11 December 1991. On 1 January 1992, the United Nations released a report which claimed Iran had suffered $97.2 billion in damages during the Iran-Iraq war and that it needed international assistance, see: *Wall Street Journal*, 2 January 1992.

NOTES FOR CHAPTER 5

1. Sir John Nott, former Tory defence secretary, quoted in *The Independent*, 16 May 1994.

2. See: Annie Laurent and Antoine Basbous, *Guerres Secretes au Liban* (Paris: Gallimard, 1987); Peter Kornbluh and Malcolm Byrne (eds.), (1993), *op. cit.*; Nicholas Tenzer and Franck Magnard, (1987), *op. cit.*; and Yves Loiseau, *Le Grand Troc: Le Labyrinthe des Otages Francais au Liban* (Paris: Hachette, 1988).

3. See: Gilbert Guillaume, "France and the Fight Against Terrorism", *Terrorism and Political Violence*, Vol.4, No.4 (Winter 1992): p.134.

4. For Buckley's position as CIA station chief, see: *Washington Post*, 25 November 1986. In January 1987, U.S. State Department confirmed the death of Buckley, see: *Ma'aretz*, 22 January 1987.

5. See: Jane Mayer and Doyle McManus, *Landslide: The Unmaking of the President 1984–88* (Boston, MA.: Houghton Mifflin, 1988).

6. For the implications of the Iran-Contra affair on U.S. relations with Arab states, see: Joseph A. Kechichian, "The Impact of American Policies on Iranian-Arab Relations", in Hooshang Amirahmadi and Nader Entessar (eds.), (1993), *op. cit.*: pp.136–7; Samuel Segev, (1988), *op. cit.*: pp.27–8; and Eric Hooglund, "The United States and Iran", in Anoushiravan Ehteshami and Manshour Varasteh (eds.), (1991), *op. cit.*: p.42.

7. See: Eric Hooglund, "The United States and Iran, 1981–9", in Anoushiravan Ehteshami and Manshour Varasteh (eds.), (1991), *op. cit.*: p.45; *Guardian*, 24 April 1990; and *Independent*, 7 May 1990.

8. See: Farhang Jahanpour, (1992), *op. cit.*: pp.33–6; and Maskit Burgin, "Western Hostages and Israeli POWs in Lebanon", in Shlomo Gazit (ed.) *The Middle East Balance 1990–1991* (Boulder, CO.: Westview Press, 1992).

9. For the overall failure of U.S. policy, see: James A. Bill, "The U.S. Overture to Iran, 1985–1986", in Nikki R. Keddie and Mark J. Gasiorowski (eds.), (1990), *op. cit.*: pp.176–7.

10. See: Pierre Pean, (1987), *op. cit.* Also see: *New York Times*, 20 September 1987.

11. See: *Independent*, 8 November 1989; and *Le Nouvel Observateur*, 13–19 May 1988.

12. *Liberation*, May 7–8, 1988; and *International Herald Tribune*, March 7, 1986.

13. See: *Maskit Burgin, Anat Kurz and Ariel Merari, (1988), op. cit.*: pp.28–9; *al-Qabas*, 28 April 1988; *Yediot Aharanot*, 5 May 1988; and *Le Monde*, 6 May 1988.

14. See: *L'Express*, 23 February 1987; and *Independent*, 8 November 1989. Also see: Fred Halliday, "An Elusive Normalization: Western Europe and the Iranian Revolution", *Middle East Journal*, Vol.48, No.2 (Spring 1994): p.313.

15. See: *Newsweek*, 16 May 1988; *Washington Post*, 5 May 5, 1988; and *Liberation*, 7–8 May 1988.

16. See: *Newsweek*, 16 May 1988; and *Economist*, 11 June 1988; and *Sunday Times*, 8 May 1988.

17. Steve M. Berry, (1989), *op. cit.*: p.22.

18. See: Gilles Delafon, *Beyrouth: Les Soldats de l'Islam* (Paris: Stock: 1989).

19. See: *Independent*, 9 August 1991; and *Independent*, 25 August 1991. Also see: John Dickie, *Inside The Foreign Office* (London: Chapmans, 1992).

20. *Time*, 23 May 23, 1988

21. See: *Independent on Sunday*, 25 August 1991.

22. For difficulty in affecting or penetrating the operational activity of Hizb'allah, see: *Times*, 5 October 1984; *Ha'aretz*, 3 November 1986; *Da'var*, 11 January 1987; Ali al-Kurani, *Tariqat Hizballah fil-amal al-islami* (Beirut: 1986); *Newsweek*, 27 February 1989; and Martin Kramer, (1988), *op. cit.*: pp.39–59.

23. For details of these operations, see: Annie Laurent and Antione Basbous, (1987), *op. cit.*: pp.299–304; Pierre Marion, *La Mission Impossible* (Paris: Calmann-Lévy, 1991): p.233; and David C. Martin and John Walcott, *Best Laid Plans: The Inside Story of America's War Against Terrorism* (New York, NY.: Harper Row, 1988): pp.133–44.

24. *New York Times*, 9 February 1984; and *Ha'aretz*, 21 June 1987.

25. *Washington Post*, 21 February 1987.

26. *Independent*, August 3, 1989.

27. The absence of Hizb'allah leaders through kidnappings or deaths are more valuable for the movement than living leaders. This was discussed in an interview with Dr Martin Kramer, Jaffee Center for Strategic Studies, Tel Aviv University, Tel Aviv, Israel, August 1991.

28. *Independent*, 18 February 1992; *Foreign Report*, 13 May 1993; *Foreign Report*, 30 April 1992; and *Ha'aretz*, 20 March 1992.

29. *New York Times*, 22 August 1989.

30. For low ratio between threats and actual executions by Hizb'allah, see: Maskit Burgin, Anat Kurz, and Ariel Merari, (1988), *op. cit.*: pp.14–17.

31. For U.S. threats against Iran, see: *FBIS*, August 7, 1989; *Independent*, August 5, 1989; *Independent*, August 7, 1989; and *New York Times*, August 5, 1989.

32. *Ha'aretz*, 18 February 1988.

33. *Ma'aretz*, 16 February 1987.

34. *Newsweek*, 9 February 1987.

35. See: David C. Martin and John Walcott, (1988), *op. cit.*: pp.213–4.

36. *Independent*, 3 August 1988; *Foreign Report*, 20 May 1993; and *Foreign Report*, 13 May 1993.

37. For Hizb'allah's own statements that martyrs strengthen the movement's cause, see: *Voice of the Oppressed*, 0530 gmt 25 May 92–BBC/*SWB* ME/1390, 26 May 1992.

38. Unattributable interview with French counterterrorism official, Paris, June 1991.

39. Unattributable interview with senior official in Israel's Ministry of Foreign Affairs, Jerusalem, August 1991.

40. On November 10, 1986, the E.C. member states, except Greece and France, adopted sanctions against Syria which included an arms embargo, suspension of high-level visits, investigation of Syrian diplomats and tightened security around the operations of Syrian airlines, see: *Washington Post*, 11 November 1986. On July 14, 1987, the E.C. lifted its ban on high-level contacts, see: *Washington Post*, 14 July 1987.

41. The major conditions by Britain were: the closure of Abu Nidal's offices in the country, the punishment of General Mohammed al-Kholi and Col. Haitham Said, the responsible intelligence officers in the Hindawi-affair and the Syrian Ambassador, Lutfallah Haydar, see: *Times*, 19 November 1991.

42. For Thatcher's obstruction of relations, see: *Independent*, 9 August 1991.

43. The main offices of Iranian arms purchases in Europe were in London under the auspices of the Iranian National Oil Company, see: Hermann Moll, *Broker of Death* (London: Macmillan, 1988): p.55. See: George Joffe, "Iran, the southern Mediterranian and Europe: Terrorism and Hostages", in Anoushiravan Ehteshami and Mansour Varasteh (eds.), (1993), *op. cit.*: p.80. An offer by Iran for renewal of British arms supplies to Iran, transferred via France, was rejected by the British government, see: *Ma'aretz*, 6 December 1987. Iran was also displeased with Saudi Arabia's conclusion of a $30 billion arms purchase agreement with Britain in mid-1988, see: Shireen T. Hunter, *Iran and the World: Continuity in a Revolutionary Decade* (Bloomington, IL.: Indiana University Press, 1990): pp.63–78.

44. See: Maskit Burgin, "Shi'ite International Terrorism", in Anat Kurz (ed.), (1989), *op. cit.*: pp.51–2.

45. Between 1977 and 1988, Syria received a total of $42 billion in external aid of which: $23 billion was supplied from the Soviet Union; $3 billion from Iran; $12 billion from Saudi Arabia, Kuwait and other Gulf states; and $4 billion from the West, see: *Wall Street Journal*, 10 August 1989. Also see: Shahram Chubin and Charles Tripp, (1988), *op. cit.*: pp.179–87.

46. The extradition treaty between the United States and West Germany was signed in June 1978, see: *AP*, 16 January 1987.

47. *New York Times*, 16 April 1988; and *Sunday Times*, 24 April 1988.

48. See: *Le Quotidien de Paris*, 27 February 1986; and *Ma'aretz*, 4 February 1987.

49. See: Michel Wieviorka, "French Politics and Strategy on Terrorism", in Barry Rubin (ed.), *The Politics of Counter-Terrorism: The Ordeal of Democratic States* (Washington, DC.: John's Hopkins Foreign Policy Institute, 1990): pp.61–90.

50. See: *Liberation*, 26–27 March 1988; and *Le Monde*, 28 March 1987.

51. For President Mitterrand's promise for the release of Naccache, see: *International Herald Tribune*, January 31, 1990. For their release, see:

Jerusalem Post, July 29, 1990; *Ma'aretz*, July 29, 1990; and *Ma'aretz*, July 31, 1990.

52. For a discussion of the sanctuary principle, the granting of concessions to terrorist groups of presence in, and free passage through, France on the understanding that no terrorist incidents would be conducted on French soil, see: Edwy Plenel, "La France et le Terrorisme: la Tentation du Sanctuaire", *Politique Étrangere*, Vol.4 (1986).

53. The Ahl al-Beit Islamic Cultural Center in Paris served as a citadel for pro-Iranian and Hizb'allah members for meetings and recruitment, as evident by the involvement of Muhajir and Salah in its activities, see: Pierre Pean, (1987), *op. cit.*: pp.289–90.

54. *Newsweek*, 14 August 1989.

55. Unattributable interview with U.S. counter-terrorism official, Washington DC, September 29, 1993. For a very useful analysis of CIA-activity in Lebanon, see: David Kennedy and Leslie Brunetta, *Lebanon and the Intelligence Community*, (Cambridge, MA.: JFK School of Government, Harvard University, 1988).

56. See: *Independent*, March 7, 1990.

57. Unattributable interview with senior IDF official, Tel Aviv, August 1991.

58. Unattributable interview with British intelligence specialist, April 1994.

59. This was discussed by the author with Col. Menarchik, Office of Secretary for Defense, U.S. Department of Defense, in 1993. For Hizb'allah financial links with BCCI, see: *Los Angeles Times*, 12 August 1991. Also see: Stephen Sackur's film "Allah's Army" shown on BBC2 series *Assignment*, 10 May 1994.

60. *Ha'aretz*, 20 November 1985; *Le Monde*, 6 May 1988; *Jerusalem Post*, 27 March 1986; and *Jerusalem Post*, 10 March 1986.

61. See: *Ha'aretz*, 20 November 1985; *Time*, 24 March 1986; and *Jerusalem Post*, 10 March 1986. A senior Pasdaran official, Mohammad Sadek (head of security), was reportedly in France in January 1986 and closely involved in the negotiations with French officials for the release of Anis Naccache, see: *Le Nouvel Observateur*, 28 March–3 April 1986. Also see: Pierre Pean, (1987), *op. cit.*: pp.169–252. For information about Raad, see declassified U.S. diplomatic cable from the American embassy in Beirut to Secretary of State (March 1986), No. 0 11 1353Z Mar 86.

62. While France offered Syria long-term international credits on easy terms for its intervention with Hizb'allah for the release of its hostages, Iranian intervention undermined any progress, see: *Foreign Report*, 5 September 1985; and Roger Faligot and Remi Kauffer, (1994), *op. cit.*: p.410.

63. See: Maskit Burgin, Anat Kurz, and Ariel Merari, (1988),: *op. cit.*: pp.28–9. This rivalry was exploited through rumours that Mitterand's emissaries had offered to pay the Hizb'allah $10 million not to release the hostages until after the French presidential elections in May 1988, see: *Liberation*, 7 May 1988.

64. Apart from Omran Adham, two other individuals close to Mitterand involved in negotiations were: Francois de Grossouvre and Eric Rouleau, see: *al-Qabas*, 28 April 1988.

65. For a profile, see: *Times*, May 6, 1988.

66. See: Michel Wieviorka, "French Politics and Strategy on Terrorism", in Barry Rubin (ed.), (1990), *op. cit.*: p.82–4. Also see: *Washington Post*, 11 July 1987; *Independent*, 8 November 1989; and *Middle East International*, 21 November 1986. The rivalry between using Iran and Syria as channels through various emissaries was revealed by the arrests of the pro-Iranian network in France in April 1987. Despite the fact that the French DST indicated Iranian involvement, the Chirac government advocated Syrian involvement, see: *Le Monde*, 27 April 1987; *Le Monde*, 6 May 1988; and *Ma'aretz*, 26 April 1987.

67. *Guardian*, 21 October 1987; and *Financial Times*, 2 December 1987.

68. See: *Sunday Times*, 8 June 1986; and *Time*, 30 June 1986.

69. Iskandar Safa was a Lebanese Christian businessman well-connected within Lebanon and the Iranian clerical establishment, see: Steve Berry, (1989), *op. cit.*: p.21. Also see: Le Nouvel Observateur, 6–12 May 1988; *Time*, 14 December 1987; and *Le Nouvel Observateur*, 13–19 May 1988. The approach used by Marchiani, backed by the security of twelve GIGN members, in meetings with Hizb'allah officials was to reveal the names of the relatives of the Hizb'allah negotiators living in France, who would be harmed in the event that anything happened to Marchiani. This was revealed in an unattributable interview with French counterterrorism official in Paris in June 1990. Apart from Marchiani, negotiations were led by Bernard Gérard, Director of the DST, and Philippe Rondot, from the disbanded paramilitary force Service d'Action Civique, see: Roger Faligot and Remi Kauffer, (1994), *op. cit.*: p.410.

70. See: *Washington Post*, 5 May 1988; *Sunday Times*, 8 May 1988; and *Liberation*, 7–8 May 1988. Adham was believed to have been behind the leaked information published by the Lebanese newspaper al-Haqiqa that Chirac's emissaries had attempted to delay the release of the French hostages until after the 1986 parliamentary elections and that a ransom of $8.8 million were paid to secure the release of two French hostages in November 1987.

71. The French government repaid a second installment of $330 million to Iran while it recalled French warships in the Persian Gulf, refused to supply Iraq with Mirage aircraft, and lifted a sixteen-month embargo against the purchase of Iranian oil, see: *Ha'aretz*, 5 April 1988; *Ma'aretz*, 8 May 1988; *Observer*, 6 December 1987; and *Yediot Aharanot*, 5 May 1988.

72. See: *Economist*, 4 August 1990; *International Herald Tribune*, 3 February 1989; and *New York Times*, 31 January 1990.

73. *International Herald Tribune*, July 28–29, 1990.

74. On 25 October 1991, France agreed to pay the outstanding debt to Iran, see: *Financial Times*, 30 December 1991.

75. *Le Monde*, 6 May 1988.

76. American Frank Regier and Frenchman Christian Joubert were freed by Amal on 15 April 1984, see: *International Herald Tribune*, 16 April 1984; and *Washington Post*, 9 May 1984.

77. See: *New York Times*, 22 June 1987; and *Sunday Times*, 30 June 1985.

78. The independent efforts to mediate by the PLO leadership was discussed with a senior PLO official in Egypt, 8 April 1994. Also see: Neil C. Livingstone and David Halevy, (1990), *op. cit.*: p.272–4.

79. For U.S. official encouragement of private initiatives in 1985, see: *Middle East Reporter*, 28 March 1985. For examples of unauthorized mediation efforts during 1988, see: *Los Angeles Times*, 19 October 1988; and *Newsweek*, 7 November 1988.
80. See: *Time*, 16 December 1991. Also see: Maskit Burgin, "Western Hostages and Israeli POWs in Lebanon", in Shlomo Gazit (ed.), (1992), *op. cit.*: pp.195–7.
81. The contacts between Picco and Iran as well as Hizb'allah was initiated in 1990, see: *Times*, 10 August 1991. Also see: Giandomenico Picco, "A Personal Journey through the Middle East", *Middle East Journal*, Vol.48, No.1 (Winter 1994): pp.108–12.
82. Prior to the release of the last American hostage, Terry Anderson, reports surfaced that the U.S. government was seeking legal indictments against the hostage-takers, see: *Independent*, 1 December 1991; and *Observer*, 8 December 1991. For Hizb'allah warning of retribution for any U.S. attempts to capture or kill hostage-takers, see: *Independent*, 21 November 1991.
83. Amir Taheri, (1987), *op. cit.*: p.197.
84. See: *Newsweek*, 9 February 1987; and Maskit Burgin, Anat Kurz and Ariel Merari, (1988), *op. cit.*: p.33.
85. For a useful overview of Waite's negotiation efforts, see: Gavin Hewitt, (1991), *op. cit.*
86. For Waite's failure to secure permission to enter Kuwait, see: *Times*, 10 November 1986; and *Observer*, 24 November 1991.
87. See: *Washington Post*, 18 November 1986; *Times*, 19 November 1991; and *Independent*, 26 March 1990. Hizb'allah's own newspaper, al-Ahd, advised Waite to leave Lebanon prior to his abduction, see: *Independent*, 19 November 1991. Terry Waite had left a message before his abduction which urged the British government not to pay any ransom for his release or use any military options, see: *Ma'aretz*, 1 February 1987. See: *Times*, May 12, 1994.
88. See: *al-Shira*, 30 December 1987; Ian Gelldard and Keith Craig, *IRA, INLA: Foreign Support and International Connections* (London: Institute for the Study of Terrorism, 1988): p.77; Martin Dillon, *The Dirty War* (London: Arrow Books, 1990): pp.430–1; *Ma'aretz*, 31 December 1987; *Independent*, 5 May 1990; and Times, 31 December 1987.
89. See: Maskit Burgin, Anat Kurz and Ariel Merari, (1988), *op. cit.*: pp.14–19.
90. This was discussed in an unattributable interview by the author with a former FCO diplomat in November 1992.
91. Robert Oakley, "International Terrorism", *Foreign Affairs*, Vol.65, No.3 (1986). Also see: Margaret G. Hermann and Charles F. Hermann, "Hostage Taking, the Presidency, and Stress", in Walter Reich (ed.), (1990), *op. cit.*: pp.211–29.
92. See: Grant Wardlaw, (1989), *op. cit.* As phrased by Peggy Say, sister of Terry Anderson: "I have to wonder if quiet diplomacy is a code word for no diplomacy", see: *Time*, May 23, 1988.
93. While U.S. public opinion polls indicated a 77 percent approval for the retaliatory actions against Libya, opposition to the action was evident in France, who refused permission for U.S. aircrafts to use French airspace,

     and in Britain, by its condemnation accounting for 59 percent of the population, see: *New York Times*, 21 April 1986; and *Time*, 28 April 1986.

94. See: *Time*, 14 August 1989.

95. See: Jane Mayer and Doyle McManus, (1988), *op. cit.*: p.292 and 437.

96. See: *New York Times*, 18 July 1987.

97. The poll, conducted on May 8, 1990, yielded over 75 percent in favour of negotiations, see: *Middle East International*, 11 May 1990.

98. See: *Economist*, 5 December 1987; and *Time*, 14 December 1987.

99. As quoted in: Robert M. Sayer, "Combatting Terrorism: American Policy and Organization", *Department of State Bulletin*, (1982): pp.1–17.

100. Also see: *Christian Science Monitor*, 26 October 1988. , see: *Economist*, 11 June 1988.

101. Ronald D. Crelinsten, "Terrorism and the Media: Problems, Solutions, and Counterproblems", *Political Communication and Persuasion*, Vol.6, No.3 (1989): p.312.

NOTES FOR CHAPTER 6

1. Statement by former Lebanese hostage Jamil Nasser, "The Uncostly War", *New Statesman*, February 20, 1987: p.10.

Select Bibliography

Abdallah, Umar F. *The Islamic Struggle in Syria* (Berkeley, CA.: University of California Press, 1983).

AbuKhalil, Asád. "Druze, Sunni, and Shiite Political Leadership in Present-day Lebanon", *Arab Studies Quarterly*, 7, No.4 (Fall 1985): 28–58.

_____. "Syria and the Shiites: Al-Asad's Policy in Lebanon", *Third World Quarterly*, Vol.12, No.2 (April 1990).

_____. "Hizbullah in Lebanon: Islamisation of Leninist Organisational Principles", *Middle Eastern Studies*, Vol.27, No.3 (July 1991).

Agha, Hussein J., and Khalidi, Ahmad S. *Syria and Iran: Rivalry and Cooperation* (London: Pinter Publishers, 1995).

Ajami, Fouad. *The Vanished Imam – Musa al Sadr and the Shia of Lebanon.* (London: I.B. Tauris, 1986).

_____. "Lebanon and Its Inheritors". *Foreign Affairs* 63 (Spring 1985): 778–99.

Akhavi, Shahrough. "Elite Factionalism in the Islamic Republic of Iran", *Middle East Journal*, Vol.40, No.2 (Spring 1987): pp.181–201.

Alnwick, Kenneth J.; Fabyanic, Thomas (eds.). *Warfare in Lebanon* (Washington, DC.: National Defense University, 1988).

Amirahmadi, H. and Entessar, N. *Iran and the Arab World* (London: Macmillan,1993).

Anderson, Sean K. "Iranian State-Sponsored Terrorism", *Conflict Quarterly* (Fall 1991): pp.19–34.

Anderson, Terry. *Den of Lions* (New York, NY.: Crown Publishers, 1993).

"An Open Letter: Hizballah Program", *Jerusalem Quarterly*, No.48 (Fall 1988): pp.111–16.

Armstrong, Scott; Byrne, Malcolm; and Blanton, Tom. *Secret Military Assistance to Iran and the Contras: A Chronology of Events and Individuals* (Washington, DC.: National Security Archive, 1987).

Auque, Roger. *Un Otage A Beyrouth* (Paris: Filipacchi, 1988).

Avi-Ran, R. *Syrian Involvement in Lebanon (1975–1985)* (Tel Aviv: Jaffee Center for Strategic Studies, 1986).

Bakhash, Shaul. *The Reign of the Ayatollahs – Iran and the Islamic Revolution* (London: I.B. Tauris, 1985).

_____. "Iraq's Underground Shi'a Movements: Characteristics, Causes and Prospects", *Middle East Studies*, Vol.35, No.4 (Autumn 1981).

Bedlington, Stanley S. *Combatting International Terrorism: U.S.-Allied Cooperation and Political Will* (Washington, DC.: The Atlantic Council of the United States, November 1986).

Behrooz, M. "Factionalism in Iran under Khomeini", *Middle Eastern Studies*, Vol.27, No.4 (1991): pp.597–614.

Bengio, Ofra. "Shi'is and Politics in Ba'athi Iraq", *Middle Eastern Studies*, Vol.21, No.1 (January 1985).

Bernstein, Alvin H. "Iran's Low-Intensity War Against the United States", *Orbis* 30, (Spring 1986): 149–167.

Berry, Steve M. "The Release of France's Last Hostages in Lebanon: An Analysis", *TVI Report* 8, No.3 (1989): 19–22.

Bell, Coral. *The Conventions of Crisis: A Study in Diplomatic Management* (London: Oxford University Press, 1971).

Black, Ian; Morris, Benny. *Israel's Secret Wars: The Untold History of Israeli Intelligence* (London: Hamish Hamilton, 1991).

Bradlee, Ben. *Guts and Glory: The Rise and Fall of Oliver North* (New York, NY.: Donald I. Fine, 1988).

Burgin, Maskit; Merari, A; and Kurz, A. (eds.) *Foreign Hostages in Lebanon*, JCSS Memorandum no.25 – August 1988 (Tel Aviv: Tel Aviv University, 1988).

_____. "Foreign Hostages in Lebanon – An Update", in *Inter: International Terrorism in 1988* (Tel Aviv: Jaffee Center for Strategic Studies, 1989).

Calabrese, John. "Iran II: the Damascus connection", *The World Today* (October 1990).

Carré, Oliver. "Quelques mots-clefs de Muhammad Husayn Fadlallâh", *Revue francaise de science politique*, Vol.37, No.4 (August 1987): pp.478–501.

_____. "La 'révolution islamique' selon Muhammad Husayn Fadlallâh", *Orient: German Journal for Politics and Economics of the Middle East*, Vol.29, No.1 (March 1988): pp.68–84.

_____; and Dumont, P. *Radicalismes islamiques* (Paris: L'Harmattan, 1985).

Christopher, Warren. *American Hostages in Iran: The Conduct of a Crisis* (New Haven, CT.: Yale University Press, 1985).

Clutterbuck, Richard. *Kidnap, Hijack and Extortion* (London: Macmillan, 1987).

_____. "Negotiating with Terrorists", *Terrorism and Political Violence*, Vol.4, No.4 (Winter 1992): pp.263–87.

Cobban, Helena. *The Shia Community and the Future of Lebanon*, Occasional Paper No.2 (Washington, DC.: American Institute for Islamic Affairs, 1985).

Cole, Juan R.I. and Nikki Keddie (eds.) *Shi'ism and Social Protest* (New Haven, CT.: Yale University Press, 1986).

Coughlin, Con. *Hostage* (London: Little and Braun, 1992).

Debock, Walter. and Deniau, Jean-Charles. *Des Armes pour l'Iran: L'Irangate Européen* (Paris: Gallimard, 1988).

Deeb, Marius. *Militant Islamic Movements in Lebanon: Origins, Social Basis and Ideology.* (Occasional Paper Series, Center for Contemporary Arab Studies, Georgetown University, Washington D.C., November 1986).

_____. "Lebanon: Prospects for National Reconciliation in the Mid 1980s", *Middle East Journal*, Vol.38 (Spring 1984).

_____. "Shia Movements in Lebanon: Their Formation, Ideology, Social Basis, and Links with Iran and Syria", *Third World Quarterly* Vol.10, No.2 (April 1988): pp.683–698.

Draper, Theodore. *A Very Thin Line: The Iran-Contra Affairs* (London: Simon & Schuster, 1991).

Ehteshami, Anoushiravan. "After Khomeini: the Structure of Power in the Iranian Second Republic", *Political Studies*, Vol.39 (1991): pp.149–57.

_____; and Varasteh, M. (eds.) *Iran and the International Community* (London: Routledge, 1991).

Esposito, John L. *The Iranian Revolution: Its Global Impact* (Miami, FL.: Florida International Press, 1990).

_____. *Islam and Politics* (Syracuse, NY.: Syracuse University Press, 1991).

_____. *The Islamic Threat: Myth or Reality?* (Oxford: Oxford University Press, 1992).

_____. (ed.) *Voices of Resurgent Islam* (New York, NY.: Oxford University Press, 1983).

Fadlallah, Ayatollah Muhammed Hussein. *Islam and the Logic of Force.* (Beirut: Al Dar Al Islamiya, 1981).

Faligot, Roger; and Remi Kauffer. *Les Maîtres Espions* (Paris: Robert Laffont, 1994).

Fisk, Robert. *Pity the Nation: Lebanon at War.* (Oxford: Oxford University Press, 1990).

Frei, Daniel. (ed.). *International Crisis and Crisis Management* (London: Saxon House, 1978).

Fuller, Graham E. *The "Center of the Universe": The Geopolitics of Iran* (Boulder, CO.: Westview Press, 1991).

George, Alexander (ed.). *Avoiding War: Problems of Crisis Management* (Boulder, CO.: Westview Press, 1991).

Glass, Charles. *Tribes With Flags* (London: Secker & Warburg, 1990).

Halawi, Majed. *A Lebanon Defied: Musa al-Sadr and the Shi'a Community* (Oxford: Westview Press, 1992).

Hamzeh, Nizar A. "Lebanon's Hizbullah: from Islamic Revolution to Parliamentary Accommodation", *Third World Quarterly*, Vol.14, No.2 (1993): pp.321–37.

Hewitt, Gavin. *Terry Waite: Why Was He Kidnapped?* (London: Bloomsbury, 1991).

Hiro, Dilip. *Iran Under the Ayatollahs* (London: Routledge, 1985).

_____. *The Longest War: The Iran-Iraq Military Conflict* (London: Paladin, 1990).

_____. *Fire and Embers – A History of the Lebanese Civil War* (London: Weidenfeld and Nicholson, 1993).

_____. *Holy Wars: The Rise of Islamic Fundamentalism* (New York, NY.: Paladin, 1989).

Hoffman, Bruce. *Recent Trends and Future Prospects of Iranian Sponsored International Terrorism.* (Santa Monica, CA.: Rand Corporation (R-3783-USDP), 1990).

Hunter, Shireen T. "Iran and the Spread of Revolutionary Islam", *Third World Quarterly*, Vol.10, No.2 (April 1988): 730–749.

_____. (ed.). *The Politics of Islamic Revivalism* (Indianapolis, IN.: Indiana University Press, 1988).

_____. *Iran and the World: Continuity in a Revolutionary Decade* (Bloomington, IN.: Indiana University Press, 1990).

_____. *Iran after Khomeini* (Westport, CT.: Greenwood Press, 1992).

Jacobsen, Eric. *Hostage: My Nightmare in Beirut* (New York, NY.: Donald I. Fine, 1991).

Jahanpour, Furhang. "Iran after Khomeini", *The World Today* 45, Nos.8–9, August 1989: 150–53.

_____. "The Roots of the Hostage Crisis", *The World Today* (February 1992): pp.33–6.

Jenkins, Brian; Robin Wright. "The Kidnappings in Lebanon", *TVI Report*, Vol.7, No.4, 1987: 2–11.

Katz, Samuel. *Soldier Spies: Israeli Military Intelligence* (Novato, CA.: Presidio Press, 1992).

_____. *Guards Without Frontiers: Israel's War Against Terrorism* (London: Arms and Armour Press, 1990).

_____. *The Elite* (New York, NY.: Pocket Books, 1992).

Katzman, Kenneth. *The Warriors of Islam: Iran's Revolutionary Guard* (Oxford: Westview Press, 1993).

Keddie, Nikki R.; Mark J. Gasiorowski (eds.). *Neither East Nor West: Iran, the Soviet Union, and the United States* (London: Yale University Press, 1990).

Keenan, Brian. *An Evil Cradling* (London: Vintage, 1993).

Kennedy, David; and Leslie Brunetta. *Lebanon and the Intelligence Community* (Cambridge, MA.: JFK School of Government, Harvard University, 1988).

Kornbluh, Peter; and Malcolm Byrne (eds.). *The Iran-Contra Scandal: The Declassified Story* (New York, NY.: The New Press, 1993).

Kramer, Martin (ed.) *Shi'ism, Resistance and Revolution* (London: Mansell Publ. Ltd. 1987).

_____. "Muhammad Husayn Fadlallah", *Orient: German Journal for Politics and Economics of the Middle East* 26, no.2 (June 1985): pp.147–9.

Laurent, Annie and Antoine Basbous. *Guerres'Secretes au Liban* (Paris: Gallimard, 1987).

Mallat, Chibli. *Shií Thought from the South of Lebanon*. Papers on Lebanon, no.7 (Oxford: Centre for Lebanese Studies, 1988).

_____. Religious Militancy in Contemporary Iraq: Muhammad Baqer as Sadr and the Sunni-Shia Paradigm", *Third World Quarterly*, Vol.10, No.2 (April 1988).

Mann, Jack and Sunnie. *Yours Till the End* (London: Heineman, 1992).

Moshe Ma'oz and Avner Yaniv (ed.) *Syria under Assad: Domestic Constraints and Regional Risks* (London: Croom Helm, 1986).

Martin, David C; and John Walcott. *Best Laid Plans: The Inside Story of America's War Against Terrorism* (New York, NY.: Harper Row, 1988).

Mayer, Jane; and Doyle McManus, *Landslide: The Unmaking of the President* (Boston, MA.: Houghton-Mifflin, 1988).

McCarthy, John; and Jill Morell. *Over Some Other Rainbow* (London: Crown, 1993).

Menashri, David (ed.) *The Iranian Revolution and the Muslim World* (Boulder, CO.: Westview Press, 1990).

_____. *Iran: A Decade of War and Revolution* (London: Holmes & Meier, 1990).

Norton, Augustus R. *Amal and the Shi'a: Struggle for the Soul of Lebanon* (Austin, TX: University of Texas Press, 1987).

_____. "Changing Actors and Leadership Among the Shiites of Lebanon", *Annals of the American Academy of Political and Social Science*. Vol.482 (November 1985): pp.109–122.

Pean, Pierre. *La Menace* (Paris: Fayard, 1987).

Picco, Giandomenico. "A Personal Journey through the Middle East", *Middle East Journal*, Vol.48, No.1 (Winter 1994): pp.108–12.

Pipes, Daniel. *Greater Syria: The History of an Ambition* (Oxford: Oxford University Press, 1990).

Piscatori, James (ed). *Islam in the Political Process* (Cambridge: Cambridge University Press, 1983).

_____. *Islam in a World of Nation-States* (Cambridge: Cambridge University Press, 1986).

_____. *The Fundamentalism Project* (Chicago, IL.: The American Academy of Arts and Sciences, 1992).

Ramazani, R.K. *Revolutionary Iran: Challenge and Response in the Middle East* (Baltimore, MD.: Johns Hopkins University Press, 1986).

Raufer, Xavier. *La Nebuleuse: Le Terrorisme du Moyen-Orient* (Paris: Librairie Arthème Fuyard, 1987).

_____. *Atlas Mondial de L'Islam Activiste* (Paris: La Table Ronde, 1991).

Raviv, Dan; and Mellan, Yossi. *Every Spy a Prince: the Complete History of Israel's Intelligence Community* (London: Houghton Mifflin, 1990).

Reich, Walter ed. *Origins of Terrorism*. Woodrow Wilson International Center for Scholars. (Cambridge: University of Cambridge Press, 1990).

Rieck, Andreas "Abschied vom 'Revolutionsexport'? Expansion und Rückgang des iranischen Einflusses im Libanon 1979–89", *Beitäge zur Konfliktforschung*, Vol.20, No.2 (1990): pp.81–104.

Rosenthal, O.; P.T. Hart; and M. Charles. *Coping with Crisis: The Management of Disasters, Riots, and Terrorism* (Springfield, IL.: Charles Thomas Books, 1989).

_____; Paul T. Hart; and Alexander Kouzmin, "The Bureau-Politics of Crisis Management", *Public Administrations*, Vol.69 (Summer 1991): pp.211–33.

Barry Rubin (ed.), *The Politics of Counter-Terrorism: The Ordeal of Democratic States* (Washington, DC.: The Johns Hopkins Foreign Policy Institute, 1990).

Sabhani, Sohrab. *The Pragmatic Entente: Israeli-Iranian Relations, 1948–1988* (New York, NY.: Praeger, 1989).

Sahliyeh, Emile (ed.) *Religious Resurgence and Politics in the Contemporary World* (Albany, NY.: State University of New York Press, 1990).

Schahgaldian, N.B. *The Clerical Establishment in Iran*. Rand/R-3788–USDP, (Santa Monica: Rand Corporation, June 1989).

Schiff, Ze'ev; Ya'ari, Ehud. *Israel's Lebanon War.* (New York, NY.: Simon and Schuster, 1984).

Schbley, Ayla H. "Resurgent Religious Terrorism: A Study of Some of the Lebanese Shi'a Contemporary Terrorism", *Terrorism* Vol.12, 1989: 213–47.

Seale, Patrick. *Assad: The Struggle for the Middle East* (Berkeley, CA.: University of California Press, 1988).

Segev, Samuel. *The Iranian Triangle: The Untold Story of Israel's Role in the Iran-Contra Affair* (New York: Free Press, 1988).

Seurat, Mary. *Les Corbeaux d'Alep* (Paris: L'Age d'Homme, 1988).

Shangaldian, N.B. *The Clerical Establishment in Iran*, Rand/R-3788-USDP (Santa Monica, CA.: Rand Corporation, June 1989).

Shapira, Shimon. "The Origins of Hizballah", *The Jerusalem Quarterly*, Vol.46, (Spring 1988): pp.115–30.

Sick, Gary. *October Surprise* (New York, NY.: Random House, 1991).

Sirriyeh, Hussein. *Lebanon: Dimensions of Conflict* (London: International Institute for Strategic Studies – Adelphi Paper 243, Autumn 1989).

Sivan, Emmanuel; and Friedman, M. *Religious Radicalism and Politics in the Middle East* (Albany, NY.: State University of New York Press, 1990).

Taheri, Amir. *Holy Terror: The Inside Story of Islamic Terrorism* (London: Sphere Books, 1987).

Tophoven, Rolf. "Der Tod eines Terroristen – Hintergründe und Konsequenzen", *Terrorismus*, Nr.3 (March 1992): pp.1–4.

_____."State-Supported Terrorism After the Gulf War: The Rôle of Iran, Iraq and Libya", 9th International Conference on "Democracy Challenged and Put to the Test – The Problem of Combating Terrorism, Drugs and Organized Crime", (London: Hans Seidel Foundation, August 1992).

Tower, John; Muskie, Edmund; Scowcroft, Brent. *The Tower Commission Report.* (New York: Bantam Books and Times Books, 1987).

Waite, Terry. *Taken on Trust* (London: Routledge, 1993).

Weir, Benjamin and Carol. *Hostage Bound, Hostage Free* (Philadelphia, PA: Westminister Press, 1987).

Wilkinson, Paul, "Hezbollah – A Critical Appraisal", *Jane's Intelligence Review* (August 1993): pp.369–70.

_____. *Terrorism and the Liberal State* (London: Macmillan, 1977, 1986).

Woodward, Bob. *Veil: The Secret Wars of the CIA, 1981–87* (New York: Simon and Schuster, 1987).

Wright, Robin. *Sacred Rage: The Wrath of Militant Islam* (London: Deutsch, 1986).

_____. *In the Name of God: the Khomeini Decade* (New York, NY.: Simon & Schuster, 1989).

NEWSPAPERS AND PERIODICALS

Agence France Presse (AFP)
Al-Ahd
Al-Anba
Al-Anwar
Al-Diyar
Al-Dustur
Al-Haqiqa
Al-Hawadith
Al-Hayat
Al-Liwa
Al-Majallah
Al-Muntalaq
Al-Musawwar
Al-Mustaqbal
Al-Nahar
Al-Safir
Al-Sharq al-Awsat
Al-Shira
Al-Watan
Al-Watan al-Arabi

Al-Taqrir
Arab Times
Associated Press (AP)
BBC Summary of World Broadcasts (1985–1995)
Christian Science Monitor
Da'var
Defense & Armament Heracles
Defense & Foreign Affairs Weekly
Der Spiegel
Die Welt
Economist
El Pais
Ettela'at
Financial Times
Foreign Broadcast Information Service (FBIS), Daily Report, Near East and South
    Asia
Foreign Report
Guardian
Ha'aretz
Hadashot
Independent
International Herald Tribune
Intelligence Newsletter
Iran Press Digest
Islamic Republic News Agency – IRNA (Teheran)
Jane's Defense Weekly (London)
Jeune Afrique
Jerusalem Post
Jerusalem Report
Kayhan
Keyhan International
Kuwait Times
La Révue du Liban
L'Evenement du Jeudi
L'Express
Le Figaro
Le Matin
Le Monde
Le Monde Diplomatique
Le Nouvel Observateur
Le Point
Le Quotidien de Paris
Le Soir
Libération
Los Angeles Times
Ma'aretz
Ma'ariv
Middle East
Middle East Defense News

Middle East Economic Digest
Middle East Insight
Middle East International
Middle East News Agency (MENA)
Middle East Reporter
Monday Morning
Newsweek
New York Times
Nouveau Magazine
Observer
Paris Lettre Persane
Richochets (IDF Spokesman)
Sunday Times
Teheran Times
The Echo of Iran
Time
The Times
US News & World Report
Valeurs Actuelles
Wall Street Journal
Washington Post
Washington Times
Yediot Aharanot

Index